Field Guide to the Wildlife of Costa Rica

Number Fifty-one, The Corrie Herring Hooks Series

Photographs by Carrol L. Henderson

Illustrations by Steve Adams

Foreword by Alexander F. Skutch

Field Guide to the

Wildlife of Costa Rica

by Carrol L. Henderson

University of Texas Press, Austin

The University of Texas Press wishes to acknowledge the generous financial support by the following foundations, individuals, and businesses that helped to underwrite the costs of producing this *Field Guide to the Wildlife of Costa Rica:*

The Dellwood Wildlife Foundation of Dellwood, Minnesota, in memory of wildlife conservationist and founder of the Dellwood Wildlife Foundation, Ramon D. (Ray) Whitney. Ray Whitney was instrumental in helping restore trumpeter swans to Minnesota, and he shared a love and appreciation for the diversity and abundance of wildlife in Costa Rica.

The Costa Rica–Minnesota Foundation of St. Paul, Minnesota, in support of cultural and natural resource initiatives fostering greater understanding, educational programs, and habitat protection for Costa Rica's wildlife.

Honorary Consul to Costa Rica from Minnesota and former CEO of the H. B. Fuller Company, Tony Andersen, who has been a tireless promoter for cooperative projects that are of benefit to Costa Rica's culture and environment.

Karen Johnson, President of Preferred Adventures Ltd. of St. Paul, Minnesota, a business that specializes in ecotourism and natural history adventures for worldwide travelers and has been especially active in promoting wildlife tourism in Costa Rica and other countries of Latin America.

Michael Kaye, President of Costa Rica Expeditions, San José, Costa Rica. Costa Rica Expeditions owns and manages Monteverde Lodge, Tortuguero Lodge, and Corcovado Lodge Tent Camp. This company has set an excellent example of high standards for protecting sensitive tropical habitats while accommodating the needs of nature tourism and adventure travelers in Costa Rica.

Dan Conaway, President of Elegant Adventures, Atlanta, Georgia. Elegant Adventures specializes in quality, customized tours to Latin American destinations, including Costa Rica. This company has served international travelers since its founding in 1986.

∞ The paper used in this book meets the minimum requirements of ANSI/ NISO Z39.48– 1992 (R1997) (Permanence of Paper).

Library of Congress Cataloging-in-Publication Data

Henderson, Carrol L.
    Field guide to wildlife of Costa Rica / by Carrol L. Henderson ; illustrations by Steve Adams ; foreword by Alexander F. Skutch.
        p.   cm.
Includes bibliographical references (p.   ).
ISBN 0-292-73128-0 (cloth : alk. paper)—ISBN 0-292-73459-x (pbk. : alk. paper)
1. Zoology—Costa Rica—Identification.   I. Title.
QL228.C8 H46   2002
591.97286—DC21   2001027916

To my wife, Ethelle, and son, Craig,
with whom I share my love of Costa Rica,

and to Drs. George Knaphus, James H. Jenkins, and Daniel H. Janzen,
my mentors

Backlit canal in rainforest

CONTENTS

79: **Beetle Family** (Scarabaeidae)

81: **Dobson Fly Family** (Corydalidae)

82: **Katydid Family** (Tettigoniidae)

83: **Orb-weaver Spider Family** (Araneidae)

85: **Giant Damselfly Family** (Pseudostigmatidae)

87: **Rock Runner Crab Family** (Grapsidae)

88: **Land Crab Family** (Gecarcinidae)

Amphibians: 90

92: **Leptodactylid Frog Family** (Leptodactylidae)

96: **Toad Family** (Bufonidae)

98: **Hylid Frog Family** (Hylidae)

100: **Poison Dart Frog Family** (Dendrobatidae)

104: **Glass Frog Family** (Centrolenidae)

Reptiles: 108

110: **Leatherback Turtle Family** (Dermochelyidae)

112: **Hard-shelled Sea Turtle Family** (Cheloniidae)

116: **Mud Turtle Family** (Kinosternidae)

117: **Semiaquatic Pond Turtle Family** (Emydidae)

119: **Lizard Family** (Iguanidae)

128: **Teiid Lizard Family** (Teiidae)

129: **Constrictor Family** (Boidae)

130: **Colubrid Snakes** (Colubridae)

133: **Viper Family** (Crotalidae)

134: **Coral Snake Family** (Micruridae)

135: **Crocodile Family** (Crocodylidae)

Birds: 142

145: **Tinamou Family** (Tinamidae)

147: **Pelican Family** (Pelecanidae)

148: **Cormorant Family** (Phalacrocoracidae)

150: **Anhinga Family** (Anhingidae)

152: **Frigatebird Family** (Fregatidae)

154: **Heron Family** (Ardeidae)

166: **Stork Family** (Ciconiidae)

170: **American Vulture Family** (Cathartidae)

176: **Ibis and Spoonbill Family** (Threskiornithidae)

179: **Duck Family** (Anatidae)

Mammals : 440

FOREWORD

To the dweller in a northern land eager to know the rich bird life of tropical America, I recommend Costa Rica. Readily accessible from the United States, Canada, or Europe, this small Central American republic supports an abundant representation of the great, exclusively New World families—tyrant flycatchers, hummingbirds, antbirds, ovenbirds, and woodcreepers—all poorly represented or absent north of Mexico.

Among the most exciting neotropical specialties are toucans, jacamars, puffbirds, and guans. With them are more familiar cosmopolitan families, including finches, sparrows, thrushes, swallows, swifts, woodpeckers, cuckoos, and others. Less strange to a visitor from the north are wintering migrants: wood warblers, vireos, orioles, and flycatchers. They are really neotropical birds returning to their ancestral homes to escape winter's snow and ice. There are also a few migrants from the south, such as the Swallow-tailed Kite, Yellow-green Vireo, and pesky Piratic Flycatcher.

Amid the rainforested Caribbean lowlands, the birder will find the richest representation of the great South American bird families, including species like the White-fronted Nunbird, Keel-billed Toucan, Lattice-tailed Trogon, and Dusky-faced Tanager.

Costa Rica's southern Pacific lowlands support a unique avifauna that it shares with western Panama. Here live such fascinating birds as the Fiery-billed Aracari, Turquoise Cotinga, Golden-naped Woodpecker, and Riverside Wren. In sharp contrast to the southern half of Costa Rica's Pacific side, the northern half has a prolonged severe dry season. Many birds range along the arid western side of Middle America from Mexico to central Costa Rica. Notable among them are the White-throated Magpie-Jay, Long-tailed Manakin, Turquoise-browed Motmot, and Banded Wren.

Isolated by the lowlands of the Isthmus of Panama and the Costa Rica–Nicaragua border, high mountains support endemic birds, including the Scintillant Hummingbird, Timberline Wren, Flame-throated Warbler, Volcano Junco, and the southern race of the Resplendent Quetzal.

All this great diversity of birds is found in a country the size of West Virginia. Good roads and comfortable lodges make them readily accessible to tourists, who nearly everywhere find helpful Costa Ricans who speak English. For an introduction to the rich neotropical avifauna, Costa Rica offers many advantages.

By their abundance, visibility, beautiful plumage, melodious songs, and endearing ways, especially as they faithfully attend their young in carefully con-

Dr. Alexander F. Skutch, left, welcomes a visitor, Dr. Walter Breckenridge, to his home, Los Cusingos, in 1995.

structed nests, birds rightfully claim much of the attention of almost everyone attracted to nature. But if we permitted them to absorb all our attention, we would miss much of nature's beauty and interest. Indeed, birds often direct our attention to flowering plants, lovely butterflies, other insects, mammals, reptiles, amphibians, and more obscure creatures that we might otherwise fail to notice. In this book, you will find accurate accounts of a liberal selection of a richly endowed tropical country's vast diversity of organisms. This field guide should interest not only visitors from other countries but also many who live in Costa Rica.

Alexander F. Skutch
July 11, 2000

PREFACE

I grew up as a farm boy near Zearing in central Iowa, and most of my early travels were within twenty-five miles of our family farm. I had quite a provincial view of life and no concept of ecosystems, biological diversity, or tropical rainforests. I just knew that I loved wildlife. I had no idea that Costa Rica, a small country thousands of miles away in Central America, would later play such a dramatic role in shaping the direction of my personal and professional life.

An early and enthusiastic interest in nature led me to major in zoology and minor in botany at Iowa State University. After completing my bachelor's degree at ISU in 1968, I enrolled in graduate school at the University of Georgia, where I studied ecology, forest and wildlife management, journalism, and public relations. During my search for a thesis topic, Dr. James H. Jenkins directed me to an Organization for Tropical Studies (OTS) course in Costa Rica.

When I began my two-month OTS course in tropical grasslands agriculture in February of 1969, I had no idea it would be such a life-changing experience. Every day was an adventure! I tried to absorb all that I could about the land,

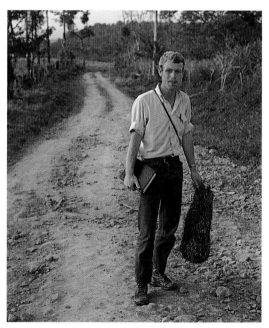

The author with an oropendola nest during an OTS course in Costa Rica, 1969

the people, and the wildlife of Costa Rica. I quickly learned that this is not a country you can visit just once. By March I had already applied for another OTS course and was subsequently accepted. In June 1969, I drove from Georgia to Costa Rica with Dr. Jenkins for an OTS course in tropical ecology.

The OTS faculty, recruited from educational institutions throughout North and Central America, included some of the most notable tropical biologists in the world. They inspired me with their knowledge and enthusiasm about tropical ecosystems. By the end of the tropical ecology course, I had fallen in love with the country, with its people, and with Ethelle González Alvarez, a student at the University of Costa Rica. I returned to Costa Rica a third time in 1969. Ethelle and I were married in December of that year and have now been married thirty-three years. We have a son, Craig, who shares our love and enthusiasm for his Tico heritage.

After returning to the University of Georgia, I wrote my master's thesis, "Fish and Wildlife Resources of Costa Rica, with Notes on Human Influences." The 340-page thesis analyzed human influences that were having significant positive or negative impacts on Costa Rica's wildlife. I also provided recommendations for changes in the game laws that would improve management of the country's wildlife.

During the thirty-three years since my first visit to Costa Rica, I have returned twenty-four times. Since 1987, our visits to the country have included leading wildlife tours. Ethelle and I have led fifteen birding and wildlife tours to Costa Rica since 1987 in coordination with Preferred Adventures Ltd. in St. Paul. We continue to see new species on every visit—and every day is still an adventure!

Each year thousands of first-time tourists are experiencing the same sense of wonder about the country's rainforests and wildlife that I did in 1969. This book is written to share my enthusiasm and knowledge about the country's wildlife with those tourists and with Costa Ricans who share our love of nature. It is written to answer questions about identification, distribution, natural history, and the incredible ecological adaptations of many wildlife species. It also provides the opportunity to recognize the people and conservation programs that have made Costa Rica a world leader in preserving its tropical forest and wildlife resources.

ACKNOWLEDGMENTS

Writing this book has been a real labor of love. It represents the culmination of thirty-three years of personal and professional relationships in Costa Rica. Special appreciation goes to my wife, Ethelle, and my son, Craig, who have traveled with me from Minnesota to Costa Rica many times and helped with everything from wildlife observations to editing and preparing the manuscript. In 1985, Karen Johnson, the owner of Preferred Adventures Ltd. in St. Paul, Minnesota, convinced us to try leading a birding trip to Costa Rica. We finally agreed and led our first trip in 1987. It was the beginning of a wonderful experience that has enabled us to meet many special people in our tour groups as well as Costa Rican tourism outfitters, guides, and ecolodge staffs. Sarah Strommen, formerly of Preferred Adventures Ltd., has helped in recent years with Costa Rica trip arrangements and with reviewing the manuscript.

Michael Kaye, the owner of Costa Rica Expeditions, has been very supportive of this project and has coordinated our travel there. He facilitated travel to visit several sites for photography purposes, including Monteverde Lodge. Carlos Gómez Nieto is the extraordinary guide who has led all but one of our Costa Rican birding trips. Carlos is the premier birder in Costa Rica, and his vast knowledge of wildlife behavior and identification has helped us accumulate our wildlife records, which now exceed 15,000 observations. Carlos reviewed the manuscript for the book, and his wife, Vicky, also accompanied us on several wildlife outings. Manuel Salas has been the driver for most of our trips and has been invaluable in spotting birds and in providing us with safe and memorable travel experiences. The birding guide Jay VanderGaast, formerly of Rancho Naturalista, and the noted ornithologist Dr. Noble Proctor also provided comprehensive reviews of the manuscript.

Other people have helped greatly with facilitating our travels, birding trips, and the collection of information and photos. They include Lisa Erb at Rancho Naturalista; Don Efraín Chacón, Rolando Chacón, and the rest of the Chacón family; Amos Bien of Rara Avis; Gail Hewson-Hull; Luis Diego Gómez; Dr. Alexander Skutch and Pamela Skutch at Los Cusingos; and Werner and Lily Hagnauer. The owners and management of La Pacífica and Hotel and Cabinas Eclipse near Quepos also provided accommodations while we collected wildlife observations and photos.

Biologists and scientists provided expertise on species identification and life history data, including Dr. Daniel Janzen, Dr. Graciela Candelas, Dr. Alexander Skutch, Brian Kubicki, Dr. Frank T. Hovore, Jorge Corrales of the Instituto Nacional de Biodiversidad (INBIO), and Dr. Jay M. Savage. Other persons who have helped us with wildlife observations, outings, and photography include Dennis Janik and Henry Kantrowitz at Zoo Ave, Lic. Jorge González Fallas, Lydia González de Alvarez, Lic. Daniel González Alvarez, Roberto Espinoza, Luis Diego Cruz, and Zoíla Cruz. Jim Lewis and Joan Galli provided information on the wildlife of Caño Negro National Wildlife Refuge. Additional editing has been provided by Pam Perry, Sarah Strommen, and Margaret Dexter. Ed and June Rogier deserve special appreciation for providing invaluable references on bird life, including accounts from *The Birds of North America* and the *Handbook of the Birds of the World*.

One bird photo in this book portrays a mounted specimen. The Milwaukee Public Museum kindly provided the opportunity to photograph a Montezuma Oropendola in a displaying posture that was mounted by Greg Septon. The only photo in this book not taken by the author, showing Dr. Dan Janzen teaching in 1967, was kindly provided by the Organization for Tropical Studies.

Special thanks and appreciation go to Nancy Warrington for her excellent job of editing the final manuscript.

And finally, special appreciation goes to all the Costa Rican travelers who have accompanied us on our birding trips and provided us with the companionship, sharp eyes, and friendships that have enriched our lives.

ABOUT THE AUTHOR

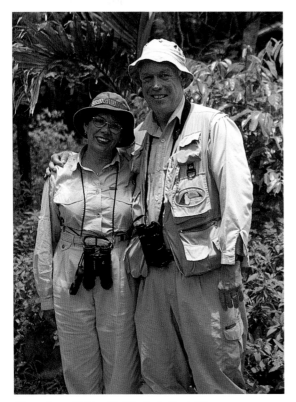

The author with his wife, Ethelle, in Costa Rica, 1999

Carrol L. Henderson, a native of Zearing, Iowa, received a bachelor of science degree in zoology from Iowa State University in 1968 and a master of forest resources degree in ecology from the University of Georgia in 1970. He did his graduate studies on the fish and wildlife of Costa Rica through the Organization for Tropical Studies (OTS) and the University of Costa Rica.

Henderson joined the Minnesota Department of Natural Resources (DNR) in 1974 as assistant manager of the Lac qui Parle Wildlife Management Area near Milan. In 1977 he became supervisor of the DNR's new Nongame Wildlife Program and continues in that role to the present. During the past twenty-five years, Henderson has developed a statewide program for the conservation of Minnesota's nongame wildlife and has had responsibility for planning and developing projects to help bring back bluebirds, Bald Eagles, Peregrine Falcons, River Otters, and Trumpeter Swans.

Henderson received the national Chevron Conservation Award in 1990, the 1992 Chuck Yaeger Conservation Award from the National Fish and Wildlife Foundation, the 1993 Minnesota Award from the Minnesota Chapter of The Wildlife Society, and the 1994 Thomas Sadler Roberts Memorial Award from the Minnesota Ornithologist's Union.

His writings include *Woodworking for Wildlife, Landscaping for Wildlife, Wild about Birds: The DNR Bird Feeding Guide,* and co-authorship of *The Traveler's Guide to Wildlife in Minnesota,* and *Lakescaping for Wildlife and Water Quality.* He is a regular contributor of feature stories in *Birder's World* magazine.

An avid wildlife photographer, Henderson has taken most of the photos in his books and is the primary photographer for the 1995 book *Galapagos Islands—Wonders of the World.* His bird photography has been featured in the *New York Times, World Book Encyclopedia of Science, Audubon* magazine, and Discovery Online and has received seven national awards from *Wild Bird* magazine between 1995 and 1998.

Henderson and his wife, Ethelle, developed their expertise in tropical wildlife by leading thirty-one birding tours to Latin America since 1987. This included fifteen trips to Costa Rica and additional trips to Panama, Belize, Trinidad, Tobago, Venezuela, Bolivia, Ecuador, Brazil, Argentina, Peru, and the Galápagos Islands.

Field Guide to the Wildlife of Costa Rica

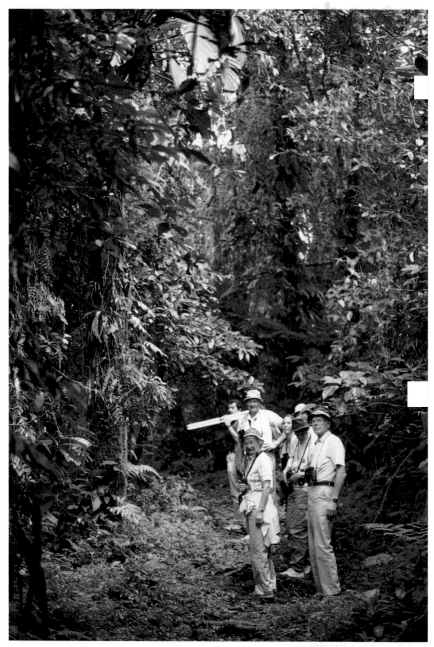

Birding group entering the rainforest

Introduction

Costa Rica! The name generates a sense of excitement and anticipation among international travelers. Among European explorers, the first recorded visitor was Christopher Columbus in 1502. On his fourth trip to the New World, Columbus landed where the port city of Limón is now located. The natives he encountered wore golden disks around their necks. He called this new place "Costa Rica," meaning "Rich Coast," because he thought the gold came from there. The gold had actually come from other countries and had been obtained as a trade item from native traders along the coast.

The name Costa Rica means "Rich Coast."

Spanish treasure seekers eventually discovered their error and went elsewhere in their quest for gold. The irony is that Christopher Columbus actually picked the perfect name for this country. The wealth overlooked by the Spaniards is the rich biological diversity that includes about 505,000 species of plants and wildlife! That species richness is an incredible natural resource that sustains one of the most successful nature tourism industries in the Western Hemisphere. It also provides the basis for a biodiversity industry of "chemical prospecting" among plants and creatures in search of new foods and medicines for humans.

For such a small country, Costa Rica gets much well-deserved international attention and has become one of the most popular tourist destinations in the Americas. The lure is not "sun and sand" experiences at big hotels on the country's beaches; it is unspoiled nature in far-flung nooks and crannies of wildlands that are accessible at rustic nature lodges throughout the country.

It is now possible to immerse yourself in the biological wealth of tropical forests during a vacation in Costa Rica. During a two-week visit you may see more than three to four hundred species of birds, mammals, reptiles, amphibians, butterflies, moths, and other invertebrates. Some vacations are planned for rest and relaxation, but who can do that in such a diverse country where there is so much nature to see and experience!

Costa Rica is a country where every day is an adventure, and where the marvelous diversity and abundance of wildlife creates an enthusiasm for nature that many people have not experienced since childhood.

The ease with which it is possible to travel to Costa Rica and enjoy wildlife in such a pristine setting makes a visitor think it has always been that way. It has not. The appealing travel and tourism conditions are the product of nearly four decades of social, educational, and cultural developments.

There was a time when Costa Rican wildlife was persecuted at every opportunity. Virtually every creature weighing "over a pound" was shot for its value as meat or for its hide. Wildlife was killed year-round from the time of settlement through the 1960s. Instead of acquiring souvenirs like T-shirts and postcards in those days, Costa Rican visitors in the 1960s found vendors selling boa constrictor hides, caiman-skin briefcases, stuffed caimans, skins of spotted cats, and sea turtle eggs.

HISTORICAL PERSPECTIVE

To appreciate the abundance of today's wildlife populations, it is necessary to understand the revolution in wildlife conservation and habitat preservation that has occurred since the 1960s. Dozens of dedicated biologists, politicians, and private citizens have contributed to Costa Rica's world leadership in tropical forest conservation, wildlife protection, and nature tourism over the past forty-plus years. This process occurred in five phases: (1) Research, (2) Education, (3) Preservation, (4) Conservation, and (5) Nature Tourism.

Research

One of the earliest advances for Costa Rica's legacy of conservation was the development of research data on Costa Rica's plants and wildlife. Without such basic knowledge, there can be little appreciation, respect, or protection for wild species. In 1941, Dr. Alexander Skutch homesteaded property in the San Isidro del General Valley along the Río Peña Blanca. Since settling there with his wife, Pamela, Dr. Skutch has studied Costa Rica's birds for sixty years and continues to observe them and record their life history in his prolific writings.

In 1954, another biologist, Dr. Archie Carr, started epic research. Dr. Carr, from the University of Florida, began a lifelong commitment to the protection and management of the green turtle at Tortuguero. That effort continues to this day through the efforts of his son, Dr. David Carr, and the work of the Caribbean Conservation Corporation, which was created in 1959.

Another significant development for Costa Rica's legacy of leadership in tropical research was the creation of the Tropical Science Center. It was founded in 1962 by Drs. Leslie R. Holdridge, Joseph A. Tosi, and Robert J. Hunter. These three scientists helped promote research on tropical ecosystems, land use, and sustainable development. Dr. Gary Hartshorn later joined the staff to add more expertise in the development of tropical forest management. The Tropical Science Center was instrumental in establishing La Selva Biological Field Station and the Monteverde Cloud Forest Reserve and in preserving Los Cusingos, the forest reserve owned by Dr. Alexander Skutch and now managed by the Tropical Science Center.

Another research catalyst for subsequent conservation and land protection was the creation of the Organization for Tropical Studies (OTS) in 1964. The OTS is a consortium of fifty-five universities and educational institutions throughout the Americas. The OTS operates three tropical research field stations—located at La Selva, Palo Verde, and San Vito. Tropical biologists from throughout the world come to these field stations to pursue pioneering studies on taxonomy, ecology, and conservation of tropical ecosystems.

For decades, people had believed it was necessary to eliminate tropical forests in order to create croplands, pastures, and monocultures of exotic trees for the benefit of society. Tropical biologists of OTS changed the way people viewed tropical forests and helped society realize the infinitely greater ecological and economic benefits that can accrue from preserving and managing tropical forests as sustainable resources.

Education

In 1963 the National Science Foundation supported an "Advanced Science Seminar in Tropical Biology," which was subsequently adapted by OTS. The OTS initiated a second part of its legacy with field courses in tropical ecology, forestry, agriculture, and land use for undergraduate and graduate students from throughout the Americas. Since its founding, the OTS has conducted over 185 field courses for over 3,000 students. For many of these students, including the author, the courses were life-changing experiences. The faculty who taught these courses were some of the most prominent ecologists in the world, including, among others, Drs. Dan Janzen, Mildred Mathias, Carl Rettenmeyer, Frank Barnwell, Rafael Lucas Rodríguez Caballero, Gordon Orions, Roy Mc-Diarmid, Larry Wolf, and Rex Daubenmire.

Another significant source of tropical education and research has been the Tropical Agricultural Center for Research and Education (Centro Agronómico Tropical de Investigación y Enseñanza; CATIE). This center was created in 1942 at Turrialba and was originally known as the Interamerican Institute of Agricultural Science (Instituto Interamericano de Ciencias Agrícolas; IICA). Graduate students come from all over Latin America to study agriculture, forestry, and wildlife management courses there.

Dr. Dan Janzen teaching an OTS course in 1967. Photo provided courtesy of the Organization for Tropical Studies.

Logging in Costa Rica, 1969

Preservation

By the 1960s, about 50 percent of Costa Rica's forests had been cut, and the clearing continued. It became apparent that national programs for protection of the remaining forests and wildlife would be necessary if they were to be preserved into the next century.

The first wildlife conservation law was decreed on July 20, 1961, and was updated with bylaws on June 7, 1965. These laws and regulations provided for the creation and enforcement of game laws, the establishment of wildlife refuges, the prohibition of commercial sale of wildlife products, the issuance of hunting and fishing licenses, the establishment of fines for violations, and the creation of restrictions on the export and import of wildlife. Complete protection was given to tapirs, manatees, White-tailed Deer does accompanied by fawns, and Resplendent Quetzals. However, the laws were not enforced.

In 1968, a Costa Rican graduate student, Mario Boza, was inspired by a visit to the Great Smoky Mountains National Park (NP). In 1969 a Forestry Protection Law allowed national parks to be established, and Mario Boza was designated as the only employee of the new National Parks Department. He wrote a master plan for the newly designated Poás Volcano NP as his master's thesis subject.

In 1970, wildlife laws were still being ignored by poachers, and wildlife continued to disappear. President "Don Pepe" Figueres visited Dr. Archie Carr and then graduate student David Ehrenfeld to see the green turtle nesting beaches at Tortuguero. He was considering a proposal to protect the area as a national park. The following account was later written by Dr. David Ehrenfeld (1989):

It was Don Pepe's first visit to the legendary Tortuguero—we had been watching a green turtle nest, also a first for him. El Presidente, a short, Napoleonic man with boundless energy, was enjoying himself enormously. Both he and Archie were truly charismatic people, and they liked and respected one another. The rest of us went along quietly, enjoying the show. As we walked up the beach towards the boca, where the Río Tortuguero meets the sea, Don Pepe questioned Dr. Carr about the green turtles and their need for conservation. How important was it to make Tortuguero a sanctuary? Just then, a flashlight picked out a strange sight up ahead.

A turtle was on the beach, near the waterline, trailing something. And behind her was a line of eggs which, for some reason, she was depositing on the bare, unprotected sand. We hurried to see what the problem was.

When we got close, it was all too apparent. The entire undershell of the turtle had been cut away by poachers who were after calipee, or cartilage, to dry and sell to the European turtle soup manufacturers. Not interested in the meat or eggs, they had evidently then flipped her back on her belly for sport, to see where she would crawl. What she was trailing was her intes-

Rainbow over the Monteverde Cloud Forest Reserve

tines. The poachers had probably been frightened away by our lights only minutes before.

Dr. Carr, who knew sea turtles better than any human being on earth and who had devoted much of his life to their protection, said nothing. He looked at Don Pepe, and so did I. It was a moment of revelation. Don Pepe was very, very angry, trembling with rage. This was his country, his place. He had risked his life for it fighting in the Cerro de la Muerte. The turtles were part of this place, even part of its name: Tortuguero; . . . She was home, laying her eggs for the last time.

Don Pepe realized that the ancient turtles, as well as the Costa Rican people, needed a safe place to live and raise their young. The poaching had to end. He declared Tortuguero National Park by executive decree in 1970. The tragic poaching incident with the nesting green turtle was probably the pivotal incident that catalyzed the national parks movement in Costa Rica. Mario Boza served under President Figueres as the National Park Service director from 1970 to 1974. By the end of 1974, the Service had grown to an organization of 100 employees with an annual budget of $600,000. A total of 2.5 percent of the country was designated as national parks and reserves.

Private preservation efforts also began in the 1970s. The scientists George and Harriet Powell and Monteverde resident Wilford Guindon created the 810-acre Monteverde Cloud Forest Reserve. They brought in the Tropical Science Center to own and manage the preserve, which now totals 27,428 acres. The Monteverde Conservation League was subsequently formed to help manage and carry out conservation projects and land acquisition.

In 1984, Dr. Dan Janzen brought more international recognition to Costa Rica when he received the Crafoord Prize in Coevolutionary Ecology from the Swedish Royal Academy of Sciences. This is the ecologist's equivalent of the Nobel Prize. Dr. Janzen received the prize for his pioneering research on entomology and ecology of tropical dry forests. This focused attention on the need for preserving tropical dry forests in the Guanacaste Conservation Area (http://www.acguanacaste.ac.cr).

Oscar Arias was elected president in 1986. He created the Ministry of Energy, Mining, and Natural Resources (MIRENEM) by merging the national land management departments to make them more efficient in managing the nation's natural resources. That agency is now referred to as the Ministry of Environment and Energy (Ministerio del Ambiente y Energía; MINAE).

Since then, Costa Rica's national system of parks and reserves has continued to grow and mature. It now consists of thirty-four protected areas, including twenty-eight national parks. Those areas total more than 1,415,000 acres—over 11 percent of the country's land area. When forest reserves and wildlife refuges are included, federal lands total about 25 percent of the country.

Dr. Dan Janzen, winner of the Crafoord Prize in 1984

Conservation

As the national park system grew and encompassed more life zones, it became clear to ecological visionaries like Drs. Dan Janzen and Rodrigo Gámez that they had an opportunity to take another bold step that would place them in a world-leadership role for conservation of biological diversity and creation of economic benefits to society from that biological diversity. They created the National Institute of Biodiversity (Instituto Nacional de Biodiversidad; INBIO). Dr. Gámez became the first director of INBIO and continues in that role to the present. The ambitious goal of this institute was to collect, identify, and catalog all of the living species in Costa Rica. Estimated at 505,000 species, this figure includes 878 birds, 228 mammals, 218 reptiles, 175 amphibians, 360,000 insects, and 10,000 plants. This represents about 5 percent of the world's species. So far, about 85,000 of those species have been described.

Following the creation of INBIO, MIRENEM developed a national system of "conservation areas" in 1990. This is referred to as SINAC (Sistema Nacional de Areas de Conservación). Eleven conservation areas were established. Personnel in the fields of wildlife, forestry, parks, and agriculture teamed up to manage the national parks and wildlands in each conservation area. Their goal is the conservation of Costa Rica's biodiversity for nondestructive use by Costa Ricans and the world populace. This national scale of "ecosystem-based management" predated efforts in more "developed" countries by years.

Nature Tourism

Beginning in the mid-1980s, and concurrent with the conservation phase, the value of Costa Rica's National Parks (NPs), National Wildlife Refuges (NWRs), and Biological Reserves (BRs) was reaffirmed in another way: as a resource for "nature tourism." Nature tourism is motivated by the desire to experience unspoiled nature: to see, enjoy, experience, or photograph scenery, natural communities, wildlife, and native plants. The first rule of nature tourism is that wildlife is worth more alive—in the wild—than dead. It has become a great incentive to protect wildlife from poachers and to conserve the forests.

Nature tourism provided new employment opportunities for Costa Ricans as travel agency personnel, outfitters, nature lodge owners and staff, drivers, and naturalist guides. The best naturalist guides can identify birds, mammals, reptiles, amphibians, flowers, butterflies, and trees. These dedicated guides share an infectious enthusiasm for the country as they help visitors experience hundreds of species during a visit. Guides like Carlos Gómez Nieto have seen over 730 of the country's bird species and can identify most of them by sight and sound.

Rainforests—and the international loss of rainforests—received an incredible amount of publicity in the 1980s. Costa Rica's NPs provided an opportunity to attract tourists to experience the mystique and beauty of those forests. Improved road systems and small airstrips throughout the country provided access to those NPs and private reserves in the rainforests. Enterprising outfitters recognized the opportunity to establish locally owned and managed nature tourism lodges to cater to this "new breed" of international tourists.

One of the best-known pioneers in nature-based tourism is Michael Kaye. Originally from New York, he was a white-water rafting outfitter in the Grand Canyon before he founded Costa Rica Expeditions in 1978. In Costa Rica he provides tourists with the opportunity for adventure tourism, including white-water rafting and wildlife viewing. Kaye built three lodges—Tortuga, Mon-

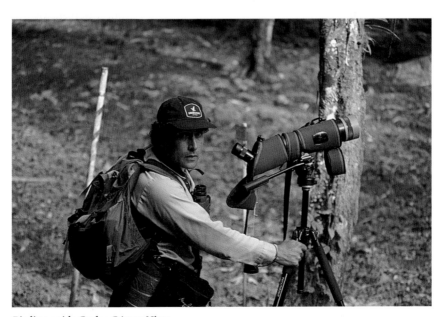

Birding guide Carlos Gómez Nieto

teverde, and Corcovado—and he provided ecologically based innovations and adaptations at these facilities that minimized their impact on the environment and sensitized visitors to the importance and vulnerability of the forests where these lodges were located. Kaye believes that tourists respond to world-class facilities and service that are provided by local ownership and management of smaller, dispersed lodging facilities. Costa Rica's tourism forte is that it is one of the best rainforest destinations in the Americas because it is safe and easily accessible; the attraction is not the beaches.

There are now dozens of other locally owned nature-based lodges throughout the country. John Aspinall founded Costa Rica Sun Tours and built the Arenal Observatory Lodge. His brother Peter founded Tiskita Jungle Lodge. Don Perry initiated the Rainforest Aerial Tram facility. John and Kathleen Erb founded Rancho Naturalista and Tárcol Lodge. John and Karen Lewis founded Lapa Ríos. Other nature lodges are Selva Verde, El Gavilán, Hacienda Solimar, Los Inocentes, La Ensenada, Villa Lapas, Rancho Casa Grande, Rara Avis, Rainbow Adventures, Río Sierpe Lodge, Savegre Mountain Lodge, Drake Bay Wilderness Resort, El Pizote Lodge, Luna Lodge, and La Laguna del Lagarto. OTS research facilities like La Selva and San Vito also provide accommodations for nature tourists.

International connections also benefited Costa Rica's nature tourism. In 1989, Preferred Adventures Ltd. was founded by Karen Johnson in St. Paul, Minnesota, with special emphasis on Costa Rican tourism. Through the efforts of Karen Johnson and Tony Andersen, Chairman of the Board and for-

Ctenosaur sharing the beach with tourists, Tamarindo

mer CEO of the H. B. Fuller Company and Honorary Consul to Costa Rica from Minnesota, these connections resulted in the creation of the Costa Rica–Minnesota Foundation, which has promoted cultural, medical, and conservation projects in Costa Rica.

As nature tourism lodges proliferated after the mid-1980s, the number of tourists arriving in Costa Rica grew steadily. In 1988, about 330,000 tourists came, and over the next eleven years the number increased to 1,027,000 people per year. During the same period, the annual number of foreign visitors entering national parks increased from about 125,000 to 269,000. From 1988 to 1998 the number of tour operators increased from 58 to 180.

Nature tourism has turned heads throughout Costa Rica and Latin America because of the amount of income it has generated. In 1991, tourism contributed $330 million to the Costa Rican national economy. By 1999 that figure had increased to $940 million and exceeded the amount generated by exports of either coffee ($408 million) or bananas ($566 million)! In addition, nature tourism has created 140,000 jobs. The best thing about nature tourism is that when it is practiced ethically and in balance with the environment, it is a sustainable natural resource use.

Costa Ricans realize that a significant part of the economic health and prosperity of their country is tied to the health and prosperity of their national parks, forests, and wildlife and to the future of the country's macaws, quetzals, Tepescuintles, Jaguars, and Green Turtles. "Don Pepe" Figueres was right. If you make the world a safe place for green turtles and other wildlife, it becomes a better place for people, too.

GEOGRAPHY

Costa Rica, a Central American country between Panama and Nicaragua, is shown in Figure 1. Considering its relatively small size, 19,653 square miles, Costa Rica has an exceptionally high diversity of plant and wildlife species. This is explained in part by the fascinating geological history of the region.

The geological history that led to the creation of Costa Rica goes back about 200 million years to the Triassic Period, when much of the earth's landmass was composed of a supercontinent called Pangaea. The supercontinent began to separate through continental drift, portrayed in Figure 2, which is the process by which the earth's landmasses essentially float upon the molten core of the earth, "drift" among the oceans, and occasionally separate or merge. Pangaea eventually separated into two supercontinents. The northern supercontinent, called Laurasia, later became North America, Asia, and Europe. The southern portion, called Gondwanaland, drifted apart and later became South America, Africa, southern Asia, and Australia.

Figure 1. Location of Costa Rica in Central America

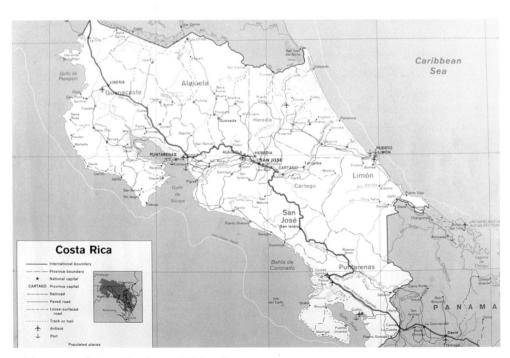

Highway map of Costa Rica. Source: U.S. State Department.

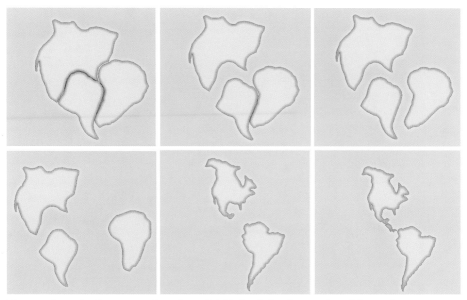

Figure 2. Stages in the process of continental drift that led to the creation of Costa Rica

About 130 million years ago the western portion of Gondwanaland began to separate into South America and Africa. Concurrently, the North American landmass drifted westward from the European landmass. Both North America and South America drifted westward, but they were still separate. By the Pliocene Period, about 3 to 4 million years ago, North America and South America were aligned from north to south, but a gap in the ocean floor between the two continents existed where southern Nicaragua, Costa Rica, and Panama are today.

About three million years ago an undersea plate of the earth's crust, called a tectonic plate, began moving north and eastward in the Pacific Ocean into the area between North and South America. This particular tectonic plate, the Cocos Plate, pushed onto the Caribbean Plate and rose above sea level to create the land bridge that now connects North and South America. That bridge became southern Nicaragua, Costa Rica, and the central and western portions of Panama.

BIOGEOGRAPHY

Biogeography is the relationship between the geography of a region and the long-term distribution and dispersal patterns of its plants and wildlife. The geological history of Costa Rica, Nicaragua, and Panama created a situation in which they became a land bridge between two continents. Plants and wildlife

Topographical relief map of Costa Rica

have been dispersing across that bridge for the last three million years; as a result, Costa Rica became a "biological mixing bowl" of species from both continents. Those dispersal patterns are shown in Figure 3.

Temperate-climate plants that have dispersed southward from North America include alders (*Alnus*), oaks (*Quercus*), walnuts (*Juglans*), magnolias (*Mag-*

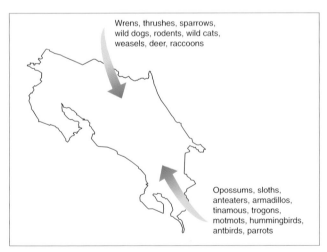

Wrens, thrushes, sparrows, wild dogs, rodents, wild cats, weasels, deer, raccoons

Opossums, sloths, anteaters, armadillos, tinamous, trogons, motmots, hummingbirds, antbirds, parrots

Figure 3. Costa Rica became a land bridge that facilitated the dispersal of wildlife from both North and South America.

nolia), blueberries (*Vaccinium*), Indian paintbrush (*Castilleja*), and mistletoe (*Gaiadendron*). Most dispersal appears to have occurred during cooler glacial periods. As the climate became warmer, these northern-origin plants became biologically "stranded" on the mountains, where the climate was cooler.

Wildlife dispersing from North America across the land bridge included coyotes, tapirs, deer, jaguars, squirrels, and bears. Birds that dispersed from North America to Central and South America included wrens, thrushes, sparrows, woodpeckers, and common dippers.

Plants that dispersed from South America toward the north included tree ferns, cycads, heliconias, bromeliads, orchids, poor-man's umbrella (*Gunnera*), *Puja,* and *Espeletia*. Wildlife that dispersed northward from South America through Costa Rica are opossums, armadillos, porcupines, sloths, monkeys, anteaters, Agoutis, and Tepescuintles. Some species expanded through Central America and Mexico to the United States. Birds that dispersed from South America to Costa Rica and beyond include tinamous, hummingbirds, motmots, trogons, spinetails, flowerpiercers, antbirds, parrots, and woodcreepers.

Migratory Birds

Northern Hemisphere Migrants

Among Costa Rica's 878 bird species, about 180 are migratory. Most migrate from North America to winter in Latin America between September and April. Many people consider that the "real home" of these migrants is in the north and that the birds fly south as if they were going on vacation each winter. They

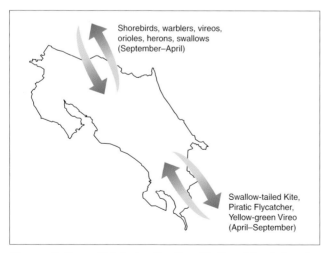

Figure 4. Patterns of bird migration from North and South America

are sometimes referred to by travelers from the United States as "our birds." Patterns of migration from the north and south are shown in Figure 4.

However, the story behind the migratory traditions and the origins of these migrants is both intriguing and surprising. Migratory birds are believed to have originated in the tropics. In tropical forests, insects are present in a great diversity of species, but the numbers of any one species are low. They can be very difficult for birds to find in adequate quantities to feed young. That is why the parents of many tropical bird species have young from previous broods that help feed their young. In northern temperate forests, the species diversity of insects is lower, but the seasonal abundance of each species can be great—as occurs in outbreaks of tent caterpillars. This is referred to as a "protein pulse" as it relates to bird food provided by insects. Such a bountiful supply of insects provides ideal conditions for parent birds to reproduce and adequately feed their young. The annual pattern of seasonal migration was likely tied to the passing of glacial periods, when mild northern summers and the increasing presence and abundance of northern insects benefited birds that migrated north to nest.

Considering that most migrants leave their breeding grounds in September and return north in April, they spend twice as much time in Costa Rica each year as in their breeding range in the north. Northern migrants include ducks, warblers, vireos, tanagers, shorebirds, herons, hawks, falcons, and orioles.

Southern Hemisphere Migrants

As most northern migrants are leaving for North America in March and April, a few birds are migrating from South America to Costa Rica to stay from April through September. The Swallow-tailed Kite, Piratic Flycatcher, Blue-and-white Swallow, and Yellow-green Vireo are migrants from South America.

Elevational Migrants

North American migrants carry out migration by changes in latitude. Some permanent residents in Costa Rica, like the Three-wattled Bellbird, do a migration each year along an elevational gradient from breeding areas in middle- and high-elevation "temperate" forests during the rainy season (April through December) to lower-elevation "tropical" forests during the dry season (January through March). The Silver-throated Tanager, the Scarlet-thighed Dacnis, and many Costa Rican moths carry out elevational migrations.

Fly-Over Migrants

Some birds migrate between wintering areas in South America and summering locations in the United States and Canada. They pass through Costa Rica but do not winter there in significant numbers. They are primarily observed

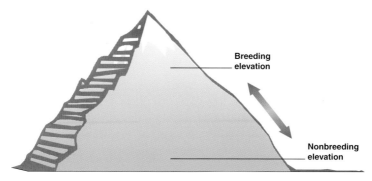

Figure 5. Some tropical insects and birds, like the Three-wattled Bellbird, carry out elevational migrations between breeding seasons and nonbreeding seasons.

during spring migratory periods from March through May and fall migratory periods from July through October. These "fly-over migrants" include Purple Martins, Barn Swallows, Dickcissels, Bobolinks, Scarlet Tanagers, Eastern Kingbirds, Cerulean Warblers, Swainson's Hawks, Swainson's Thrushes, Black-poll Warblers, and many shorebirds.

In addition to fly-over migrants, there are many birds, such as Broad-winged Hawks, Peregrine Falcons, Ospreys, and shorebirds, that winter in Costa Rica as well as Panama and countries of South America.

Migrants/Nonmigrants

Some birds (and the Monarch Butterfly) in Costa Rica are nonmigratory residents that also occur in the United States and Canada. The Hairy Woodpecker, Eastern Meadowlark, House Wren, Red-winged Blackbird, dipper, and several wading birds are nonmigratory permanent residents in Costa Rica that are also found in northern latitudes. Birds that nest in Costa Rica and are also present as migrants during the wintering period from October through April are the White-winged Dove, Red-tailed Hawk, Turkey Vulture, Common Nighthawk, Cattle Egret, Green Heron, Tricolored and Little Blue Herons, and Yellow-crowned Night-Heron.

ENDEMIC SPECIES

An endemic species is one found in one country or region and nowhere else in the world. Costa Rica has three "zones of endemism" in which unique species and subspecies are found. These zones occur because geographic barriers created by mountains, arid zones, or oceans have created genetic isolation from other populations of a species until they finally evolved into separate species through natural selection.

Endemic Wildlife of the Highlands

The mountain ranges and volcanoes of Costa Rica and western Panama include about 160 species of birds out of the 878 species present in the country. The concept of endemic species is often applied to species in a single country, but the Talamanca Mountains are contiguous with those of western Panama. For the purposes of this book, it is considered a single endemic zone. Many birds have evolved into distinctive species or subspecies because they were reproductively isolated from the same species or similar species in the mountains of Guatemala and southern Mexico and from birds in the mountains of eastern Panama and Colombia. This highland endemic zone is portrayed in Figure 6.

An impressive 47 birds are endemic to the mountains and foothills of Costa Rica and western Panama. They include the Black Guan; Black-breasted Wood-Quail; Buff-fronted Quail-Dove; Sulphur-winged Parakeet; Red-fronted Parrotlet; Dusky Nightjar; White-crested Coquette; Black-bellied, Fiery-throated, Scintillant, and Volcano Hummingbirds; Coppery-headed and White-tailed Emeralds; Gray-tailed and White-bellied Mountain-gems; Magenta-throated Woodstar; and Costa Rican Pygmy-Owl.

Other endemics include the Lattice-tailed and Orange-bellied Trogons, Prong-billed Barbet, Ruddy Treerunner, Streak-breasted Treehunter, Silvery-fronted Tapaculo, Dark and Ochraceous Pewees, Black-capped and Golden-

Figure 6. Highland zone of endemic species in Costa Rica and western Panama

bellied Flycatchers, Silvery-throated Jay, Timberline Wren, Sooty Robin, Black-faced Solitaire, and Black-billed Nightingale-Thrush.

Additional endemic birds are the Long-tailed Silky-Flycatcher; Yellow-winged Vireo; Collared Redstart; Black-cheeked and Flame-throated Warblers; Zeledonia (Wrenthrush); Golden-browed Chlorophonia; Spangle-cheeked Tanager; Sooty-capped Bush-Tanager; Black-thighed Grosbeak; Large-footed, Peg-billed, and Yellow-thighed Finches; Slaty Flowerpiercer; and Volcano Junco.

Two species are found only in Costa Rica's mountains—the Coppery-headed Emerald and the Poás Mountain Squirrel (*Syntheosciurus poasensis*).

Many birds, like the Resplendent Quetzal, Magnificent Hummingbird, and Band-tailed Pigeon, are separate subspecies from those found farther north. There are over fifty subspecies of birds in the Costa Rica/western Panama highlands that are different from subspecies in the mountains of Mexico/Guatemala or in eastern Panama and the Andes of northern South America.

Examples of subspecies unique to this highland region are the Sulphur-winged Parakeet, and Black-and-yellow Silky-Flycatcher. Over geologic time, some of these birds can be expected to continue to differentiate from other subspecies and be designated as new species.

Endemic Species of the Southern Pacific Lowlands

Costa Rica's mountain ranges serve as a giant barrier that separates moist and wet lowland rainforest birds and other species that originally dispersed from South America to both the Caribbean lowlands and the southern Pacific lowlands. The mountains have caused reproductive isolation between populations of species that occurred in both areas. Over geologic time, the species diverged into separate species. This has contributed to a second zone of endemic species in Costa Rica: the southern Pacific lowlands. There are several interesting "pairs" of species with a common ancestor that are separated by the mountains between the Caribbean lowlands and the southern Pacific lowlands. Since the ranges of each pair of species do not overlap, these are referred to as allopatric species.

This divergence of two species from a common ancestor is a continuing process, as evidenced by the recent decision by taxonomists to split the Scarlet-rumped Tanager into the Cherrie's Tanager in the Pacific lowlands and the Passerini's Tanager in the Caribbean lowlands. The males are identical, but the females are distinctive. Other birds designated as endemic subspecies include the Masked Yellowthroat (Chiriquí race) and the Variable Seedeater (Pacific race). One day they may eventually become different enough from the Caribbean subspecies to be designated as new species.

Additional endemic species of the southern Pacific lowlands that do not

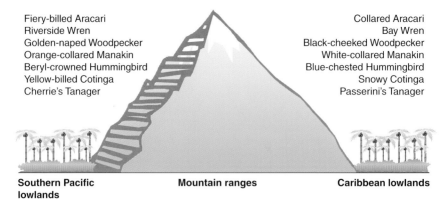

| Southern Pacific lowlands | Mountain ranges | Caribbean lowlands |

Figure 7. Closely related pairs of allopatric species of the Caribbean and Pacific lowlands that share a common ancestor but are now separated by Costa Rica's mountains

have a corresponding closely related species in the Caribbean lowlands include the Baird's Trogon, Black-cheeked Ant-Tanager, Granular Poison Dart Frog, Mangrove Hummingbird, and Red-backed Squirrel Monkey.

Endemic Species of Cocos Island

A third zone of endemism is Cocos Island. This island is 600 miles out in the Pacific, and three endemic birds have evolved there: Cocos Finch, Cocos Cuckoo, and Cocos Flycatcher. Cocos Island is an extension of the Galápagos Island archipelago but it is owned by Costa Rica. There are thirteen finches on the Galápagos Islands commonly referred to as Darwin's finches. The Cocos Finch is actually the fourteenth Darwin's finch.

MAJOR BIOLOGICAL ZONES

The most detailed and traditional classification of the habitats in Costa Rica includes twelve "life zones," as described by the late Dr. Leslie Holdridge of the Tropical Science Center. Those life zones are based on average annual precipitation, average annual temperature, and evapotranspiration potential. Evapotranspiration potential involves the relative amount of humidity or aridity of a region.

For tourism planning purposes, that classification system has been simplified in this book from twelve to six biological zones. These zones, the first five of which are shown in Figure 8, coincide with the distribution of many Costa Rican wildlife species and are designed for trip planning by wildlife tourists. The sixth zone consists of the entire coastline of both the Pacific and the Caribbean coasts. A good trip itinerary should include at least three biological zones in addition to the Central Plateau.

Tropical Dry Forest

The tropical dry forest in northwestern Costa Rica is a lowland region that generally coincides with the boundaries of Guanacaste Province. It extends eastward to the Cordilleras of Guanacaste and Tilarán, southeast to Carara NP, and north to the Nicaragua border. This zone extends from sea level to approximately 2,000 feet in elevation.

This region is characterized by a pronounced dry season from December through March. The deciduous trees include many plants that lose their leaves during the dry season and flower during that leafless period. Common trees are bullhorn acacia (*Acacia*), *Tabebuia*, strangler fig (*Ficus*), *Guazuma*, kapok (*Ceiba*), *Bombacopsis*, buttercup tree (*Cochlospermum*), *Anacardium*, and the national tree of Costa Rica—the Guanacaste tree (*Enterolobium cyclocarpum*). The tallest trees approach 100 feet in height. Rainfall ranges from 40 to 80 inches per year.

Epiphytes are not a major component of the dry forest canopy, as they are in the moist and wet forests. However, some trees are thickly covered with vines like monkey vine (*Bauhinia*) and *Combretum*. The ease with which this forest can be burned and cleared for agricultural purposes has made the tropical dry forest the most endangered habitat in the country.

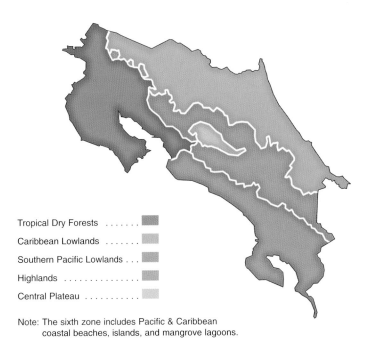

Tropical Dry Forests . . . .
Caribbean Lowlands . . . .
Southern Pacific Lowlands . . .
Highlands . . . .
Central Plateau . . . .

Note: The sixth zone includes Pacific & Caribbean
coastal beaches, islands, and mangrove lagoons.

Figure 8. Five biological zones of Costa Rica. In addition, the country's entire coastline, beaches, and mangrove lagoons make up a sixth zone of biological importance.

Tropical dry forest in Guanacaste

An important habitat within the dry forest consists of the riparian forests along the rivers, also called gallery forests. They maintain more persistent foliage during the dry season.

Wetlands, estuaries, islands, and backwaters of this region's rivers are also a major habitat for wetland wildlife. Especially important are lands along the Río Tempisque, its tributaries, and the wetlands of Palo Verde NP. Birds found predominantly in the forests and wetlands of Guanacaste are the Wood Stork, Jabiru, Blue-winged Teal, Black-bellied Whistling-Duck, Roseate Spoonbill, Muscovy Duck, Snail Kite, Crested Caracara, White-bellied Chachalaca, Double-striped Thick-Knee, White-winged Dove, Inca Dove, Orange-fronted Parakeet, White-fronted Parrot, Black-headed Trogon, White-lored Gnatcatcher, and Yellow-naped Parrot. Other dry forest birds are the Pacific Screech-Owl, Cinnamon Hummingbird, Spot-bellied Bobwhite, Turquoise-browed Motmot, Ivory-billed Woodcreeper, Long-tailed Manakin, White-throated Magpie-Jay, Rufous-naped Wren, Scrub Euphonia, and Stripe-headed Sparrow. The Crested Caracara, Wood Stork, and Muscovy Duck are found in lower numbers in the Caribbean lowlands.

Important examples of tropical dry forest habitat are preserved in Guanacaste Province; Santa Rosa, Las Baulas, and Palo Verde NPs; and Lomas Barbudal BR. The northeastern limit of this zone appears to be at Los Inocentes Lodge. If one travels east from that ranch, the flora and fauna are typical of the

Caribbean lowlands, but if one travels west, the flora and fauna are typical of the Guanacaste dry forest. Some species of the dry forest, including migrant Scissor-tailed Flycatchers and Mourning Doves, Double-striped Thick-Knees, and White-tailed Kites, now appear to be extending their ranges east to the agricultural lands of Los Chiles south of Lake Nicaragua. The southeastern limit of this region is at Carara NP, which has a combination of wildlife characteristic of both the dry forest and the southern Pacific lowlands.

Southern Pacific Lowlands

The southern Pacific lowlands include the moist and wet forested region from Carara NP through the General Valley, Osa Peninsula, and Golfo Dulce lowlands to the Panama border and inland to the premontane forest zone at San Vito.

The moist and wet forests of this region receive 80 to 200 inches of rainfall per year, with a more pronounced dry season from December through March than occurs in the Caribbean lowlands. These forests have fewer epiphytes than are found in Caribbean lowland forests. The tallest trees exceed 150 feet in height.

Among tree species are the kapok (*Ceiba*), *Anacardium,* strangler fig (*Ficus*), wild almond (*Terminalia*), purpleheart (*Peltogyne purpurea*), *Carapa,* buttercup tree (*Cochlospermum vitifolium*), *Virola,* balsa (*Ochroma*), milk tree (*Brosimum*), *Raphia,* garlic tree (*Caryocar costaricense*), and *Hura*. Understory plants include species like bullhorn acacia (*Acacia*), walking palm (*Socratea*), *Bactris,* and *Heliconia*. Most trees maintain their foliage throughout the year.

Much of this region has been converted to pastureland and plantations of pineapple, coconut, and African oil palm. Among the most significant reserves remaining in natural habitat are Carara, Manuel Antonio, and Corcovado NPs. Corcovado NP is one of the finest examples of lowland wet forest in Central America, and it has excellent populations of wildlife species that are rare in other regions—Scarlet Macaws, Jaguars, tapirs, and White-lipped Peccaries.

Additional private reserves include one near San Isidro del General at Los Cusingos, home of Dr. Alexander Skutch. It is managed by the Tropical Science Center. The Wilson Botanical Garden at San Vito is an excellent example of premontane wet forest and is owned and operated by the Organization for Tropical Studies.

The southern Pacific lowland area is of biological interest because it is the northernmost range limit for some South American species, examples of which are the Yellow-headed Caracara, Smooth-billed Ani, Masked Yellowthroat, Thick-billed Euphonia, and Streaked Saltator. Some of these birds are dispersing further into Costa Rica. The Yellow-headed Caracara has recently been seen in southern portions of Guanacaste and in the Pacific lowlands approaching

Monteverde. The Pearl Kite, Southern Lapwing, and Crested Oropendola are new arrivals and have dispersed from Panama to this region since 1999.

Premontane (middle-elevation) sites like the Wilson Botanical Garden at San Vito are included in this biological region because many of the species typical of this region are found up to about 4,000 feet along the western slopes of the Talamanca Mountains. Premontane forests, like those preserved at the Wilson Botanical Garden, are the second most endangered life zone in Costa Rica, after tropical dry forests.

Southern Pacific lowland forest, Manuel Antonio National Park

Central Plateau (Central Valley)

The Central Plateau contains the human population center of Costa Rica. The capital, San José, and adjoining suburbs are located in this relatively flat plateau at an elevation of approximately 3,900 feet. It is bordered on the north and east by major volcanoes of the Central Cordillera: Barva, Irazú, Poás, and Turrialba. To the south is the northern end of the Talamanca Mountains.

Rainfall ranges from 40 to 80 inches per year, and the original life zone in this area was premontane moist forest, but that forest has been largely cleared. The climate of the region, about 68 degrees Fahrenheit year-round, made it ideal for human settlement, and the rich volcanic soils made it an excellent region for growing coffee and sugarcane. The region is also important for production of fruits, vegetables, and horticultural export products like ferns and flowers.

Central Plateau overlooking San José and suburbs

Although premontane moist forests of the Central Plateau are largely gone, extensive plantings of shrubs, flowers, and fruiting and flowering trees throughout the San José area have made it ideal for adaptable wildlife species. Shade coffee plantations are preferred habitats for songbirds, including neotropical migrants. Living fence posts of *Erythrina* and *Tabebuia* are excellent sources of nectar for birds and butterflies. Private gardens abound with butterflies and Rufous-tailed Hummingbirds. Remaining natural places, like the grounds of the Parque Bolívar Zoo in San José, host many wild, free-living butterflies and songbirds.

Among wildlife commonly encountered in backyards, woodlots, and open spaces of the Central Plateau and San José are the Clay-colored Robin, Rufous-tailed Hummingbird, Blue-crowned Motmot, Tennessee Warbler, Blue-gray and Summer Tanagers, White-tailed Kite, Cattle Egret, Turkey and Black Vultures, Rufous-collared Sparrow, Great-tailed Grackle, Broad-winged Hawk, Red-billed Pigeon, Crimson-fronted Parakeet, Groove-billed Ani, Ferruginous Pygmy-Owl, Common Pauraque, Hoffmann's Woodpecker, Tropical Kingbird, Social Flycatcher, Great Kiskadee, Gray-breasted Martin, Blue-and-white Swallow, Brown Jay, House Wren, Baltimore Oriole, and Variegated Squirrel.

Caribbean Lowlands

The Caribbean lowlands include moist and wet lowland forests from the Caribbean coast westward to the foothills of Costa Rica's mountains. The Caribbean lowland fauna extends from Los Inocentes Lodge southeastward to Cahuita and the Panama border. For the purposes of this book, the region extends from sea level to the upper limit of the tropical zone at about 2,000 feet elevation. The premontane forest, at least up to about 3,200 feet, also contains many lowland species. This region receives 80 to 200 inches of rainfall annually.

The trees grow to a height of over 150 feet. This is an evergreen forest that receives precipitation throughout the year and does not have a pronounced dry season like the moist and wet forests of the southern Pacific lowlands. Trees include coconut palms (*Cocos*), raffia palms (*Raffia*), *Carapa*, *Penta-clethra*, kapok (*Ceiba*), swamp almond (*Dipteryx panamensis*), *Alchornea*, walking palm (*Socratea*), and *Pterocarpus*. Tree branches have many epiphytes, such as bromeliads, philodendrons, and orchids. The complexity of the forest canopy contributes to a high diversity of plant and animal species in the treetops. Plants of the understory and forest edge include passion flower (*Passiflora*), *Hamelia*, *Heliconia*, palms, *Costus*, and *Canna*.

Much of this region has been cleared and settled for production of cattle and bananas. Remaining forest reserves include Tortuguero and Cahuita NPs, Gandoca-Manzanillo NWR, Hitoy-Cerere BR, lower elevations of La Amistad and Braulio Carrillo NPs, and Caño Negro NWR. Tortuguero NP is one of the most extensive reserves and one of the best remaining examples of rainforest in Central America. Canals at Tortuguero and open water of the Río Frío and at Caño Negro provide excellent opportunities for viewing wildlife from boats. The grounds of Rara Avis also provide an excellent protected reserve at the upper elevational limit of this biological zone. La Selva Biological Field Station, owned and managed by the OTS, has an exceptional boardwalk and trail system that allows easy viewing of rainforests.

Lower levels of Braulio Carrillo NP offer excellent examples of moist and wet lowland forest, but some trails there are unsafe because of a history of armed robberies of tourists. Inquire with Costa Rican outfitters before using those areas.

The Caribbean lowlands are significant as an excellent example of tropical habitat that supports "classic" rainforest species in all their complex diversity, beauty, and abundance: Great Green Macaws, Chestnut-mandibled and Keel-billed Toucans, trogons, jacamars, manakins, antbirds, parrots, tinamous, Collared Peccaries, tapirs, howler monkeys, spider monkeys, white-faced monkeys, Two- and Three-toed Sloths, bats, morpho and owl butterflies, Strawberry Poison Dart Frogs, and Red-eyed Tree Frogs.

Caribbean lowland wet forest, Tortuguero National Park

Highlands

The highland biological zone comprises Costa Rica's four mountain ranges. This zone includes lower montane, montane, and subalpine elevations generally above 4,200 to 4,500 feet in elevation.

Five volcanoes near the Nicaragua border form the Cordillera of Guanacaste: Orosi, Rincón de la Vieja, Santa María, Miravalles, and Tenorio.

The second group of mountains is the Cordillera of Tilarán. It includes the still-active Arenal Volcano, which exploded in 1968, and mountains that are part of the Monteverde Cloud Forest.

Third is the Cordillera Central that includes three large volcanoes that encircle the Central Plateau—Poás, Irazú, and Barva—and Volcano Turrialba southeast of Barva. Poás is active, and Irazú last erupted in 1963.

The fourth highland region is composed of the great chain of mountains from Cartago to the Panama border. They are the Talamanca Mountains and Cerro de la Muerte, which are of tectonic origin rather than volcanic. Included is Cerro Chirripó, the highest point in Costa Rica at 15,526 feet. These mountains were formed when the Cocos Tectonic Plate pushed up from beneath the ocean onto the Caribbean Tectonic Plate about three to four million years ago. Much of this mountain range is protected as Tapantí NP (11,650 acres), Chirripó NP (123,921 acres), and La Amistad Costa Rica–Panama International Park (479,199 acres).

Crater of Poás Volcano

Talamanca Mountains, Cerro de la Muerte

Species Diversity

Species diversity decreases with elevation. Out of Costa Rica's 878 species of birds, about 130 species can be expected above 6,000 feet. About 105 species can be expected above 7,000 feet; about 85 can be found above 8,000 feet; and about 70 bird species can be expected above 9,000 feet.

Humboldt's Law

The South American explorer Alexander von Humboldt recognized an interesting relationship in tropical countries with high mountains. As one travels up a mountain, the average annual temperature decreases by one degree Fahrenheit for each increase of 300 feet in elevation. As one travels northward from the equator, the mean annual temperature decreases by one degree Fahrenheit for each 67 miles of change in latitude. So an increase of 300 feet elevation on a mountain in the tropics is broadly comparable to traveling 67 miles north. This relationship is portrayed in Figure 9 and is referred to as Humboldt's Law.

Some interesting changes in plant and animal life become apparent in travel up a mountain in the tropics that biologically resemble northward travel in lat-

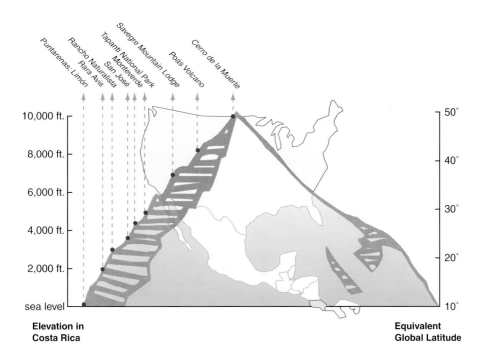

Figure 9. Humboldt's Law: Each 300 feet of ascent on a tropical mountain is comparable to traveling 67 miles north in latitude in terms of the changes in average annual temperature.

itude. The relationship of latitude and elevation becomes apparent at higher elevations because there are many temperate-origin plants and birds in the
highlands. For example, the avifauna present at 8,000 feet elevation on Costa
Rica's mountains includes a higher proportion of temperate-origin thrushes,
finches, juncos, and sparrows than found in the tropical lowlands.

Many plants of higher elevations in Costa Rica are in the same genera as
plants found in the northern United States and Canada, including alders
(*Alnus*), oaks (*Quercus*), blueberries (*Vaccinium*), blackberries (*Rubus*), bay-
berries (*Myrica*), dogwoods (*Cornus*), bearberry (*Actostaphylos*), Indian paintbrush (*Castilleja*), and boneset (*Eupatorium*). Of course, in temperate areas
there is a great deal more variation above and below the annual average temperature than in tropical areas, where there is little variation throughout the
year, and in Costa Rica there has never been a snowfall.

Elevational Zones

To understand the role that elevation plays in plant and animal distribution, it
is useful to understand the main categories by which biologists classify elevations and how those zones relate to the "highlands." These elevational zones
are shown in Figure 10 and described below.

Tropical lowlands: The tropical "lowland" zone ranges from sea level to
about 2,300 feet on the Pacific slope and 2,000 feet on the Caribbean slope.
The lowland zone includes dry forests like those in Guanacaste as well as moist
and wet forests of the southern Pacific and Caribbean lowlands.

Premontane zone: This zone is called the "foothills" or "subtropical" zone
and is also referred to as the "middle-elevation zone." Some birds and other
animals are only found in the foothills. Examples are Speckled and Silver-
throated Tanagers. This zone ranges from about 2,300 feet to 4,900 feet on the

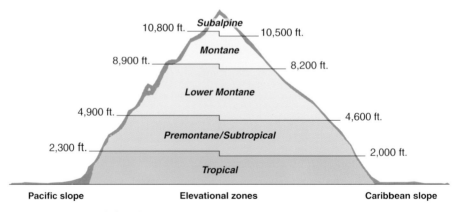

Figure 10. Costa Rica's five elevational zones

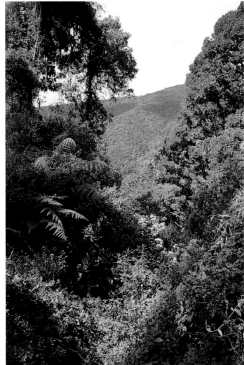

Cloud forest vegetation, Monteverde   Montane wet forest, Cerro de la Muerte

Pacific slope and 2,000 feet to 4,600 feet on the Caribbean slope. It could also be called the coffee zone because it is the zone in which the conditions are ideal for coffee production—and for human settlement.

Lower montane zone: The lower montane zone is part of the "highlands." It includes the region from 4,900 feet to 8,500 feet on the Pacific slope and 4,600 feet to 8,200 feet on the Caribbean slope. One special habitat that occurs within this zone, and in upper levels of the premontane zone, is "cloud forest." The cloud forest occurs roughly from 4,500 to 5,500 feet. A cloud forest, like that at Monteverde, is characterized by fog, mist, and high humidity as well as high precipitation—about 120 to 160 inches per year.

Orchids, bromeliads, philodendrons, and dozens of other epiphytes grow in lush profusion among the branches of cloud forest trees. The Resplendent Quetzal is a well-known bird of the cloud forest as well as lower montane and montane forests.

Montane zone: The montane zone ranges from 8,500 feet to 10,800 feet on the Pacific slope and from 8,200 feet to 10,500 feet on the Caribbean slope. Among plants of lower montane and montane zones are many of northern temperate origins: oak (*Quercus*), blueberry (*Vaccinium*), bearberry (*Arc-*

Subalpine rainforest paramo

tostaphylos), bamboo (*Chusquea*), alder (*Alnus*), bayberry (*Myrica*), magnolia (*Magnolia*), butterfly bush (*Buddleia*), elm (*Ulmus*), mistletoe (*Gaiadendron*), boneset (*Eupatorium*), dogwood (*Cornus*), Indian paintbrush (*Castilleja*), and members of the blueberry family (Ericaceae) like *Satryia, Cavendishia,* and *Psammisia*. Other conspicuous plants are *Oreopanax, Senecio, Miconia, Clusia, Bomarea,* giant thistle (*Cirsium*), *Monochaetum, Poikilocanthos,* wild avocado (*Persea*), poor-man's umbrella (*Gunnera*), and tree ferns.

    Subalpine paramo: Above the montane zone is the area above the treeline called the paramo. It has short, stunted, shrubby vegetation, including bamboo (*Chusquea*), many composites (like *Senecio*), and plants of South American origin from the Andes: a terrestrial bromeliad called *Puya dasylirioides* and a yellow-flowered composite with fuzzy white leaves called lamb's ears (*Espeletia*).

Coastal Beaches, Islands, and Mangrove Lagoons

The sixth biological zone, not portrayed on the map of biological regions (Fig. 8), includes all Pacific and Caribbean coastlines that extend from Nicaragua to Panama. This shoreline habitat consists of the beaches to the high-tide line and adjacent forests, offshore islands, rocky tidepools exposed at low tide,

Río Tárcoles estuary

coral reefs, and mangrove lagoons. Among the more notable islands are Caño Island and Cocos Island. The only coral reef is at Cahuita NP.

Coastal beaches and river estuaries are extremely important as habitat for migratory shorebirds, many of which—such as the Willet, Whimbrel, Wandering Tattler, and Ruddy Turnstone—winter along Costa Rica's beaches. Peregrine Falcons also winter along the coasts and prey on the shorebirds. American Oystercatchers nest along the shorelines above the high-tide line. Lesser Nighthawks nest along Pacific beaches. Brown Boobies, Magnificent Frigatebirds, and Brown Pelicans nest on offshore islands and feed in shallow water near shore. Costa Rica's beaches are extremely important as nesting sites for Green Turtles on the Caribbean coast and for Ridley Turtles and Leatherback Turtles on the Pacific coast.

Other important coastal habitats that are critically endangered by foreign beachfront developers and pollution are those of the mangrove lagoons and mangrove forests. These are important nurseries for fish and wildlife. Significant mangrove lagoons exist at Tamarindo, Playas del Coco, Gulf of Nicoya, Parrita, Golfito, Chomes, Boca Barranca, Quepos, and the 54,362-acre Mangrove Forest Reserve of the Ríos Térraba and Sierpe. They provide exceptional wildlife-watching opportunities during guided boat tours.

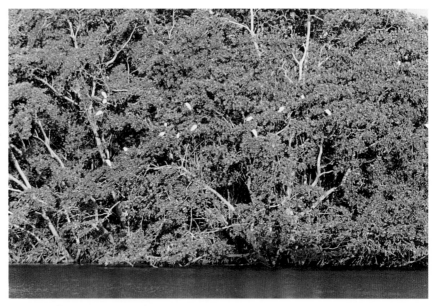

Mangrove lagoon at Tamarindo

WILDLIFE OVERVIEW AND SPECIES COVERAGE

The fauna of Costa Rica includes thousands of birds, mammals, reptiles, amphibians, butterflies, moths, and other invertebrates. This diversity can be both overwhelming and inspiring to a nature enthusiast. Even the casual tourist is drawn to the tropical beauty and appeal of monkeys, motmots, and morphos.

This book has been written to help Costa Rica's visitors know more about the identity and ecology of both common and unusual wildlife. There are field guides just for birds or butterflies, but most tourists are interested in all kinds of wildlife. This field guide includes birds, mammals, reptiles, amphibians, butterflies, moths, and other selected invertebrates.

One of the greatest challenges of writing this book was narrowing down the species list. Species were selected by a process that was both objective and subjective. About two-thirds of the accounts are for birds. This is an arbitrary choice that reflects the strong interest that people have in Costa Rica's diverse bird fauna. About a fifth of the country's 878 birds are included. About 85 percent of the birds included have been seen on 60 percent or more of all Henderson birding trips. Species are selected based on abundance, unique ecological relationships, conspicuousness, or special interest as a rare, endemic, or endangered species. Except for those of very common species, most bird accounts are for residents rather than migrants. Special efforts have been made to include "gee-whiz" facts about life history that make learning fun. Reproductive details have been included for some species that have interesting or unusual reproductive strategies.

Each species account includes a summary of how many trips out of fifteen a species has been encountered on, and the cumulative number of times that the species was recorded during those fifteen trips. For example, "13/15 trips; 59 sightings" for the Brown Pelican indicates that the Brown Pelican was encountered on thirteen out of fifteen trips and recorded 59 times. The highest number of sightings recorded for any species was the Turkey Vulture with 194 sightings. A "sighting" is a record of one or multiple individuals of a species encountered on a walk, boat trip, or drive during a single outing. Among more uncommon species that were included are owls, antbirds, and mammals like the jaguar and tapir that are the subject of keen interest by nature enthusiasts even though chances of seeing them are low.

The amount of life-history information available for Costa Rica's wildlife varies greatly among species. Some have been well studied and others are largely unknown. A large amount of scientific literature has been reviewed and represents the best information available. Much information was obtained from Dr. Dan Janzen's monumental work *Costa Rican Natural History* (1983), the *Handbook of the Birds of the World*, Volumes 1–6 (1992), by Josep del Hoyo, Andrew Elliott, and Jordi Sargatal, and from species accounts in *The Birds of North America* (1992–2001), *A Guide to the Birds of Costa Rica* (1989) by Gary Stiles and Alexander Skutch, and *The Butterflies of Costa Rica and Their Natural History*, Volumes 1–2 (1987/1997), by Philip J. DeVries. All literature used is included in the respective Literature Cited sections.

Each account is preceded by the species's common name, scientific name, Costa Rican name(s), number of trips on which the species has been sighted and number of sightings, migratory or resident status (for birds), length and (where available) weight, vocalization tapes with the songs or calls of the species, geographic range, and elevational range. Appendix C is a detailed list of the vocalization tapes referred to in the species accounts.

During our fifteen birding tours to Costa Rica, we visited 46 sites and subsequently compiled an Excel spreadsheet of 15,500 wildlife sightings from those tours. The 292 species selected for this book represent about 60 percent of those sightings. All sites are shown in Figure 11. Details for each site are in Appendix B. Both elevations and Geographic Position System (GPS) readings of latitude and longitude were taken so these observations could be used to compile distribution maps, which have been prepared for selected invertebrates and for all vertebrates. They mainly portray sightings recorded on fifteen Henderson birding trips to Costa Rica. Concentrations of dots within a biological zone portray the general distribution of a species, but there are obviously many areas we have not visited where these species also occur. There is a seasonal bias to these sightings, as most were recorded in January and February.

Photos by the author have been used to illustrate all species accounts. These photos represent the best available from a personal collection of 33,000 Costa Rican and Latin American nature and wildlife images. It is felt that the postures, behavior, and natural colors provided by these photos provide the best reference for nature enthusiasts because paintings usually fail to capture the stunning iridescence of many tropical birds and butterflies. Also, paintings frequently fail to convey correct color, proportions, and postures of the creatures involved because they are often painted from dead or faded museum specimens.

All photos were taken with Pentax 35-millimeter cameras (k-1000, sf-10, sf-1n, and pz-1). Lenses included a Pentax 100–300 mm. telephoto lens and Sigma 400 mm. apo telephoto lens (sometimes with a 1.4x Sigma teleconverter). Close-up photos of butterflies and hummingbirds were taken with a Tamron 90 mm. macro lens and 1.7x Pentax teleconverter. Flash units included a Pentax af400ftz for telephoto flash (used with a Lepp Project-A-Flash) and a Pentax af240ft for macro photography. Fuji 100 Sensia i and Sensia ii film was used for the photos. More information on the author's collection of Latin American wildlife and natural history images is available at his Green Book web site: http://www.agpix.com/carrolhenderson.

Over 70 percent of the wildlife images included in this book were photographed in the wild, primarily in Costa Rica. Some have been photographed in the wild in other countries of Latin America, but they are the same species or subspecies that occur in Costa Rica. The remainder were taken in captive settings either in Latin America or in the United States. Some photos have been enhanced through the use of Adobe Photoshop to highlight identification marks and remove distracting background features.

Figure 11. Wildlife tourism sites referred to in the text and on species distribution maps

LITERATURE CITED

Beletsky, Les. 1998. *Costa Rica: The Ecotravellers' Wildlife Guide.* San Diego, Calif.: Academic Press. 426 pp.

Boza, Mario A. 1987. *Costa Rica National Parks.* San José, Costa Rica: Fundación Neotrópica. 112 pp.

_____. 1988. *Costa Rica National Parks.* San José, Costa Rica: Fundación Neotrópica. 272 pp.

Cahn, Robert. 1984. An Interview with Alvaro Ugalde. *The Nature Conservancy News* 34(1): 8–15.

Carr, Archie, and David Carr. 1983. A Tiny Country Does Things Right. *International Wildlife* 13(5): 18–25.

Cornelius, Stephen E. 1986. *The Sea Turtles of Santa Rosa National Park.* San José, Costa Rica: Fundación de Parques Nacionales. 64 pp.

Ehrenfeld, David. 1989. Places. *Orion Nature Quarterly* 8(3): 5–7.

Franke, Joseph. 1997. *Costa Rica's National Parks and Preserves: A Visitor's Guide.* Seattle: The Mountaineers. 223 pp.

Gómez, Luis Diego, and Jay M. Savage. 1989. Searchers on That Rich Coast: Costa Rican Field Biology, 1400–1980. In *Costa Rican Natural History,* ed. Daniel H. Janzen, 1–11. Chicago: Univ. of Chicago Press. 816 pp.

Henderson, Carrol L. 1969. Fish and Wildlife Resources of Costa Rica, with Notes on Human Influences. Master's thesis, Univ. of Georgia, Athens. 340 pp.

Holdridge, Leslie R. 1967. *Life Zone Ecology.* San José, Costa Rica: Tropical Science Center. 206 pp.

INICEM. 1998. Costa Rica: Datos e Indicadores Básicos. Costa Rica at a Glance. Miami: INICEM Group. Booklet. 42 pp.

Janzen, Daniel H. 1990. Costa Rica's New National System of Conserved Wildlands. Mimeographed report. 15 pp.

_____. 1991. How to Save Tropical Biodiversity: The National Biodiversity Institute of Costa Rica. *American Entomologist* 36(3): 159–171.

Kohl, Jon. 1993. No Reserve Is an Island. *Wildlife Conservation* 96(5): 74–75.

Lewin, Roger. 1988. Costa Rican Biodiversity. *Science* 242: 1637.

Lewis, Thomas A. 1989. Daniel Janzen's Dry Idea. *International Wildlife* 19(1): 30–36.

Market Data. 1993. Costa Rica: Datos e Indicadores Básicos. Costa Rica at a Glance. San José, Costa Rica. 36 pp.

McPhaul, John. 1988. Peace, Nature: C. R. Aims. *The Tico Times* 32(950): 1, 21.

Meza Ocampo, Tobías A. 1988. *Areas Silvestres de Costa Rica.* San Pedro, Costa Rica: Alma Mater. 112 pp.

Murillo, Katiana. 1999. Ten Years Committed to Biodiversity. *Friends in Costa Rica* 3: 23–25.

Pariser, Harry S. 1998. *Adventure Guide to Costa Rica.* 3rd ed. Edison, N.J.: Hunter. 546 pp.

Pistorius, Robin, and Jeroen van Wijk. 1993. Biodiversity Prospecting: Commercializing Genetic Resources for Export. *Biotechnology and Development Monitor* 15: 12–15.

Pratt, Christine. 1999. Tourism Pioneer Wins Award, Hosts Concorde. *The Tico Times* 43(1507): 4.

Rich, Pat V., and T. H. Rich. 1983. The Central American Dispersal Route: Biotic History and Paleogeography. In *Costa Rican Natural History,* ed. Daniel H. Janzen, 12–34. Chicago: Univ. of Chicago Press. 816 pp.

Sandlund, Odd Terje. 1991. Costa Rica's INBIO: Towards Sustainable Use of Natural Biodiversity. Norsk Institutt for Naturforskning. Notat 007. Trondheim, Norway. Report. 25 pp.

Sekerak, Aaron D. 1996. *A Travel and Site Guide to Birds of Costa Rica.* Edmonton, Alberta: Lone Pine. 256 pp.

Skutch, Alexander F. 1971. *A Naturalist in Costa Rica.* Gainesville: University of Florida Press. 378 pp.

_____. 1984. Your Birds in Costa Rica. Santa Monica, Calif.: Ibis. Brochure. 8 pp.

Sun, Marjorie. 1988. Costa Rica's Campaign for Conservation. *Science* 239: 1366–1369.

Tangley, Laura. 1990. Cataloging Costa Rica's Diversity. *BioScience* 40(9): 633–636.

Ugalde, Alvaro F., and María Luisa Alfaro. 1992. Financiamiento de la Conservación en los Parques Nacionales y Reservas Biológicas de Costa Rica. Speech presented at the IV Congreso Mundial de Parques Nacionales, Caracas, Venezuela, February. Mimeographed copy. 16 pp.

Zúñiga Vega, Alejandra. 1991. Archivo de riqueza natural. *La Nación,* Section B, Viva, February 4.

_____. 1991. Estudios de los manglares. *La Nación,* Section B, Viva, February 4.

Butterflies and Moths

The abundance and diversity of butterflies bring extra life and beauty to Costa Rica's forests and gardens. Butterflies, as well as moths, are dependent on tropical plants as caterpillar food, and they are essential to plants because of their role as flower pollinators.

There are at least 1,250 species of butterflies in Costa Rica and at least 8,000 moths. Butterflies and moths may be enjoyed during any time of year, but they are most apparent in the rainy season, primarily June and July.

Much of the beauty of these creatures lies not just in their colors and designs but in their amazing adaptations for survival and reproduction. Swallowtails have caterpillars that mimic bird droppings! Heliconius butterflies warn predators of toxic chemicals in their bodies with bright warning coloration. Caligo butterflies have deceptive eyespots that trick attacking birds. Dozens of butterflies have complicated "mimicry complexes" whereby edible species mimic inedible species that have warning coloration and toxic body chemicals. Some apparent butterflies and wasps are actually moths, and some moths undergo extensive migrations that rival the monarch migrations of North America.

Half of the enjoyment of learning about tropical moths and butterflies comes not just from watching them but from photographing them, identifying them, and learning about their fascinating life histories. Don't limit your observations to daytime. Although most butterflies are most active in the morning and early afternoon, Caligo butterflies are most active at dawn and dusk. Some tropical lodges like Rancho Naturalista provide special lights to attract moths and other insects at night so you can see and marvel at their beauty and adaptations. Other rainforest lodges have security lights at night that also attract nocturnal insects.

A total of twenty-four butterflies and moths are covered in the following accounts. This is only a very small representation of the thousands of species present in Costa Rica, but they include some of the more abundant or conspicuous species that may be encountered while traveling in that country. One problem with butterflies is that many tropical species do not have common names, and their Costa Rican names typically apply to many different butterflies. To avoid confusion, the scientific name is provided for most species accounts unless there is a common name in use from more northerly populations. For more details on the butterflies, see volumes 1 and 2 of *The Butterflies of Costa Rica and Their Natural History* (1987 and 1997), by Philip J. DeVries, and *Costa Rican Natural History* (1983), edited by Daniel H. Janzen. To view photos of Costa Rican caterpillars, see <http://janzen.sas.upenn.edu>.

SWALLOWTAIL FAMILY (Papilionidae)

Thoas Swallowtail

Heraclides thoas
(formerly *Papilio thoas*)

    WINGSPREAD: 4.5–4.8 inches.

    RANGE: Nicaragua to Brazil.

    ELEVATIONAL RANGE: Sea level to
3,600 feet.

The Thoas Swallowtail is a large butterfly that is conspicuous as it flies through tropical forests. There are thirteen swallowtail species in the country, and one of them, the Giant Swallowtail (*Papilio cresphontes*), is very similar to this species. This butterfly is most common in moist and wet forests of the Caribbean lowlands and on the southern Pacific slope, but it may also be seen in Guanacaste. Habitat includes forest edges, clearings, or areas along streams where sunlight penetrates the forest canopy.

Adults are fast fliers and are adept at avoiding predation by birds. Among flowers visited for nectar are *Stachytarpheta* and *Lantana*. Males visit wet sand to sip the moisture for salt concentrations that are apparently needed for development. Host plants include members of the piper family (*Piper* and *Pothomorphe* spp.). Eggs are laid singly and hatch into remarkable caterpillars that look like bird droppings! This is a very effective camouflage that discourages birds from eating them.

Thoas Swallowtail adult

Thoas Swallowtail caterpillar

Hamadryas guatemalena

Hamadryas februa

BRUSH-FOOTED BUTTERFLY FAMILY (Nymphalidae)

Guatemalan Cracker and Gray Cracker

Hamadryas guatemalena
and *H. februa*

> COSTA RICAN NAMES: *Calicó; soñadora común.*
> WINGSPREAD: 2.6–3.5 inches.
> RANGE: Mexico to Costa Rica.
> ELEVATIONAL RANGE: Sea level to 3,300 feet.

The camouflage markings of "cracker" or "calico" butterflies help these species "disappear" when they land on a tree trunk. They rest upside down and are known for an unusual "cracking" sound that they make in flight—often as they chase away other butterflies. The sound can be heard up to sixty feet away and was first reported by Charles Darwin when he explored South America. The Guatemalan Cracker (*H. guatemalena*) is found only on the Pacific slope in dry, moist, and wet forests but is most common in the dry forests of Guanacaste. The Gray Cracker (*H. februa*), the most common cracker butterfly in Costa Rica, is distinguished from the previous species by red crescents on the tiny eyespots of the hindwing margins. It occurs throughout the country in the lowlands of both slopes but is most common in forests of Guanacaste.

There are nine kinds of cracker butterflies in the country. Six have the mottled gray or brownish camouflage markings, including *H. guatemalena* and *H. februa*. Since they depend on camouflage for survival, they do not have protective chemical defenses in their bodies. They are preyed on by Rufous-tailed Jacamars. Adults do not feed on flower nectar. They sip juices of rotting fruit, fermented sap from leguminous trees, and animal dung. The only host plants on which females lay eggs are members of the euphorbia family: *Dalechampia* spp.

Similar Species: *Hamadryas laodamia saurites*

Hamadryas laodamia saurites is also in the genus of cracker butterflies, but it is black with iridescent blue spots. DeVries (1987) refers to it as the "starry night" hamadryas. Eggs are laid on a euphorbia called *Dalechampia triphylla*. The caterpillar apparently sequesters bad-tasting toxic chemicals from this plant because this butterfly is avoided by jacamars. The bright blue highlights serve as a warning coloration.

The distribution includes Caribbean and Pacific slopes to an elevation of about 3,300 feet, but it is most common in the middle and upper canopy of Caribbean lowland forests. While at rest, *H. laodamia saurites* rests upside down on tree trunks with the wings open. It feeds on juices of rotting fruits.

Hamadryas laodamia saurites adult

Marpesia berania

Marpesia berania

> WINGSPREAD: 2.4–2.5 inches.
> RANGE: Mexico through Brazil.
> ELEVATIONAL RANGE: Sea level to
> 3,300 feet.

Marpesia berania is one of eight "daggerwing" butterflies in Costa Rica. Common throughout the country, it is characterized by distinctive tails on the hindwing, an orange base color, and slender longitudinal brown bands on the wings. The distribution includes both Caribbean and Pacific lowlands in a wide variety of habitats. It is most common in moist and wet lowland forests and less common in the tropical dry forests of Guanacaste. Adults visit the blossoms of *Cordia* and *Croton* bushes.

Males may gather in large numbers along riverbanks, where they feed on moisture in the sand. *Marpesia berania* sleeps in groups of up to fifty butterflies. This daggerwing lives much longer than many butterflies—up to five months. Host plants are all in the family Moraceae, but the host species on which this daggerwing lays its eggs is unknown.

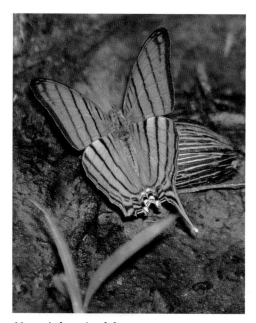

Marpesia berania **adult**

Adelpha cytheria marcia

Adelpha cytheria marcia

WINGSPREAD: 1.8–2.0 inches.

RANGE: Guatemala to Colombia.

ELEVATIONAL RANGE: Sea level to 3,000 feet.

This common butterfly inhabits disturbed habitats. It is brown with white bands on the hindwings and is one of many tropical butterflies that have prominent orange bands on the forewings aligned with continuous white bands on the posterior of the forewings and adjacent hindwings. Inhabiting moist and wet lowlands of the Caribbean and southern Pacific regions, this butterfly is absent from Guanacaste's dry forests. It frequents forest edges, beaches, and forest openings. The host plant is a species in the coffee family (Rubiaceae) called *Sabicea villosa,* found in disturbed places. Adults feed on the juices of rotting fruits and the nectar of asters and hot lips (Cephaelis). There are thirty species in the genus *Adelpha* in Costa Rica, and they can be difficult to identify.

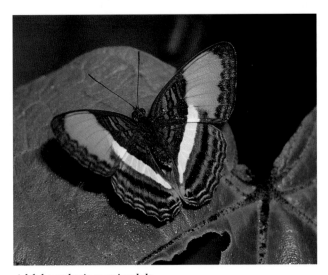

Adelpha cytheria marcia **adult**

Similar Species: *Doxocopa laure*

Doxocopa laure is similar to *Adelpha cytheria*. This butterfly is also brown with white bands through the wings and orange on the forward portion of each white band. This coloration would appear to be an example of mimicry, but since these butterflies do not contain toxic chemicals that deter predators, the

Doxocopa laure **adult male**

reason for this resemblance is unknown. The male has iridescent purple and blue highlights adjacent to the white bands. Host plants are trees and shrubs in the elm family (Ulmaceae), including *Celtis pallida*.

Doxocopa laure occurs on the Pacific and Caribbean slopes, including Guanacaste's dry forests. Adults visit *Croton* and *Cordia* flowers as well as wet sand and fresh mammal droppings. Among locations where this butterfly can be seen are Santa Rosa NP and Monteverde.

Hypanartia arcaei

Hypanartia arcaei
> WINGSPREAD: 2.2–2.3 inches.
> RANGE: Costa Rica and Panama.
> ELEVATIONAL RANGE: 4,000–7,200 feet.

Hypanartia arcaei is a medium-sized brown butterfly of higher elevations with a conspicuous orange patch on each forewing and a short tail on each hindwing. This butterfly is usually encountered in Cerro de la Muerte, in the Talamanca Mountains, and in the San Gerardo de Dota region, including Savegre Mountain Lodge. Host plants for this genus include plants in the nettle family (Urticaceae) and elm family (Ulmaceae), but the host plant species is unknown. Preferred habitats include cloud forests and montane oak forests.

This attractive butterfly is usually solitary and may be found at wet sites like river edges and water seepages. It will also visit the large yellow flowers of *Senecio megaphylla*. At one site in Cerro de la Muerte, this butterfly landed on the binoculars of persons in our birding group and spent several minutes perched there, suggesting that it was attracted to salt concentrations from perspiration deposits.

***Hypanartia arcaei* adult**

Malachite

Siproeta stelenes

WINGSPREAD: 3.5–3.8 inches.

RANGE: South Florida and Texas to Brazil.

ELEVATIONAL RANGE: Sea level to 4,600 feet.

The Malachite is a medium-sized butterfly with greenish spots and blotches on the dorsal and ventral wing surfaces. One of the most common butterflies in Central America, it lives along forest edges, among disturbed second growth, and in rural and urban gardens. This butterfly is conspicuous on sunny days and occurs on both the Caribbean and Pacific slopes at lower and middle elevations.

In addition to visiting flowers, *Siproeta stelenes* visits rotting fruits, carrion, and bat dung under bat roosts. Adults roost in groups on shrubs close to the ground. Females lay single eggs on new leaves of plants in the Acanthaceae family, including *Ruellia coccinea* and *R. metallica; Justicia candalerianae* and *J. carthaginensis;* and *Blechum brownei, B. blechum,* and *B. pyramidatum.*

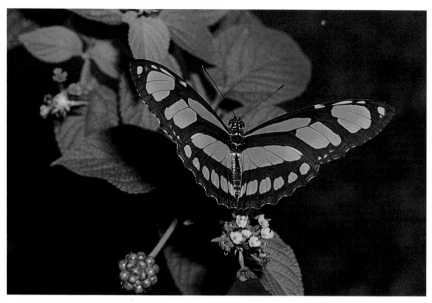

Malachite adult

Banded Peacock

Anartia fatima

Costa Rican name: ***Cocinera.***
Wingspread: 2.1–2.4 inches.
Range: Mexico to Eastern Panama.
Elevational range: Sea level to 4,900 feet.

The Banded Peacock is the most common butterfly in Costa Rica and is found in meadows; along roadsides, pastures, and riverbanks; and in deforested areas. It occurs in Guanacaste and in Caribbean and southern Pacific regions. It lives as high as middle elevations like the Wilson Botanical Garden at San Vito and Monteverde. The medium brown to dark brown wings have conspicuous yellow or white bands and red highlights on the hindwings. Newly emerged male butterflies have yellow bands that eventually fade to white. Newly emerged females may have yellow or white bands, but the yellow-banded females also fade to white.

Caterpillars feed primarily on plants in the Acanthaceae family, including *Blechum brownei* and *Blechum pyramidatum,* found in disturbed places. Other host plants include *Justicia candalerianae, Dicliptera unguiculata,* and *Ruellia.* This butterfly is active in sunny areas throughout the day and feeds primarily

Banded Peacock adult

on nectar of second-growth plants like *Lantana, Emilia,* and *Cosmos.* An adult may live about two weeks.

Not protected by toxic chemicals, this butterfly is preyed upon by spiders, praying mantises, frogs, lizards, birds, and mammals. Males are so overzealous in defending territories that they pursue not only other males of their species, but other butterfly species, birds, and even humans!

Julia Butterfly (Orange Longwing)

Dryas iulia
>WINGSPREAD: 3–5.6 inches.
>RANGE: Southern Texas and Florida to Brazil.
>ELEVATIONAL RANGE: Sea level to 5,900 feet.

The bright orange Julia Butterfly is one of the most common and easily identified butterflies in the American tropics. Its elongated orange wings with black highlights distinguish it from other passionflower butterflies. The male is bright orange with a slender black marking along the leading edge of the forewing. The female is dull orange with more black edging on the forewing. A species of disturbed areas, forest edges, and forest canopy, the Julia Butterfly is often observed in openings along forest roads and trails where passionflowers and vines (*Passiflora*) occur.

Julia Butterfly adult female

Adults visit many flowers for nectar, including *Lantana*. The host plants on which eggs are laid are limited to the genus *Passiflora*. The Julia Butterfly also visits mud puddles and sandy, wet stream edges to sip mineral-laden moisture. This butterfly is found in the lowlands of both the Pacific and Caribbean slopes. Though usually seen near the ground, it also flies in the forest canopy. Individuals of this butterfly species live only a few weeks.

Similar Species: *Dione juno*

Another passionflower butterfly, *Dione juno*, resembles *Dryas iulia*. The wings are bright orange, but the black edging is more pronounced than for the Julia Butterfly, and the posterior edge of each forewing is jagged. This butterfly is less common than *Dryas iulia*, and the wingspread is slightly smaller (about 2.8–3.2 inches). It is found from sea level to about 3,900 feet on Caribbean and

Pacific slopes. Habitat includes open and disturbed areas, forest edges, and trail sides. It also inhabits the canopy of primary rainforest. This butterfly can be found throughout the year, but it is most abundant during the rainy season. As with *Dryas iulia*, host plants for the eggs and caterpillars include members of the genus *Passiflora*.

Dione juno **adult**

Zebra Longwing

Heliconius charitonia

Costa Rican name: ***Zebra; zebrita.***

Wingspread: 3.0–3.5 inches.

Range: Southern Texas and Florida
to Peru.

Elevational range: Sea level to
4,200 feet; occasionally to 8,200 feet.

The Zebra Longwing is one of fourteen Heliconius butterflies in Costa
Rica. The genus is well known for its
host-plant relationships to passionflowers and its fascinating mimicry patterns. This species is the only member of this genus with a pattern of yellow
stripes and spots on a black background.

Adults visit *Lantana, Stachytarpheta, Cissus, Rytidostylis,* and *Hamelia.* This
butterfly gathers pollen on its proboscis, as do *Heliconius hecale zuleika* and *H.
erato.* The improved nutrition from the pollen helps them live up to three
months and allows females to lay up to 1,000 eggs! Without pollen, they may
live only a month. Adults roost in groups of up to seventy individuals at night.

The caterpillars have some incredible adaptations. They feed on *Passiflora*
flowers that are toxic or deadly to other butterflies of this genus, including *P. lo-
bata, P. biflora, P. menispermifolia, P. adenopoda,* and *P. pulchella.* This is the
only butterfly that can feed on leaves of the plant *Tetrastylis.* Adult male Zebra
Longwings have one other unusual habit. They mate with the female before
she emerges from her chrysalis! The Zebra Longwing is found on both slopes
at lower and middle elevations. Less common in the southern Pacific region
and at high elevations, it is a species of open areas, pastures, gardens, forest
edges, coffee plantations, and roadside ditches.

Zebra Longwing adult

Heliconius hecale zuleika adult

Heliconius hecale zuleika

Heliconius hecale zuleika
WINGSPREAD: 3.3–3.9 inches.
RANGE: Nicaragua to Panama.
ELEVATIONAL RANGE: Sea level to
5,600 feet.

This passionflower butterfly is one of the most common "classic" black, orange, and yellow Heliconius butterflies in Costa Rica. It is found at lower and middle elevations on both Caribbean and Pacific slopes. As with other Heliconius butterflies, the bright colors are a warning to birds that they contain toxic chemicals that will make them sick if eaten.

They contain cyanogenic glycosides—a cyanide poison that the caterpillars manufacture from passionflower leaves. Other insects cannot eat passionflower leaves, but Heliconius butterflies have the ability to process these poisons. Birds exposed to such toxins respond by retching, vomiting, bill wiping, fluffing and flattening of the feathers, and exhibiting a sickly composure.

This butterfly lays eggs on passionflowers, including *Passiflora vitifolia, P. platyloba, P. oerstedii, P. filipes,* and *P. auriculata.* Upon hatching, adults feed on *Psiguria, Gurania, Lantana, Psychotria, Hamelia,* and *Anguria.* In addition to feeding on the nectar, this butterfly collects pollen on its proboscis. It makes a thick slurry in the rolled proboscis. Amino acids leach into the nectar, and this is drunk by the butterfly. The high protein content of the amino acids from the pollen gives this butterfly an increased life span and greater reproductive potential. Although most butterflies live only about ten days, individuals of this species may live up to nine months.

Heliconius erato petiverana

Heliconius erato petiverana
  WINGSPREAD: 2.4–2.9 inches.
  RANGE: Mexico to Brazil.
  ELEVATIONAL RANGE: Sea level to
  5,300 feet.

Heliconius erato petiverana is the most common Heliconius butterfly in Costa Rica. Its black, yellow, and red pattern is conspicuous as it visits flowers of disturbed forest edges, second-growth forests, roadsides, coffee plantations, and gardens. Occurring on both Pacific and Caribbean slopes, this butterfly, like other members of its genus, is long-lived because it feeds on pollen as well as nectar. Adults visit flowers of *Psiguria, Lantana, Psychotria, Cissus, Anguria, Rytidostylis,* and *Hamelia.*

Eggs are laid singly at the tips of passionflower leaves, and host species include *Passiflora talamancensis, P. coriacea, P. costaricensis,* and *P. biflora.* Adults roost in groups of up to ten individuals near the ground in second-growth vegetation.

Similar Species: Heliconius melpomene

Heliconius melpomene is a nearly identical "Müllerian mimic" of *Heliconius erato.* Both share toxic qualities if eaten, and birds avoid both species since they look alike. This is one of the most incredible mimicry complexes in

Adult *Heliconius erato*

Heliconius butterfly with pollen slurry on its proboscis

Adult *Heliconius melpomene*

Latin America. Processes of natural selection have resulted in the development of twelve different color patterns, or subspecies, for *H. erato* throughout the range of this species from Mexico to Brazil. In eleven of twelve cases, the distinctive color pattern of each *H. erato* subspecies is almost perfectly mimicked by the color patterns of *H. melpomene* in the same area.

The subtle differences in these two butterflies include the yellow stripe on the underside of the hindwing. This stripe extends to the top of the hindwing when the butterfly is at rest with the wings closed in *H. erato,* and it stops short of the upper edge of the hindwing on *H. melpomene.* Also, there are four tiny red spots on the underside of the hindwing where the wing attaches to the thorax on *H. erato* and only three tiny red spots on *H. melpomene.*

Comparison of underwing markings of *H. erato,* left, and *H. melpomene,* right

Greta oto

Greta oto

> COSTA RICAN NAME: *Espejitos.*
> WINGSPREAD: 2.2–2.4 inches.
> RANGE: Mexico to Panama.
> ELEVATIONAL RANGE: 1,600–5,200 feet.

Greta oto adult

Greta oto is one of the most common of more than twenty small "clearwing" butterflies in the subfamily Ithomiinae. The transparent wings make it difficult for a predatory bird to track it in flight. An insect of middle elevations, this butterfly is regularly encountered in gardens around San José and forest openings and disturbed habitats of the Caribbean and Pacific slopes. This clearwing undergoes elevational migratory movements and at times can be very abundant.

Adults visit common flowers like *Lantana*. Eggs are laid on flowers of *Cestrum lanatum* and *C. standleyi* in the nightshade family (Solanaceae). From these plants the caterpillars acquire toxic alkaloids and an undesirable taste that discourages predation by birds. The pupae of this butterfly are silver and contribute to its Costa Rican name *espejitos,* meaning "little mirrors." The caterpillars develop into very toxic adults that also discourage predation due to their taste and effects on birds that eat them.

Caligo (Owl) Butterfly

Caligo eurilochus sulanus
and *Caligo atreus dionysos*

> COSTA RICAN NAME: **Buhito pardo**.
> WINGSPREAD: 5.4–7.2 inches.
> RANGE:
> *C. e. sulanus*—Guatemala to Panama.
> *C. a. dionysos*—Costa Rica to Panama.
> ELEVATIONAL RANGE:
> *C. e. sulanus*—Sea level to 5,300 feet.
> *C. a. dionysos*—Sea level to 4,300 feet.

The huge Owl Butterfly is one of the best-known insects of tropical lowland forests. The "eyespot" on the hindwing is the most conspicuous identification feature and is shared by all five species of Caligo. Though primarily a rainforest butterfly, some species also occur in the dry forests of Guanacaste. The wingspread can exceed five inches, although this butterfly is typically observed with the wings closed as it rests on the side of a tree.

Caligo butterflies have an exceptional strategy for surviving attacks by birds. The eyespot provides a type of "startle" strategy for evading predatory birds. When a bird attacks, the "eye" provides a "startling" effect on the bird that disrupts the attack and tricks the bird into attacking the eyespot rather than the real body of the butterfly. The butterfly has such huge wings that it can still fly to escape and live to reproduce even if the hindwing is damaged.

The caterpillars have two interesting survival adaptations. The young green caterpillars are inconspicuous because they align themselves along the main veins of leaves on host plants like *Heliconia,* banana (*Musa*), and *Calathea.* Before forming a pupa, they become conspicuous because of their size (over four inches long), but the larger caterpillars have a protective gland that is everted and used to release an offensive chemical when attacked. Owl butterflies are most active at dawn and dusk. They feed on rotting fruits like bananas, tree sap, mammal droppings, and even carrion. Adults may live up to five weeks.

Although banana plants (*Musa*) are not native to Costa Rica, they are heavily used by Caligo caterpillars. This butterfly is considered an agricultural pest by banana growers. Caligo butterflies can be seen in Tortuguero NP and at La Selva Biological Field Station on the Caribbean slope. On the Pacific slope, look for them at Carara NP, Tiskita Jungle Lodge, Corcovado NP, and the Wilson Botanical Garden at San Vito.

Adult *Caligo eurilochus*

Adult *Caligo atreus* showing wing damage from a bird attack

Caterpillar of *C. eurilochus* camouflaged along the midvein of a leaf

Morpho peleides

Morpho peleides

> Costa Rican names: **Celeste común; morfo.**
>
> Wingspread: 5.0–6.1 inches.
>
> Range: Mexico to Colombia and Venezuela.
>
> Elevational range: Sea level to 5,900 feet.

The stunning Morpho Butterfly is the most conspicuous and well-known rainforest butterfly. Its swift, erratic flight and iridescent blue wings create brilliant flashes of blue amid lush rainforest vegetation. This butterfly is frequently seen along forest trails, on coffee and banana plantations, and along woodland streams in lowland and middle elevations of the Caribbean and Pacific slopes. Most adults in the Caribbean lowlands are iridescent blue on the dorsal surface of the wings. In the southern Pacific lowlands they have more brown on the wings, and some in the Central Plateau are nearly all brown. In addition to *Morpho peleides,* there are five other morphos in the country, including one white species.

It is believed that the iridescent blue wings with contrasting brown markings below serve as an effective defense against predatory birds because morphos have a fast, irregular "dipsy-doodling" flight that makes the butterfly difficult to pursue. Because it has these escape strategies, the morpho does not have toxins in its body like Heliconius butterflies do. This butterfly is eaten by Rufous-tailed Jacamars and large flycatchers.

Morpho butterflies do not visit flowers. They feed only on rotting fruits like bananas, on fruit peels, and on sap that flows from cuts in the bark of trees and vines. Eggs are laid singly on rainforest plants, including *Mucuna* vines and plants in the genera *Pterocarpus, Lonchocarpus, Machaerium, Platymiscium, Andira, Heteropteris, Swartzia,* and *Dalbergia.* Newly hatched caterpillars are yellow and red.

Morphos can be observed in Tortuguero NP, La Selva Biological Station, Braulio Carrillo NP, and at La Virgen del Socorro on the Caribbean slope. On the Pacific slope, they can be observed at Carara and Tapantí NPs, Monteverde, Corcovado NP (including the Sirena Biological Station), Corcovado Lodge Tent Camp, Tiskita Jungle Lodge, and the Wilson Botanical Garden at San Vito.

Morpho peleides adult, dorsal view

Morpho peleides adult, ventral view showing eyespots

GIANT SILKWORM MOTH FAMILY (Saturniidae)

Rothschildia Silkmoth

Rothschildia lebeau
and *Rothschildia triloba*

WINGSPREAD: 4.5–5.3 inches.

RANGE: Rio Grande Valley of Texas to Brazil.

ELEVATIONAL RANGE:
R. *lebeau*—Sea level to 3,200 feet.
R. *triloba*—Sea level to 4,500 feet.

Rothschildia Silkmoths are among the most beautiful Costa Rican insects. The transparent, triangular "windows" in the forewings and hindwings distinguish them from other moths. *R. lebeau* has grayish wings with white, black, and brown highlights. The female's wings are more rounded than those of the male. *R. triloba* is larger and more reddish. The host plants of *R. lebeau* include *Zanthoxylum, Salix,* and *Prunus.* The adults do not feed. Adults of *R. lebeau* emerge from their cocoons in early evening and mate from about 10:00 P.M. to 12:00 midnight. Egg laying begins on the following night and continues for several more nights. Broods are produced from February through April and from September through November. *Rothschildia* Silkmoths are found in all Costa Rican forests and have been encountered at night-lights at Monteverde Lodge and Rancho Naturalista.

Adult *Rothschildia lebeau*

Adult *Rothschildia triloba*

NOCTUID MOTH FAMILY (Noctuidae)

Black Witch Moth

Ascalapha odorata
(formerly *Erebus odora*)

Costa Rican name:
Bruja negra.
Wingspread: 5.9 inches.
Range: South Florida to Brazil.
Elevational range: Sea level to
10,000 feet.

The huge Black Witch Moth is a great traveler and is so adaptable that it is found from south Florida to Brazil. It can be encountered at night-lights of coastal areas at sea level and high in the Andes of South America. This large brown moth has a dark comma-shaped mark on each forewing, and females have a prominent purplish-pink bar across each forewing and hindwing. The name Black Witch Moth apparently comes from Mexican folklore, which suspiciously considers it the "butterfly of death."

Adults feed at night on overripe fruit like bananas and on native fruits high in the rainforest canopy. It can be attracted to lights at night. By day it roosts in

Black Witch Moth adult

dark sheltered places like hollow trees and rocky crevices. It is most abundant during the rainy season, but also survives well during the dry season in moist microhabitats of forests along rivers and shaded ravines.

Host plants are primarily in the bean family (Fabaceae): *Mora, Cassia, Acacia,* and *Pithecellobium.* This moth undergoes sporadic dispersal movements each year from August to October into the United States. It can show up in states ranging from California to Minnesota and New York. There is even a record from Canada.

URANIID MOTH FAMILY (Uraniidae)

Green Page Moth (Green Urania)

Urania fulgens

CostaRican name:
Colipato verde.
Wingspread: 2.3–3.2 inches.
Range: Veracruz, Mexico, to Brazil.
Elevational Range: Sea level to at
least 4,000 feet.

The green jewel-like iridescence and elegant swallow-tail design of the diurnal Green Page Moth make it one of the most stunning lepidopterans in Costa Rica. Most people consider it a butterfly because it flies during the day, but it is a diurnal moth. This moth has its origins primarily in the wet swamps and forests of the Osa Peninsula, where its host plant is abundant. The plant is a rainforest vine in the euphorbia (spurge) family called *Omphalea diandra*.

The breeding season begins in May and up to five generations may be produced before the end of the rainy season in November to December. Every few

Green Page Moth adult

years there is an enormous migration of this moth across the country. Hundreds of thousands fly from the Osa Peninsula across the Central Plateau into the lowlands north of San Carlos, and others fly from breeding areas in Panama through Costa Rica's Caribbean lowlands and along the coast. Others fly from Guatemala south to Colombia. The migration begins in July to August and may last several months. The frequency of migrations may be every four to eight years. Very large migrations occurred in 1983, 1995, and 1998. As the moths stage for migration in the forests of Corcovado NP, thousands can blanket the trees in much the same way that monarchs cover roosting trees during migration in North America.

The reason for the migration seems related to the extent to which the *Urania* caterpillars eat the *Omphalea* leaves. These leaves provide a low amount of toxic chemicals that the caterpillar incorporates into its system to discourage predation. However, as the amount of foraging increases, the plants begin producing higher concentrations of toxic chemicals that can subsequently kill the caterpillars. Adults must then move to a new region where they can find vines whose leaves have not recently been exploited by this moth. In March following a migration, there is a much smaller migration back to the original breeding area. Adults feed primarily on the nectar of white flowers like *Inga, Leucania, Eupatorium,* and guava (*Psidium*). The female may lay clusters of up to eighty eggs on *Omphalea* leaves.

LITERATURE CITED

Aiello, Annette. 1992. Dry Season Strategies of Two Panamanian Butterfly Species, *Anartia fatima (Nymphalinae)* and *Pierella luna luna (Satyrinae)*. In *Insects of Panamá and Mesoamerica: Selected Studies,* ed. Diomedes Quintero and Annette Aiello, 573–575. New York: Oxford Univ. Press. 692 pp.

Brower, Lincoln P. 1983. Chemical Defense in Butterflies. In *Coevolution,* ed. Douglas J. Futuyma and Montgomery Slatkinn, 109–134. Sunderland, Mass.: Sinauer Assoc. 555 pp.

Carter, David. 1992. *Butterflies and Moths.* Eyewitness Handbooks. New York: Dorling Kindersley. 304 pp.

Corrales, Jorge F. 1996. Las mariposas *Heliconius* de Costa Rica. Heredia, Costa Rica: Instituto Nacional de Biodiversidad. Booklet. 34 pp.

———. 1999. *Mariposas comunes, Area de Conservación Tempisque, Costa Rica.* Santo Domingo de Heredia: Instituto Nacional de Biodiversidad. 116 pp.

DeVries, Philip J. 1983a. *Heliconius hecale.* In *Costa Rican Natural History,* ed. Daniel H. Janzen, 730–731. Chicago: Univ. of Chicago Press. 816 pp.

———. 1983b. *Morpho peleides.* In *Costa Rican Natural History,* ed. Daniel H. Janzen, 741–742. Chicago: Univ. of Chicago Press. 816 pp.

———. 1987. *The Butterflies of Costa Rica and Their Natural History.* Vol. 1, *Papilionidae, Pieiridae, Nymphalidae.* Princeton, N.J.: Princeton Univ. Press. 327 pp.

———. 1997. *The Butterflies of Costa Rica and Their Natural History.* Vol. 2, *Riodinidae.* Princeton, N.J.: Princeton Univ. Press. 288 pp.

Holland, W. J. 1968. *The Moth Book: A Guide to the Moths of North America.* New York: Dover. 479 pp.

Lemaire, Claude. 1988. *The Saturniidae of America: Ceratocampinae.* San José, Costa Rica: Museo Nacional de Costa Rica. 480 pp.

Monge-Najera, Julián. 1992. Clicking Butterflies, *Hamadryas,* of Panama: Their Biology and Identification. In *Insects of Mesoamerica and Panama,* ed. Diomedes Quintero and Annette Aiello, 567–572. New York: Oxford Univ. Press. 692 pp.

Murawski, Darlyne A. 1993. A Taste for Poison. *National Geographic* 184(6): 122–137.

Norman, David. 1995. Moths Brighten Sky in Mysterious Migration. *The Tico Times* 39(1335): 14. September 8.

Scott, James A. 1986. *The Butterflies of North Americia: A Natural History and Field Guide.* Stanford, Calif.: Stanford Univ. Press. 583 pp.

Silberglied, Robert. 1983. *Anartia fatima.* In *Costa Rican Natural History,* ed. Daniel H. Janzen, 682–683. Chicago: Univ. of Chicago Press. 816 pp.

Smith, Neal G. 1983. *Urania fulgens.* In *Costa Rican Natural History,* ed. Daniel H. Janzen, 775–776. Chicago: The Univ. of Chicago Press. 816 pp.

———. 1992. Reproductive Behaviour and Ecology of *Urania (Lepidoptera: Uraniidae)* Moths and of Their Larval Food Plants, *Omphalea* spp. In *Insects of Panama and Mesoamerica: Selected Studies,* ed. Diomedes Quintero and Annette Aiello, 576–593. New York: Oxford Univ. Press. 692 pp.

Struttman, Jane M. 1999. *Rothschildia lebeau: Moths of North America*. N. Prairie Wildlife Research Center, Jamestown, N.D. U.S. Geological Survey, <www.npwrc. usgs.gov/resource/distr/depid/MOTHS/usa/1003.html>.

Turner, John R. G. 1983. Mimicry: The Palatability Spectrum and Its Consequences. In *Coevolution*, ed. Douglas J. Futuyma and Montgomery Slatkin, 141–161. Sunderland, Mass.: Sinauer Assoc. 555 pp.

Tveten, John, and Gloria Tveten. 1996. *Butterflies of Houston and Southeast Texas*. Austin: Univ. of Texas Press. 292 pp.

Young, Allen M. 1991. *Sarapiquí Chronicle. A Naturalist in Costa Rica*. Washington, D.C.: Smithsonian Institution Press. 361 pp.

Other Invertebrates

Invertebrates other than butterflies and moths constitute the bulk of Costa Rica's biological diversity. There are tens of thousands of invertebrates in every life zone and at every level of the forest that are even now poorly known and largely unidentified. Ants, bees, beetles, bugs, wasps, katydids, and thousands of microscopic invertebrates are a rich heritage of Costa Rica's tropical forests. One study in Panama revealed that 950 species of beetles inhabited a single rainforest tree, so single trees are habitat for thousands of insects. The National Biodiversity Institute (INBIO) is making huge efforts to collect, catalog, and identify the country's invertebrates. Of the estimated 505,000 species in the country, 1,481 are vertebrates, 10,000 are plants, and the remaining 493,000-plus species are invertebrates! The fifteen creatures featured here are only a tiny sampler of Costa Rica's invertebrate fauna and are included because they traditionally capture the attention of wildlife travelers.

BEE FAMILY (Apidae)

Stingless Bees

Trigona sp.

> Costa Rican name: ***Abeja atarrá; abeja jicote.***
> Length: 0.2–0.3 inches.
> Range: Southern Mexico to Brazil.
> Elevational range: Sea level to middle elevations.

Stingless Bees are inconspicuous insects of tropical forests until you learn how to spot their colonies. They build a faucetlike tube that sticks out perpendicular to the trunks of large trees— usually about one to six feet above the ground. These tubes are usually four to six inches long and may be straight or have a down-turned angle that prevents rain from entering. Each colony of Stingless Bees contains three to ten thousand individuals and is safely located within a hollow tree or in subterranean cavities among the roots of a tree. Stingless Bee colonies inhabit the dry forests of Guanacaste and moist and wet forests of the Caribbean lowlands and the southern Pacific lowlands. The bee *Trigona fulviventris* is among the most common and widespread of sixty Stingless Bee species in Costa Rica. Each colony defends a territory with an average radius of 300 feet and collects pollen and nectar from a wide variety of flowers within that area.

Although this bee is harmless and has no stinger, it can create a unique problem. Its attack pheromone is citronella, so if you use shampoo with a citronella base while visiting in a tropical forest, Stingless Bees may become entangled in your hair!

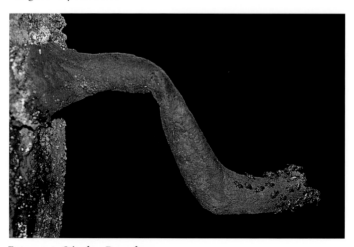

Entrance to Stingless Bee colony

Leafcutter Ants carrying leaf portions

ANT FAMILY (Formicidae)

Leafcutter Ants

Atta cephalotes
>   Costa Rican name: ***Zompopas.***
>   Length: 0.08–0.8 inches.
>   Range: Southern Mexico to Northern Argentina.
>   Elevational range: Sea level to 6,600 feet.

Leafcutter Ants are among the most well-known rainforest insects. Their four- to six-inch-wide trails are conspicuous on the forest floor because the ground looks like it has been cleaned with a vacuum. The ants form a continuous procession as worker ants carry circular portions of leaves back to the colony. These are all daughters of the queen and are called media workers. Sometimes aggressive little minima workers ride on the leaf portions. As "bodyguards," they protect the media workers from parasitic flies in the family Phoridae. These flies attempt to lay eggs on the neck of the media worker. If successful, the fly larva burrows into the ant's head and kills the ant. The ant colonies are also protected by large sol-dier ants that are over three-fourths of an inch long.

Once the ant reaches the underground nest, the leaf portions are cleaned and chewed into tiny portions. Saliva and ant fecal material, which contain en-zymes that help break down the leaf, are then added. Tiny portions of a special fungus are also added so that the leaf creates a substrate for the growth of the fungus. These ants cannot eat or digest the leaves directly. Instead, they eat the fungus, which grows only in the colonies of Leafcutter Ants and is an example of symbiosis. Within the chambers of the colony, the fungus gardens grow into a spongy globular mass that may be six to twelve inches in diameter.

One colony may contain as many as five million ants and a queen that may live from seven to twenty years. The colony is apparent on the surface of the ground because many ant trails converge at a large mound of dirt, leaf litter, dead ants, and other debris. One mound was estimated to contain almost thirty cubic yards of soil and organic material that were brought to the surface over a six-and-one-half-year period. Because of this excavation practice, leaf-cutters are important in recycling treetop nutrients. The nutrients become available to other organisms after use by the ants.

Leafcutter Ants can be seen at most forest reserves and NPs in the Caribbean and Pacific lowlands, including Tortuguero NP, Tortuga Lodge, La Selva Biological Field Station, Monteverde, Las Baulas NP near Tamarindo, Palo Verde NP, Santa Rosa NP, Guanacaste NP, lower levels of Braulio Carrillo NP, Rancho Naturalista, Corcovado NP, and Tiskita Jungle Lodge.

Leafcutter Ant, media worker

Bullet Ants

Paraponera clavata

CostA Rican name: **Bala.**
LENGTH: 0.6–0.9 inches.
Range: Nicaragua to Brazil.
ELEVATIONAL RANGE: Sea level to
1,600 feet.

The notorious Bullet Ant is the largest ant in Central America. This large black ant is a solitary hunter found only in the Caribbean lowlands. It is especially common at La Selva Biological Field Station and should be looked for on tree trunks and trail-marker pipes during hikes in the Arboretum area. This ant should be avoided because it can give an extremely painful sting that gives the ant its Costa Rican name, *bala,* meaning "bullet." Although individuals can be encountered during the daytime, this species hunts smaller insect-type prey mainly at night. It hunts from ground level up to the canopy.

Nests of this ant are made of complex subterranean tunnels and chambers with an entrance hole at the base of large trees like *Pentaclethra macroloba.* The oval entrance holes are about 0.8 inch wide by 2.4 inches high. Each colony contains from 700 to 1,400 worker ants that hunt for the colony.

Bullet Ant adult

Bullhorn Acacia Ants

Pseudomyrmex spinicola

> Costa Rican name: ***Hormiga de cornizuelo.***
>
> Length: 0.2 inch.
>
> Range: Southern Mexico to Colombia.
>
> Elevational range: Sea level to 4,000 feet.

Bullhorn Acacia Ants demonstrate symbiosis (mutualism) in the form of the mutually beneficial relationship that exists between them and the bullhorn acacia shrubs that provide their home. The bullhorn acacia (*Acacia* sp.) includes several species of short, thorny shrubs in the Pacific lowlands and middle elevations, including the Central Plateau. It is most abundant in the tropical dry forests of Guanacaste and can be seen in Palo Verde, Santa Rosa, and Guanacaste NPs; Lomas Barbudal BR; La Pacífica; Hacienda Solimar; La Ensenada Lodge; and south to Carara and Corcovado NPs.

The shrub has large paired hollow thorns that look like "bullhorns," from which the plant gets its name. New growth has small circular "nectaries" on the top side of the leaf petioles that provide nectar for the ants. At the tips of new leaflets are circular brown structures called Beltian bodies that provide a nutritious protein diet for the ants. The hollow "horns" provide a home for the ants, which chew an entry hole into the horn at the tip. All of these features have developed through natural selection to accommodate the ants' basic needs for survival. One shrub can support one colony, which includes one queen, ten to fifteen thousand worker ants, a couple thousand males, a thousand virgin queens, and up to fifty thousand larvae. The queen may live twenty years.

Mutualism is the process whereby two species mutually benefit each other's survival. In this case, the ants benefit from the special features of the acacia, and in return they protect the plant from animals that might eat the stems or leaves. Whenever an animal tries to climb the shrub or lands on its branches, it is attacked and stung by the ants. The ants also kill other plants that sprout within four to six feet of the base of the shrub by cutting off new sprouts so the acacia does not have to compete for sunlight or for nutrients in the soil. However, orioles, Great Kiskadees, Yellow-olive Flycatchers, and Rufous-naped Wrens build nests on these shrubs. The ants tolerate them and protect the birds' nests.

Pseudomyrmex ants at entrance to "bullhorn" on *Acacia* plant

"Beltian bodies" on the tips of new leaflets: food for ants

Army Ants

Eciton burchelli

Costa Rican name: ***Hormiga arriera.***

Length: 0.1–0.6 inch.

Range: Southern United States to Northern Argentina.

Elevational range: Sea level to 6,500 feet.

Army Ants are well known for their legendary raids in which tens of thousands of ants spread across the forest floor in a fan-shaped column to capture whatever small living creatures are unable to escape. Army Ants collectively include about 150 tropical species of ants, but the best-known is *Eciton burchelli*. These ants occur in colonies that may include from thirty thousand to over one million individuals. Each colony contains one queen. The colonies include different "castes" of ants that each have different duties. The most conspicuous and largest are soldier ants, which have large pincer-like mandibles. The males are the only caste with wings.

Army Ants killing a cockroach

Army Ants eat other ants, wasps, cockroaches, katydids, crickets, and other arthropods. The headquarters of a colony is known as a bivouac. It is formed from a solid mass of ants that link their bodies together with their feet into a living structure that conceals the queen, eggs, and larvae. Army Ants begin raids early in the morning and form a fan-shaped column that may be ten to fifty feet wide.

Many creatures follow ant swarms and capture invertebrates flushed by the ants: Great Tinamous; Bicolored, Chestnut-backed, Immaculate, Ocellated, and Spotted Antbirds; Black-crowned Antpittas; Barred and Slaty Antshrikes; Black-faced Antthrushes; Barred, Plain-brown, Ruddy, and Tawny-winged Woodcreepers; Roadside Hawks; Cattle Egrets; Blue-crowned Motmots; Summer Tanagers; Squirrel Cuckoos; Buff-throated Saltators; and Ruddy Foliagegleaners.

Parasitic flies follow the ants to lay eggs or larvae on escaping insects. Barred Forest-Falcons follow the swarm to prey on antbirds and woodcreepers. *Melinaea ethra* butterflies follow Army Ant swarms in search of antbird droppings, because the females need to feed on the amino acids of the droppings so their eggs can develop. Other insects that accompany ant swarms are mites, silverfish, beetles, flies, and wasps. Some prey on the ants, and others live in mutualistic relationships with the ants.

Army Ant swarms may be encountered in many Caribbean and Pacific lowland and middle-elevation sites, including dry forest reserves in Guanacaste, cloud forests at Monteverde, Corcovado Lodge Tent Camp and Corcovado NP on the Osa Peninsula, Tapantí NP, Wilson Botanical Garden, and Rancho Naturalista near Turrialba.

LONG-HORNED BEETLE FAMILY (Cerambycidae)

Harlequin Beetle

Acrocinus longimanus

> COSTA RICAN NAME: *Arlequín*.
> LENGTH: 3.0 inches, excluding antennae.
> RANGE: Southern Mexico to Brazil.
> ELEVATIONAL RANGE: Sea level to 3,600 feet.

The Harlequin Beetle is one of the most distinctive lowland rainforest beetles. Named for its harlequin color pattern, it is also distinguished by antennae over four inches long. This beetle can utilize several trees as host plants for egg laying, including strangler fig (*Ficus*), *Lonchocarpus, Artocarpus, Guazuma, Chorisia, Enterolobium, Urostigma, Castilla, Chlorophora, Brosimum,* and *Parahancornia.*

Adults are most active during the rainy season (July–September). Females usually select trees that have a bracket fungus. The markings of the fungus provide camouflage for the beetles and perhaps are characteristic of wood that is at the right point of decay to provide good habitat for the larvae. Each female lays fifteen to twenty eggs. It takes about twelve months from the time eggs are laid until adults emerge. Adults can be attracted to lights at night and also to dripping sap at tree wounds. They are especially attracted to the sap of *Bagassa guianensis.* An interesting example of commensalism—which means that both species involved in this (symbiotic) relationship benefit from their interaction—is that pseudoscorpions are frequently found living under the wing covers (elytra) of this beetle.

Harlequin Beetle adult showing intricate camouflage pattern

Harlequin Beetle adult showing long antennae

Hercules Beetle adult

BEETLE FAMILY (Scarabaeidae)

Hercules Beetle

Dynastes hercules

    COSTA RICAN NAME: *Cornizuelo*.

    LENGTH: 5.1 inches.

    RANGE: Mexico to Bolivia and Brazil.

    ELEVATIONAL RANGE: 2,600–6,600 feet.

The impressive Hercules Beetle is distinguished by a body that is almost 1.5 inches wide and 5 inches long, including a huge rhinoceros-like "horn" on the males. Although not common, it is one of the most imposing insects of the American tropics. A species of middle elevations, it lives in moist and wet forests and cloud forests, where the larvae develop in the rotting trunks of fallen trees. It takes about two years for the larva to develop into a beetle. Adult beetles are mainly nocturnal, but they are sometimes encountered at dawn and dusk. They can be attracted to lights at night, particularly during the rainy season (July–September).

Golden Beetle

Plusiotis resplendens

LENGTH: 0.8–0.9 inch.

RANGE: Costa Rica and Panama.

ELEVATIONAL RANGE: 1,300–9,200 feet.

The stunning Golden Beetle looks like it has been gold-plated. A species of middle to high elevations, it occurs in both wet forests and coffee planta-tions. Although the golden coloration may seem very conspicuous, the mirror-like surface of the beetle reflects the subdued green colors of its surrounding vegetation and camouflages it very well.

There are seventy-eight members of the genus *Plusiotis* in the American tropics, and twenty-two of those are known from Costa Rica. Many members of this genus occur at higher elevations because host plants include oaks (*Quercus*) and alder (*Alnus*). In spite of the attraction of this beetle's beauty, details of the life history are poorly known. Adults are seldom seen in the forest because they spend much of their life in the canopy, but the females fly down from the forest canopy to lay eggs in partially rotten tree trunks, where the lar-vae then feed on decomposing wood. The length of time from egg laying to emergence from the pupa is approximately one year.

This beetle is most apparent when it is attracted to night-lights early in the rainy season: May and June. Most records for *Plusiotis resplendens* are from mountains of the Monteverde area, Volcano Arenal, montane forests and coffee plantations in the vicinity of the Poás and Barva volcanoes, and northern re-gions of the Talamanca mountain range.

Golden Beetle adult

DOBSON FLY FAMILY (Corydalidae)

Dobson Fly (Fish Fly)

Corydalus sp.
> WINGSPREAD: 6.3 inches.
> LENGTH: 2.8 inches.
> RANGE: Southern Canada to Brazil.
> ELEVATIONAL RANGE: Sea level to at least 5,000 feet.

The ferocious-looking pincers of male Dobson Flies make them appear quite intimidating. The huge pincers are used for "dueling" among males during battles for females and for "prodding" the females during subsequent courtship rituals. Male Dobson Flies may also drum on their abdomens as part of those rituals. The females lack large pincers. Adults do not feed, and they live for only one or two weeks.

Dobson Flies are extremely adaptable insects, as evidenced by their occurrence throughout much of the temperate and tropical regions of North and South America. Their larval form is perhaps better known than the adults. Larvae are called hellgrammites and are a voracious aquatic predator in ponds and streams. In some areas hellgrammites are used as fish bait.

Females lay masses of 300 to 3,000 eggs near water. The aggressive larvae prey on small invertebrates, fishes, and amphibians. In northern regions, the life cycle of the Dobson Fly is one to five years, but the length of the life cycle is not known in tropical regions. This species occurs primarily along streams and is rarely encountered except when attracted to lights at night. At such lights, like those at Rancho Naturalista, it is possible to examine the impressive design of these conspicuous insects.

Dobson Fly adult male

KATYDID FAMILY (Tettigoniidae)

Lichen Katydid

Markia hystrix

LENGTH: 2.2 inches.

RANGE: Costa Rica and Panama.

ELEVATIONAL RANGE: Lowlands to at least 3,200 feet.

Katydids comprise a diverse group of insects and are particularly well adapted to survival in rainforests because of their exceptional camouflage. Most are nocturnal and extremely difficult to find. At night they come out of their hiding places to feed, "sing," and mate. There are probably more than 150 species in Costa Rica, and a total of 162 species are known in Panama. The large number of species, their abundance in many habitats, and their lack of chemical defenses make them an important food for lizards, birds, bats, monkeys, frogs, spiders, praying mantises, Army Ants, and other invertebrates.

Most katydids are well camouflaged with brown or leaflike green markings. The Lichen Katydid, however, has one of the most incredible camouflages of all. It resembles the pale greenish-white lichens on which it lives in rainforest treetops. Not only does the color match the lichens, but the body and legs have a bizarre assortment of spines and points that blend well with lichens. This is an extraordinary example of how the processes of natural selection over thousands of years have resulted in camouflage colors and structures that match the katydid's habitat so well that this insect is extremely difficult for predators to find.

This nocturnal katydid eats flower parts and young leaves and is capable of flights shorter than one hundred feet. The best chance to see the Lichen Katydid is where lights are put out at night with an adjacent sheet to attract nocturnal insects in the rainforest. The specimen shown here was attracted to a night-light at Rancho Naturalista.

Lichen Katydid adult

Adult female Golden Orb-weaver eating Caligo butterfly

ORB-WEAVER SPIDER FAMILY (Araneidae)

Golden Orb-weaver

Nephila clavipes

> Costa Rican name: ***Araña de oro.***
> Length: 0.2–2.5 inches, including legs.
> Range: South Florida and Texas to Panama.
> Elevational range: Sea level to 3,000 feet.

The Golden Orb-weaver is one of the largest spiders in Central America and is the largest orb-weaving spider in the New World. The females have bodies about one inch long, and when the legs are included, they average over 2.5 inches long. In contrast, the tiny males do not exceed a quarter inch in length, including the legs. When you encounter one of these spider webs, look carefully in an area within several inches of the conspicuous female. You will discover a tiny spider nearby, which is the male! The large webs of this spider may be up to two feet across and are distinguished by very strong golden yellow

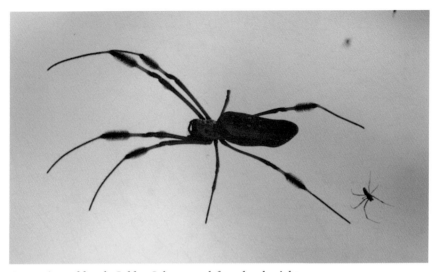

Comparison of female Golden Orb-weaver, left, and male, right

silk. This silk has incredible strength considering its diameter, and it has been used for industrial purposes like crosshairs in some telescopes.

This spider is found in forest openings, along trails, and in second-growth forest areas where there is enough sunlight reaching the forest floor to provide good habitat for many second-growth insects that serve as prey. Webs are usually within several feet of the ground. This spider is found in lowland forests of both the Caribbean and Pacific slopes. Golden Orb-weavers prey on flies, beetles, moths, and butterflies. Once an insect is caught in the web, the spider bites it with a venom that has digestive enzymes. The victim is wrapped in silk and taken back to the hub of the web where the spider eats it. Some small spiders, wasps, damselflies, and hummingbirds routinely steal prey from the webs of these spiders.

GIANT DAMSELFLY FAMILY (Pseudostigmatidae)

Helicopter Damselfly
(Giant Damselfly)

Mecistogaster sp.
and *Megaloprepus coerulatus*

    Costa Rican name: ***Gallito azul.***
    Wingspread: 7.5 inches.
    Length: 4 inches.
    Range: Mexico to Brazil.
    Elevational range: Sea level to at least 3,900 feet.

Helicopter Damselflies are one of the most mystifying—and enchanting—insects of the rainforest. These huge damselflies defy all logical explanations for the principles of flight because the four wings appear to beat slowly in four directions at once and at different rates as the damselfly floats through the air among forest understory plants.

There are two different genera of Helicopter Damselflies. The genus *Megaloprepus* has blue to purple bands on its clear wings. The male has a white patch in front of the bluish patch. The second genus, *Mecistogaster,* is characterized by clear wings that have yellow tips. These insects are found primarily in the moist and wet forests of the Caribbean lowlands and in the southern Pacific lowlands. Examples of good places to see them are in the Arboretum at La Selva Biological Station, in the rainforests of Tortuguero NP, and in Corcovado NP on the Osa Peninsula. The damselfly *Megaloprepus coerulatus* may also be observed at higher elevations in the premontane forests of the Wilson Botanical Garden near San Vito.

The eggs of this genus are laid in the water tanks of bromeliads and in water-filled tree holes. The predatory nymphs mature in these tiny water reservoirs, where they eat small aquatic organisms like mosquito larvae. Larger larvae eat tadpoles of frogs and syrphid fly larvae. They also eat larvae of their own species, which reduces competition for limited food resources in these small water cavities. Since there are about 250 tropical species of wildlife that complete at least part of their life cycle in these bromeliad water tanks, there is apparently no shortage of food for damselfly larvae. The larvae develop over a period of four to eight months.

Adult damselflies prey on spiders. The transparent wings make them largely invisible to spiders resting on their webs. The damselfly hovers a couple of feet from the spider as it prepares to attack. With great swiftness and agility, the damselfly swoops at the spider and captures it with its forelegs. It then flies backward from the web and goes to a nearby perch, where it consumes all of the spider except the legs.

Helicopter Damselfly adult, *Mecistogaster* sp.

Helicopter Damselfly adult, *Megaloprepus coerulatus*

ROCK RUNNER CRAB FAMILY (Grapsidae)

Sally Lightfoot Crab

Grapsus grapsus

COSTA RICAN NAME: **Cangrejo.**

CARAPACE LENGTH: 3.25 inches.

RANGE: Florida to Brazil; Mexico to Peru; Galápagos Islands.

The widespread Sally Lightfoot Crab is a type of "rock runner" that is seen on both Pacific and Caribbean beaches. The carapace, round and flattened, is purplish brown with fine cream-colored spots. This active crab frequents rocky shorelines and beaches at and above the spray line.

Sally Lightfoot Crab adult

LAND CRAB FAMILY (Gecarcinidae)

Mouthless Crab
(Jack-o-Lantern Crab)

Gecarcinus quadratus

COSTA RICAN NAME: ***Cangrejo***.

CARAPACE LENGTH: 2.0 inches.

RANGE: Mexico to Northwestern South America.

The colorful Mouthless Crab is found along the length of the Pacific coast and leaves little doubt about its identity. It has a black carapace, orange legs, and purple chelipeds (front claw-bearing legs). The name "Jack-o-Lantern Crab" comes from the facelike pattern of three yellow spots on the front of the crab. One is between the eye stalks, and the others are above and outside the eyestalks. A nocturnal species, this crab can be observed with flashlights by walking the beach and nearby forests at night. It forages on the sand and in adjacent upland mangrove forests and underbrush. It is common in the Tamarindo area near the beaches used by nesting Leatherback Turtles and along the beaches of Corcovado NP and Corcovado Lodge Tent Camp on the Osa Peninsula.

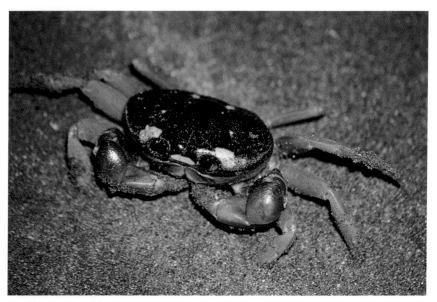

Mouthless Crab adult

Ayensu, Edward S. 1980. *The Life and Mysteries of the Jungle*. New York: Crescent Books. 200 pp.

Emmons, Katherine M., et al. 1996. *Cockscomb Basin Wildlife Sanctuary: Its History, Flora, and Fauna*. Cay Caulker, Belize: Producciones de la Hamaca. 334 pp.

Fincke, Ola M. 1992. Behavioural Ecology of the Giant Damselflies of Barro Colorado Island, Panama. In *Insects of Panama and Mesoamerica: Selected Studies,* ed. Diomedes Quintero and Annette Aiello, 102–113. New York: Oxford Univ. Press. 692 pp.

Henry, Charles S., Norman D. Penny, and Phillip A. Adams. 1992. The Neuropteroid Orders of Central America (Neuroptera and Megaloptera). In *Insects of Panama and Mesoamerica: Selected Studies,* ed. Diomedes Quintero and Annette Aiello, 432–458. New York: Oxford Univ. Press. 692 pp.

Horwich, Robert H., and Jonathan Lyon. 1990. *A Belizean Rain Forest: The Community Baboon Sanctuary*. Gays Mills, Wis.: Orangutan Press. 420 pp.

Kaplan, Eugene H. 1988. *Southeastern and Caribbean Seashores*. Peterson Field Guides. Boston: Houghton Mifflin. 425 pp.

Morón, Miguel-Angel. 1990. *The Beetles of the World*. Vol. 10, *Rutelini, Part 1: Plusiotis, Chrysina, Chrysophora, Pelidnotopsis, Ectinoplectron*. Venette, France: Sciences Nat., Imprimerie de Compiègne. 280 pp.

————. 1997. *Atlas de los Escarabajos de México: Coleoptera: Lamellicornia*. Vol. 1, *Familia Melolonthidae: Subfamilias Rutelinae, Dynastinae, Cetoniinae, Trichiinae, Valginae, y Melolonthinae*. Mexico City: CONABIO. 145 pp.

Nickle, David A. 1992. Katydids of Panama. In *Insects of Panama and Mesoamerica: Selected Studies,* ed. Diomedes Quintero and Annette Aiello, 142–184. New York: Oxford Univ. Press. 692 pp.

Solís, Angel. 1998. Los Escarabajos Dorados (*Plusiotis*) de Costa Rica. Santo Domingo de Heredia, Costa Rica: INBIO. 2 pp.

Stevens, George C. 1983. Leafcutter Ant (*Atta cephalotes*). In *Costa Rican Natural History,* ed. Daniel H. Janzen, 688–691. Chicago: Univ. of Chicago Press. 816 pp.

Stout, Jean. 1983. Helicopter Damselflies (*Megaloprepus*) and (*Mecistogaster*). In *Costa Rican Natural History,* ed. Daniel H. Janzen, 734–735. Chicago: Univ. of Chicago Press. 816 pp.

Amphibians

There are about 175 amphibians in Costa Rica, including frogs and toads, which have incredible adaptations for reproduction and survival. Many frogs have reproductive strategies that enable them to avoid raising tadpoles in ponds inhabited by fishes. Because fishes eat frog eggs and tadpoles, survival chances are increased for frogs that can find "fishless water" in which to raise their young. Poison dart frogs lay their eggs in forest litter and then transport them to the water tanks of bromeliads. *Eleutherodactylus* frogs lay their eggs in moist ground litter where their tadpoles can grow without threat from fish.

Some amphibians are well camouflaged for survival, and others, like *Dendrobates* frogs, are brightly colored to warn predators of their toxicity. Survival strategies include semitransparency in Glass Frogs, which allow them to blend with their backgrounds, as well as toxic chemicals in toads and poison dart frogs that discourage predation.

Don't rush to judgment on the identity of most amphibians. There are thirty-five different species of *Eleutherodactylus* frogs, twenty-six *Hyla* frogs, thirteen *Centrolenella* Glass Frogs, and ten kinds of *Bufo* toads. In most cases, you must be content to identify amphibians to genus. You can enjoy their beauty and adaptations regardless of their identity. Ten frogs and toads are included in the following accounts. The endemic Golden Toads of Monteverde are not included because they have not been observed since 1988 and are believed extinct. Several theories have been put forth about why that extinction occurred, but biologists have not yet arrived at a decision about the cause.

LEPTODACTYLID FROG FAMILY (Leptodactylidae)

Rain Frog (Fitzinger's Litter Frog)

Eleutherodactylus fitzingeri

COSTA RICAN NAME: **Rana de lluvia; ranita piedrita.**

TOTAL LENGTH: 2.0 inches.

RANGE: Northeastern Honduras to central Colombia.

ELEVATIONAL RANGE: Sea level to 5,000 feet.

The Rain Frog is a common and widely distributed frog found the length of the Pacific and Caribbean lowlands. The body, light to medium sandy brown, has a fine pebbly texture. Many show narrow black bands that begin at the point of the nose and extend through the eyes and the top of the tympanum. This band then turns downward and ends just behind the tympanum. Some individuals have a narrow light stripe down the center of the back, and most show indistinct, parallel brownish bands across the thighs. The Rain Frog also shows a prominent gold horizontal bar through the top edge of the eye. The best distinguishing mark for this highly variable frog is yellow spots on the back of the thighs.

This terrestrial frog can be encountered in Tortuguero NP, including the trails at Tortuga Lodge, and also at Cahuita NP. It occurs in Corcovado NP and can be discovered in leaf litter along the trails at Sirena Biological Station. Other locations include La Selva Biological Station, Carara and Manuel Antonio NPs, Rainforest Aerial Tram property, and lower levels of Braulio Carrillo NP. It can be found in the leaf litter during the day and can be found calling as it rests on leaves of low vegetation at night.

Rain Frog adult

Bransford's Litter Frog adult

Bransford's Litter Frog

Eleutherodactylus bransfordii
    Costa Rican name: ***Rana***.
    Total length: 1.2 inches.
    Range: Nicaragua to Panama.
    Elevational range: Sea level to
    3,900 feet.

This frog, perhaps the most common
frog in Costa Rica, is found on the forest floor throughout lowlands and
middle elevations in Guanacaste dry

forests and moist and wet forests of the Caribbean and Pacific regions. The
specimen shown here is tan with a cream-colored line down the back, and it
has a black band through the side of the face, eye, and shoulder area. However,
many different colors and skin textures are known for this frog, which provide
camouflage on widely varying colors and textures of the forest litter. The posterior edge of the thigh is reddish. The genus *Eleutherodactylus* is represented
by thirty-five species throughout the country, so identification to species is difficult.

    This diurnal frog eats ants, mites, beetles, hemipteran bugs, insect larvae,
and spiders. *E. bransfordii* breeds at night and lays eggs on moist sites on the
ground where there is enough moisture to keep them from drying out. The
embryos develop within the eggs and hatch as froglets. This frog can be seen at
La Selva Biological Station, and the similar *E. stejnegrerianus* can be seen at the
Wilson Botanical Garden and the Sirena Biological Station in Corcovado NP.

Smoky Jungle Frog

Leptodactylus pentadactylus

COSTA RICAN NAME: **Rana ternero**.

TOTAL LENGTH: Up to 6.3 inches.

RANGE:

Caribbean slope—Northern Honduras to Colombia and Ecuador.

Pacific slope—Northern Nicaragua to Brazil.

ELEVATIONAL RANGE: Sea level to at least 3,900 feet.

The Smoky Jungle Frog is the largest frog and the second largest amphibian in Costa Rica. Only the Giant Toad (*Bufo marinus*) is larger. It is distinguished by its huge size, medium brown back and sides, brown-to-black splotches along the upper lip, narrow black stripe through the eye that extends above the tympanum, yellowish belly, and symmetrical golden brown squiggly lines on the back and sides. It has a large gland in the groin area. Frequently found near streams and ponds, this frog inhabits burrows in the ground and in rock crevices. Habitats include dry and riparian forests in Guanacaste and moist and wet lowlands and middle elevations of both Caribbean and Pacific regions.

The frog has an appetite for other frogs, insects, crabs, crayfish, and snakes up to twenty inches long! It has interesting defenses: the skin secretes very irritating toxins that cause a predator to quickly drop it. It also gives out a loud scream that may serve to warn other frogs, but it also seems to attract nearby caimans! It is believed that the approach of a caiman may subsequently scare off the frog's predator.

Eggs are laid in huge foam masses that can exceed a gallon of foam. The masses are located on the edge of temporary woodland pools or dry depressions in streambeds where they are not exposed to predatory fish. The foam prevents the eggs from drying out while the tadpoles develop. The partially carnivorous tadpoles eat the eggs and tadpoles of other frogs. This frog may be encountered in Corcovado NP, Lapa Ríos, Corcovado Lodge Tent Camp, and Tiskita Jungle Lodge.

Smoky Jungle Frog adult

Litter Toad adult

TOAD FAMILY (Bufonidae)

Litter Toad

Bufo haematiticus

> Costa Rican name: *Sapo*.
> Total length: 2.0 to 2.75 inches.
> Range: Eastern Honduras to central Ecuador.
> Elevational range: Sea level to 4,200 feet.

A small smooth-skinned toad, *Bufo haematiticus* has no cranial crests and is coppery brown above with a thin copper-colored line that passes from the nose, above each eye, and along each side of the body to the base of the hind legs. There are one to four small, dark brown, paired crescent-shaped or apostrophe-shaped marks on the back. Huge parotoid glands on the sides of the neck produce a milky venom that deters predators. When calling, the male produces a series of chirps that sound like a chick in search of food.

This toad is found in moist and wet lowland and middle-elevation forests of the Caribbean and southern Pacific regions, including La Selva Biological Station, Drake Bay Wilderness Resort, Corcovado NP, and Wilson Botanical Garden. Strings of eggs are laid in small pools of water that remain in streambeds during the dry season. Adults are found on the forest floor foraging for small insects and other arthropods in the leaf litter.

Giant Toad (Marine Toad)

Bufo marinus

    Costa Rican name: ***Sapo grande***.

    Total length: 7.9 inches.

    Weight: 2.6 pounds.

    Range: Southern Texas to central Brazil.

    Elevational range: Sea level to 6,600 feet.

This huge, well-known toad is the largest toad in the Americas. It is most common in yards, gardens, farms, and other human settlements. There is a very large parotoid gland on each side of the neck that contains a toxic chemical that deters predators and is powerful enough to kill a dog. This toad has another effective defense: if you pick one up, it copiously urinates on you! This amphibian has become an exotic pest in many tropical and subtropical countries where it has been introduced by humans.

Bufo marinus is best known for its enormous appetite—it seems to eat just about anything: small mammals, smaller marine toads, spiders, hemipteran bugs, beetles, millipedes, ants, wasps, and vegetable matter. Natural population densities may be about ten per acre, but populations around human dwellings exceed one hundred per acre. Marine Toads remain concealed during the day under logs, rocks, and other objects and emerge at night to feed. Individual toads feed only once every three to four days. They are most active for the first several hours after dark.

This toad is very prolific. At the end of the dry season, it lays masses of eggs in shallow edges of pools and ponds. The number of eggs laid may vary from 5,000 to 25,000, depending on the size of the female. A toxic coating on the surface of the eggs protects them from predation. This toad reaches sexual maturity at one year of age. Females grow rapidly for three to four years and become larger than males, whose growth slows after one year. As with all amphibians, these toads continue to grow throughout their lives.

Giant Toad adult

HYLID FROG FAMILY (Hylidae)

Red-eyed Tree Frog (Gaudy Tree Frog)

Agalychnis callidryas

COSTA RICAN NAME:
Rana calzonuda.

TOTAL LENGTH: 2.8 inches.

RANGE: Southern Mexico to Panama.

ELEVATIONAL RANGE: Sea level to
3,280 feet.

The Red-eyed Tree Frog is often featured in rainforest literature and in Costa Rican tourism brochures. The expressive, bright red eyes with black elliptical pupils; green body; and blue, white, and orange highlights make it one of the most colorful rainforest creatures. The frog may be found in moist and wet lowland forests of the Caribbean and southern Pacific regions. Unfortunately, it is rarely seen by tourists.

Red-eyed Tree Frog adult

Adults inhabit the upper canopy of the forest for most of the year, but they come down to lower canopy levels with the onset of the rainy season in March to April. The males locate small, temporary rainforest pools (pools that lack predatory fish), and then they give a mating call that attracts the females. After mounting the female, the mating pair descends to the pool, where the female absorbs water through the skin into her bladder. Then the pair, with the male still on the back of the female, climbs to the upper or underside of a leaf over-hanging the pool. The female lays a mass of 11 to 104 eggs, and the male fertil-izes the eggs as they are laid. The female releases the water from her bladder onto the newly fertilized eggs, creating a foam that covers the eggs and keeps them from drying out. The female returns to the pool with the male still on her back, refills her bladder, and climbs back up to repeat the process. She may lay three to five clutches of eggs in one night. After five to eight days, the eggs hatch into tadpoles that drop from the egg mass into the pond. They feed on plank-ton and develop into frogs in about eighty days.

Red-eyed Tree Frogs eat small insects, moths, and other arthropods. They are eaten by birds, coatis, Kinkajous, and Fringe-lipped Bats (*Trachops cirrho-sus*). The bats locate the frogs by the calls of the males. The adults and egg masses are also eaten by Cat-eyed Snakes (*Leptodiera* spp.). Red-eyed Tree Frogs can sometimes be located at night on foliage adjacent to ponds in the courtyard at Tortuga Lodge. Another place to look for them—on guided night walks primarily in late March and early April—is on emergent vegetation next to boardwalks over the woodland pools along Sendero Cantarana at La Selva Biological Station.

Green and Black Poison Dart Frog adult

POISON DART FROG FAMILY (Dendrobatidae)

Green and Black Poison Dart Frog

Dendrobates auratus

  Costa Rican name: ***Rana venenosa***.

  Total length: 1.6 inches.

  Range: Southeastern Nicaragua to northwestern Colombia.

  Elevational range: Sea level to 1,900 feet.

Poison dart frogs derive their name from the Golden Poison Dart Frog (*Phyllobates terribilis*) of western Colombia. Their skin contains an alkaloid poison called batrachotoxin so dangerous that a two-inch frog has enough poison to kill eight humans. Chocó Indians of western Colombia treat their blowgun darts with juice from the skin of these frogs. Although other frogs in this family are not used to treat blowgun darts, their skin contains a potent but milder venom called pumiliotoxin-C.

The Green and Black Poison Dart Frog inhabits southern Pacific lowlands, including the Osa Peninsula and forests on the east side of the Golfo Dulce near the Panamanian border. It is also found in the northeastern lowlands, including Selva Verde and La Laguna del Lagarto. There it is active throughout the day among leaf litter on the forest floor and on logs, stumps, trees, and shrubs to a height of fifty feet. A major portion of its diet consists of ants and termites.

Reproduction is a complex process by which the male calls a female to him on the forest floor. After laying four to six eggs, she leaves. The male covers the eggs with sperm and tends the fertilized eggs for the next four to thirteen days. Meanwhile, he calls more females, entices them to lay eggs, and takes care of those egg masses as well. During this period, he sits in small puddles to absorb water and then sits on the eggs to keep them moist. Females lay eggs about every two weeks throughout the breeding season.

As each egg hatches, the tadpole climbs up a hind leg of the male and onto its back. The tadpoles are transported one at a time to tree cavities, bromeliad water tanks, and water-filled cavities in logs. The tadpoles eat aquatic organisms like protozoans, rotifers, and mosquito larvae. They develop into frogs in about twelve weeks. This frog may live four years or more. It may be observed in Corcovado NP, Lapa Ríos, at Sirena Biological Station, and on the grounds of Corcovado Lodge Tent Camp and Tiskita Jungle Lodge. It is best observed when ground conditions are moist to wet.

Strawberry Poison Dart Frog

Dendrobates pumilio

Costa Rican name: **Ranita roja; rana venenosa.**

Total length: 0.8–0.9 inch.

Range: Nicaragua to northwestern Panama.

Elevational range: Sea level to 3,200 feet.

The brightly colored Strawberry Poison Dart Frog demonstrates warning coloration to potential predators. If a snake bites such a frog, it immediately releases the frog, scrapes its mouth against the ground, and may writhe or lie comatose for several hours. Snakes, birds, and mammals do not die from this experience, but they do learn not to eat brightly colored little frogs.

This frog has many color patterns, but in Costa Rica the body is bright red and the legs are usually blue. Sometimes referred to as the "red frog wearing blue jeans," this species is found in Caribbean lowland rainforests and is most active in the morning. Ants, termites, mites, and tiny insects make up its diet. It is believed that toxic pumiliotoxin-C in the skin may be derived from chemicals in the ants in its diet, because the toxicity of the skin significantly declines in captivity when the frog doesn't have access to rainforest ants.

The reproductive behavior of this frog is one of the most incredible stories in the rainforest. Males establish territories on logs and stumps at a spacing of about ten feet. Their mating call is a cricketlike buzz that pulses at a rate of four to five buzzes per second, deterring males while attracting females. If another male approaches, the two males rise up and grapple with each other like little sumo wrestlers. When a female approaches, the male leads her to a nesting site in the ground litter, where he deposits sperm on a leaf and she deposits two to five eggs on it. He guards the eggs and keeps them moist for about seven days until they hatch.

When the eggs hatch, the female instinctively returns, and the tadpoles climb onto her back. They cling to her by using their mouths as suckers. She climbs trees and backs into the water tanks of bromeliads or water-filled plant cavities. The tadpoles slide into the water, and the female returns for the other tadpoles until she has placed all young ones. She visits each tadpole every one to nine days for the fifty days it takes to develop. When the tadpole senses its approaching mother, it vibrates its tail. Then she backs into the water and lays an unfertilized egg for the tadpole to eat! She provides seven to eleven eggs for each tadpole during its development. This incredible process is an adaptation

Strawberry Poison Dart Frog adult

that tropical frogs have developed to avoid raising tadpoles in ponds that contain fish. The most dependable place to view this frog is along the nature trail at Tortuga Lodge near Tortuguero. It may also be seen along the trails at La Selva Biological Station when rainy weather keeps the ground cover moist.

Similar Species: Granular Poison Dart Frog
(Dendrobates granuliferus)

The Granular Poison Dart Frog is endemic to Costa Rica and is found in the Pacific lowland rainforests of the Golfo Dulce region. It is a lowland species found from sea level to about 2,300 feet. This frog, closely related to *Dendrobates pumilio,* is red except for its green legs, sides, and belly. The skin has a granular texture, hence its name. The skin glands contain the toxin that is so potent in protecting the frog. The life history is similar to the Strawberry Poison Dart Frog. Look for this frog in Corcovado NP on the Osa Peninsula and along trails at Tiskita Jungle Lodge.

Granular Poison Dart Frog adult

GLASS FROG FAMILY (Centrolenidae)

Glass Frogs

Centrolenella sp./
Hyalinobatrachium sp.

> COSTA RICAN NAME: **Ranita de vidrio.**
> TOTAL LENGTH: Up to 1.5 inches.
> RANGE: Southern Mexico to Paraguay and northern Argentina.
> ELEVATIONAL RANGE: Sea level to over 6,000 feet.

In contrast to poison dart frogs that advertise their presence with bright colors, Glass Frogs are protected from predation by a greenish translucent body that shows the color of their background. Through the transparent skin on some species can be seen the beating heart as well as the stomach, intestines, and blood vessels. The thirteen Glass Frogs in Costa Rica are arboreal and are found primarily along streams in moist and wet Caribbean and Pacific lowland forests. A few are found at middle and high elevations.

A distinctive feature of Glass Frogs is that they typically lay their egg masses on or under leaf tips suspended over streams. The eggs develop in eight to twenty days. During that period, the males of some Glass Frogs guard the eggs. Some of these frogs have a blotched yellow-and-green pattern on their backs that resembles an egg mass. The tadpoles drop from the egg mass on the tip of the leaf into the stream during heavy rainfall. The rainfall and resulting turbidity provide concealment for the tadpoles. If tadpoles dropped into calm water, they would immediately be noticed by fish and eaten. Once in the stream, the tadpoles conceal themselves under leaf litter on the bottom and live for several months until metamorphosing into frogs. Look for this frog in moist and wet lowland rainforests on vegetation along streams. Examples of good habitat are in Tortuguero NP and in the Arboretum at La Selva Biological Station.

Glass Frog adult

Beletsky, Les. 1998. *The Ecotravellers' Wildlife Guide: Costa Rica*. San Diego, Calif.: Academic Press. 426 pp.

Crump, Marty L. 1983. Poison Dart Frogs (*Dendrobates granuliferus*) and (*Dendrobates pumilio*). In *Costa Rican Natural History,* ed. Daniel H. Janzen, 396–398. Chicago: Univ. of Chicago Press. 816 pp.

Emmons, Katherine M., Robert H. Horwich, et al. 1996. *Cockscomb Basin Wildlife Sanctuary: Its History, Flora, and Fauna for Visitors, Teachers, and Scientists*. Caye Caulker, Belize: Producciones de la Hamaca, and Gays Mills, Wis.: Orang-utan Press. 334 pp.

Janzen, Daniel H. 1983. *Costa Rican Natural History*. Chicago: Univ. of Chicago Press. 816 pp.

Kubicki, Brian. 2000. The Centrolenidae Family of Neotropical Glass Frogs. *Reptiles* 8(8): 48–60.

McDiarmid, Roy W. 1983. *Centrolenella fleischmanni*. In *Costa Rican Natural History,* ed. Daniel H. Janzen, 389–390. Chicago: Univ. of Chicago Press. 816 pp.

Norman, David. 1998. Common Amphibians of Costa Rica. Heredia, Costa Rica: Published by the author. Apdo. 387-3000. 96 pp.

Pounds, J. A., Michael P. L. Fogden, Jay M. Savage, and G. C. Gorman. 1997. Tests of Null Models for Amphibian Declines on a Tropical Mountain. *Conservation Biology* 11(6): 1307–1322.

Scott, Norman J. 1983a. Red-eyed Tree Frog (*Agalychnis callidryas*). In *Costa Rican Natural History,* ed. Daniel H. Janzen, 374–375. Chicago: Univ. of Chicago Press. 816 pp.

_____. 1983b. Litter Toad (*Bufo haematiticus*). In *Costa Rican Natural History,* ed. Daniel H. Janzen, 385. Chicago: Univ. of Chicago Press. 816 pp.

_____. 1983c. Bransford's Litter Frog (*Eleutherodactylus bransfordii*). In *Costa Rican Natural History,* ed. Daniel H. Janzen, 399. Chicago: Univ. of Chicago Press. 816 pp.

_____. 1983d. Smoky Jungle Frog (*Leptodactylus pentadactylus*). In *Costa Rican Natural History,* ed. Daniel H. Janzen, 405–406. Chicago: Univ. of Chicago Press. 816 pp.

Walls, Jerry G. 1994. *Jewels of the Rainforest—Poison frogs of the Family Dendrobatidae*. Neptune City, N.J.: T. F. H. Publications. 288 pp.

_____. 1996. *Red-eyes and Other Leaf Frogs*. Neptune City, N.J.: T. F. H. Publications. 64 pp.

Zug, George. 1983. Giant Toad (*Bufo marinus*). In *Costa Rican Natural History,* ed. Daniel H. Janzen, 386–387. Chicago: Univ. of Chicago Press. 816 pp.

Ctenosaur and tourist

Reptiles

Costa Rica's fauna includes at least 218 reptiles: marine and freshwater turtles, geckos, lizards, crocodilians, and snakes. Reptiles demonstrate impressive adaptations to the diverse tropical habitats of Costa Rica. They may be encountered from high mountains to coastal rainforests and the dry forests of Guanacaste. As with mammals, some are readily seen in the daytime, but others are best seen on guided night hikes. Many lizards depend on sunny days to warm their bodies, so iguanas, Ctenosaurs, and *Norops* and *Ameiva* lizards are readily observed. Along lowland streams, freshwater turtles and basiliscus lizards can be seen basking along the shore.

Caimans can be observed during day- and nighttime boat trips along the canals of Tortuguero NP, along the Río Frío, and at La Laguna del Lagarto. Crocodiles are best seen from the Río Tárcoles bridge by the entrance to Carara NP, in Tortuguero NP, at La Ensenada Lodge, and at Estero Madrigal on Hacienda Solimar. These reptilians are prehistoric reminders of how long these creatures have inhabited the earth and of how important these tropical habitats are in perpetuating their existence.

An excursion to see nesting marine turtles on a peaceful moonlit beach is an unforgettable lifetime experience. Nocturnal guided tours to observe nesting Leatherback and Green Turtles are offered at Las Baulas NP (January to February) and Tortuguero NP (June to November), respectively.

Many people breathe a sigh of relief when they learn that snakes are seldom seen, even by enthusiastic naturalists who are intentionally looking for them. Most are nocturnal and live underground or in the treetops, where they are inaccessible. Although a few species like the Bushmaster generate fear and misunderstanding, the danger posed by venomous reptiles is far less than that posed by aggressive drivers on Costa Rican roads. Snakes are seldom encountered and are harmless if left alone.

A total of twenty-five reptiles have been selected for coverage, including freshwater and marine turtles, lizards, snakes, and two crocodilians.

LEATHERBACK TURTLE FAMILY (Dermochelyidae)

Leatherback Turtle

Dermochelys coriacea

COSTA RICAN NAME: ***Baula***.

4/15 trips; 4 sightings.

TOTAL LENGTH: 70.8 inches.

WEIGHT: Up to 1,300 pounds, one record of 2,000 pounds.

RANGE: Atlantic, Pacific, and Indian Oceans, including tropical and temperate waters.

The Leatherback Turtle is the largest reptile in the world. A male accidentally caught off the coast of Wales measured 9 feet long and weighed 2,000 pounds. In contrast to most other sea turtles, which have hard shells, the Leatherback's shell has a firm, leathery texture. The upper shell (carapace) has seven parallel dorsal ridges and averages 63 inches long and 44 inches wide.

The flexible shell is an adaptation for diving as deep as 3,330 feet, where the pressure exceeds 1,500 pounds per square inch. Another adaptation is that they store oxygen in muscle tissues when they dive because the pressure would crush their lungs. They dive to these depths in search of jellyfish. Other foods

Leatherback Turtle adult female ashore for nesting at Playa Grande

Adult female, close-up of head

include sea urchins, squid, crustaceans, mollusks, fish, blue-green algae, and seaweeds. Sometimes they die from eating discarded plastic bags and balloons, which to them resemble jellyfish.

Playa Grande near Tamarindo on the Pacific coast is one of thirteen primary Leatherback nesting beaches in the world. Up to 1,600 Leatherbacks have nested there in one season, which extends from October through February. Individual females come ashore repeatedly at ten-day intervals, and each female may nest from three to six times during the nesting season. Nesting typically occurs at night during high tide. About one hundred eggs are deposited in a nest hole that is dug with the hind flippers. The eggs hatch after sixty days.

This endangered species faces threats from ocean garbage, egg poaching, predation on hatchlings by dogs and pigs, illegal killing for meat by commercial fishermen, and lights on beaches that disorient the young after hatching. The world population is estimated to have declined from 115,000 to 34,500 since 1980. The half-mile-long nesting beach at Playa Grande was designated as Las Baulas NP in 1995. A few Leatherbacks also nest on the beaches at Tortuguero NP and along the coast of the Osa Peninsula and at Corcovado Lodge Tent Camp.

Since Leatherbacks nest during the peak of Costa Rica's tourist season, this is the species most easily seen in January and February. It is worth the pilgrimage to Tamarindo to see the Leatherbacks. Sea turtles have been on this earth for at least 150 million years. That is why sitting on a Costa Rican beach at night watching a sea turtle plod ashore, dig its nest, and lay its eggs becomes a mystical, almost religious, experience. It transports you back in time millions of years; it connects you with ancient rhythms and natural processes that help you understand and appreciate the incredible diversity of life that is preserved in Costa Rica's national park system. Check with nature tourism companies in Costa Rica or with hotels in the Tamarindo vicinity to arrange for turtle-watching tours at Playa Grande. At Playa Grande you must be escorted by guides from the National Park Service to see the turtles.

HARD-SHELLED SEA TURTLE FAMILY (Cheloniidae)

Green Turtle

Chelonia mydas and C. agassizii

> COSTA RICAN NAMES: ***Tortuga verde; tortuga blanca***.
>
> TOTAL LENGTH: 60.2 inches (shell length averages 39.3 inches).
>
> WEIGHT: 130 to 440 pounds; largest record is 850 pounds.
>
> RANGE: Atlantic, Pacific, and Indian Oceans.

The Green Turtle is one of four hard-shelled sea turtles found along Costa Rica's coasts. Others include the Hawksbill, Olive Ridley, and Loggerhead. Although the Green Turtle nests at other beaches in the Caribbean, the Tortuguero site is one of the most significant in the world. It hosts from 5,000 to 15,000 turtles along its twenty-two-mile beach from June through November, with a peak in late August.

Females may reproduce only once every two to three years. After mating offshore, females go ashore to nest three to seven times at thirteen-day intervals. The peak of nesting is at night during high tide. About 100–150 eggs are laid each time. The eggs hatch after incubating in the sand for forty-five to sixty days. The sex of the baby turtles is determined by temperature. Warmer temperatures create more females, and cooler temperatures create more males.

Green Turtles mainly eat plants. Extensive turtle-grass beds along the Mosquito Coast off Nicaragua are a primary feeding area. They also eat mangrove roots and leaves and green, brown, and red algae. Occasional animal foods include small mollusks, crustaceans, sponges, and jellyfish. These turtles may live thirty to fifty years, but they have become endangered because they are killed for their meat. Their eggs are also collected for use as food and as an aphrodisiac.

Costa Rica has a worldwide reputation as a major Green Turtle nesting area because of the pioneering work done at Tortuguero since 1954 by the late Dr. Archie Carr. His book *So Excellent a Fishe* documents his conservation story. As many as 15,000 people now come to Tortuguero each year to see nesting Green Turtles. Contact the Caribbean Conservation Corporation at 1-800-678-7853 for details on helping turtles and how to see them there. (Remember that Green Turtles are not nesting during the main tourist season from January through March.)

The Green Turtles in the Caribbean are mainly brown and do not have indentations on the carapace above the hind legs. Green Turtles are also found along the Pacific coast of tropical America and are sometimes regarded as a separate species: *Chelonia agassizii*. They are more greenish to olive-brown and have conspicuous indentations on the carapace above the hind legs. Most of these turtles are very dark brown or black on the upper portions of the soft parts. The head scales are light-margined in *C. mydas* and uniformly dark on *C. agassizii*. In the Galápagos Islands, these are referred to as "Black Turtles."

Green Turtle adult

Olive Ridley (Pacific Ridley) Sea Turtle

Lepidochelys olivacea

> COSTA RICAN NAMES: **Lora** (Playa Ostional); **carpintera** (Playa Nancite).
>
> TOTAL CARAPACE LENGTH: 25.1–28 inches.
>
> WEIGHT: 88.2 pounds.
>
> RANGE: Atlantic, Indian, and Pacific Oceans in tropical regions.

Olive Ridley Turtles, the most abundant of all Costa Rican turtles, are well known for their *arribadas* in the Guanacaste region at the Nancite and Ostional beaches on the Pacific coast. During an *arribada*, as many as 120,000 Ridley turtles formerly emerged to nest during four- to eight-day periods from July through December. However, the numbers have declined in recent years. The *arribadas* occur at two- to four-

Hatchling Olive Ridley Turtles at Tamarindo beach

week intervals. Smaller *arribadas* occur at these beaches from January through June. A few Olive Ridley Turtles nest along the Pacific coast south to Panama, and tracks leading from their nests may be seen regularly on the beaches from the Sirena Biological Station to Carate on the Osa Peninsula during January and February.

When a female Ridley comes ashore, she digs a hole fifteen to twenty inches deep with her hind flippers. About one hundred eggs are deposited and covered using the hind flippers. A female normally nests two times in one season at an interval of twenty-eight to thirty days. The incubation period is about fifty days. Hatchling turtles have many predators: frigatebirds, coatis, coyotes, feral dogs, pigs, raccoons, opossums, vultures, sharks, and even crabs. Few hatchlings—probably less than one percent—survive their first year.

At Playa Ostional, 20 to 30 million eggs may be laid during one season. Eggs laid during the first days of an *arribada* are dug up by turtles nesting later. Since many of these eggs go to waste, the villagers of Ostional are organized into the Ostional Development Corporation and are authorized by the government to collect and sell eggs laid at the beginning of an *arribada*. They collect a quota of 3 million eggs per year and receive about $95,000 in income. Some of the money is used to staff the Ostional turtle research station, and the remainder has been used to build a new school and a health clinic. Turtle eggs from Ostional are sold in small bags that are labeled to show their legal origin. Otherwise, it has been illegal to take or sell sea turtle eggs in Costa Rica since 1966. The Ostional area is now threatened by development of a large hotel and by squatters along the beachfront property.

Ridley turtles are carnivores and dive as deep as 500 feet to eat shrimp, crabs, snails, sea urchins, jellyfish, and fish eggs. Studies of turtle migration show that Ridleys seasonally move south to feeding areas offshore from Ecuador. Although the Olive Ridley is protected in Costa Rica, fishermen off the coast of Ecuador kill this turtle in large numbers. Because of the difficulty of predicting when an *arribada* will occur and the remoteness of Playas Nancite and Ostional, it is difficult to experience the wonder of an *arribada*. However, during the main nesting period from July through December, a few turtles can be seen nesting every night. Nesting appears to peak during the waning quarter moon of months in the nesting season, especially in July. Visits to Nancite must be coordinated with Santa Rosa NP Service officials and visits to Ostional, with Ostional turtle research station biologists.

MUD TURTLE FAMILY (Kinosternidae)

White-lipped Mud Turtle

Kinosternon leucostomum

Costa Rican names: ***Tortuga caja; tortuga amarilla; candado pequeño.***

2/15 trips; 2 sightings.

Total carapace length: 7 inches.

Range: Veracruz, Mexico, to Colombia, Ecuador, and Peru.

Elevational range: Sea level to 4,000 feet.

Among the more interesting freshwater turtles in Costa Rica is a mud turtle that is a box turtle. It has two hinges on its plastron that allow the turtle to completely close its shell when approached by danger. The high-domed shell has a single keel along the midline of the carapace and an elongated oval profile when viewed from above. Both features are characteristic of this species. The overall body color is dark brown to blackish on the carapace, and the plastron is dark yellow. The jaws and chin are yellowish. Males have a relatively long tail, and females have a very short tail.

Nesting occurs twice each year, with major nesting activity in July and October. Multiple clutches of one to five eggs (usually one) are laid on the ground and covered with leaf litter. The eggs hatch in 126 to 148 days. This turtle is considered nocturnal, but it can occasionally be found crossing roads between wetlands during the day. The White-lipped Mud Turtle eats aquatic plants, mollusks, insects, worms, carrion, and aquatic invertebrates.

This turtle is found in quiet waters of marshes, swamps, ponds, rivers, and streams in lowlands and middle elevations of the Caribbean and Pacific slopes. It can also be found on adjacent upland sites. It can be seen in the wetlands of Palo Verde and Carara NPs; La Selva Biological Station; Caño Negro NWR; Corcovado, Cahuita, Manuel Antonio, and Tortuguero NPs; and at wetlands near San Vito.

White-lipped Mud Turtle

Ventral view showing two hinges that allow plastron to close

Black River Turtle adults basking

SEMIAQUATIC POND TURTLE FAMILY (Emydidae)

Black River Turtle
(Black Wood Turtle)

Rhinoclemmys funerea

COSTA RICAN NAMES: **Tortuga negra del río; Jicote.**

8/15 trips; 8 sightings.

TOTAL CARAPACE LENGTH: 12.8–14.0 inches.

WEIGHT: 10 pounds.

RANGE: Caribbean lowlands on the Honduras/Nicaragua border to Panama.

ELEVATIONAL RANGE: Sea level to 3,240 feet.

The Black River Turtle is the largest and most conspicuous turtle in the Caribbean lowlands and middle elevations. This aquatic turtle frequents ponds, rivers, and swamps, where it can typically be seen basking on partially submerged logs. The Black River Turtle has a high-domed shell that is dark brown to black. The head, neck, and edges of the shell have yellow highlights.

This turtle eats fruits, grasses, and broad-leaved plants. The nesting season extends from March through August. A female lays eggs one to four times per season, with an average clutch of three eggs. The incubation period is 98 to 104 days. Eggs are laid on the ground and covered with leaves. This turtle is commonly seen during the day on boat trips along the canals of Tortuguero NP or the Río San Juan and its tributaries, from the Stone Bridge at La Selva Biological Field Station, and along the boat canal from Limón to Tortuguero.

Orange-eared Slider

Trachemys scripta venusta
and *T. s. emolli*

COSTA RICAN NAME:
Tortuga resbaladora.

2/15 trips; 2 sightings.

TOTAL CARAPACE LENGTH: Up to
15.0 inches.

RANGE: Mexico to northern
Argentina.

ELEVATIONAL RANGE: Sea level to
3,000 feet.

Slider turtles of the species *Trachemys scripta* include fourteen subspecies that range from Virginia to Brazil. In northern regions, it is called the Red-eared Slider because of the red mark above and behind the eyes. The two Costa Rican subspecies are very similar and have orange markings. They can be seen basking on floating logs in freshwater wetlands and along lowland rivers of the Caribbean and Pacific slopes. This turtle seems to prefer wetlands with muddy or murky bottoms. Sometimes they can be seen "stacked" several turtles deep on their favorite basking logs.

Young turtles eat tadpoles, small fish, crayfish, shrimp, and snails. As they mature, their diet broadens to include herbaceous plants and algae. The nesting season extends from December to May. A female will lay several clutches of two to thirty-five eggs during the dry season. The young hatch after sixty-nine to one hundred and twenty-three days. This turtle should be looked for along the canals of Tortuguero NP and in nearby woodland ponds and backwaters like those at Tortuga Lodge.

Orange-eared Slider adult showing orange "ear" marking

LIZARD FAMILY (Iguanidae)

Norops Lizard (Anolis Lizard)

Norops (Anolis) limifrons; N. oxylo-
phus; and *Dactyloa (Anolis) insignis*
COSTA RICAN NAME: **Lagartija.**
6/15 trips; 6 sightings.
TOTAL LENGTH: 4–6 inches.
RANGE:
N limifrons—Belize to Panama.
N. oxylophus—Nicaragua to
    Costa Rica.
D. insignis—Costa Rica to Panama.
ELEVATIONAL RANGE: Sea level to
montane levels, depending on species.

There are more than twenty-five species of *Norops* (*Anolis*) Lizards in Costa Rica. The Giant Anoles (*Dactyloa*) are related forms. Most have brownish markings, but some females have prominent white stripes or diamond-shaped markings on their backs. Their most conspicuous feature is a colorful dewlap on the throat that males extend as a territorial display against other males. These lizards are conspicuous in low shrubs and on wood piles as males extend and retract their dewlaps and bob their heads up and down. The dewlaps are colored differently in different species.

Some *Norops* breed year-round, producing about one egg per week during the rainy season and one egg every two weeks during the dry season. Young hatch after fifty days and become sexually mature in three to four months. If this lizard is attacked by a predator, the tail will break off and twitch. This dis-

Adult *Norops limifrons* at La Selva

Adult *Dactyloa insignis* displaying at Corcovado Lodge Tent Camp

Adult *Norops oxylophus* with regenerating tail

tracts the predator and allows the lizard to escape. It is common to see distinctly colored new tails on these lizards. Predators include praying mantises, katydids, trogons, pygmy-owls, motmots, vine snakes, and other lizards. *Norops* Lizards eat butterfly and moth caterpillars, crickets, katydids, grasshoppers, and cockroaches.

These small lizards can be encountered throughout the country in many of Costa Rica's lowland and middle-elevation forests, plantations, ranches, and farms.

Basiliscus Lizard
(Jesus Christ Lizard)

Basiliscus plumifrons; B. basiliscus;
and *B. vittatus*

> COSTA RICAN NAMES: **Chisbala;**
> **chirbala.**
>
> 10/15 trips; 16 sightings.
>
> TOTAL LENGTH: Up to 28 inches.
>
> WEIGHT: Up to 1 pound 4 ounces.
>
> RANGE: Tamaulipas, Mexico, to
> Venezuela, Colombia, and Ecuador.
>
> ELEVATIONAL RANGE: Sea level to
> 3,000 feet.

The memorable "Jesus Christ Lizard" is renowned for its ability to run across the water upright on its hind legs. A young Basiliscus Lizard can run over fifty feet across a stream or pond if flushed from its perch on a branch overhanging the water.

There are three species, including the Common Basiliscus (*Basiliscus basiliscus*) found in the Pacific lowlands from Guanacaste southeast through the Osa Peninsula. The latter is brown with a prominent crest. A similar but bright green species lives in the Caribbean lowlands and southwestern Costa Rica and is called the Double-crested Basiliscus (*B. plumifrons*). The Striped Basiliscus (*B. vittatus*) in the Caribbean lowlands is brown and has narrow white horizontal stripes through the face. The prominent crests on Common

Adult *Basiliscus plumifrons* in night roosting posture

Adult *Basiliscus basiliscus*

Adult *Basiliscus vittatus*

Young *Basiliscus vittatus* ("Jesus lizard") running on the water

Young *Basiliscus plumifrons* in typical resting posture overhanging water (in the water is an Orange-eared Slider resting on a Black River Turtle)

and Double-crested Basiliscus Lizards make them look like miniature dinosaurs. It is likely that these crests aid in dissipating heat in hot weather.

Basiliscus lizards lay five to eight clutches of eggs during a ten-month breeding season from April through January. Each clutch contains six to eighteen eggs that hatch after sixty to ninety days. Females become sexually mature at eighteen months of age. These lizards may live three to six years and continue to grow throughout their lives. These omnivorous lizards are active during the day and eat insects, newly hatched iguanas and Ctenosaurs, *Norops* lizards, snakes, small birds, small mammals, fish, flowers, and fruits. Predators include snakes, hawks, and opossums, but the basiliscus' ability to run across water makes them difficult to catch.

Look carefully for these well-camouflaged lizards resting on small branches overhanging streams and ponds. One way to discover them is to watch for their long slender tails hanging from these branches, usually no more than one or two feet above the water. Look for them on ponds and canals of Tortuguero NP and of La Selva, Santa Rosa, and Palo Verde NPs in Guanacaste; on streams of the Río Frío and Caño Negro NWR; and on pond edges in Corcovado NP on the Osa Peninsula. In good habitat they can be very common—their density can reach 80–160 per acre.

Ctenosaur
(Spine-tailed Lizard; Black Iguana)

Ctenosaura similis

COSTA RICAN NAMES: **Garrobo;
iguana negra.**

10/15 trips; 27 sightings.

TOTAL LENGTH: Up to 40 inches.

WEIGHT: 1 pound 5 ounces–2 pounds
5 ounces.

RANGE: Southern Mexico to Panama.

ELEVATIONAL RANGE: Sea level to
1,000 feet.

The Ctenosaur is the most abundant and conspicuous large lizard on the Pacific slope of northwestern Costa Rica. During sunny days it spends most of its time basking on the tops of fence posts, rock piles, roofs, and tree branches. The body is tan and dark brown, and there may be a deep reddish tinge on the back during the mating season. Juveniles are bright green.

Adult Ctenosaur showing "rings of spines" on the
tail, Guanacaste

123

Adult Ctenosaur of Manuel Antonio National Park showing splotchy black-and-white markings that differ from those on Ctenosaurs in Guanacaste

This lizard could be mistaken for the Green Iguana, but the latter are more greenish, have longer tails, and have a large circular "scale" on the jaw area behind the eye. Iguanas are usually found by water, but Ctenosaurs occur throughout the landscape, including ranches, backyards, and gardens. The tail of the Ctenosaur is ringed by rows of large, pointed scales that give them the name Spine-tailed Iguana. Sometimes Ctenosaurs are hunted as small game species and they, as well as iguanas, are referred to as the "chicken of the tree," in reference to their chicken-like meat.

Although most abundant in the dry forests of Guanacaste, this lizard is found along the entire Pacific coast to the moist and wet forests of the Osa Peninsula and adjacent Panama. Its diet consists of fresh-growing plant material, such as leaves, flowers, field crops, and fruits, as well as small rodents, small lizards, eggs of lizards and birds, frogs, insects, and other invertebrates. The diet changes from largely animal food for young to largely plant food for adults. Ctenosaurs are eaten by raccoons, coatis, raptors, and boa constrictors. As with most other lizards, the tail will grow back if broken off by a predator.

The breeding season begins in December, and males may be seen defending their territories with conspicuous head-bobbing displays. Females lay a single clutch of about forty eggs in underground burrows. The young hatch from April through July. Females reach sexual maturity at the age of two. This adaptable lizard may be seen high in the treetops; on low shrubs, posts, and branches; or foraging on the ground. It is common at ranches, resorts, and beachfront hotels throughout the Guanacaste region. Ctenosaurs can be seen at close range along trails at Manuel Antonio NP; at La Pacífica, La Ensenada Lodge, and Hacienda Solimar; and in the picnic area near the headquarters of the OTS research station at Palo Verde NP.

Green Iguana

Iguana iguana

Costa Rican name: ***Iguana.***

13/15 trips; 30 sightings.

Total length: Up to 82.7 inches.

Weight: Up to 15 pounds.

Range: Northern Mexico to Paraguay and Southern Brazil.

Elevational range: Sea level to 1,000 feet.

The "dinosaur-like" Green Iguana adds a touch of primitive wildness to tropical forests as it peers from treetop foliage. It is a symbol of rainforests well known locally as "chicken of the tree" because of its use for meat. An iguana can be green to grayish, with rust-colored highlights. Large males are most frequently seen perched high in a tree, exposed in the sunlight, bobbing their heads in territorial displays. A large dewlap under the chin flaps conspicuously during the head bobs. This dewlap is absent on Ctenosaurs. There is also a large, circular scale on the jaw area that is absent on Ctenosaurs. The iguana tail is longer and more slender than the Ctenosaur's, with alternating bands of grayish green and dark gray to black along the tail.

The iguana usually occupies sites overlooking rivers, canals, and wetlands. An adult male maintains a territory of about 0.2 acre, and females and young

Close-up of adult male Green Iguana showing dewlap and large circular scale on the jaw area

maintain territories of 0.5 to 0.6 acre. The iguana is a vegetarian throughout life. Iguanas eat flowers, newly sprouted leaves, and fruits. When the mating season begins in December, male iguanas turn bright reddish orange and head-bobbing displays become conspicuous. A male may mate with one to four females in his territory. After mating, each female lays twenty-four to seventy-two eggs in an underground burrow. The young hatch after ten to fourteen weeks, in late April through May. At two to three years of age, iguanas reach sexual maturity. Iguanas may live up to fifteen years.

Research and educational efforts have been under way to promote saving tropical rainforests by raising Green Iguanas for meat. This is a land-use alternative for local farmers who would otherwise cut the rainforest to raise cattle. One acre of rainforest can produce 300 pounds of iguana meat per year, but if cleared, will produce only 33 pounds of beef per year.

Look for iguanas along the canals of Tortuguero NP, from the Stone Bridge over the Río Sarapiquí at La Selva Biological Station, from the bridge over the river in the town of Muelle, along the Río Tempisque and its tributaries in Guanacaste (including Palo Verde, Santa Rosa, and Guanacaste NPs), and in rainforest habitats of the southern Pacific lowlands, including Corcovado NP and Tiskita Jungle Lodge. The best place to see big iguanas up close is at the picnic area near the headquarters of the OTS field station at Palo Verde NP.

Spiny Lizard (Malachite Lizard)

Sceloporus malachiticus

> COSTA RICAN NAME:
> *Lagartija espinosa.*
> 8/15 trips; 12 sightings.
> TOTAL LENGTH: 7 inches.
> RANGE: Veracruz, Mexico, to Panama.
> ELEVATIONAL RANGE: 1,900–9,200 feet.

As the colorful Spiny Lizard basks in the midday sun, it becomes bright malachite green. The color darkens during cooler portions of the day, and at night it turns blackish. This adaptable high-elevation lizard inhabits rocky outcrops, exposed dirt banks along highways, garden walls, patios, and rural backyards. The Spiny Lizard usually clings to rocks, banks, or tree trunks in a vertical posture.

The diet includes insects, flowers, fruits, and plant sprouts. The Spiny Lizard has a unique adaptation whereby eggs develop and hatch inside the female. The heat needed by the eggs for incubation is derived from the basking activi-

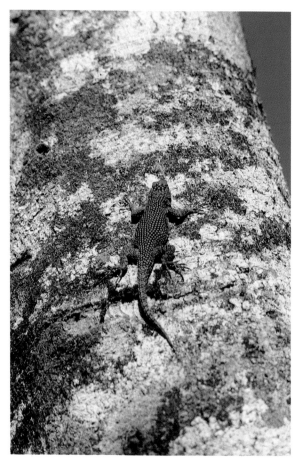

**Spiny Lizard adult showing bright malachite color
during heat of midday**

ties of the female, because the soil is too cool at high elevations for the eggs to develop. She gives birth to an average of six young each year—usually in January and February. Watch for this small but brightly colored lizard around garden and patio areas of the Central Plateau and highland farms, hotels, and nature resorts like those at Monteverde, Savegre Mountain Lodge at San Gerardo de Dota, and Hotel El Pórtico in San José de la Montaña.

TEIID LIZARD FAMILY (Teiidae)

Ameiva Lizard

Ameiva festiva

COSTA RICAN NAME: **Chisbalas.**
5/15 trips; 5 sightings.
TOTAL LENGTH: 8 to 9 inches.
Range: Tabasco, Mexico, to Colombia.
ELEVATIONAL RANGE: Sea level to
4,900 feet.

The *Ameiva* Lizard is a medium-sized speckled lizard of Costa Rica's Caribbean and southern Pacific lowlands. Except for large males, the species has a prominent light stripe down the center of the back and is conspicuous when sunning along rainforest trails. There are three other members of this genus in the country: *A. quadrilineata* (Caribbean and southern Pacific lowlands), *A. undulata* (northwestern Costa Rica and the Central Plateau), and *A. leptophrys* (southwestern Costa Rica). *Ameiva festiva* is the most widely distributed. It feeds primarily on the ground of forest edges, where it digs and explores among leaves and twigs for small insects, insect eggs, and insect larvae.

A female produces three to four clutches of eggs per year, with an average of two to three eggs per nest. Predators include hawks, motmots, opossums, coatis, and other medium-sized carnivores. The *Ameiva* Lizard may be seen at La Selva Biological Station and Rancho Naturalista in the Caribbean lowlands and at Carara and Corcovado NPs in the southern Pacific lowlands.

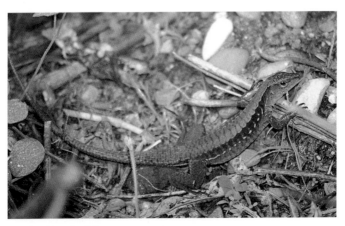

Ameiva Lizard adult

CONSTRICTOR FAMILY (Boidae)

Boa Constrictor

Boa constrictor

> COSTA RICAN NAMES: ***Boa; béquer***.
> 3/15 trips; 3 sightings.
> TOTAL LENGTH: 10–15 feet; record is 19.7 feet.
> WEIGHT: 66.1–88.2 pounds.
> RANGE: Sonora and Tamaulipas, Mexico, to Argentina and Paraguay.
> ELEVATIONAL RANGE: Sea level to 3,800 feet.

The Boa Constrictor is the largest snake in Costa Rica. Although the prospect of seeing a snake that can exceed ten feet in length might create anxiety, this reptile is uncommonly seen and feeds primarily on small mammals and birds. It is not a threat to people. An adaptable snake, the boa inhabits dry and riparian forests in Guanacaste and lowland and middle-elevation forests of the Caribbean and southern Pacific regions. It occurs in pristine forests as well as in cleared areas and on farms and ranches. Sometimes one will take up residence in the rafters of a building with a thatched roof, where it helps control rodents at night—rather like a six-foot-long cat with scales.

As the name "constrictor" implies, this reptile kills prey by coiling around it, suffocating it, and swallowing it head first. Prey includes small deer, coatis, raccoons, Tamanduas, Agoutis, Tepescuintles, bats, Ocelots, lizards, and birds. Dogs and poultry may also be taken. The boa hunts primarily at night and at dawn and dusk. It will remain motionless on a tree branch or in an animal's burrow and await the passage of a bird or mammal.

This snake gives birth to twenty to sixty-four live young from March

Boa Constrictor adult

through August. The young are about eighteen inches long at birth and disperse with no parental care. A boa becomes sexually mature at a length of five to six feet. This snake may live more than thirty years, but in the past it has been killed indiscriminately by people for its hide and by people who fear snakes.

COLUBRID SNAKES (Colubridae)

Vine Snake

Oxybelis brevirostris

COSTA RICAN NAME: **Bejuquillo**.

5/15 trips; 5 sightings.

TOTAL LENGTH: Up to 72 inches.

RANGE: Mexico to Brazil.

ELEVATIONAL RANGE: Sea level to 2,600 feet.

Vine Snakes are well camouflaged, pencil-thin snakes that drape them-selves over thin branches and mimic a slender vine as they wait for small lizards. They are difficult to discern in vege-tation, so sightings are uncommon. The term "vine snake" is a generic term that refers to several long, slender arboreal snakes, including three species in the genus *Oxybelis*: *O. aeneus* (a gray species found on the Pacific slope in dry forests of the north and humid forests of the south), *O. brevirostris* (shown here, a brown-green and white species found in Caribbean lowlands, including Tortuguero NP and La Selva), and *O. fulgidus* (a green species of the Gua-nacaste dry forest and northeastern Caribbean lowlands).

These snakes have an extremely slender body. The color is green, brownish, or grayish above and creamy white or greenish below. The head is long, slen-der, and pointed. The round pupil is black. If approached, *O. aeneus* opens its mouth as a bluff and exposes a black mouth lining. It is a rear-fanged snake that can bite, chew, and inject a mild venom that may cause local blisters and swelling.

Vine Snake adult camouflaged among plant stems

Adult *Leptophis mexicanus* in Guanacaste

Similar Species: Green-headed Tree Snakes (*Leptophis mexicanus* and *Leptophis ahaetulla*)

Green-headed Tree Snakes include snakes in the genus *Leptophis*. This genus includes five snakes in Costa Rica: *L. ahaetulla* (shown here; Caribbean and southern Pacific humid lowlands), *L. depressirostris* and *L. nubulosus* (Caribbean and southern Pacific lowlands), *L. mexicanus* (shown here; Guanacaste dry forest and Caribbean lowlands), and *L. riveti* (southern Pacific lowlands and foothills).

Leptophis mexicanus has a green head, yellowish white sides, and black lateral stripes that extend the length of the body. Also shown is *Leptophis ahaetulla,* which is greenish above and pale yellow below. Short black lateral stripes pass from the nose *through* the eyes to the back of the head. These snakes have round, black pupils and are rear-fanged snakes with a mild venom. They feed primarily on tree frogs. They usually do not exceed 36 inches in length and do not pose a threat to people.

Adult *Leptophis ahaetulla* in Tortuguero National Park

VIPER FAMILY (Crotalidae)

Eyelash Viper (Palm viper)

Bothriechis schlegelii
(formerly *Bothrops schlegelii*)

COSTA RICAN NAMES: ***Bocaracá;
oropel*** (golden morph).

3/15 trips; 3 sightings.

TOTAL LENGTH: 19.7 inches.

RANGE: Southern Mexico to Ecuador
and Venezuela.

ELEVATIONAL RANGE: Sea level to
1,700 feet.

The Eyelash Viper is a small but very venomous snake of Costa Rica's Caribbean and southern Pacific lowlands and foothills and the forests of the Santa Elena region at Monteverde. The name "eyelash" refers to the hoodlike scales over each eye, and "palm viper" refers to the fact that this arboreal species spends much of its life resting motionless on palm tree trunks, branches, and fruits awaiting its prey. This amazing snake comes in six colors: green, brown, rust, gray, light blue, and gold. The golden morph is known only from Costa Rica and blends well when concealed on ripe yellow palm fruits.

Prey includes small lizards, frogs, hummingbirds, and small rodents. Because this snake is so well camouflaged, it is difficult to spot. Bites can occur if a person tries climbing trees or vines or reaches into tree branches or clusters of tropical fruits without inspecting them first. Several fatalities occur in Costa Rica each year as a result of bites from this snake.

Adult Eyelash Viper, golden morph

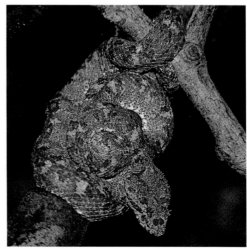

Adult Eyelash Viper, dark green morph

CORAL SNAKE FAMILY (Micruridae)

Coral Snake

Micrurus nigrocinctus

CostA RicAN NAMES: *Coral; coralillo.*

3/15 trips; 5 sightings.

TOTAL LENGTH: 24–36 inches.

RANGE: Southern Mexico to north-western Colombia.

ELEVATIONAL RANGE: Sea level to 4,000 feet.

The brightly colored Coral Snake is a widely distributed but seldom seen snake with alternating red, yellow, and black rings around the body. Although this snake is venomous, it is nocturnal and burrows under leaf litter, so encounters with humans are infrequent. The bright colors provide warning coloration that deters large predators. There are four Coral Snakes in Costa Rica. Others are *M. mipartius* (bicolored with black-white and black-pink), *M. clarki,* and *M. alleni.* Each has a different arrangement of brightly colored rings around their bodies.

Daytime hours are spent concealed in leaf litter, hollow logs, or ant hills. If approached, a Coral Snake warns of its presence by raising its coiled tail and waving it back and forth; it also swings the head from side to side with the mouth open.

This snake occupies dry and riparian forests in Guanacaste, moist and wet forests of the Caribbean and southern Pacific lowlands, and forests of middle

elevations. The Coral Snake feeds by crawling under leaf litter and biting small lizards, snakes, and amphibians. The prey are immobilized by nerve toxin in the venom and then swallowed. This venom can be fatal to humans, but the Coral Snake has such a small mouth that it is difficult for this small snake to bite a human. Most biting incidents are caused by careless people trying to handle Coral Snakes.

Coral Snake adult

Spectacled Caiman adult

CROCODILE FAMILY (Crocodylidae)

Spectacled Caiman

Caiman crocodilus

> Costa Rican names: **Caimán; lagarto; baba; babilla**.
>
> 7/15 trips; 11 sightings.
>
> Total length: 4–6 feet.
>
> Range: Southern Mexico to Ecuador and central Brazil.
>
> Elevational range: Sea level to 1,000 feet.

The Spectacled Caiman is related to alligators, but it is smaller than the American Alligator and does not pose a threat to humans. The caiman occupies lowland wetlands, rivers, marshes, ponds, and even water-filled roadside ditches of the Caribbean and Pacific slopes. Prey consists of fish and amphibians, though other kinds of wildlife may be eaten as carrion. Newly hatched caimans eat insects. Young caimans are eaten by Jabirus, Wood Storks, Great Egrets, and raccoons. Adult caimans have no predators except human poachers.

Nesting mainly occurs during February and March. Females lay and bury twenty to forty eggs in a nest mound near the water's edge. The eggs hatch after seventy-three to seventy-five days. Upon hatching, the 8- to 9-inch-long young call the parents, who open the nest and carry the young to the water in their mouths. The young are defended by the parents for at least four months after hatching.

Caimans may be viewed from boats along the canals of Tortuguero NP,

Close-up of head

along lowland rivers, and on wetlands at La Laguna del Lagarto Lodge. During the day, caimans lie quietly in beds of water hyacinth so that only their eyes and nostrils are exposed. At night the eyes reflect light like red coals along river and pond edges when spotlights are shined on them.

American Crocodile

Crocodylus acutus

> Costa Rican name: ***Cocodrilo***.
> 10/15 trips; 14 sightings.
> Total length: Usually 10–12 feet; record is 23 feet.
> Range: Florida to Ecuador.
> Elevational range: Sea level to 650 feet.

The American Crocodile adds an imposing and prehistoric presence to Costa Rica's rivers, swamps, and wetlands. Although the caiman seldom exceeds six feet, the crocodile is frequently twice that length. A crocodile can be distinguished from a caiman by the shape and structure of the snout. The snout is more pointed on a crocodile, and the canine teeth of the lower jaw are visible because they fit in grooves on the sides of the upper jaw. The snout of the caiman is more broadly rounded, and the canines of the lower jaw are not visible because they fit into pits in the upper jaw.

As with caimans, the American Crocodile builds a nest mound near the water's edge that contains about twenty eggs. Upon hatching, the young call to the female, who digs them out and gently transports them to the water in her enormous mouth. The young are protected by the adult for an extended period after hatching.

This is an endangered species because it has been relentlessly killed in the past. Protection has allowed the crocodile to make an impressive recovery. It occurs in salt, brackish, and freshwater habitats. The diet includes fishes, turtles, and mammals up to the size of deer. When a crocodile swallows its prey, it must tip its head upward because it cannot swallow with its head in a horizontal position. As recently as the late 1990s, crocodiles have killed three people in Costa Rica when they swam in rivers occupied by crocodiles.

Among places where crocodiles can be seen are the canals in Tortuguero NP, along the Río Colorado and Río San Juan, the marshes of Palo Verde NP, the Río Tempisque and its tributaries in Guanacaste, the Río General southeast of San Isidro del General, and even such unlikely places as the city water treatment lagoons at San Isidro del General. There are four excellent places to safely observe crocodiles. The first is from the bridge over the Río Grande de Tárcoles near the entrance to Carara NP on the Pacific coast. Over a dozen crocodiles can routinely be observed sunning themselves on sand bars near the bridge. The second location, at Hacienda Solimar, is the lagoon at Estero Madrigal surrounding the heronry. The third is in the mangrove lagoons and wetlands at La Ensenada Lodge, and the fourth is during boat tours in the mangrove lagoons near Quepos.

American Crocodile adult basking in Tortuguero National Park

Close-up of head of American Crocodile

Acuña Mesén, Rafael Arturo. 1998. *Las tortugas continentales de Costa Rica*. 2d ed. San José, Costa Rica: Editorial de la Universidad de Costa Rica. 92 pp.

Andrews, Robin M. 1983. *Norops polylepis*. In *Costa Rican Natural History*, ed. Daniel H. Janzen, 409–410. Chicago: Univ. of Chicago Press. 816 pp.

Bartlett, R. D., and Patricia Bartlett. 1997. *Lizard Care from A to Z*. Hauppauge, N.Y.: Barron's. 178 pp.

Carr, Archie. 1967. *So Excellent a Fishe: A Natural History of Sea Turtles*. Garden City, N.Y.: Natural History Press. 248 pp.

_____. 1983. *Chelonia mydas*. In *Costa Rican Natural History*, ed. Daniel H. Janzen, 390–392. Chicago: Univ. of Chicago Press. 816 pp.

Carr III, Archie. 1998. The Big Green Seafood Machine. *Wildlife Conservation* 101(4): 16–23.

Coborn, John. 1994. *Green Iguanas and Other Iguanids*. Neptune City, N.J.: T. H. F. Publications. 64 pp.

Cornelius, Stephen E. 1983. Olive Ridley Sea Turtle (*Lepidochelys olivacea*). In *Costa Rican Natural History*, ed. Daniel H. Janzen, 402–405. Chicago: Univ. of Chicago Press. 816 pp.

_____. 1986. *The Sea Turtles of Santa Rosa NP*. San José, Costa Rica: Fundación de Parques Nacionales. 65 pp.

Crump, Marty L. 1983. Poison Dart Frogs (*Dendrobates granuliferous*) and (*Dendrobates pumilio*). In *Costa Rican Natural History*, ed. Daniel H. Janzen, 396–398. Chicago: Univ. of Chicago Press. 816 pp.

Dixon, Jim R., and Maureen A. Staton. 1983. Spectacled Caiman (*Caiman crocodilus*). In *Costa Rican Natural History*, ed. Daniel H. Janzen, 387–388. Chicago: Univ. of Chicago Press. 816 pp.

Echternacht, Sandy C. 1983. Ameiva Lizard (*Ameiva*) and (*Cnemidophorus*). In *Costa Rican Natural History*, ed. Daniel H. Janzen, 375–379. Chicago: Univ. of Chicago Press. 816 pp.

Emmons, Katherine M., Robert H. Horwich, et al. 1996. *Cockscomb Basin Wildlife Sanctuary: Its History, Flora, and Fauna for Visitors, Teachers, and Scientists*. Gays Mills, Wis.: Orang-utan Press. 334 pp.

Ernst, Carl H. 1983. Black River Turtle (*Rhinoclemmys funerea*). In *Costa Rican Natural History*, ed. Daniel H. Janzen, 417–418. Chicago: Univ. of Chicago Press. 816 pp.

Ernst, Carl H., and Roger W. Barbour. 1989. *Turtles of the World*. Washington, D.C.: Smithsonian Institution Press. 313 pp.

Fitch, Henry S., and Jenny Hackforth-Jones. 1983. Ctenosaur (*Ctenosaura similis*). In *Costa Rican Natural History*, ed. Daniel H. Janzen, 394–396. Chicago: Univ. of Chicago Press. 816 pp.

Flaschendrager, Axel, and Leo Wijffels. 1996. *Anolis*. Berlin, Germany: Terrarien Bibliothek. 207 pp.

Greene, Harry W. 1983a. Boa Constrictor (*Boa constrictor*). In *Costa Rican Natural History*, ed. Daniel H. Janzen, 380–382. Chicago: Univ. of Chicago Press. 816 pp.

_____. 1983b. *Micrurus nigrocinctus*. In *Costa Rican Natural History,* ed. Daniel H. Janzen, 406–408. Chicago: Univ. of Chicago Press. 816 pp.

Janzen, Daniel H. 1983. *Costa Rican Natural History*. Chicago: Univ. of Chicago Press. 816 pp.

Robinson, Douglas C. 1983. Malachite Lizard (*Sceloporus malachiticus*). In *Costa Rican Natural History,* ed. Daniel H. Janzen, 421–422. Chicago: Univ. of Chicago Press. 816 pp.

Rudloe, Anne, and Jack Rudloe. 1994. Sea Turtles: In a Race for Survival. *National Geographic* 185(2): 94–121.

Scott, Norm J. 1983. Vine Snake (*Oxybelis aeneus*). In *Costa Rican Natural History,* ed. Daniel H. Janzen, 410–411. Chicago: Univ. of Chicago Press. 816 pp.

Seifert, Robert P. 1983. Eyelash Viper (*Bothrops schlegelii*). In *Costa Rican Natural History,* ed. Daniel H. Janzen, 384–385. Chicago: Univ. of Chicago Press. 816 pp.

Tyson, Peter. 1997. High-tech Help for Ancient Turtles. *MIT's Technology Review* 10(8): 54–60.

Van Devender, R. Wayne. 1983. Basiliscus Lizard (*Basiliscus basiliscus*). In *Costa Rican Natural History,* ed. Daniel H. Janzen, 379–380. Chicago: Univ. of Chicago Press. 816 pp.

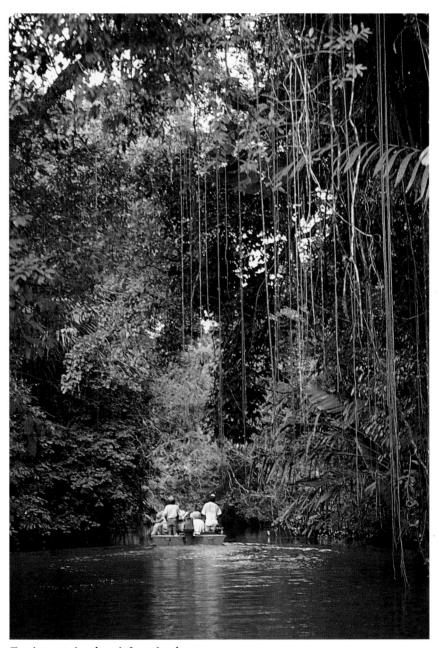
Tourists entering the rainforest in a boat

Birds

Among the memorable experiences of exploring Costa Rica are encounters with birds that possess a kaleidoscope of stunning colors and a repertoire of the most beautiful, and sometimes bizarre, natural sounds in the world. This relatively small country, only one-fourth the size of Minnesota, has 878 species of birds! In comparison, about 850 species of birds are known for all of North America north of Mexico! This diversity includes 78 different bird families. For most visitors, many of these bird families are new to them and provide exciting memories—trogons, motmots, macaws, potoos, toucans, jacamars, woodcreepers, antbirds, becards, cotingas, and manakins.

Some people enjoy making a list of the birds they see, or they may enjoy photographing, recording, or sketching the wildlife. It is easy to be overwhelmed by the abundance of birds! Newcomers should take time to enjoy the birds and absorb the essence of the tropical forests. One of the best observation techniques is to hire a naturalist guide. Be sure to bring your binoculars. It is also productive to sit or stand for extended periods at places that attract wildlife—near a pool or drinking site, a fruiting or flowering tree, or near feeders—and let the wildlife come to you.

Many people place too much emphasis on trying to see the birds. Listen to the forest. Many birds can be identified by listening for their songs and subsequently locating the birds. Where vocalizations of bird songs or calls are commercially available, species accounts in this book refer to such tapes or CDs, listed with full information in Appendix C. You can prepare for a trip to Costa Rica by purchasing one or more of the tapes or CDs and listening to them before you go. Particularly comprehensive selections of Costa Rican bird sounds are included on *Costa Rican Bird Song Sampler* and *Voices of Costa Rican Birds: Caribbean Slope,* two audiotapes by David Ross. The species accounts included here represent about one-fifth of the country's bird life. They include many of the most common, conspicuous species and some of the more unusual and unique species for which there is keen interest on the part of birders and nature enthusiasts. Although some neotropical migrants are included, there is an intentional bias to include species that are permanent residents. Reproductive details are included for species that exhibit polyandry, lek behavior, fledgling care by young from previous broods, or use of unusual nesting sites. For general reproductive details, the reader is referred to Stiles and Skutch (1989).

Included in the following accounts are references to the total number of sightings recorded on fifteen Henderson Birding Trips. A sighting includes one or more individuals of a species encountered on a walk, drive, or outing on trips that typically involve three outings per day. Based on this data, the dozen most commonly sighted birds in Costa Rica are listed in Table 1. You can benefit from reviewing the identification features of these common birds before making your first visit to the country. All these birds are included in the species accounts.

Table 1. The twelve most commonly sighted birds in Costa Rica (during January and February) 1987-2000.

1. Turkey Vulture
2. Black Vulture
3. Cattle Egret
4. Tropical Kingbird
5. Blue-gray Tanager
6. Great Kiskadee
7. Clay-colored Robin
8. Great-tailed Grackle
9. Baltimore Oriole
10. Rufous-tailed Hummingbird
11. Chestnut-sided Warbler
12. Rufous-collared Sparrow

For other birds, their apparent abundance could be grouped by the cumulative number of sightings as follows: 1 to 10 sightings = uncommon; 11 to 50 sightings = common; 51 to 120 sightings = abundant; and 121 to 200 sightings = very abundant. The Turkey Vulture was sighted more than any other bird during our fifteen trips: 194 times.

TINAMOU FAMILY (Tinamidae)

Great Tinamou

Tinamus major

>   CInstr Rican names: ***Gongolona; tinamú grande; gallina de monte; perdiz.***
>
>   9/15 trips; 30 sightings.
>
>   Status: Permanent resident.
>
>   Length: 15.7–18.0 inches.
>
>   Weight: 1 pound 8 ounces–2 pounds 11 ounces (700–1,142 grams).
>
>   Vocalization tapes: B, D, I, Q, T, V, Z, BB, CC.
>
>   Range: Southern Mexico to central Brazil.
>
>   Elevational range: Sea level to 5,600 feet.

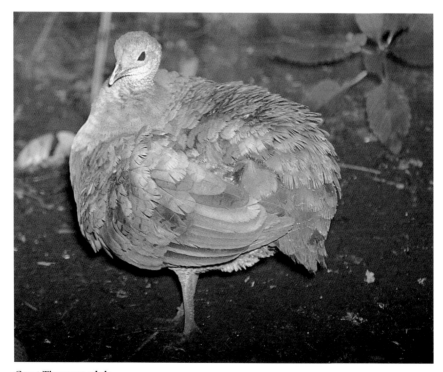

Great Tinamou adult

The well-camouflaged Great Tinamou is one of the most characteristic but seldom seen birds of the rainforest. Its presence is regularly detected, however, by its beautiful, flutelike call—three paired tremulous notes—which is most often heard at sunset. Dr. Alexander Skutch, Costa Rica's premier ornithologist, wrote of the tinamou's song: "All the beauty of the tropical forest, all its mystery . . . find expression in these exquisite notes." Tinamous, closely related to rheas and ostriches, are represented by five species in Costa Rica: Great, Highland, Little, Slaty-breasted, and Thicket. Tinamous evolved from a primitive family that dates back 10 million years. They even have unique reptilian qualities, including similar blood proteins.

The Great Tinamou, about the size of a chicken, lives a solitary life on the forest floor. Individuals move slowly among the undergrowth, eating fruits, seeds, frogs, small lizards, spiders, worms, and other insects. A Great Tinamou may accompany army ants to catch insects flushed by the ants.

When mating season arrives in December, the female lays three to five huge bright blue eggs with a glossy porcelain-like finish in a shallow depression on the ground—usually by the base of a tree or log. The male incubates the eggs for nineteen to twenty days and cares for the young for another twenty days before seeking out another female so it can mate again and renest. Meanwhile, the female has sought out other males, and they raise families as well. A female may keep as many as four males busy raising chicks during the nesting season, which extends to August. This reproductive behavior is called polyandry.

On the Caribbean slope, Great Tinamous may be heard at Tortuguero NP, La Selva Biological Station, Rara Avis, and Rancho Naturalista. On the Pacific slope, they occur at Carara NP, Wilson Botanical Garden at San Vito, Corcovado NP, and Tiskita Jungle Lodge. The best place to see Great Tinamous in Costa Rica is at La Selva Biological Station, where they can be observed at close range along trails in the Arboretum, along Sendero Tres Ríos, and on the river trail to the successional plots. Listen for them early in the morning and late in the afternoon.

PELICAN FAMILY (Pelecanidae)

Brown Pelican

Pelecanus occidentalis

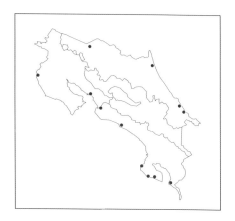

COSTA RICAN NAMES: ***Pelícano pardo; buchón; pelicano; alcatraz.***

13/15 trips; 59 sightings.

STATUS: Permanent resident.

LENGTH: 41.3–59.8 inches.

WINGSPREAD: 79.9–89.8 inches.

WEIGHT: 6 pounds 10 ounces–7 pounds 11 ounces.

RANGE: Pacific coast from Washington to Peru, and the Caribbean coast from Florida to Venezuela.

ELEVATIONAL RANGE: Sea level.

The Brown Pelican is the largest waterbird in Costa Rica. The adult is dark grayish brown with whitish highlights over the back. The head and neck are white. The immature bird is brownish. Pelicans fly with grace and elegance as they skim the wave tips in follow-the-leader formations. Also impressive when diving for fish, a pelican will fly no more than ten to thirty feet above the water, bank sharply, and plunge downward. As it strikes the water, the wings fold backward to decrease water resistance as the bird thrusts its open bill over a fish. Prey consists primarily of small fish. Pelicans may live up to thirty-one years.

On the Caribbean coast, Brown Pelicans are regularly seen in the vicinity of Cahuita NP, Limón, and along the coast at Tortuguero NP. There are at least four breeding colonies of Brown Pelicans on islands along the Pacific coast, including the largest on Isla Guayabo. Along the Pacific coast, they can be seen from nearly any beach.

Brown Pelican adult, banking to dive

Brown Pelican adult, swimming

CORMORANT FAMILY (Phalacrocoracidae)

Neotropic Cormorant
(Olivaceous Cormorant)

Phalacrocorax brasilianus
(*P. olivaceus*)

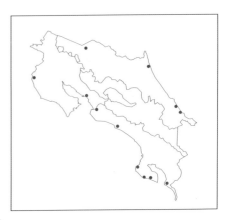

COSTA RICAN NAMES: *Cormorán
neotropical; pato chancho; pato de
agua.*

14/15 trips; 41 sightings.

STATUS: Permanent resident.

LENGTH: 22.8–28.7 inches.

WEIGHT: 4.0 pounds (1,814 grams).

RANGE: Southwestern United States to
southern South America.

ELEVATIONAL RANGE: Sea level to
2,000 feet (in Costa Rica).

Neotropic Cormorant adult

The Neotropic Cormorant is a black fish-eating waterbird closely related to pelicans. The only cormorant in Costa Rica, it is the size of a large duck and is often seen sitting on trees, posts, or rocks with the wings outspread in a "choir director" pose. In sunlight, the black plumage shows bluish-purple highlights. The long, pointed bill has a downturned hook at the tip, and the legs are positioned far back on the body to provide greater propulsion when pursuing fish. Cormorants are found in coastal saltwater areas, freshwater marshes, rivers, and brackish ponds. Their presence lends a prehistoric touch to wetlands, because fossil evidence for cormorants dates back about 30 million years. Although this bird is generally seen in Costa Rica's lower elevations, it occurs to elevations of over 15,000 feet on Andean lakes of South America.

Cormorants usually fish individually but sometimes form a line and flail the water with their wings to drive fish into shallow water. Then they dive to catch fish that are usually three to four inches long. Cormorants also eat frogs, crustaceans, tadpoles, shrimp, and aquatic insects. They can plunge-dive like Brown Pelicans. While swimming, cormorants sit low in the water with a slightly upturned bill and a posture similar to that of an Anhinga. When perched, both species sit in an upright posture. However, the neck of a cormorant is shorter and thicker than the "snakelike" neck of the Anhinga, and the body of the Anhinga is more slender.

In Caribbean lowlands, cormorants may be seen along the beach and canals of Tortuguero NP and from Limón south to Cahuita NP. Cormorants may also be seen along the Río Sarapiquí near La Selva Biological Station and along the Río Frío. On the Pacific coast, they occur along beaches from the Nicaragua border south to Panama. They also inhabit freshwater marshes of the Guanacaste region like those at Palo Verde NP and Caño Negro NWR.

ANHINGA FAMILY (Anhingidae)

Anhinga

Anhinga anhinga

Costa Rican names: ***Pato aguja; aninga.***

12/15 trips; 40 sightings.

Status: Permanent resident.

Length: 31.9–35.8 inches.

Wingspread: 47.2 inches.

Weight: 3.0 pounds (1,350 grams).

Range: Florida to northern Argentina.

Elevational range: Sea level to 2,000 feet.

The Anhinga has a snakelike head and neck that make it distinctive among Costa Rican waterbirds. The appearance and posture of this species resemble those of the Neotropic Cormorant, but the cormorant has a shorter and thicker neck. The tip of the bill is hooked on the cormorant and pointed on the Anhinga. The Anhinga has unique plumage that allows the feathers to become waterlogged very quickly. This helps them assume a very low profile when swimming. When only the head and neck are exposed, an Anhinga looks like a snake moving through the water.

This bird inhabits shallow fresh and brackish water of lowland rivers, ponds, marshes, and mangrove lagoons. An Anhinga hunts underwater for small fish among submerged vegetation, paddling slowly with its feet and holding the wings slightly outspread for stability. Modified neck vertebrae allow the neck to be cocked back in an S-shaped profile, enabling the Anhinga to thrust its bill forward to spear its quarry. After swimming, an Anhinga dries its feathers by perching in an upright posture with the wings outspread like a cormorant. Anhingas may also be seen soaring high overhead among vultures and Wood Storks and are distinguished by the long neck extended forward and a widespread fan-shaped tail.

The Anhinga is fairly common in Caribbean lowlands, including canals of Tortuguero NP, in rivers and ponds from Limón south to Cahuita NP, and in the Río Sarapiquí near La Selva Biological Station. In the Pacific lowlands, this waterbird is regularly encountered in Palo Verde NP, at La Ensenada Lodge, and along the Río Tárcoles from Carara NP to its mouth at Tárcol Lodge. Anhingas also occur in the Río Frío region and in Lake Arenal.

Anhinga adult

FRIGATEBIRD FAMILY (Fregatidae)

Magnificent Frigatebird

Fregata magnificens

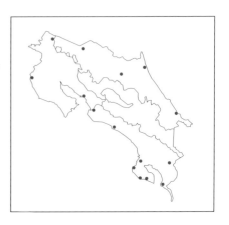

Costa Rican names: *Rabihorcado magno; tijereta del mar; zopilote de mar.*

12/15 trips; 57 sightings.

Status: Permanent resident.

Length: 35.0–44.9 inches.

Wingspread: 85.4–96.0 inches.

Weight: 2 pounds 6 ounces–3 pounds 8 ounces (1,100–1,587 grams).

Range: Southern California to Peru in Pacific; Florida to northern Argentina in Atlantic.

Elevational range: Sea level to 4,000 feet.

Magnificent Frigatebird adult male displaying

Adult female showing flight silhouette

Flight silhouette showing aerodynamic profile

The Magnificent Frigatebird is aerodynamically stunning. Considering that a frigatebird weighs only as much as a mallard duck, the amount of lift provided by the four-foot-long angular wings demonstrates their perfect flight adaptations for life at sea. The bones are so light that they represent only 5 percent of the bird's body weight and weigh less than the bird's feathers. This low percentage of bone weight is unequaled by any other bird. The deeply forked tail provides great agility in flight. This is the only frigatebird regularly seen along Costa Rican beaches of the Caribbean and Pacific Oceans. This bird has a purplish sheen on its black plumage.

Frigatebirds fly low over the water and dip their heads to grasp flying fish, squid, jellyfish, hatchling sea turtles, crabs, and small fish. On land, they prey on the eggs and nestlings of birds, including other frigatebirds. Frigatebirds are well known for aerial piracy. They harass terns, gulls, boobies, and tropicbirds and force them to drop or regurgitate any fish they may be carrying. When the fish falls, the frigatebirds acrobatically catch the fish in their bills.

Frigatebirds have impressive courtship displays. While sitting on top of a bush in the colony, a male inflates its huge red throat pouch, spreads its wings, points its bill to the sky, and waits for a female to fly overhead. When one is sighted, the male drums its bill against its throat pouch, quivers its wings, and gives a loud "winnowing" sound. Frigatebirds nest only on a few islands along the Pacific coast. The reproductive cycle is longer than for any other seabird. Parental care continues for four and a half to seven months in the nest and for nine to twelve months after the chick leaves the nest.

Frigatebirds may be observed along the beaches of Tortuguero and Cahuita NPs on the Caribbean coast and along the entire Pacific coast. They may even be seen flying overland at sites like La Selva Biological Station, Poás Volcano, and the Wilson Botanical Garden at San Vito as they cross between the Caribbean and the Pacific.

HERON FAMILY (Ardeidae)

Bare-throated Tiger-Heron

Tigrisoma mexicanum

COSTA RICAN NAMES: ***Garza-tigre cuellinuda; martín peña; pájaro vaco***.

11/15 trips; 41 sightings.

STATUS: Permanent resident.

LENGTH: 28.0–31.9 inches.

WEIGHT: 2 pounds 10 ounces (1,200 grams).

RANGE: Northern Mexico to Colombia.

ELEVATIONAL RANGE: Sea level to 3,600 feet.

The Bare-throated Tiger-Heron is a large, elegantly marked heron of Caribbean and Pacific marshes, lakes, streams, and mangrove lagoons. This heron often stands in a bitternlike posture along the water's edge and is distinguished by fine gray vermiculations that give a "herringbone" appearance to its plumage. This is the most common of three tiger-herons in Costa Rica. Others are the Fasciated and Rufescent Tiger-Herons.

A resident of fresh and brackish water habitats, this tiger-heron is usually found in quiet waters of lowland and middle-elevation wetlands. Prey includes small fish, frogs, and crayfish. Feeding occurs primarily in early morning, late evening, and at night. Tiger-herons stand quietly in shallow water and wait for prey to move within striking range of their sharp beaks. They may also stalk slowly along wetland edges in search of food. Although usually silent, tiger-herons may squawk loudly when flushed, and the males are known for a loud, booming roar at dusk or at night during the breeding season.

Among the best places to see this bird are along the canals of Tortuguero NP and in the Río Frío region on the Caribbean slope. In Pacific lowlands, it may be encountered in wetlands throughout Guanacaste, including those at Palo Verde NP, Estero Madrigal on Hacienda Solimar southwest of Cañas, La Ensenada Lodge, Caño Negro NWR, and Carara NP, in wetlands near Manuel Antonio NP, and in lowland rivers of Corcovado NP. It is especially abundant at Estero Madrigal. A pair has traditionally nested in a tree above the Villa Lapas Lodge near Carara NP.

Bare-throated Tiger-Heron adult

Bare-throated Tiger-Heron immature

Yellow-crowned Night-Heron adult

Yellow-crowned Night-Heron immature

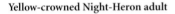

Yellow-crowned Night-Heron

Nyctanassa violacea

> Costa Rican name: **Martinete cabecipinto**.
>
> 11/15 trips; 41 sightings.
>
> Status: Permanent resident and migrant.
>
> Length: 20.0–27.6 inches.
>
> Weight: 1 pound 6 ounces (652 grams).
>
> Range: Central United States to Brazil; Galápagos Islands.
>
> Elevational range: Sea level to 1,000 feet.

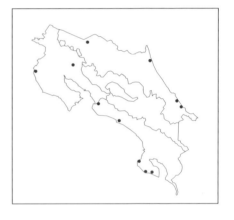

The Yellow-crowned Night-Heron is a medium-sized waterbird of Caribbean and Pacific lowlands. The gray body, thick bill, and black-and-white striped head make it easy to distinguish. The immature bird, brown speckled with white, is similar to a young Black-crowned Night-Heron. In flight, the feet of a Yellow-crowned Night-Heron extend farther beyond the tail, because they are proportionally longer than the feet of a Black-crowned Night-Heron.

Preferred habitats include brackish water in mangrove lagoons and fresh-water lowland streams, marshes, ponds, and estuaries of rivers entering both the Caribbean and the Pacific. The thick bill is an adaptation for feeding on crabs and crayfish. Frogs, insects, snails, mussels, and fish are also eaten. This night-heron is usually nocturnal or crepuscular but may feed in daytime when tidal water levels are ideal for feeding.

Look for this bird in Caribbean lowlands along canals in Tortuguero NP and in estuaries along the highway between Limón and Cahuita NP. Along the Pacific coast, it may be seen in mangrove lagoons near Tamarindo, at the mouth of the Río Tárcoles, in Carara NP, along the Río Corobicí near La Pacífica, in Manuel Antonio NP, along the Ríos Térraba and Sierpe, in Corcovado NP, and on islands offshore from the Osa Peninsula.

Boat-billed Heron

Cochlearius cochlearius
> Costa Rican names: *Pico cuchara; chocuacua; cuaca.*
> 10/15 trips; 14 sightings.
> Status: Permanent resident.
> Length: 17.7–20.0 inches.
> Weight: 1 pound 5 ounces.
> Vocalization tapes: D, V.
> Range: Mexico to northern Argentina.
> Elevational range: Sea level to 1,000 feet.

The Boat-billed Heron, probably the most memorable of all Costa Rican herons, has a huge, broad bill and enormous eyes that give it an almost comical appearance. This medium-sized wading bird occupies Caribbean and Pacific lowlands in habitat with shallow, quiet, or slow-moving water. This includes mangrove lagoons, ponds, and small streams. It is found in small, noisy colonies that are usually heard before they are seen. Individuals make a variety of croaks, quacks, and squawks, as well as popping noises that are made with the bill.

The large eyes are an adaptation for hunting in shallow water at dawn, dusk, and at night. Standing quietly in shallow water, it looks for prey and uses the bill to scoop up small fish, shrimp, frogs, insects, and even small mammals. This is the only heron that scoops up its prey instead of spearing it with a sharp bill.

Because Boat-billed Heron sites are often in thick cover, it is generally necessary to have a naturalist guide or boatman locate them. They can be seen in Tortuguero, Carara, and Palo Verde NPs; Río Frío; Estero Madrigal at Hacienda Solimar; La Ensenada Lodge; and along the Río Corobicí near La Pacífica. Care should be taken not to enter nesting colonies because disturbance could cause them to abandon the area. An easily viewed colony is located at the CATIE (Centro Agronómico Tropical de Investigación y Enseñanza) agricultural and forestry education facility near Turrialba. The pond inside the entrance has long been famous for its waterbirds. There is a bamboo thicket on the small island where Boat-billed Herons nest. A permit is required to visit the CATIE grounds for birding. Call ahead at 506-558-2275 or 506-558-2000 for a permit or fax 506-556-1533 to obtain the permit. Permits can also be requested by e-mail at *lsalas@catie.ac.cr*.

Boat-billed Heron adult

Close-up showing bill detail

Cattle Egret

Bubulcus ibis

COSTA RICAN NAMES: *Garcilla bueyera; garza del ganado*.

15/15 trips; 182 sightings.

STATUS: Permanent resident; a few migrants from the north.

LENGTH: 18.1–22.0 inches.

WINGSPREAD: 34.6–37.8 inches.

WEIGHT: 11.2–14.4 ounces (340–390 grams).

RANGE: Southern Canada to southern Argentina and Chile; southern Europe, Africa, Asia, and Australia.

ELEVATIONAL RANGE: Sea level to 7,000 feet.

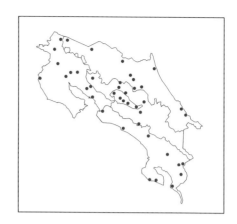

The Cattle Egret is the most widespread and adaptable egret in the world. It is a small white egret with a short thick neck, yellowish bill, and buffy to coppery tinges over the head, chest, and back. This egret spread from Africa to north-

Cattle Egret adult

Adult feeding by horse

eastern South America in about 1877 and has since dispersed south to Chile and Argentina and northward to Canada. It first appeared in Costa Rica in 1954 and is now the most common egret in the country.

Originally a bird that evolved with roaming herds of African wildlife, the Cattle Egret has adapted to regions occupied by cattle and horses. It accompanies livestock and eats grasshoppers, small lizards, crustaceans, frogs, and other invertebrates flushed by grazing animals. It also seeks insects and small creatures flushed by fires or by tractors as people plow or cultivate croplands.

The most dramatic aspect of this bird's natural history is the sight of a communal roosting tree adorned with dozens or hundreds of Cattle Egrets. In early morning and late evening, small flocks of Cattle Egrets can be seen flying across the countryside between feeding pastures and night roosts. Normally seen in small flocks of one or two dozen birds during the day, Cattle Egrets roost communally at night in large trees that afford nocturnal protection from predators. The Cattle Egret may be seen throughout most of Costa Rica, from lowland wetlands and pastures in both Caribbean and Pacific regions to the Central Plateau and highlands with mixed forests and pastures.

Cattle Egret night roost

Green Heron adult

Green Heron (Green-backed Heron)

Butorides virescens (*Butorides striatus virescens*)

COSTA RICAN NAMES: **Garcilla verde; chocuaco; martín peña**.

14/15 trips; 74 sightings.

STATUS: Permanent resident and northern migrant.

LENGTH: 13.8–18.9 inches.

WINGSPREAD: 20.5–23.6 inches.

WEIGHT: 4.8–8.8 ounces (135–250 grams).

VOCALIZATION TAPE: D.

RANGE: Southern Canada to northern Argentina; Africa, Malaysia, India, Galápagos Islands, and Australia.

ELEVATIONAL RANGE: Sea level to 6,000 feet.

The Green Heron, like the Cattle Egret, is widely distributed across tropical and temperate regions. The species occurring in Costa Rica, *Butorides virescens,* is found from southern Canada to Panama. The adult has a black cap and crest, chestnut neck and shoulders, metallic greenish-blue back, a white streak down the center of the breast, yellow eyes, and yellow legs. The immature Green Heron is similar to the adult, but the plumage on the back is dark brownish with less iridescence than on the adult.

This small, common heron is found in lowlands of the Caribbean and Pacific slopes to premontane levels. A solitary heron, this bird can be found wherever shallow fresh, brackish, and salt water provides an opportunity for capturing small fishes, shrimp, insects, and frogs.

Look for the Green Heron in Caribbean lowlands along the edges of canals and ponds in Tortuguero NP, Puerto Viejo en Sarapiquí, Guapiles, and La Selva Biological Station. In the Pacific lowlands, it may be seen at lagoons in Puntarenas, Carara and Palo Verde NPs, Río Tárcoles estuary, San Isidro city lagoons, Manuel Antonio NP, and the lagoons near the San Vito airport.

Little Blue Heron

Egretta caerulea

COSTA RICAN NAME: ***Garceta azul.***

14/15 trips; 97 sightings.

STATUS: A few permanent residents; mostly northern migrants.

LENGTH: 20.0–29.9 inches.

WINGSPREAD: 39.4–41.3 inches.

WEIGHT: 12.3–12.8 ounces (296–364 grams).

RANGE: Massachusetts to southern Brazil.

ELEVATIONAL RANGE: Sea level to 5,000 feet.

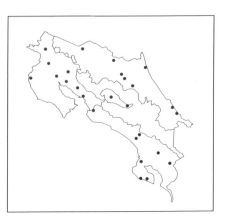

Little Blue Heron adult

Little Blue Heron immature showing bluish-gray, black-tipped bill

The Little Blue Heron, a common migrant from September through April, offers a challenge in identification. It resembles other herons, and the adults and immatures have different plumages. Adults have slaty-blue plumage and a maroon-colored neck. The bill is bluish gray with a black tip. Immature birds are white with bluish-gray, black-tipped bills. Immature birds often have grayish blotches on the tips of the white feathers over the back. These feathers, as well as the bill color, help distinguish them from other white wading birds such as Snowy Egrets, Great Egrets, and Cattle Egrets. Also, this heron sometimes flies with the neck extended forward, while other herons usually fly with the neck recurved. The Great Blue Heron, a migrant from North America, can be distinguished from the Little Blue Heron by its height (about three feet) and yellowish bill. The Great Blue Heron also has a white head with a black stripe behind the eyes that extends to plumes behind the head.

The Little Blue Heron is diurnal and feeds by stalking slowly in shallow water or along marshy edges. It may feed singly, in small groups, or in the company of white ibises. Among the most common food items are small fish, crayfish, crabs, shrimp, frogs, tadpoles, grasshoppers, beetles, and crickets. A few Little Blue Herons nest in Costa Rica from June through September.

This heron may be encountered in the Caribbean lowlands along the canals and wetlands of Tortuguero and Cahuita NPs, wetlands in the vicinity of

Guapiles and La Selva Biological Station, and in estuaries along the highway from Limón to Cahuita. The Little Blue Heron can be seen in wetlands, estuaries, and mangrove lagoons in Guanacaste and along the entire length of the Pacific coast.

Snowy Egret

Egretta thula

> Costa Rican name: **Garceta nivosa**.
>
> 14/15 trips; 49 sightings.
>
> Status: A few permanent residents; mostly northern migrants.
>
> Length: 18.7–26.8 inches.
>
> Weight: 13.8 ounces (370 grams).
>
> Range: Northern United States to northern Argentina.
>
> Elevational range: Sea level to 3,900 feet.

The Snowy Egret is a stately white wading bird with elegant plumes at the back of the head, on the chest, and over the back. It has a black bill with contrasting yellow face and yellow eyes. The black legs have contrasting yellow feet that give it the nickname "golden slippers." The Great Egret is also white, but stands almost three feet tall compared to the Snowy Egret, which is about two feet tall. The Great Egret has black feet and a yellow bill.

The Snowy Egret is a bird of fresh- and saltwater habitats including ponds, marshes, mangrove lagoons, estuaries, and coastal beaches. Feeding typically occurs in shallow water in the company of other wading birds. The Snowy Egret uses more feeding strategies than any other heron or egret: It actively moves around to stir up the bottom with its yellow feet to find small fish, shrimp, frogs, and crayfish. It may capture prey during low flights over water, and flocks may also follow livestock to capture insects in a manner similar to that used by Cattle Egrets. So don't assume all egrets near cattle are Cattle Egrets. Some Snowy Egrets nest in Costa Rica, but most are wintering migrants present from October through March.

This bird is common in Caribbean lowlands, in Tortuguero NP, and in estuaries and wetlands from Limón south to Cahuita NP. The Snowy Egret is also common in the Guanacaste region and along the entire Pacific coast. It is also found inland near San Isidro, along the Río Térraba, San Vito, and in the Central Plateau in the vicinity of the Cachí Reservoir.

Snowy Egret adult showing black legs with yellow feet

STORK FAMILY (Ciconiidae)

Wood Stork

Mycteria americana

    Costa Rican names: ***Cigueñón; garzón; guairón.***

    13/15 trips; 46 sightings.

    Status: Permanent resident.

    Length: 32.7–40.2 inches.

    Wingspread: 59.0 inches.

    Weight: 4 pounds 6.5 ounces–6 pounds 9.7 ounces (2,000–3,000 grams).

    Range: South Carolina to northern Argentina.

    Elevational range: Sea level to 2,500 feet.

The Wood Stork is the second tallest bird in Costa Rica—exceeded only by the Jabiru. Although similar to a Great Egret, it is more closely related to vultures than to egrets or herons. Several significant features distinguish it from wading

Wood Stork immature

Adult in flight showing black wingtips and pink feet

birds. The Wood Stork is larger; the bill is much heavier; the wing tips and secondary feathers are black, whereas all egrets and the immature Little Blue
Heron have white wing tips; the head and neck are vulturelike: black and un-
feathered; and finally, in flight, storks fly with their neck extended, whereas
herons and egrets usually fly with their neck recurved. Since Wood Storks are
often seen soaring, the black primaries and secondaries and the extended neck
are good identification marks. The most unique markings of the Wood Stork
at close range are black legs highlighted by pink toes.

Whereas herons and egrets feed by spearing their prey, the Wood Stork
feeds by moving through shallow water with the submerged bill partially open.
Whenever the bill comes in contact with prey, the bill snaps shut on it. Sometimes Wood Storks feed in a group. They feed in shallow freshwater and saltwater wetlands, mangrove lagoons, ponds, streams, and flooded fields along
the Pacific coast. Prey includes small- to medium-sized fish, crayfish, frogs, insects, snakes, and even hatchling caimans! One pair of Wood Storks and their
three to four nestlings will consume 440 pounds of prey during the nesting
season.

The Wood Stork is most abundant in the Guanacaste region. Look for it in
Palo Verde NP, Estero Madrigal at Hacienda Solimar, La Ensenada Lodge, the
Puntarenas lagoons, and the Río Tárcoles and estuary near Carara NP. It can
occasionally be encountered in the Caribbean lowlands.

Jabiru

Jabiru mycteria

COSTA RICAN NAMES: *Jabirú; galán sin ventura; veterano*.

3/15 trips; 4 sightings.

STATUS: Permanent resident.

LENGTH: 48.0–55.1 inches.

WINGSPREAD: 90.6–102.4 inches.

WEIGHT: 16 pounds 9 ounces (8 kilograms).

RANGE: Southern Mexico to northern Argentina.

ELEVATIONAL RANGE: Sea level to 1,000 feet.

Jabiru adult

The stately Jabiru, standing nearly five feet tall and with a wingspread exceeding eight feet, is the largest bird in Costa Rica. It is an endangered species, with only about twelve pairs nesting in the country. The Jabiru may be seen soaring high overhead, but, unlike the wings of the Wood Stork, which have black tips, the Jabiru's wings are all white.

This stork inhabits shallow wetlands and flooded fields of the Guanacaste region. It often feeds in the company of Wood Storks, White Ibises, Roseate Spoonbills, herons, and egrets. Wading through shallow water, the Jabiru uses its huge bill to splash the water and flush prey as well as to clamp shut on fish, frogs, snakes, young caimans, eels, crabs, and small turtles.

The Jabiru nests at the beginning of the dry season so it can capitalize on the availability of aquatic creatures that become stranded as shallow wetlands dry up. Solitary nesters, a pair of Jabiru storks build an enormous stick nest high in a tree. The young are cared for in the nest for eighty to ninety-five days and continue to be fed by the par-

Adult with two young in nest

Close-up of head

ents for two months after leaving the nest. Jabiru storks have been known to live up to thirty-six years. A good place to look for the Jabiru is in Palo Verde NP. There is also a recent nest record from Caño Negro NWR. The Mata Redonda lagoons in Guanacaste are being managed by Ducks Unlimited. At that wetland, a total of 86 Jabirus were counted in 2000. A Jabiru also showed up for the first time at La Ensenada Lodge wetlands in 2000.

AMERICAN VULTURE FAMILY (Cathartidae)

Turkey Vulture

Cathartes aura

COSTA RICAN NAMES: ***Zopilote cabecirrojo; zonchiche; noneca.***

15/15 trips; 194 sightings.

STATUS: Permanent resident and northern migrant.

LENGTH: 25.1–31.9 inches.

WINGSPREAD: 70.9–78.7 inches.

WEIGHT: 1 pound 14 ounces–4 pounds 6.5 ounces (850–2,000 grams).

RANGE: Southern Canada to southern Argentina.

ELEVATIONAL RANGE: Sea level to over 10,000 feet.

The Turkey Vulture is a large black bird with a bare red head that may be seen soaring throughout Costa Rica, from beaches to the highest peaks of the Talamanca Mountains. Although usually not appreciated by humans, vultures are fascinating. Closely related to storks, the Turkey Vulture is one of the only birds with a well-developed sense of smell. It will often fly low over the forest to locate the carcasses of dead animals by smell. Black Vultures and King Vultures may watch the movements of Turkey Vultures to locate carrion.

Because vultures occur over a broad range of cold and hot climates, they have interesting adaptations for dealing with extreme temperatures. The bare, wrinkled head is easier to keep clean while eating carrion and also helps radiate excessive body heat. A vulture may also urinate onto its legs, as the cooling effect of evaporation on the legs serves to dissipate heat. At night, the body temperature drops to conserve energy, and in the morning, the black body color helps absorb heat from the sun.

The large surface of the wings compared to the relatively light body weight allows a Turkey Vulture to soar for hours without flapping its wings. In flight, the Turkey Vulture holds its wings slightly uplifted in a shallow V-profile. This is in contrast to Black Vultures, which hold their wings in a horizontal posture. Also, the tail of the Black Vulture is distinctly shorter and more fan-shaped when viewed in flight. There is a bluish-white band across the back of the head of the resident Turkey Vulture subspecies, *C. aura ruficollis*. The migrant race is red on the back of the head. This scavenger feeds on carcasses of freshly dead animals, primarily mammals. It may go for two weeks without food or water. The digestive system of the Turkey Vulture has the remarkable ability to kill disease organisms associated with carrion—like anthrax and cholera.

Resident Turkey Vultures may be seen throughout Costa Rica all year. Some migratory Turkey Vultures winter in Costa Rica, but most pass through en route to South America from September through October and return north from January through May.

Turkey Vulture adult

Adult, flight silhouette

Black Vulture adult

Black Vulture

Coragyps atratus

COSTA RICAN NAMES: *Zopilote negro; gallinazo; zoncho*.

15/15 trips; 183 sightings.

STATUS: Permanent resident.

LENGTH: 22.0–26.8 inches.

WINGSPREAD: 53.9–59.1 inches.

WEIGHT: 2 pounds 6.8 ounces–4 pounds 3.0 ounces (1,100–1,900 grams).

RANGE: Southeastern United States to southern Argentina.

ELEVATIONAL RANGE: Sea level to 9,300 feet.

The Black Vulture is a common scavenger throughout the country and often soars in the company of Turkey Vultures. In flight, this vulture flaps its wings more frequently than the Turkey Vulture and holds its wings horizontally. The short fan-shaped tail is a good identification mark. The head, which is black in contrast to the red head of the Turkey Vulture, also dissipates body heat. This species also urinates onto its legs to cool itself in hot weather.

The Black Vulture hunts by sight and has a poor sense of smell. It is well adapted to cities, backyards, and garbage dumps where waste food and meat scraps can be obtained. This is a benefit to some small rural villages, where the vultures perform sanitation duties. In addition to feeding on carrion, this scavenger will kill newborn or weakened prey, including newly hatched sea turtles. Other food items include bananas and fruits of African oil palms. When a dead animal is encountered, Black Vultures dominate Turkey Vultures for feeding preference. Turkey Vultures feed after Black Vultures have eaten their fill. In some cases, dozens or hundreds of Black Vultures will surround a single cow or horse carcass.

Populations of Black Vultures have increased where they have had access to garbage dumps and dead livestock on farms and ranches. This bird may be seen during daylight hours anywhere in the country, but it is most abundant in the lowlands.

Black Vulture adult, flight silhouette showing short, fan-shaped tail

King Vulture

Sarcoramphus papa

> COSTA RICAN NAMES: ***Zopilote rey; rey gallinazo; rey de zopilotes***.
>
> 12/15 trips; 33 sightings.
>
> STATUS: Permanent resident.
>
> LENGTH: 28.0–31.9 inches.
>
> WINGSPREAD: 70.9–78.0 inches.
>
> WEIGHT: 6 pounds 9.7 ounces–8 pounds 4.2 ounces (3,000–3,750 grams).
>
> RANGE: Southern Mexico to northern Argentina.
>
> ELEVATIONAL RANGE: Sea level to 4,000 feet.

King Vulture adult

Close-up of head

The sight of a King Vulture circling above the rainforest is one of the highlights of birding in the American tropics. The effortless soaring flight and white body contrasting with the black primaries and secondaries make it easy to identify. The Wood Stork has a similar plumage pattern, but the long neck and legs make soaring Wood Storks distinctive even at great distances. When viewed close-up, the King Vulture's head and neck are an incredible combination of orange, yellow, purple, blue, red, and black patterns amid assorted wattles and wrinkles. Immature King Vultures are black with a small neck ruff and an orange tinge on the bill.

This imposing scavenger, found in Caribbean and Pacific lowlands, may be seen soaring above undisturbed and partially deforested forests where dead mammals can be encountered. Like the Turkey Vulture, this raptor can locate carrion by smell.

The King Vulture may be seen soaring above Tortuguero NP and in the vicinity of La Selva in the Caribbean lowlands. Among the best places to see King Vultures, however, are at Corcovado Lodge Tent Camp, Lapa Ríos, Carara NP, Villa Lapas, Sirena Biological Station in Corcovado NP, and Tiskita Jungle Lodge.

IBIS and SPOONBILL FAMILY (Threskiornithidae)

White Ibis

Eudocimus albus

Costa Rican names: **Ibis blanco; coco**.

11/15 trips; 19 sightings.

Status: Permanent resident.

Length: 22.0–28.0 inches.

Weight: 1 pound 10.4 ounces– 2 pounds 5.0 ounces (750–1,050 grams).

Range: North Carolina to Venezuela and Peru.

Elevational range: Sea level to 1,000 feet.

The White Ibis, a medium-sized wading bird with a white body, a red face, and a long, slender, down-curved bill, is regularly encountered in mangrove lagoons and shallow wetlands in Guanacaste and the Pacific coastal region. The male is about 35 percent larger than the female. In flight, the long down-curved bill and black tips on the four outermost primary wing feathers provide good identification marks. The White Ibis flies in lines or V-formations. The species is characterized by alternate wing flapping and gliding. Immature White Ibises are brown with white splotches over the head and neck. Their rumps and bellies are white. Green and Glossy Ibises are less common.

Ibis pair, with larger male on left and smaller female on right

This wading bird forages singly or in flocks on mud flats, river estuaries, shallow wetlands, flooded fields, or ponds and among tree roots of mangrove swamps. It picks up crayfish, crabs, shrimp, small fish, snails, small snakes, beetles, and grasshoppers with dexterous movements of its long bill. Nesting and night roosting are colonial activities involving dozens or hundreds of birds.

The White Ibis is most common in the Río Tempisque basin, including Palo Verde NP, Estero Madrigal at Hacienda Solimar, and wetlands of La Ensenada Lodge, Caño Negro in the Río Frío area, coastal wetlands from the Tamarindo area south to Puntarenas, the Río Tárcoles estuary near Carara NP, and Tárcol Lodge. Large numbers of White Ibises congregate at shrimp-production ponds near Puntarenas. This ibis may be seen in smaller numbers on river estuaries along the coast of Corcovado NP.

Roseate Spoonbill

Ajaia ajaja

Costa Rican names: ***Espátula rosada; garza rosada.***

11/15 trips; 18 sightings.

Status: Permanent resident.

Length: 26.8–34.1 inches.

Weight: 3 pounds 1.3 ounces (1,400 grams).

Range: Florida to northern Argentina.

Elevational range: Sea level to 1,000 feet.

The Roseate Spoonbill is a memorable wading bird that is stately, beautiful, and bizarre. The pink body and spoon-shaped bill make identification easy. A close look at the bare facial details reveals prehistoric, almost reptilian, features. Standing nearly three feet tall, this large bird is typically seen feeding among other waterbirds in shallow wetlands and flooded fields. The spoonbill feeds alone or in small flocks by walking through shallow water, swinging its head from side to side with the bill slightly open. The bill snaps shut whenever prey is encountered. Food items include shrimp, crayfish, crabs, small fish, aquatic beetles, snails, slugs, plant stems, and roots of sedges.

The greatest concentration of Roseate Spoonbills is in the Río Tempisque basin in the vicinity of Palo Verde NP. This bird may also be seen in wetlands near Tamarindo, Estero Madrigal at Hacienda Solimar, La Ensenada Lodge, scattered ponds throughout Guanacaste, the lagoons at Puntarenas, along the Río Tárcoles and its estuary at Tárcol Lodge, and at river estuaries of Corcovado NP near the Sirena Biological Station.

Roseate Spoonbill adult

Roseate Spoonbill adult in flight

DUCK FAMILY (Anatidae)

Black-bellied Whistling-Duck

Dendrocygna autumnalis

Costa Rican names: **Piche; pijije común.**

11/15 trips; 18 sightings.

Status: Permanent resident and northern migrant.

Length: 16.9–20.9 inches.

Weight: 1 pound 6.9 ounces–1 pound 15.9 ounces (650–1,020 grams).

Vocalization tape: D.

Range: Southern Texas to northern Argentina.

Elevational range: Sea level to 4,000 feet.

The Black-bellied Whistling-Duck is the most abundant of three whistling-ducks in Costa Rica. Others are the Fulvous and White-faced Whistling-Ducks. These birds form an interesting genus different from other ducks: drakes and hens are identical, and the drakes help incubate the eggs and care for the young. This vocal duck is well known for its squealing call that sounds like "peechee" or "peechichichi," giving it the local name *piche*.

Like the Wood Duck in North America, this duck nests in tree cavities, so it adapts well to nest boxes. The Black-bellied Whistling-Duck feeds on sprouting rice in upland fields, grass, seeds of moist-soil plants like smartweed, insects, snails, and other invertebrates. Feeding takes place in daytime or at night.

Nesting occurs from May through October. A hen lays twelve to sixteen eggs in tree cavities, nest boxes, or on the ground. The drake and hen mate for life, and the male assists with incubation and brood rearing. The young leave the nest within one to two days after hatching and are cared for by both parents for about two months.

The wetlands at Palo Verde NP, Mata Redonda, La Ensenada Lodge, and Caño Negro NWR are good places to see this duck. Scan the flocks closely to see if any Fulvous or White-faced Whistling-Ducks are present. Other places where it can be observed are wetlands near La Pacífica, Hacienda Solimar, and Los Inocentes Lodge; Río Bebedero; small ponds throughout Guanacaste; the Río Frío region; and wetlands of Carara NP. A few are reported nesting near Cartago and in the Reventazón Valley in the Central Plateau.

Black-bellied Whistling-Ducks, pair of adults, sexes identical

Muscovy Duck

Cairina moschata

Costa Rican names: ***Pato real;
pato perulero.***

4/15 trips; 6 sightings.

Status: Permanent resident.

Length: 26.0–33.1 inches.

Weight: 2 pounds 6.8 ounces–
8 pounds 13.0 ounces (1,100–4,000
grams).

Range: Southern Texas to northern
Uruguay.

Elevational range: Sea level to
1,000 feet.

The Muscovy Duck is often perceived as a huge, tame farm duck across much
of North and South America. In Costa Rica, it is possible to see and appreciate
this duck as a wary, wild, fast-flying waterfowl species. It lives along wooded
wetlands, streams, and swamps, and nests in large hollow trees. The male,
more than twice as large as the female, has black plumage with green iridescent
highlights and a fleshy face characterized by red and black warty caruncles. It
can raise a prominent crest on top of its head when confronting other males. In
flight, the shoulder areas on the upper surface of the wings show large white
patches.

Muscovy Duck adult male

The best habitat for this duck is in the Guanacaste region along forested streams and rivers. It is also found in mangrove lagoons and wooded swamps. The Muscovy feeds on roots, seeds, leaves, and stems of aquatic plants like water lily and mangrove and on rice and corn. Animal foods include small fish, frogs, tadpoles, crabs, small lizards, spiders, termites, and crayfish.

The best places to observe the Muscovy Duck include marshes at Palo Verde NP, Caño Negro NWR, and Estero Madrigal at Hacienda Solimar. It can also be seen along the Río Tárcoles, in Carara NP, and rarely at Tortuguero NP.

Blue-winged Teal

Anas discors

COSTA RICAN NAMES: *Cerceta aliazul; zarceta; pato canadiense*.

6/15 trips; 9 sightings.

STATUS: Northern migrant.

LENGTH: 13.8–16.1 inches.

WEIGHT: 9.4–14.4 ounces (266–410 grams).

RANGE: Alaska to Venezuela and Peru.

ELEVATIONAL RANGE: Sea level to 4,000 feet; to 9,800 feet in migration.

The Blue-winged Teal is the most abundant duck in Costa Rica during the wintering season from September through April. This small North American prairie wetland duck migrates farther than most other waterfowl and demonstrates how important it is for conservationists to preserve both summer and winter habitats for migratory birds. Wetland drainage for crop production has greatly reduced habitat for Blue-winged Teal in the prairie wetlands of the north and in tropical wetlands of the Guanacaste region. Identification marks for this small duck include pale blue patches on the shoulder areas of the upper wing surfaces and white crescents on the blue-gray face of the drakes.

This duck is an aquatic plant feeder. Foods include seeds, roots, and leaves of aquatic and moist-soil grasses, sedges, algae, pondweed, duckweed, smartweed, and rice in paddies. Some insects and small crustaceans are also eaten.

The best habitats for Blue-winged Teal include Río Tempisque basin marshes like those at Palo Verde NP, La Ensenada Lodge, and the Mata Redonda lagoon. More winter in Caño Negro NWR in the Río Frío region. This duck may be encountered at Las Concavas Marsh near Cartago and in wetlands near the San Vito airport. Scan flocks of Blue-winged Teal closely to look for Cinnamon Teal in winter plumage.

Blue-winged Teal pair of adults, male on left and female on right

OSPREY FAMILY (Pandionidae)

Osprey

Pandion haliaetus

> Costa Rican names: ***Aguila pescadora; gavilán pescador.***
> 13/15 trips; 50 sightings.
> Status: Northern migrant.
> Length: 21.7–22.8 inches.
> Wingspread: 57.1–66.9 inches.
> Weight: 2 pounds 10.3 ounces–4 pounds 6.5 ounces (1,200–2,000 grams).
> Vocalization tapes: C, F, X.
> Range: Winters from Florida to Argentina.
> Elevational range: Sea level to 5,000 feet.

The Osprey is one of the largest and most conspicuous migratory raptors in Costa Rica. It is regularly seen along coastal and inland waters where it can catch fish in shallow water. The brown body, white breast, and brown mask through the eye, and its association with water make identification easy. In flight, the wings are long and have a distinctive bend at the wrist joint.

Osprey adult

Osprey adult in flight

As an Osprey hunts, it flies slowly over shallow water and can hover when prey is sighted. It plummets with the wings folded back and the legs extended downward as it strikes the water to capture the fish, which may be a foot or two below the surface. Most fish caught weigh from one-third to two-thirds of a pound. On some occasions, small lizards, mammals, or birds may be taken.

The Osprey has several adaptations for its fish-eating lifestyle. The outer toe of each foot is "reversible" so that when a fish is caught, two toes point forward and two point back so the fish can be gripped with the head pointed forward. The fish is carried head first for easier flight. The toes have spiny pads that aid in holding slippery fish, the claws are especially long and curved, and the nostrils have valves that shut as the Osprey strikes the water. The Osprey migrates into Costa Rica beginning in September. Some birds stay to winter, but most continue to wintering destinations that range from Panama to Bolivia and Brazil. The return migration occurs in March and April.

Look for wintering Ospreys in the Caribbean lowlands, along canals and beaches of Tortuguero NP, in estuaries and wetlands from Limón to Cahuita, and along the Río Sarapiquí in the vicinity of La Selva. On the Pacific slope, they may be seen in mangrove lagoons and along beaches of the Tamarindo region, in Palo Verde NP, at La Ensenada Lodge, along the Río Corobicí near Cañas, and from Playa Doña Ana southeast to Panama.

ACCIPITER FAMILY (Accipitridae)

Swallow-tailed Kite

Elanoides forficatus

COSTA RICAN NAMES: ***Elanio tijereta; tijerilla; gavilán tijerilla***.

13/15 trips; 49 sightings.

STATUS: Permanent resident, northern migrant, and southern migrant.

LENGTH: 22.0–26.0 inches.

WINGSPREAD: 51.2 inches.

WEIGHT: 13.2 ounces (375 grams).

VOCALIZATION TAPES: D, AA.

RANGE: South Carolina to northern Argentina.

ELEVATIONAL RANGE: Sea level to 6,000 feet; occasionally to 10,000 feet.

The deeply forked tail, graceful flight, and elegant black-and-white markings of the Swallow-tailed Kite make it one of the most impressive raptors in the Americas. With great precision, this bird of prey plucks small creatures on the wing or from treetop foliage. Cicadas, lizards, bats, hummingbirds, small snakes, frogs, and nestling birds are all adeptly snatched from their nests or perches. Fruits are also eaten.

Swallow-tailed Kite adult in flight

The Swallow-tailed Kite is a breeding resident in wet lowlands of the Caribbean and southern Pacific slopes, including the Monteverde Cloud Forest Reserve and Corcovado NP on the Osa Peninsula. Migratory birds are also present. Some may be northern kites that nest as far north as South Carolina and Florida and migrate to South America. Most are apparently migrants from South America that enter Costa Rica from the southeast in January and February to reproduce in Costa Rica. Those birds leave from July to September. One of the most unique behaviors of this raptor is that the wintering birds sleep in communal roosts as a means of protection from predators. Communal roosts have been observed in forests of the Monteverde area (Mariano Arguedas, personal communication 1996).

A few kites may be seen in the Caribbean lowlands from Limón to Cahuita, in Tortuguero NP, at La Virgen del Socorro, and near Rincón de la Vieja. Most sightings are from San Isidro del General southeast to the Panama border. Some Swallow-tailed Kites may also be seen migrating in late January at Villa Mills in Cerro de la Muerte, at Vista del Valle Restaurant at kilometer 119 along the Pan American Highway (PAH), and at Savegre Mountain Lodge. In late January and early February, sightings are most frequent at the Wilson Botanical Garden near San Vito, Corcovado NP, Lapa Ríos, Corcovado Lodge Tent Camp, and Tiskita Jungle Lodge. Mating birds have been observed in late January near San Pedrillo at the northwest end of Corcovado NP.

Double-toothed Kite

Harpagus bidentatus

CostaRican name: ***Gavilán gorgirrayado***.

13/15 trips; 33 sightings.

Status: Permanent resident.

Length: 13 inches.

Weight: 5.9 to 8.1 ounces (168–229 grams).

Vocalization tapes: W, CC.

Range: Southern Mexico to southeastern Brazil.

Elevational range: Sea level to 5,000 feet.

The attractive Double-toothed Kite is one of the easiest raptors to identify in flight because of the fluffy white feathers on its vent and under-tail coverts. It gives an appearance of having "bloomers" that are visible even when soaring at great heights. The back is slate gray, and the throat is white with a slender dark stripe down the center of the white throat patch—resembling a slender necktie. The upper chest is chestnut rufous, and the white thighs have rufous barring. This kite spends much time soaring.

The Double-toothed Kite inhabits mature moist and wet lowland and middle-elevation forests and older second-growth forests. It also frequents forest edges and openings, where it watches for prey from a perch and then launches itself like an accipiter to fly down and snatch its unsuspecting prey. Prey items include small lizards, frogs, cicadas, bats, and larger insects. This kite follows troops of squirrel and white-faced monkeys so it can catch insects and other creatures that are flushed by the monkeys.

On the Caribbean slope, the Double-toothed Kite can be seen at La Virgen del Socorro, Tortuga Lodge, Tortuguero NP, Guapiles, Puerto Viejo en Sarapiquí, La Selva Biological Station, Rainforest Aerial Tram, and lower levels of Braulio Carrillo NP. On the Pacific slope, this kite occurs at Carara NP, Villa Lapas, San Isidro del General, Los Cusingos, Corcovado NP, Lapa Ríos, Drake Bay Wilderness Resort, Corcovado Lodge Tent Camp, Tiskita Jungle Lodge, and the Wilson Botanical Garden at San Vito.

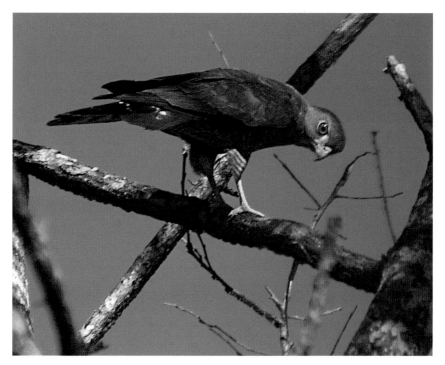

Double-toothed Kite adult

White Hawk

Leucopternis albicollis

    COSTA RICAN NAME: ***Gavilán blanco***.

    12/15 trips; 21 sightings.

    STATUS: Permanent resident.

    LENGTH: 18.2–20.1 inches.

    WEIGHT: 1 pound 5.1 ounces–1 pound 6.9 ounces (600–650 grams).

    VOCALIZATION TAPE: CC.

    RANGE: Mexico to central Brazil.

    ELEVATIONAL RANGE: Sea level to 4,600 feet.

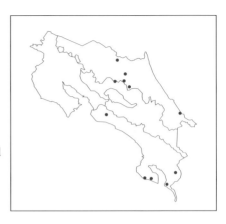

Looking like a white phantom in the treetops, the White Hawk is one of Costa Rica's most memorable raptors. Many birds of prey are varying shades of gray or brown, but the White Hawk provides beautiful contrast: snow white plumage with black wing highlights and a black band across the tip of the tail.

The White Hawk is a raptor of lowland and middle-elevation forests—especially in hilly terrain. It prefers habitat in moist and wet forests of the Caribbean slope and southern Pacific lowlands. From a perch on a vantage point at the edge of the forest, this hawk watches for snakes, lizards, frogs, and small mammals. Snakes make up much of its diet. This hawk is frequently seen soaring above the rainforest. Males defend a territory of about 500 acres.

The best place to see the White Hawk is at Tiskita Jungle Lodge, where a pair traditionally nests near the lodge. Other sites include Braulio Carrillo NP and the vicinity of the Rainforest Aerial Tram, La Virgen del Socorro, Villa Lapas, Corcovado Lodge Tent Camp, Rara Avis, and Sirena Biological Station.

White Hawk adult

Gray Hawk

Asturina plagiata (formerly *Buteo nitidus* and *Asturina nitida*)

COSTA RICAN NAMES: **Gavilán gris; gavilán pollero.**

11/15 trips; 22 sightings.

STATUS: Permanent resident.

LENGTH: 15.0–16.9 inches.

WEIGHT: 1 pound 0.4 ounce–1 pound 3.5 ounces (465–554 grams).

VOCALIZATION TAPES: D, F.

RANGE: Southern Texas to western Ecuador.

ELEVATIONAL RANGE: Sea level to 3,300 feet.

The fine, pearly-gray barring on the breast of the Gray Hawk makes it easy to identify. Primarily a bird of open country and partially forested habitat, this hawk is readily seen as it perches on roadside power lines. The Gray Hawk has a loud whistled call.

This raptor hunts by watching ground cover and vegetation for movements of small lizards, rodents, large insects, or small birds. Very agile in flight, it is able to snatch lizards or birds off their perches. When the nesting season begins in December, mated pairs perform dramatic aerial displays near their nests that include steep climbs, dives, and pursuits.

The Gray Hawk can be seen along roads from La Selva and Puerto Viejo en Sarapiquí to La Virgen del Socorro in the Caribbean lowlands and foothills. It is more abundant, however, on the Pacific slope, including the Guanacaste region. Sightings are frequent near Carara NP, Villa Lapas, Quepos, Rancho Casa Grande, and Manuel Antonio NP. This hawk also occurs at Corcovado Lodge Tent Camp, Lapa Ríos, Tiskita Jungle Lodge, and the Wilson Botanical Garden near San Vito.

Gray Hawk adult

189

Roadside Hawk adult

Roadside Hawk

Buteo magnirostris

COSTA RICAN NAME: **Gavilán chapulinero.**

14/15 trips; 69 sightings.

STATUS: Permanent resident.

LENGTH: 13.0–16.1 inches.

WEIGHT: 8.8–10.7 ounces (251–303 grams).

VOCALIZATION TAPES: B, D, E, T, X, BB.

RANGE: Southern Mexico to northern Argentina.

ELEVATIONAL RANGE: Sea level to 4,000 feet.

The Roadside Hawk is one of the most common hawks in Costa Rica, and, true to its name, it is usually seen perched along roadsides. An adult Roadside Hawk has a pale gray head and shoulders and rusty barring across the breast, whereas an adult Broad-winged Hawk has a dark brown head, a rufous patch on the upper breast area, and variable amounts of rusty barring on the belly. Immatures are similar, but the Roadside Hawk has fine rufous barring on the thighs. In flight, rufous primaries are conspicuous. The call of the Roadside Hawk is a high-pitched whistle, described as "seeuu."

The Roadside Hawk is found in lowland and middle-elevation deforested areas and has increased as forests were cut to create cropland, pastures, and plantations. It hunts by sitting on a low perch and dropping onto prey such as insects, frogs, snakes, lizards, and small mammals. It may also catch prey escaping from fires or army ants.

Roadside Hawks may be seen in the Caribbean lowlands from Tortuguero NP southeast to Cahuita. This raptor is more abundant throughout Guanacaste and along the Pacific lowlands through San Isidro del General, Quepos, Corcovado NP, Corcovado Lodge Tent Camp, and southeast to Tiskita Jungle Lodge. At middle elevations, it may occasionally be observed at the Wilson Botanical Garden near San Vito, Turrialba, and La Virgen del Socorro.

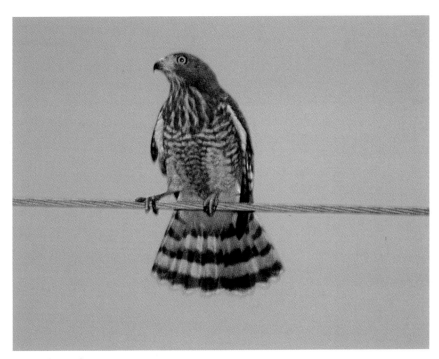

Roadside Hawk immature

Broad-winged Hawk

Buteo platypterus

> Costa Rican names: ***Gavilán aludo; gavilán pollero***.
>
> 14/15 trips; 63 sightings.
>
> Status: Northern migrant.
>
> Length: 13.4–17.3 inches.
>
> Wingspread: 33.9–39.3 inches.
>
> Weight: 9.3 ounces–1 pound 3.7 ounces (265–560 grams).
>
> Vocalization tapes: A, C, F, X.

Broad-winged Hawk adult

RANGE: Breeding—Central Canada to
Texas; wintering—Guatemala to Brazil.
ELEVATIONAL RANGE: Sea level to
6,500 feet.

The Broad-winged Hawk is the most abundant migratory raptor in Costa Rica and may be seen from late September through March. Broad-wings pass through Costa Rica en route to wintering sites in South America, but many winter in the country. This hawk soars much more than the similar Roadside Hawk, and the head and shoulders are more brownish than the grayish head of the Roadside Hawk. The tail has alternating black and white bands, and the upper chest area is rufous. The call is a long, high-pitched whistle.

The Broad-winged Hawk watches ground cover from a tree, post, or power line at the edge of fields, pastures, or forest openings. It swoops down to capture small mammals, lizards, birds, frogs, and insects like grasshoppers and dragonflies.

This hawk can be observed throughout Caribbean and Pacific lowlands in many of the same habitats as the Roadside Hawk. However, it is more common than the Roadside Hawk in the Caribbean lowlands, and it is much more common in middle- and high-elevation areas like Monteverde, Poás and Braulio Carrillo NPs, Savegre Mountain Lodge, Rancho Naturalista, Cerro de la Muerte, the Central Plateau, and San Vito. Tens of thousands of Broad-winged Hawks can be seen in mid- to late October each year migrating through Cahuita and Puerto Viejo near the Panama border en route to wintering areas in South America.

Short-tailed Hawk

Buteo brachyurus
COSTA RICAN NAME:
Gavilán colicorto.
10/15 trips; 18 sightings.
STATUS: Permanent resident and
northern migrant.
LENGTH: 14.6–18.1 inches.
WINGSPREAD: 35.4 inches.
WEIGHT: 15.9 ounces–1 pound 2.7
ounces (450–530 grams).
RANGE: Southern Florida and eastern
Mexico to northern Argentina.
ELEVATIONAL RANGE: Sea level to
5,900 feet.

Short-tailed Hawk adult

Although the Short-tailed Hawk is in the genus *Buteo,* this small hawk hunts like an accipiter. It flies 300 to 600 feet above open and semiopen habitats and dives to snatch small- and medium-sized birds, mammals, lizards, and insects from their perches. It may hover like a kite while scanning for prey. Birds up to the size of kestrels and mourning doves are included in the diet.

Markings include a dark brown head, cheek area, and back; narrowly barred tail with a dark terminal band; white throat and breast; and a chestnut patch on the lower sides of the neck. The White-tailed Hawk is similar, with a dark brown patch on the sides of the face and a white breast and belly, but the tail is white with a black terminal band. Some Short-tailed Hawks are sooty black "melanistic" birds that are white only on the face.

Short-tailed Hawks are present as residents and as migrants that pass through the Caribbean lowlands. In migration, this bird may be seen flying with Swallow-tailed and Plumbeous Kites. Preferred habitats include the foothills of the Caribbean slope, like the area around La Virgen del Socorro. On the Pacific slope, the Short-tailed Hawk may be seen in hilly terrain of the Río Térraba watershed near San Isidro del General, San Vito, Quepos, Lapa Ríos, Corcovado Lodge Tent Camp, and Tiskita Jungle Lodge.

FALCON FAMILY (Falconidae)

Crested Caracara

Caracara plancus
(formerly *Polyborus plancus*)

COSTA RICAN NAMES: ***Caracara cargahuesos; cargahuesos; querque; quebrantahuesos.***

13/15 trips; 44 sightings.

STATUS: Permanent resident.

LENGTH: 19.2–23.2 inches.

WINGSPREAD: 47.2–52.0 inches.

WEIGHT: 1 pound 13.4 ounces–2 pounds 1.6 ounces (834–953 grams).

VOCALIZATION TAPE: F.

RANGE: Arizona, Texas, and Florida to Tierra del Fuego and the Falkland Islands.

ELEVATIONAL RANGE: Sea level to 2,500 feet.

Crested Caracara adult

Costa Rica has three species of caracara: Crested, Yellow-headed, and Red-throated. The Crested Caracara, the most common, is found primarily throughout Guanacaste and along Pacific coastal areas southeast to Quepos. It continues to spread south. This is the national bird of Mexico—the "Mexican eagle" that was highly regarded as part of the Aztec culture. The Crested Caracara inhabits dry forest and savanna habitats, where it preys on small creatures or feeds on carrion. It eats dead animals, human garbage, snakes, lizards, turtles, hatchling caimans, small mammals, beetles, crabs, grubs, earthworms, coconut meat, and even nestling egrets and Roseate Spoonbills.

The Crested Caracara sometimes feeds in groups by walking around in recently cultivated fields in search of insects, worms, and grubs or by feeding on dead livestock. This opportunistic bird searches for roadkills along highways or will pursue vultures, other caracaras, or pelicans in the air until they regurgitate their food. The acrobatic caracara will catch the falling "meal" in flight. Preferred habitats include ranch land, pastures, gallery forests, savannas, wet fields, marshes, and brushlands. This caracara may also fly low over an area and catch small animals by stooping at them.

The Crested Caracara can be observed at Guanacaste, Palo Verde, and Santa Rosa NPs, Lomas Barbudal BR, along Pacific coastal areas southeast to Carara and Manuel Antonio NPs, and in the San Isidro del General region. A few Crested Caracaras have moved into the Caribbean lowlands, including the San Carlos region and around Puerto Viejo en Sarapiquí. Sightings have been made since 1998 at EARTH University, the agricultural school located near Guapiles.

Crested Caracara adult in flight

Yellow-headed Caracara

Milvago chimachima

COSTA RICAN NAME: ***Caracara cabigualdo.***

12/15 trips; 39 sightings.

STATUS: Permanent resident.

LENGTH: 15.7–14.7 inches.

WINGSPREAD: 29.1 inches.

WEIGHT: 11.1–11.8 ounces (315–335 grams).

RANGE: Costa Rica to northern Argentina.

ELEVATIONAL RANGE: Sea level to 5,900 feet.

The southern Pacific lowlands are of special significance because some wildlife species of South American origin have extended their range into this region. Examples are the Yellow-headed Caracara, Blue-headed Parrot, Fork-tailed Flycatcher, and Smooth-billed Ani. The Yellow-headed Caracara was first recorded in Costa Rica in 1973 and is identified by the dark brown body and yellowish head and breast. It has since been expanding its range into the lowlands and foothills of the Pacific slope. In 1999 one was observed along the PAH south of Cañas. A pair nested along the road that goes to Monteverde in 1998.

Yellow-headed Caracara adult

This unusual raptor is adapted to open pastureland, meadows, and cleared forest land where livestock are present. It may sit on the back of horses and cattle to pick ticks from them, or it may hunt on the ground in a manner similar to that of Cattle Egrets, capturing insects, caterpillars, lizards, frogs, or small rodents as they are flushed by grazing animals. Other food items include roadkills, fledglings in bird nests, African oil palm fruits, and corn.

Yellow-headed Caracaras may be observed throughout much of the southern Pacific lowlands and foothills, including cleared areas around Carara NP, San Isidro del General, and the San Vito area; Corcovado Lodge Tent Camp; Corcovado NP; Lapa Ríos; and Tiskita Jungle Lodge.

Laughing Falcon

Herpetotheres cachinnans

Costa Rican name: ***Guaco***.

13/15 trips; 40 sightings.

Status: Permanent resident.

Length: 17.7–20.9 inches.

Weight: 1 pound 4.0 ounces–
1 pound 12.2 ounces (567–800 grams).

Vocalization tapes: B, D, I, S, T, BB, CC.

Range: Mexico to northern
Argentina.

Elevational range: Sea level to
6,000 feet.

The Laughing Falcon is one of the most memorable—and vocal—raptors in Costa Rica. Its loud, wild raucous calls pierce the woodlands with sounds resembling their local Spanish name: *guaco*. Sometimes a mated pair will call back and forth to each other in a noisy duet. Three features make this raptor easy to identify: the call, the deep chestnut mask, and the creamy-buff throat, breast, and belly.

This falcon inhabits savannas and woodland mixed with meadows and pastures. A snake-eating specialist, the Laughing Falcon sits in a tree where it can scan the surrounding tree branches and ground cover for the movement of snakes. When one is spotted, the falcon drops to grasp the snake in its talons and then flies back to a perch, where it decapitates the snake with its sharp bill and eats it. Both venomous and nonvenomous snakes are eaten as well as rodents and lizards.

Beginning in February, the Laughing Falcon lays an egg in a large tree cavity, in a cavity on a cliff face, or in an abandoned hawk nest. After hatching, the young is protected by one adult while the other parent catches snakes and brings them to the nest.

In the Caribbean lowlands, this falcon may be observed in Tortuguero NP, along the highway from Guapiles to Limón, and along the coast from Limón south to Cahuita NP. It may also be seen in the vicinity of Puerto Viejo en Sarapiquí, La Selva, and La Virgen del Socorro. In the Pacific lowlands, it can be seen in Guanacaste, but most occur in the moist and wet mixed forest and pastures from Puntarenas to Carara NP, Villa Lapas, Rancho Casa Grande, Quepos, Manuel Antonio NP, San Isidro del General, Talari Mountain Lodge, Wilson Botanical Garden at San Vito, Lapa Ríos, Corcovado NP, and Tiskita Jungle Lodge.

Laughing Falcon adult

CHACHALACA, GUAN, and CURASSOW FAMILY
(Cracidae)

Gray-headed Chachalaca

Ortalis cinereiceps

> Costa Rican names: **Chachalaca cabecigrís; chacalaca; pavita.**
>
> 9/15 trips; 24 sightings.
>
> Status: Permanent resident.
>
> Length: 18.1–22.8 inches.
>
> Weight: 1 pound 1.3 ounces–1 pound 3.0 ounces (490–540 grams).
>
> Vocalization tape: S.
>
> Range: Eastern Honduras to northwestern Colombia.
>
> Elevational range: Sea level to 3,600 feet.

The chachalaca is an uncommon but noisy chicken-sized bird of lowland and middle-elevation forests in the Caribbean and Pacific regions of Costa Rica. There are two species in the country: the White-bellied Chachalaca (formerly Plain Chachalaca) in the dry forests of Guanacaste and the Gray-headed Chachalaca throughout the remaining wetter portions of the country. In Costa Rica, a person who talks "too much" is referred to as a *chachalaca*. The Gray-headed Chachalaca is less vocal than other chachalacas. Its calls include par-

Gray-headed Chachalaca adult

rotlike squawks, squeaks, clucks, and peeping tones. The primary wing feathers are chestnut on this species but gray on the White-bellied Chachalaca.

The preferred habitat of the Gray-headed Chachalaca is along brushy edges of forests, plantations, and second-growth forests where there is an abundance of fruits like guava (*Psidium guajava*), pokeweed (*Phytolacca*), and *Miconia*. It also eats *Cecropia* fruits. This bird lives in small flocks of six to twelve or more individuals that follow each other through the trees in search of fruit by hopping, flapping, and gliding in an unsynchronized follow-the-leader procession.

The chachalaca nests from January to July and is one of the only gallinaceous birds that feeds the precocial young for an extended period after hatching. It passes fruits to the chicks instead of allowing them to peck for their own food.

Because this bird has been heavily hunted, it is seldom seen. It may be seen in protected reserves, such as La Selva Biological Station, Carara NP, and Dr. Alexander Skutch's reserve, Los Cusingos, near San Isidro del General, and on the grounds of Talari Mountain Lodge near San Isidro del General. The best place to see the Gray-headed Chachalaca at close range is at Rancho Naturalista, where a flock regularly visits the feeders in the courtyard.

Crested Guan

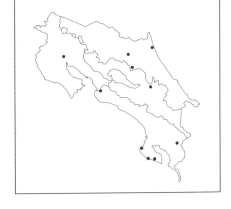

Penelope purpurascens

COSTA RICAN NAMES: ***Pava crestada; pava.***

9/15 trips; 26 sightings.

STATUS: Permanent resident.

LENGTH: 28.3–35.8 inches.

WEIGHT: 3 pounds 9.1 ounces– 5 pounds 5.6 ounces (1,620–2,430 grams).

VOCALIZATION TAPES: T, BB, CC.

RANGE: Southern Mexico to western Ecuador and northern Venezuela.

ELEVATIONAL RANGE: Sea level to 6,000 feet.

The Crested Guan is a large, brown, turkeylike bird most frequently seen peering down from the treetops as it searches for fruits and leaves that make up its diet. As its name implies, this bird has a crest that is frequently raised as it relates to nearby guans or to potential danger. A conspicuous red dewlap hangs from the throat. Slud (1964) described the call of this bird as a single- or double-note

Crested Guan adult showing dewlap on throat

honk that sounds like an old-fashioned automobile horn or a mixture of a goose's honk and a clucking hen.

A bird of primary and mixed lowland and middle-elevation habitats, the Crested Guan occurs in dry, moist, and wet forests of the Caribbean and Pacific slopes. Guans walk along high horizontal branches as single birds or in small groups of up to six individuals. They silently leap from one branch to the other or flap and glide through the treetops. Where foliage conceals the birds, their presence is sometimes revealed by debris falling from the branches. Among fruits eaten by this guan are figs, berries, *Cecropia, Spondias, Guatteria,* and wild papayas. The Crested Guan eats the fruits of wild nutmeg (*Virola surinamensis*) and disperses the plant by later regurgitating the seeds.

The best place to look for the Crested Guan is in forests where they are protected from hunting: Tortuguero, Braulio Carrillo, Palo Verde, Carara, and Corcovado NPs; La Selva Biological Station; El Gavilán Lodge; Rancho Naturalista; and the Wilson Botanical Garden at San Vito. The Río Pavo Trail at the Sirena Biological Station in Corcovado NP is named for this bird and is an excellent place to see it in the rainforest.

Black Guan

Chamaepetes unicolor

COSTA RICAN NAME: ***Pava negra***.

9/15 trips; 12 sightings.

STATUS: Permanent resident; endemic highland species.

LENGTH: 24.4–27.2 inches.

WEIGHT: 2 pounds 8 ounces (1,135 grams).

VOCALIZATION TAPES: AA, BB.

RANGE: Costa Rica and western Panama.

ELEVATIONAL RANGE: 3,000–8,200 feet.

The Black Guan, a turkey-sized bird of the cloud forest and high mountains, is endemic to the highlands of Costa Rica and western Panama. It is black with a blue face, red eyes, and red legs. The habitat includes unbroken forest and disturbed forest with scattered openings and second growth. This bird may be seen moving through the forest canopy as individual birds, in pairs, or in small groups. When in flight, the narrow, sharp-pointed primary feathers make a loud "crackling" sound. Although usually quiet, the Black Guan can make low, deep-toned groaning sounds, grunts, or piping calls.

The seeds of many forest fruits are dispersed in the droppings of this guan, so the bird is important for the propagation of many tropical trees. Among

Black Guan adult

fruits eaten by the Black Guan are wild avocado (*Persea*), *Urera, Ardisia,* holly (*Ilex*), *Guarea, Beilschmiedia, Guettarda, Chamaedorea, Citharexylum,* and *Cecropia.*

This big black bird may be seen gliding from one tree to another or perched in the middle to upper canopy of montane forests and cloud forests, including those at the Monteverde Cloud Forest Reserve, Tapantí NP, Savegre Mountain Lodge, in the forested river valley east of Tuís, and in Cerro de la Muerte along the PAH at kilometers 66, 80, 86, and 96.

Great Curassow

Crax rubra

COSTA RICAN NAMES: *Pavón grande; pavón; granadera.*

6/15 trips; 9 sightings.

STATUS: Permanent resident.

LENGTH: 30.7–36.2 inches.

WEIGHT: 6 pounds 13.3 ounces– 10 pounds 9.2 ounces (3,100–4,800 grams).

VOCALIZATION TAPES: B, T, CC.

RANGE: Southern Mexico to western Ecuador.

ELEVATIONAL RANGE: Sea level to 4,000 feet.

Like the Jaguar and White-lipped Peccary, the Great Curassow is an indicator of undisturbed tropical forests. It is eagerly hunted by settlers as roads are built into primary forests. Unlike chachalacas and guans, which spend most of their time in treetops, the Great Curassow forages primarily on the ground. The turkeylike male is black, with a prominent crest of curled feathers, a white belly, and a conspicuous yellow, knobby cere. The chestnut-colored hen has a black-and-white head and crest and a barred tail. These birds are usually encountered as individuals, pairs, or small groups of up to six. The Great Curassow has an interesting repertoire of vocalizations that includes a high-pitched "peet" that sounds like a small bird; a deep, resonant humming sound; a high-pitched descending whistle; and an alarm call that sounds like the yipping of a little dog.

The Great Curassow lives like a turkey, searching for seeds and fruits that have fallen to the ground, including *Spondias, Chione,* and *Casimira,* and some insects. It occurs in protected, extensive dry forests of Guanacaste and lowland and middle elevations of moist and wet primary forests of the Caribbean and

Great Curassow adult male

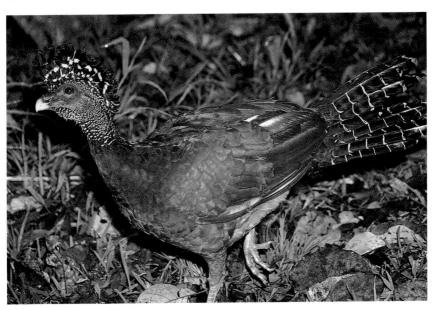

Great Curassow adult female

southern Pacific slopes. This bird can exist in secondary forests, but generally disappears in such areas because, due to overhunting, it does not survive where humans have settled. Curassow eggs are among the largest of all rainforest birds, almost 3.5 inches long. Curassow pairs are monogamous and nest from March through May. The Great Curassow is very long-lived. Individuals may live and reproduce to the age of twenty-three years.

Tourists may occasionally see a Great Curassow along the canals of Tortuguero NP, La Selva Biological Station, and at the woodland waterhole near the entrance to the OTS field station at Palo Verde NP. The best location to encounter a Great Curassow is in Corcovado NP—especially along the trails of the Sirena Biological Station. They may also be seen along the forest trail leading from Corcovado Lodge Tent Camp to the Río Madrigal in Corcovado NP.

Close-up of Great Curassow male's head

Depredated Curassow egg with fang punctures from large snake

RAIL FAMILY (Rallidae)

Gray-necked Wood-Rail

Aramides cajanea

COSTA RICAN NAMES: *Rascón cuelligrís; chirincoco; pone-pone; pomponé; cocaleca; cacaleo.*

10/15 trips; 26 sightings.

STATUS: Permanent resident.

LENGTH: 13.0–15.7 inches.

WEIGHT: 12.3 ounces–1 pound 0.4 ounce (350–466 grams).

VOCALIZATION TAPES: B, D, E, I, S, V, Z, BB, CC.

RANGE: Central Mexico to northern Argentina.

ELEVATIONAL RANGE: Sea level to 4,600 feet.

One of the loudest and most memorable sounds in tropical wetlands and marshy areas comes from the Gray-necked Wood-Rail. Early and late in the day, a ventriloquial, resonant, and somewhat chickenlike call pierces the swamp or marshland. The phrase sounds somewhat like the expression "kick-walk, kick-walk, kick-walk, cow-cow-cow-cow." The size of a small chicken, this rail stands about ten inches high and is seen more often than other rails. The rich earth tones of its olive, gray, and rufous plumage, highlighted by its yellow bill and red eyes and legs, make this one of the most striking waterbirds in the country.

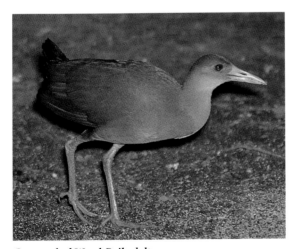

Gray-necked Wood-Rail adult

The Gray-necked Wood-Rail is found in swampy forests, edges of forest streams, wet second-growth forests, mangrove forests, marshes, swampy thickets, wet meadows, pastures, and rice and sugarcane fields with standing water. It is resident throughout lowland and middle elevations of both slopes, including the Central Plateau. The diet consists of crabs, snails, spiders, cockroaches, grasshoppers, frogs, small snakes, berries, palm fruits, bananas, rice, and corn. Some feeding occurs at night. This wood-rail may follow army ant swarms so it can catch escaping insects, arthropods, and small vertebrates.

Most rails are incredibly hard to spot, but the patchy characteristics of the habitat occupied by this bird provide viewing opportunities as it walks along wetland edges or as it walks from one patch of marshy cover or bamboo thicket to another. Although heard more often than seen, the Gray-necked Wood-Rail can be seen from boats in the canals of Tortuguero NP, in wet meadows near San Isidro del General, at Talari Mountain Lodge, on the walkways of Selva Verde Lodge, and in the Wilson Botanical Garden at San Vito by the bamboo thickets near the Heliconia garden. They are also very common at Zoo Ave at La Garita and come out of the forest after 4:00 each afternoon to eat at feeders that have been placed for free-ranging birds on the grounds.

Purple Gallinule

Porphyrula martinica

> COSTA RICAN NAMES: *Gallareta morada; calamón morada; gallina de agua*.
>
> 14/15 trips; 25 sightings.
>
> STATUS: Permanent resident.
>
> LENGTH: 10.6–14.1 inches.
>
> WEIGHT: 7.2–10.7 ounces (203–305 grams).
>
> RANGE: Central and eastern United States to northern Argentina.
>
> ELEVATIONAL RANGE: Sea level to 5,000 feet.

One of Costa Rica's most colorful waterbirds is the Purple Gallinule, which inhabits marshes, ponds, and lake edges with thick emergent vegetation. With its long toes grasping the plants, this gallinule walks among the floating leaves in search of pondweed, sedges, willow leaves, water lily fruits, berries, rice, small fish, frogs, dragonflies, grasshoppers, flies, spiders, insect larvae, and even the eggs and young of Northern Jacanas. It deftly turns over lily pads to feed on invertebrate eggs and larvae attached beneath the leaves.

Purple Gallinule adult

Nesting occurs during the rainy season in Guanacaste, but in some areas the Purple Gallinule nests every two to four months year-round. The young may be cared for by extended families—both parents and immature birds from previous broods.

This bird is found in marshy wetlands throughout the Caribbean and Pacific slopes at both lowland and middle elevations. Among places where the Purple Gallinule may be seen are Tortuguero NP, wetlands near La Selva Biological Station at Puerto Viejo en Sarapiquí, on the pond just inside the entrance to the CATIE tropical agricultural education and research center at Turrialba, Palo Verde NP, the airport lagoons at San Vito, and wetlands east of Quepos.

SUNBITTERN FAMILY (Eurypygidae)

Sunbittern

Eurypyga helias

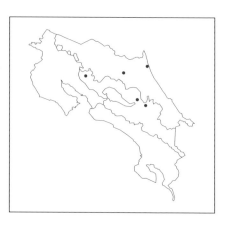

COSTA RICAN NAMES: *Garza del sol; sol y luna; ave canasta.*

3/15 trips; 4 sightings.

STATUS: Permanent resident.

LENGTH: 16.9–18.9 inches.

WEIGHT: 6.6 ounces (188.5 grams).

VOCALIZATION TAPES: V, CC.

RANGE: Southern Mexico to central Brazil.

ELEVATIONAL RANGE: 300–5,000 feet.

One of the most unusual, and beautiful, waterbirds in Costa Rica is the elusive Sunbittern. It is, however, neither a bittern nor a heron. It belongs to an avian family, Eurypygidae, for which there is only one species. The most closely related bird is the bizarre Kagu from New Caledonia near Australia. These two birds had a common ancestor that existed on the supercontinent Gondwanaland in the Mesozoic Period—before continental drift caused the supercontinent to separate into the continents we know today. The most stunning features of the Sunbittern are the eyeball patterns on the primary wing feathers. When the Sunbittern is faced by a threat, the wings and tail are spread to display the eyeball patterns and intimidate potential predators into thinking the Sunbittern is larger than it really is.

The Sunbittern inhabits Caribbean and southern Pacific wet lowlands and middle elevations. It is associated with small, rocky, fast-flowing streams in forested foothills about 2,000 to 4,000 feet in elevation. Prey is captured by stalking slowly in shallow water and thrusting the bill forward to spear its quarry. Foods include Dobson fly larvae (*Corydalus* sp.), small fish, eels, frogs, toads, snails, shrimp, lizards, earthworms, crayfish, crabs, dragonflies, cockroaches, katydids, beetles, flies, and spiders. This long-lived bird may live up to thirty years.

The Sunbittern is difficult to see because few tourism lodges provide viewing opportunities along the foothill streams and wetlands utilized by Sunbitterns. It can rarely be seen along canals in Tortuguero NP and on the Caribbean slope along small streams and wetlands in the vicinity of Turrialba and east of Tuís, Rancho Naturalista, Puerto Viejo en Sarapiquí near Selva Verde, Monte Verde and La Selva Biological Station.

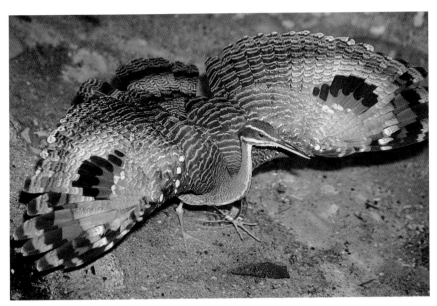

Sunbittern adult in display posture

Sunbittern adult

JACANA FAMILY (Jacanidae)

Northern Jacana

Jacana spinosa

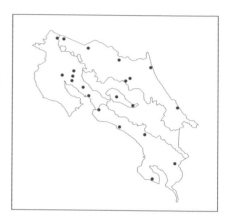

Costa Rican names: *Jacana centroamericana; cirujano; gallito de agua; mulita.*

15/15 trips; 63 sightings.

Status: Permanent resident.

Length: 6.7–9.1 inches.

Weight: 3.2–5.7 ounces (91–161 grams).

Vocalization tapes: D, S.

Range: Southern Texas to western Panama.

Elevational range: Sea level to 5,000 feet.

One of the most common and interesting waterbirds of Costa Rica's shallow marshy wetlands is the Northern Jacana. The black and russet body is highlighted by yellow wing feathers, a yellow bill, a yellow frontal shield on the forehead, and unusual yellow spurs that are briefly visible at the wrist joint of the

Northern Jacana adult

Northern Jacana immature

wings each time the bird alights. The sexes are identical, but the females are about 40 percent larger than the males. Young jacanas are colored so differently that they almost look like a different species. The back is pale brown, the throat and breast are white, and the cap and back of the neck are dark brown. The wing feathers are yellow like those of the adult.

The jacana has extremely long toes and toenails that enable it to walk on lily pads and other floating vegetation as it searches for aquatic insects and other invertebrates, tiny fishes, snails, and water lily seeds that have been exposed by Purple Gallinules. The most unusual feature of the jacana is that the females are polyandrous. Each female defends a marshy area that contains one to four males. She mates with all of them, and each male incubates four eggs on small, wet, floating platforms of aquatic vegetation. The female defends the male as he incubates the eggs, but the male raises the young after they hatch.

The Northern Jacana is readily seen in shallow wetlands of both coasts and in marshes of the Central Plateau. It is common in Tortuguero, Carara, and Palo Verde NPs; marshes of the Guanacaste region; and wetlands near San Vito. In the southern Pacific lowlands, check the jacanas carefully, as there is also a record of the Wattled Jacana, a South American species, at the water treatment lagoons at San Isidro del General.

OYSTERCATCHER FAMILY (Haematopodidae)

American Oystercatcher

Haematopus palliatus

CostA RicAN NAME:
Ostrero americano.

2/15 trips; 3 sightings.

STATUS: Permanent resident on Pacific coast and northern migrant.

LENGTH: 15.7–17.3 inches.

WEIGHT: 1 pound 4.0 ounces–1 pound 6.5 ounces (567–638 grams).

VOCALIZATION TAPES: C, F.

RANGE: Northeastern United States and northern Mexico to southern Argentina and Chile.

ELEVATIONAL RANGE: Sea level.

The only large shorebird in Costa Rica with a long, bright red bill is the American Oystercatcher. The black head and neck, dark back, white breast, and pink legs make this shorebird easy to identify. The legs are short and stout. The bill, usually held pointing downward at a slight angle, is an adaptation for feeding on marine invertebrates in coastal tidepools. That includes clams, snails, crabs, limpets, and oysters. The thin, bladelike tip of the bill is deftly inserted into the edge of a slightly open clam shell to snip the muscles that hold the clam shut. Then it opens the clam and eats the meat. This shorebird may live more than twenty years.

The American Oystercatcher may be seen singly, as pairs, or in small groups on sandy or gravelly beaches or exposed rocky tidepools at low tide. Feeding occurs in these areas during the day or night and may be timed to match the exposure of prey items in tidepools at low tide.

Look for the American Oystercatcher along beaches of the Guanacaste region, including rocky tidepools in the Tamarindo area and beaches in the Gulf of Nicoya. It can also be seen at tidepools along the coast of Corcovado NP, like the one near the mouth of the Río Llorona. Migrant oystercatchers can be seen along the Caribbean and Pacific coasts from August to October and from April through May.

American Oystercatcher adult

Black-necked Stilt adult, with Spectacled Caiman in background

STILT FAMILY (Recurvirostridae)

Black-necked Stilt

Himantopus mexicanus
  Costa Rican names: ***Cigüeñuela
  cuellinegro; soldadito.***
  10/15 trips; 17 sightings.
  Status: Permanent resident and
  northern migrant.
  Length: 13.8–15.7 inches.
  Weight: 5.9–7.2 ounces (166–205
  grams).
  Vocalization tape: F.
  Range: Western and southeastern
  United States to southern Chile and
  Argentina.
  Elevational range: Sea level to
  1,000 feet.

The slender, elegant lines and bold black-and-white markings of the Black-necked Stilt make it one of the most conspicuous and memorable shorebirds in the Americas. The long legs, long neck, and long slender bill are all adaptations that allow the stilt to wade in deeper water than most other shorebirds. It feeds in small flocks, striding through the water and sweeping its bill from side to side to capture aquatic insects, mollusks, crustaceans, annelid worms, tadpoles, and small fish. The bill is extremely sensitive and is also used to probe mud for prey.

The Black-necked Stilt is mainly found in Costa Rica's coastal lowland ponds, marshes, mangrove lagoons, estuaries, and tidal mud flats. Black-necked Stilts may be seen on shallow wetlands throughout the Río Frío and Guanacaste regions, in Palo Verde NP, on marshes near Cañas and Bebedero, at La Ensenada Lodge, in Carara NP, and at the nearby Río Tárcoles estuary. In addition to the resident population, migrants may be encountered in the lowlands of both the Caribbean and Pacific slopes from October through May.

THICK-KNEE FAMILY (Burhinidae)

Double-striped Thick-knee

Burhinus bistriatus

COSTA RICAN NAMES: *Alcaraván
americano; alcaraván.*

6/15 trips; 16 sightings.

STATUS: Permanent resident.

LENGTH: 16.9–18.9 inches.

WEIGHT: 1 pound 11.5 ounces (780
grams).

VOCALIZATION TAPES: D, BB.

RANGE: Southern Mexico to northern
Brazil.

ELEVATIONAL RANGE: Sea level to
2,000 feet.

The unusual Double-striped Thick-knee is a well-camouflaged bird of the
tropical dry forest found in pastures, burned fields, grain stubble, and savanna
habitats of the Guanacaste region and south of Lake Nicaragua. It is the only
Costa Rican representative in the family Burhinidae, which includes nine
species worldwide. The huge eyes have an almost comical appearance and are
an adaptation for seeing and feeding at night.

Double-striped Thick-knee adult

The short, thick bill is adapted for capturing insects, small lizards, frogs, snails, worms, and mollusks on the ground. Thick-knees rest by day in open fields and heavily grazed pastures and can be difficult to spot. They are usually encountered as pairs because they are monogamous and have strong pair bonds. Dozens of birds may sometimes be seen on disked fields where recent cultivation has exposed invertebrates. Because of the medium brown color of the birds and the tendency for pairs to sit on the ground, the best search technique for spotting them is to look for "pairs of cow-pies" out in the pastures. At night, thick-knees are quite vocal and create intriguing trills, cackles, and piping calls that carry for great distances. The sounds may resemble the "winnowing" of a Common Snipe.

The Double-striped Thick-knee is found only in Guanacaste and is one of the distinctive birds of that area. Look for it near Liberia, Cañas, Bebedero, Lomas Barbudal BR, Guanacaste, Palo Verde and Santa Rosa NPs, Hacienda Solimar, La Ensenada Lodge, and pastures south of Los Chiles. The courtyard at Hacienda Solimar is an excellent place to listen for the calling of thick-knees after dark.

PLOVER FAMILY (Charadriidae)

Semipalmated Plover

Charadrius semipalmatus

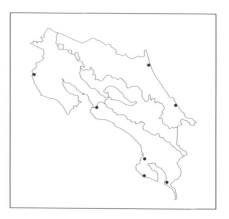

COSTA RICAN NAMES: ***Chorlitejo semipalmado; chorlito; turillo.***

7/15 trips; 14 sightings.

STATUS: Northern migrant.

LENGTH: 6.7–7.5 inches.

WEIGHT: 1.0–2.4 ounces (28–69 grams).

VOCALIZATION TAPES: C, F.

RANGE: Breeds Alaska and northern Canada; winters from southeastern and southwestern United States to central Chile and southern Argentina.

ELEVATIONAL RANGE: Sea level to 5,000 feet.

The Semipalmated Plover is one of seven plovers in Costa Rica. Others are the Killdeer and the Lesser Golden-, Black-bellied, Wilson's, Snowy, and Collared Plovers. In contrast to sandpipers, plovers have compact, short-necked bodies and short, thick bills. This plover has a short orange bill tipped with black, a single black breast band, a black bar across the forehead, and a black bar across the face above the bill. These marks differentiate it from the larger Killdeer, which has two breast bands; from the Snowy Plover, which has no breast bands; and from the Wilson's and Collared Plovers, which have single breast bands but no orange on the bills. The bill of the Wilson's Plover is longer and thicker than that of the Semipalmated Plover, and the profile suggests the Wilson's Plover is "smoking a little cigar."

This plover migrates through Costa Rica, primarily along the Pacific coast, from August through November and from March through May. Some winter along both coasts and may be seen on mudflats, sandy and rocky beaches, river estuaries, mangrove lagoons, and even pond or lake edges in the Central Plateau. As these plovers run in small groups, they pause and peck for polychaete worms, gastropods, grasshoppers, beetles, and ants.

This shorebird can be seen along the canals in Tortuguero NP, in river estuaries south of Limón, along the beach at Tamarindo, in the Río Tárcoles estuary by Tárcol Lodge, in rocky tidepools near Sirena Biological Station in Corcovado NP, and in beach tidepools near Tiskita Jungle Lodge.

Semipalmated Plover adult, winter plumage

SANDPIPER FAMILY (Scolopacidae)

Whimbrel

Numenius phaeopus

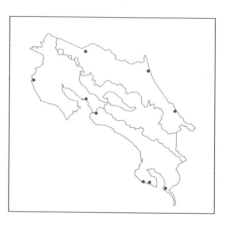

COSTA RICAN NAMES: ***Zarapito trinador; cherelá; zarceta.***

11/15 trips; 21 sightings.

STATUS: Northern migrant.

LENGTH: 15.7–18.1 inches.

WEIGHT: 9.4 ounces–1 pound 3.4 ounces (268–550 grams).

VOCALIZATION TAPES: C, F.

Range: Breeds Alaska, northern Canada and Eurasia; winters southwestern and southeastern United States to southern Brazil and Chile.

ELEVATIONAL RANGE: Sea level.

No sandpipers nest in Costa Rica, but twenty-nine species migrate through the country en route to South American wintering grounds. Some winter in the country. One of the largest and most common shorebirds is the Whimbrel. It has a long, down-curved bill (2.9–4.1 inches long) and black-and-white stripes through the head that differentiate it from other large sandpipers.

Whimbrel adults, winter plumage

The Whimbrel is a type of curlew that migrates along Costa Rica's coasts from August to September and from March to May. Some Whimbrels winter along the country's coastline and wetland edges. It is usually seen singly or in small numbers as it walks along the water's edge in search of ghost and fiddler crabs, crayfish, mollusks, polychaete worms, small fish, and lizards. The long bill is used to reach into fiddler crab (*Uca* sp.) burrows in search of the crabs. The curvature of the Whimbrel's bill matches the curvature of fiddler crab burrows. Loud piping notes, whistled calls, or trills are characteristic of this shorebird.

This shorebird can be seen along the beaches of Tortuguero NP and along the Caribbean coastline, including Cahuita NP. Along the Pacific coast, Whimbrels are regularly seen at Sugar Beach, Tamarindo, La Ensenada Lodge, Playa Doña Ana near Puntarenas, the Río Tárcoles estuary, along the beaches of Corcovado NP, and at Tiskita Jungle Lodge.

Willet

Catoptrophorus semipalmatus

COSTA RICAN NAME: **Pigüilo**.

12/15 trips; 33 sightings.

STATUS: Northern migrant.

LENGTH: 13.0–16.1 inches.

WEIGHT: 6.1–13.2 ounces (173–375 grams).

VOCALIZATION TAPES: C, F.

RANGE: Southern and eastern Canada to northern United States and Gulf Coast states; winters from southern United States to Galápagos Islands, northern Chile, and Brazil.

ELEVATIONAL RANGE: Sea level.

The Willet is a large, pale gray sandpiper with a straight, thick bill and prominent black and white bars on the wings. It is among the most common sandpipers along Costa Rica's Caribbean and Pacific beaches. The Willet has a noisy repertoire of loud shreiking "keeek" or "whreek" sounds.

This sandpiper migrates through Costa Rica from August through September and from March through May as it travels to and from wintering sites in Panama and on the coasts of South America. Some Willets winter along Costa Rica's beaches. The Willet lives on mudflats, mangrove lagoons, river estuaries, and rocky shorelines. It may walk in shallow water, pecking and probing for fiddler crabs, marine worms, and aquatic insects. It may also run through shallow water swishing the bill from side to side to capture small fish.

A few Willets may be encountered on the Caribbean coast at Tortuguero NP and on estuaries south of Limón, but most occur along Pacific beaches. Good places to observe them include Sugar Beach, Tamarindo, La Ensenada Lodge, Puntarenas, Playa Doña Ana, the Río Tárcoles estuary at Tárcol Lodge, Quepos, Manuel Antonio and Corcovado NPs, and beaches at Tiskita Jungle Lodge.

Willet adult in flight showing white wing bars

Willet adult, winter plumage

Adult, winter plumage showing no spots on breast

Spotted Sandpiper

Actitis macularia

> Costa Rican names: ***Andarríos maculado; alzacolita; piririza; tigüiza.***
>
> 15/15 trips; 77 sightings.
>
> Status: Northern migrant.
>
> Length: 7.1–7.9 inches.
>
> Weight: 1.3–1.4 ounces (37–40 grams).
>
> Wingspread: 14.6–15.7 inches.
>
> Vocalization tapes: C, F.
>
> Range: Breeds from Alaska to central United States; winters from southern United States to northern Argentina.
>
> Elevational range: Sea level to 7,200 feet.

The Spotted Sandpiper is the most common sandpiper in Costa Rica. In the northern breeding range, this bird is distinctly marked with black speckles on the breast and is characterized by continual "rump-bobbing." When present in Costa Rica, however, the Spotted Sandpiper becomes the "Spotless" Sandpiper because the bird's winter plumage includes a white, unmarked breast. However, the "rump-bobbing" behavior readily identifies the bird. Other identification marks include brownish smudges on the sides of the upper breast, a light horizontal stripe through the top of the eye, and a brownish bill that is yellow at the base.

Unlike many other sandpipers found on marine beaches, the Spotted Sandpiper is also found along the edges of freshwater inland ponds, marshes, and lakes of lowlands, middle elevations, and highlands up to 7,200 feet. The Spotted Sandpiper runs along the water's edge and on beaches to pursue crustaceans, mollusks, fish, fly larvae, beetles, grasshoppers, and caterpillars.

Studies have revealed that, on their northern nesting grounds in the United States and Canada, Spotted Sandpipers are polyandrous like Northern Jacanas and tinamous. The females are larger and defend territories where they mate with three to four males. Each male has its own nest, where it incubates the eggs and raises about four young.

Some Spotted Sandpipers migrate through Costa Rica en route to Panama and South America from August through October and return through Costa Rica from April to May. Many winter in the country and may be seen along both coasts, at wetlands throughout the Guanacaste region and the San Isidro valley, in inland wetlands of the Caribbean lowlands, and along highland streams like the Río Savegre at Savegre Mountain Lodge.

Ruddy Turnstone

Arenaria interpres

Costa Rican name: **Vuelvepiedras rojizo.**

7/15 trips; 10 sightings.

Status: Northern migrant.

Length: 8.3–10.2 inches.

Weight: 3.0–6.7 ounces (84–190 grams).

Vocalization tapes: C, F.

Range: Breeds in Alaska and northern Canada; winters from both U.S. coasts to Tierra del Fuego.

Elevational range: Sea level.

While the Ruddy Turnstone in breeding plumage is one of the most distinctly marked of all sandpipers, its nonbreeding plumage on its wintering grounds, which include Costa Rica, is much more cryptic. The back and head are grayish brown, the belly is white, and the breast is grayish. The bill, short and thick at the base, is slightly upturned and is adapted for turning over rocks and seaweed to expose marine invertebrates.

The Ruddy Turnstone winters singly or in small flocks along Caribbean and Pacific beaches. It may be encountered on mudflats at river estuaries, on rocky or sandy beaches, or on shallow wetlands and fields near coastal beaches. A flock of a dozen or more birds will walk along the shoreline and flip over stones and other debris in search of crustaceans, mollusks, worms, and insects. They will also eat small fish, eggs of fish and birds, human food scraps, and dead creatures that have washed up on the beach.

This sandpiper migrates along Costa Rica's coastlines from August through October en route to wintering sites in Panama and South America. It returns north from March through May. Small numbers remain on the country's coasts. They can be seen in rocky tidepools at low tide at Tamarindo, at the mouth of the Río Tárcoles near Tárcol Lodge, at Quepos, and along the beaches of Corcovado NP.

Ruddy Turnstone adult, winter plumage

Flock of twenty-one adults camouflaged among rocks

GULL and TERN FAMILY (Laridae)

Laughing Gull

Larus atricilla

Costa Rican name:
Gaviota reidora.

10/15 trips; 17 sightings.

Status: Northern migrant.

Length: 15.3–18.1 inches.

Weight: 8.5–14.1 ounces (240–400 grams).

Wingspread: 40.2–42.1 inches.

Vocalization tapes: C, F.

Range: Breeds from eastern Canada and southern California to Texas, West Indies, and Venezuela; winters from North Carolina to southern Peru.

Elevational range: Sea level.

The Laughing Gull is the most common migrant gull in Costa Rica. Other gulls in the country are the Ring-billed, Herring, Franklin's, Bonaparte's, Heermann's, and Sabine's Gulls. Don't look for the conspicuous black head and wing tips that are typical of this bird in breeding plumage. In winter, adults have a white head and grayish hood on the back of the head. The back is gray; the bill and legs are black; the primaries and secondaries are dark; and the tail is white. First-year subadults have a light brownish to speckled head and are brownish gray over the back, with a white rump, a white trailing edge on the wings, and a broad, black terminal band across the tail. First-year subadults do not have a well-defined light gray hood over the back of the head. Second-year subadults have a whitish head with a pale gray hood over the back of the head.

Laughing Gulls are found on both coasts from September through May but are more abundant on the Pacific coast. They are commonly seen on sandy beaches and mudflats. The Laughing Gull catches small fish, aquatic insects, and shrimp in shallow water; captures insects on the wing; pursues crabs on the beach; scavenges waste materials and fish parts from fishing boats; eats carrion and garbage in seacoast communities; and follows tractors in fields to capture worms and grubs exposed by cultivation. It will also land on the head of a Brown Pelican that has just dived for a fish and try to grab the fish out of the pelican's bill as the pelican raises its head from the water.

The Laughing Gull both winters in Costa Rica and also migrates through Costa Rica from September through November en route to wintering sites in Panama and South America. It returns north from April through May. On the

Laughing Gull adult, winter plumage

Laughing Gull first-year subadult, left, and second-year subadult, right

229

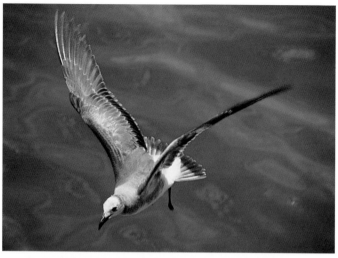

Laughing Gull first-year subadult showing flight characteristics, including broad, black terminal band on tail

Caribbean coast, this gull may be seen migrating or wintering along the beach at Tortuguero NP and south from Limón to Cahuita NP. They are common from September through May on Pacific beaches like those at Tamarindo, Puntarenas, the Río Tárcoles estuary by Tárcol Lodge, Quepos, Manuel Antonio NP, and along the beaches of Corcovado NP.

Royal Tern

Sterna maxima

    COSTA RICAN NAME: ***Pagaza real.***

    11/15 trips; 25 sightings.

    STATUS: Northern migrant and permanent resident.

    LENGTH: 17.7–20.0 inches.

    WEIGHT: 11.3 ounces–1 pound 1.6 ounces (320–500 grams).

    VOCALIZATION TAPE: F.

    RANGE: Breeds from southwestern and eastern United States to Mexico and Uruguay; winters from southern United States to Peru and Argentina.

    ELEVATIONAL RANGE: Sea level.

The Royal Tern is the most common of fifteen terns in Costa Rica. In breeding plumage, the top of the Royal Tern's head, including the eyes, is black, and the bill is bright orange. In winter plumage, the forehead is white, and the crest on

Royal Tern adult, winter plumage

the top and back of the head is black, but the black does not extend forward to the eye. Other characteristics include a large orange bill, black feet, and a deeply forked tail.

In comparison, the similar Caspian Tern has black streaking over both the crest and forehead, a thick red bill, and a tail that is not deeply forked. The Elegant Tern has a long orange bill that is more slender than that of the Royal Tern and a black crest with a black stripe that extends forward to the eyes. The second most abundant tern in Costa Rica, the Sandwich Tern, is often present with Royal Terns. Smaller than the Royal Tern, it has a black bill with a yellow tip and a short tail.

The Royal Tern feeds by flying over shallow coastline waters and estuaries in search of small fish, squid, shrimp, and crabs. From a height of 15 to 30 feet above the water, the tern plunge-dives to capture its prey but does not submerge. It may also skim the surface and dip its head to capture fish.

The Royal Tern is not known to breed in Costa Rica, but some birds in breeding and nonbreeding plumage are present from May to August. From September through December, migrants pass along the coasts to Panama and South America. Some Royal Terns in winter plumage remain in Costa Rica from December through March. In April and May the terns migrate back to Mexico and the United States. This bird may be seen along the Caribbean coast on the beaches of Tortuguero NP and along estuaries and beaches from Limón to Cahuita NP. More common on the Pacific coast, the Royal Tern is regularly seen at Guanacaste beaches, Puntarenas, the Río Tárcoles estuary, Quepos, and Corcovado NP.

Sandwich Tern

Sterna sandvicensis

COSTA RICAN NAME:
Pagaza puntiamarilla.

9/15 trips; 13 sightings.

STATUS: Northern migrant; non-breeding summer resident.

LENGTH: 16 inches.

WEIGHT: 6.7 ounces (190 grams).

RANGE: Eastern U.S. coast to Uruguay; British Isles to Caspian Sea; Pacific coast from Oaxaca, Mexico, to Peru.

ELEVATIONAL RANGE: Sea level.

The Sandwich Tern is an attractive, slender tern of the Caribbean and Pacific coasts that is regularly encountered with Laughing Gulls and Royal Terns. It is distinguished by its black bill, which usually has a yellow tip. The Elegant Tern is similar but has a slender orange bill and is uncommon. The Royal Tern is significantly larger and has a thicker orange bill. The very large Caspian Tern has a reddish bill.

When hunting, the Sandwich Tern plunge-dives for small fish, shrimp, and squid at the surface. Migrants are common along both coasts from September through November and from April through May. Some migrants pass through Costa Rica en route to Panamanian and South American coasts; others winter on Costa Rica's coasts. Some nonbreeding birds remain in the country during the remainder of the year.

Look for the Sandwich Tern from Limón southeast to Cahuita at estuaries where streams flow into the Caribbean, like Quebrada Westfalia. On the Pacific coast, it may be seen on the beaches at Tamarindo and Playa Grande, Puntarenas, at the Río Tárcoles estuary near Tárcol Lodge, and along beaches of the Osa Peninsula, including those near Carate and Corcovado Lodge Tent Camp.

Sandwich Tern adult showing the black bill with yellow tip

DOVE and PIGEON FAMILY (Columbidae)

Band-tailed Pigeon

Columba fasciata

COSTA RICAN NAME:
Paloma collareja.
13/15 trips; 37 sightings.
STATUS: Permanent resident.
LENGTH: 13.0–15.7 inches.
WEIGHT: 8.0 ounces–1 pound 0.2 ounce (226–460 grams).
VOCALIZATION TAPE: M.
RANGE: Southwestern Canada to northern Argentina.
ELEVATIONAL RANGE: 3,000–10,000 feet.

The dove and pigeon family is well represented in Costa Rica and includes twenty-five doves, pigeons, and quail-doves. The large Band-tailed Pigeon lives in mountainous regions. This handsome bird has a grayish-purple body, a white bar across the back of the neck, and an iridescent greenish patch below the white neck bar. Although this pigeon is found from Canada through Argentina, the Band-tailed Pigeon of Costa Rica and western Panama is a darker, separate subspecies (*Columba fasciata crissalis*). On this subspecies, the bill is yellow with a pale grayish tip, while the more northern subspecies has a black-tipped bill.

The Band-tailed Pigeon is usually seen as a high, fast-flying flock of ten to thirty birds passing over forested regions of the volcanoes surrounding the

Band-tailed Pigeon adult showing the white collar on the back of the neck

Central Plateau and montane forests of Cerro de la Muerte and the Talamanca Mountains. When perched, this pigeon usually sits at the top of trees. It is easy to identify because it is the only dove or pigeon with a white bar across the back of the neck. Acorns are a preferred food, as well as fruits of bayberry (*Myrica*) and pokeweed (*Phytolacca*).

Nesting takes place from March through June. Usually one egg is laid and requires nineteen to twenty days for incubation. The chick, called a squab, is fed "pigeon milk"—a nutritious material produced by the inner lining of the crop—by the male for the first nineteen days and by the female and male thereafter until the chick fledges at twenty-eight days of age.

Look for flocks of Band-tailed Pigeons on Poás and Barva Volcanoes, in the Monteverde Cloud Forest Reserve, along the PAH in Cerro de la Muerte from kilometers 62 to 96, and along the road that descends from the PAH at kilometer 80 to Savegre Mountain Lodge.

Red-billed Pigeon

Columba flavirostris

COSTA RICAN NAMES: *Paloma morada; paloma piquirroja.*

13/15 trips; 31 sightings.

STATUS: Permanent resident.

LENGTH: 12 inches.

WEIGHT: 9.4–14.9 ounces (268–424 grams).

VOCALIZATION TAPES: D, F, M.

Red-billed Pigeon adult

RANGE: Northwestern Mexico to Costa Rica.

ELEVATIONAL RANGE: Sea level to 7,000 feet.

The Red-billed Pigeon is a large pigeon with a white to whitish-yellow bill that is pinkish-red at the base. The head, neck, and breast are a deep wine-red color, the back is grayish, the shoulders are brownish, the tail is black, and the feet are red. The iris is deep orange. Males are larger than females, and the wine red of the head and neck area is a richer color than that of the female.

This pigeon inhabits open and agricultural country. It is most common in the dry forests and brushy pastures of Guanacaste Province; the Central Plateau; middle elevations of Poás, Irazú, and Barva Volcanoes; and nearby foothills. Single birds, pairs, or small flocks may be seen perched in trees while feeding on berries, buds, figs (*Ficus*), and guava (*Psidium*). Ground foraging is also common. In Guanacaste, flocks may be seen eating spilled grain along the PAH. In agricultural sites, it may be considered a pest because it eats new sprouts of corn and sorghum.

The Red-billed Pigeon can be seen in Guanacaste at Palo Verde, Santa Rosa, and Guanacaste NPs; Tamarindo; Liberia; La Pacífica; and southeast to Carara NP. In the highlands and Central Plateau, it occurs at Monteverde, Hotel El Pórtico at San José de la Montaña, San José, Sarchí, Hotel Xandari, Orosí, and Curridabat. On the Caribbean slope, this pigeon is found in the lowlands east of Los Inocentes Lodge and at La Virgen del Socorro, Rancho Naturalista, Puerto Viejo en Sarapiquí, La Selva Biological Station, El Gavilán Lodge, and Selva Verde Lodge.

White-winged Dove

Zenaida asiatica

COSTA RICAN NAME: *Paloma aliblanca.*

10/15 trips; 23 sightings.

STATUS: Permanent resident and northern migrant.

LENGTH: 9.8–12.2 inches.

WEIGHT: 4.4–6.6 ounces (125–187 grams).

VOCALIZATION TAPES: D, F, BB.

RANGE: Southwestern United States to Panama.

ELEVATIONAL RANGE: Sea level to 1,650 feet.

Like the Double-striped Thick-knee, Orange-fronted Parakeet, White-fronted and Yellow-naped Parrots, and Rufous-naped Wren, the White-winged Dove is characteristic of the Guanacaste dry forest. This dove is sandy brown with conspicuous white patches on the wings that are visible both at rest and in flight. Flocks of this dove may be seen flying over savannas, shrubby areas, pastures, and grain fields as they search for waste grain and seeds on the ground. The species may roost in large flocks in scattered trees.

The White-winged Dove feeds by walking on the ground and foraging for grit, small seeds, rice, and corn. The resident nesting population of White-winged Doves is a nonmigratory subspecies that occurs only in Costa Rica and western Panama (*Zenaida asiatica australis*). Migratory doves from the Rio Grande Valley of Texas and northern Mexico arrive in Guanacaste in November and depart in May.

The White-winged Dove is common throughout most of Guanacaste south to Puntarenas. It is particularly tame and common around Puntarenas. It is encountered in Guanacaste, Santa Rosa, and Palo Verde NPs and in grain fields, pastures, and woodlands near Cañas, Liberia, Filadelfia, Bebedero, and drier parts of the Central Valley, including Hatillo 1 southwest of San José.

White-winged Dove adult

Inca Dove adult

Inca Dove

Columbina inca
(formerly *Scardafella inca*)

COSTA RICAN NAMES: ***Tortolita colilarga; San Juan.***

12/15 trips; 34 sightings.

STATUS: Permanent resident.

LENGTH: 7.4–8.7 inches.

WEIGHT: 1.1–2.0 ounces (30–58 grams).

VOCALIZATION TAPES: D, F.

RANGE: Southwestern United States to northwestern and central Costa Rica.

ELEVATIONAL RANGE: Sea level to 4,500 feet.

Only two members of the dove and pigeon family in Costa Rica have a strongly scaled plumage—the Scaled Pigeon, which is a large, reddish woodland species, and the small, pale gray Inca Dove. The Inca Dove is a tropical dry forest bird that expanded into Costa Rica from the north in 1928. Since then it has spread throughout Guanacaste, south to Quepos and eastward to

Cartago and Paraíso in the Central Plateau. This small dove has a loud two-note call described as "cow-coo."

The Inca Dove inhabits open terrain of dry forests, second-growth scrubland, backyards, woodlots, and grassy areas. It searches the ground for small seeds, waste grain, and grit and feeds singly or in small numbers. Nesting occurs primarily during the rainy season.

The Inca Dove is a common bird that can be encountered on ranches and around residences throughout Guanacaste. It is also present in Pacific coastal areas south to Puntarenas and Quepos.

Ruddy Ground-Dove

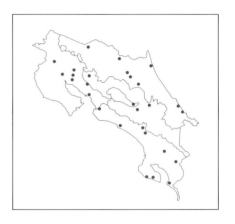

Columbina talpacoti

COSTA RICAN NAMES: ***Tortolita rojiza; tortolita; palomita colorada***.

14/15 trips; 72 sightings.

STATUS: Permanent resident.

LENGTH: 5.5–7.1 inches.

WEIGHT: 1.2–2.0 ounces (35–56 grams).

VOCALIZATION TAPES: D, M.

RANGE: Mexico to northern Argentina.

ELEVATIONAL RANGE: Sea level to 4,600 feet.

Ruddy Ground-Dove adult male

The small, rust-colored Ruddy Ground-Dove is a common and easily identified dove that frequents yards, gardens, and pastures of Costa Rica. The male has a rufous body and a bluish-gray cap. The female is browner and less distinct, but it is frequently seen in association with the male. They may perch so closely that they touch each other. The call is described as "kitty-woo."

The Ruddy Ground-Dove is present in the Caribbean lowlands in locations like Guapiles and Puerto Viejo en Sarapiquí but is most common in the moist Pacific lowlands southeast of the Gulf of Nicoya. Look for it in Cañas, Puntarenas, Carara NP, Quepos, Manuel Antonio NP, San Isidro del General, and the vicinity of La Ensenada Lodge, Villa Lapas, Rancho Casa Grande, Lapa Ríos, Corcovado Lodge Tent Camp, and Tiskita Jungle Lodge.

White-tipped Dove

Leptotila verreauxi

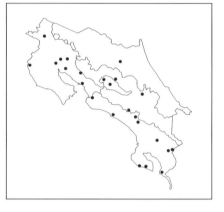

Costa Rican names: ***Paloma coliblanca; yuré; coliblanca.***

15/15 trips; 78 sightings.

Status: Permanent resident.

Length: 9.3–11.6 inches.

Weight: 3.4–5.5 ounces (96–157 grams).

Vocalization tapes: A, D, F, U, BB.

Range: Southern Texas to central Argentina.

Elevational range: Sea level to 7,200 feet.

Common throughout the American tropics, the White-tipped Dove is a medium-sized bird with a plain gray-brown body, black bill, red legs, blue eye-ring, and an orange iris. The outer feathers of the tail are tipped with white and are the source of the bird's name. These white tips show up well in flight.

The White-tipped Dove occurs throughout the Central Plateau, along the Pacific lowlands from Nicaragua to Panama, and east from the Central Plateau into the Reventazón watershed down to middle elevations of the Caribbean slope. It is absent from the Caribbean lowlands. This dove is adapted to disturbed habitats like second-growth forest, brushlands, farms, and backyards. It can be quite tame in backyard settings. It does not occur in undisturbed forest. The White-tipped Dove feeds by walking on the ground in search of small seeds, berries, and insects. Sorghum and corn are included in the diet. The call of this dove is a ventriloquial "hoop" that simulates the sound of blowing across the mouth of a bottle.

In Guanacaste, look for the White-tipped Dove in Guanacaste, Palo Verde, and Santa Rosa NPs; Lomas Barbudal BR; and the Cañas vicinity. It is more common in the southern Pacific lowlands. It is very tame along the beaches of Manuel Antonio NP. Some White-tipped Doves can be seen in the highlands at Savegre Mountain Lodge, Hotel El Pórtico at San José de la Montaña, Sarchí, and southeast of Turrialba at Rancho Naturalista.

White-tipped Dove adult

PARROT FAMILY (Psittacidae)

Scarlet Macaw

Ara macao

CostaRican names: ***Lapa roja; lapa colorada***.

10/15 trips; 31 sightings.

Status: Permanent resident.

Length: 33.1–35.0 inches.

Weight: 1 pound 15.7 ounces–
3 pounds 4.5 ounces (900–1,490
grams).

Vocalization tapes: V, BB.

Range: Southeastern Mexico to
central Brazil.

Elevational range: Sea level to
2,600 feet.

Scarlet Macaw adult

One of the most spectacular and beautiful birds in Costa Rica is the endangered Scarlet Macaw. Its large size and gaudy colors make it a favorite of even the most casual birder. The Scarlet Macaw is usually heard before it is seen. Its coarse, raucous squawks carry great distances as mated pairs fly from roosts and nesting sites to trees ripe with fruits and nuts.

The Scarlet Macaw has been ruthlessly endangered by people who have sought it only as a pretty bird to be taken from the wild for use as a pet. For decades, nesting trees have been cut down and the chicks stolen to sell to the local and international pet trade. Costa Rica is, however, a place where it is once again possible to see this magnificent species in flight, squawking back and forth with its lifetime mate and raising its young in huge hollow trees.

Scarlet Macaws live in dry, moist, and wet tropical lowland forests of the Pacific slope where large mature trees provide nesting cavities and diverse crops of wild nuts, fruits, and flowers. Among the foods eaten are fruits and flowers of *Jacaranda, Hymenaea, Guarea, Hura,* wild beach almond (*Terminalia*), *Virola, Erythrina,* balsa (*Ochroma*), *Spondias, Eschweilera, Inga, Bursera,* fig (*Ficus*), *Dipteryx,* and *Enterolobium.* The heavy bill of the macaw is very efficient for breaking open nuts and palm fruit. Scarlet Macaws mate for life and may live more than sixty years in captivity but less in the wild.

A few remaining pairs of Scarlet Macaws are found in protected dry forests of Guanacaste, like those in Palo Verde NP. In addition, a few Scarlet Macaws were first sighted in early 1999 in Tortuguero NP. They may represent birds dispersing from rainforests of southeastern Nicaragua. If so, these are the first Scarlet Macaws to occur in the Caribbean lowlands in decades. Sightings have continued there in 2000 and 2001.

There are several places to see these birds in the southern Pacific lowlands. If you arrive at the bridge over the Río Tárcoles by the entrance to Carara NP at sunrise, it is possible to see and hear pairs of Scarlet Macaws leaving their roosting areas and dispersing over the forest. Within that national park and at the nearby Villa Lapas, it is also possible to see them feeding in fruiting trees and at their nesting cavities. The best place to see them in abundance is at Sirena Biological Station in Corcovado NP and along the beaches of that park, at Drake Bay Wilderness Resort, and at Corcovado Lodge Tent Camp. Along the beaches, they can be observed feeding on wild beach almond (*Terminalia catappa*) fruits.

Great Green Macaw adult

Great Green Macaw

Ara ambigua

> Costa Rican names: *Lapa verde; guacamayo verde mayor*.
>
> 2/15 trips; 5 sightings.
>
> Status: Permanent resident.
>
> Length: 33.5–35.4 inches.
>
> Weight: 2 pounds 12.6 ounces–3 pounds 2.4 ounces (1,265–1,430 grams).
>
> Vocalization tape: CC.
>
> Range: Eastern Honduras to western Ecuador.
>
> Elevational range: Sea level to 2,500 feet.

The Great Green Macaw is an endangered and beautiful bird of Caribbean lowland rainforests. Its last stronghold appears to be along the Nicaraguan border near Laguna del Lagarto Lodge and Tortuguero NP. The intense green-

and-blue body, highlighted by red tail feathers, make this imposing member of the parrot family a stunning symbol of the country's diminishing rainforests. Unfortunately, it is a victim of both deforestation and the illegal pet trade. This macaw ranges widely across the Caribbean lowlands in search of food, but the amount of suitable remaining nesting habitat appears very small, the number of feeding trees is declining, and the number of birds left is very low—probably only thirty to thirty-five pairs. The nationwide population count declined from 549 in 1998 to 210 in 2000.

The bill of this macaw is larger than that of the Scarlet Macaw and is adapted to cracking open the very tough nuts of the swamp almond tree (*Dipteryx panamensis*). The life cycle of this macaw appears to be tied very closely to *Dipteryx* trees, because it nests in hollow cavities of this tree and depends on its fruits as a major food.

These macaws may live more than sixty years. The only places that offer a fair opportunity to see the Great Green Macaw are Tortuguero NP, Boca Tapada, and Laguna del Lagarto Lodge. However, because this macaw ranges widely in search of ripe *Dipteryx* nuts, it is not regularly observed. Other possible locations are La Selva Biological Station, the EARTH University property near Guapiles, Rara Avis, and the Rainforest Aerial Tram property. The Tropical Science Center is working to save the last nesting areas of this species through research and creation of a new reserve to be called Maguenque National Park. More information can be obtained by calling Julio César Calvo at the Tropical Science Center at 506-253-3267 or 506-225-2649. His e-mail address is lapa@cct.or.cr.

Orange-fronted Parakeet

Aratinga canicularis

Costa Rican names: ***Catano; periquito; zapoyol; perico. frentinaranja.***

10/15 trips; 25 sightings.

Status: Permanent resident.

Length: 9.1–9.8 inches.

Weight: 2.4–3.8 ounces (68–80 grams).

Vocalization tape: D.

Range: Western Mexico to central Costa Rica.

Elevational range: Sea level to 3,300 feet.

Three members of the parrot family have a reference to "fronted" in their common name: White-fronted Parrot, Crimson-fronted Parakeet, and Orange-fronted Parakeet. In each case, "front" refers to the forehead. The Orange-fronted Parakeet has a bright orange forehead and blue on top of the head. The tail is long and pointed.

A common bird of the dry forest, this parakeet is found in savannas, pastures, and deciduous forests. It feeds on the fruits of *Ficus, Bursera,* and *Brosimum* trees; on flowers of *Combretum* and *Gliricidia;* and on seeds of *Ceiba* and *Inga* trees. As with other parakeets, this bird sleeps in communal roosts that may contain hundreds of individuals.

The Orange-fronted Parakeet is one of many Costa Rican birds that excavates a nest cavity within a termite nest. These are the large gray structures commonly seen on the sides of tree trunks or on the tops of fence posts. The benefits of this nesting structure include protection from rain and insulation from hot weather. Chicks are often stolen from their nests by local residents who use them as pets. This parakeet can be seen throughout Guanacaste, along the road that leads from the PAH to Monteverde and south to Quepos.

Orange-fronted Parakeet adult showing orange "front" and white eye-ring

Orange-fronted Parakeet adult excavating nest cavity in a termitary at La Pacífica

Orange-chinned Parakeet

Brotogeris jugularis

> Costa Rican names: *Catano;*
> *zapoyolito; perico; periquito*
> *barbinaranja.*
>
> 14/15 trips; 64 sightings.
>
> Status: Permanent resident.
>
> Length: 7.1–7.5 inches.
>
> Weight: 1.9–2.3 ounces (53–65
> grams).
>
> Vocalization tapes: A, D, CC.
>
> Range: Southwestern Mexico to
> Colombia and Venezuela.
>
> Elevational range: Sea level to
> 4,000 feet.

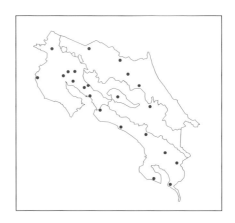

The Orange-chinned Parakeet is one of the most common and smallest members of the parrot family in Costa Rica. This parakeet has a small orange patch on the "chin," but that patch often is not visible. More conspicuous identification features include a short, compact appearance; brownish shoulder areas; a very short, pointed tail; and yellow linings under the wings, which are visible in flight. This parakeet is often encountered in flocks of four to five individuals.

The Orange-chinned Parakeet was originally a bird of open, savanna-like habitat in dry forests, pastures with scattered trees, and gallery forests of the

Orange-chinned Parakeet adult showing orange chin and brown shoulders

Guanacaste region. However, many of the fruits and flowers it eats grow in deforested areas. Lowland and middle-elevation moist and wet forests of the Caribbean and Pacific slopes that have been cleared for pastures, fields, and plantations now provide habitat for the Orange-chinned Parakeet. Foods include fruits and seeds of figs (*Ficus*), *Ceiba, Byrsonima, Cecropia, Bombax,* and *Muntingia* and the flowers and nectar of *Erythrina*, guava (*Psidium guajava*), *Bombacopsis,* and balsa (*Ochroma lagopus*).

Orange-chinned Parakeets may be observed in the Caribbean lowlands at La Selva and Guapiles. They come to the feeders at Tilajari Resort Hotel near Muelle of San Carlos to eat papayas. On the Pacific slope, this bird is common throughout the Guanacaste region and at Quepos, San Isidro, San Vito, Corcovado NP, and Tiskita Jungle Lodge. Small flocks can be seen flying around in San José, including the grounds of the University of Costa Rica and the Parque Central.

White-crowned Parrot

Pionus senilis

COSTA RICAN NAMES: **Chucuyo;**
loro coroniblanco.

14/15 trips; 77 sightings.

STATUS: Permanent resident.

LENGTH: 9.4 inches.

WEIGHT: 6.8–8.1 ounces (193–229 grams).

VOCALIZATION TAPES: A, T, CC.

RANGE: Northeastern Mexico to western Panama.

ELEVATIONAL RANGE: Sea level to 5,250 feet.

The seven parrots found in Costa Rica are the Brown-hooded, White-crowned, Blue-headed, White-fronted, Red-lored, Yellow-naped, and Mealy. The White-crowned Parrot is a conspicuous and abundant small parrot of the humid lowlands in the Caribbean and southern Pacific slopes. It frequently sits atop a palm tree in an upright "Maltese falcon" pose. The white crown is distinctive, the head is dark bluish green, and the shoulders are coppery brown. In flight, the wing beats show deeper strokes than most other parrots, which have shallow wing beats. It frequently travels in flocks of more than fifty birds.

This parrot usually keeps to the treetops and is associated with second-growth forests, forest openings, plantations, and croplands. Foods include palm fruits and seeds of *Dendropanax, Inga,* and *Erythrina.* The White-crowned Par-

White-crowned Parrot adult

rot is sometimes considered a pest by farmers because it eats corn, grain sorghum, and *pejivalle* palm fruits.

White-crowned Parrots may be observed in the Caribbean lowlands at Guapiles, Puerto Viejo en Sarapiquí, La Selva Biological Station, La Virgen del Socorro, Tortuguero and Cahuita NPs, and Limón. In the Pacific lowlands, sightings are common in San Isidro del General, Wilson Botanical Garden at San Vito, and Carara, Manuel Antonio, and Corcovado NPs. These birds also range to the Central Plateau outside of the breeding season in search of food and may be seen at middle- and higher-elevation sites like Rara Avis, Rancho Naturalista, and the Sarchí area.

Blue-headed Parrot

Pionus menstruus

COSTA RICAN NAMES: **Chucuyo; loro cabeciazul**.

7/15 trips; 16 sightings.

STATUS: Permanent resident.

LENGTH: 9.5–11.0 inches.

WEIGHT: 7.4–10.4 ounces (209–295 grams).

VOCALIZATION TAPE: V.

RANGE: Eastern Costa Rica to eastern Brazil.

ELEVATIONAL RANGE: Sea level to 3,900 feet.

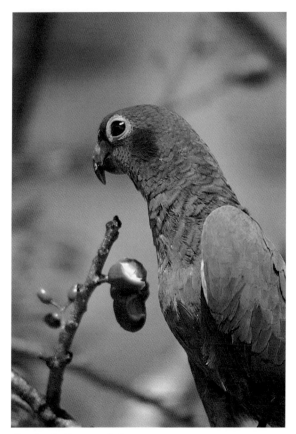

Blue-headed Parrot adult

The Blue-headed Parrot is one of the easiest parrots to identify, as it is the only parrot with a blue head. A small parrot of South American origin, it has expanded into Costa Rica within the last one hundred years. This parrot is in the same genus as the White-crowned Parrot, but in flight the wing beat is shallower than that of the White-crowned Parrot.

This parrot is adapted to lowland rainforests but also thrives in deciduous forests, second-growth forests, pastures, plantations, and woodlands. It expanded into Costa Rica in association with the cutting of lowland rainforest because it eats seeds and fruits of plants that grow after mature forest is cut. Among its foods are palm fruits and seeds of *Anacardium, Hura, Clusia,* wild avocado (*Persea*), *Inga, Brosimum,* and fig (*Ficus*), as well as flowers of *Erythrina* and *Psidium.*

Look for this distinctive parrot in Cahuita NP and along the highway from Limón to Cahuita. It is also present in the vicinity of the Wilson Botanical Garden and the San Vito area.

Red-lored Parrot
(Red-lored Amazon)

Amazona autumnalis

COSTA RICAN NAMES: ***Lora; loro frentirrojo***.

10/15 trips; 28 sightings.

Status: Permanent resident.

LENGTH: 12.6–13.8 inches.

WEIGHT: 11.1 ounces–1 pound 1.1 ounces (314–485 grams).

VOCALIZATION TAPES: D, T, CC.

RANGE: Eastern Mexico to north-western Brazil.

ELEVATIONAL RANGE: Sea level to 3,300 feet.

Many tropical birds play a role in dispersing seeds of rainforest plants by swallowing fruits whole and regurgitating the seeds or passing the intact seeds in their droppings. However, parrots, macaws, and parakeets, including the Red-lored Parrot, are "seed destroyers"—like peccaries. They crush the seeds in order to digest the nutrients. The Red-lored Parrot is a large parrot that has a conspicuous red forehead and blue on top of the head. When the bird is in flight, it is possible to see red patches in the secondary wing feathers.

This parrot inhabits moist and wet lowland forests and adjacent middle elevations of the Caribbean and southern Pacific slopes. Preferred habitats include forest openings, second growth, pastures, and plantations mixed with

Red-lored Parrot adult

forests. Foods include palm fruits, figs (*Ficus*), *Virola, Casearia, Protium, Cordia lutea, Stemmadenia, Spondias,* mangoes, and oranges. This parrot has regularly been poached for use as pets.

On the Caribbean slope, look for the Red-lored Parrot in treetop feeding sites in the vicinity of Cahuita and Tortuguero NPs, Puerto Viejo en Sarapiquí, La Selva Biological Field Station, and in tropical lowlands east of Los Inocentes Lodge. On the Pacific slope, this parrot can be seen near Quepos, Manuel Antonio, Carara, and Corcovado NPs and Drake Bay Wilderness Resort, Corcovado Lodge Tent Camp, Lapa Ríos, Villa Lapas, Rancho Casa Grande, and Tiskita Jungle Lodge.

Yellow-naped Parrot
(Yellow-naped Amazon)

Amazona auropalliata

COSTA RICAN NAMES: ***Lora; lora de nuca amarilla***.

9/15 trips; 19 sightings.

STATUS: Permanent resident.

LENGTH: 13.8–15.0 inches.

WEIGHT: 12.0 ounces–1 pound 2.9 ounces (340–535 grams).

VOCALIZATION TAPES: BB.

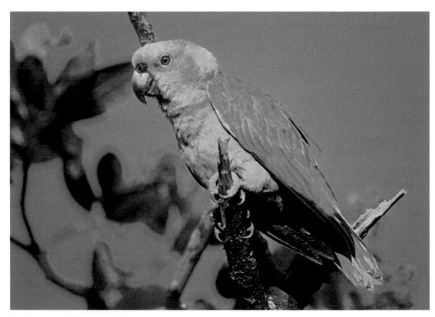

Yellow-naped Parrot adult

RANGE: Southern Mexico to north-western Costa Rica.

ELEVATIONAL RANGE: Sea level to 2,000 feet.

The Yellow-naped Parrot is one of ten closely related but distinctive Yellow-crowned Parrots (*Amazona ochrocephala*) found from Mexico to Brazil and Peru. Some taxonomists consider this a subspecies of the Yellow-crowned Parrot (*Amazona o. auropalliata*), but the Yellow-naped Parrot is treated here as a separate species. Identification marks include a yellow nape, black cere, and pale eye-ring. In flight, red patches are visible on the secondary wing feathers. The wing beats are characterized by very shallow strokes, so it appears as if only the wing tips are beating. Because this bird is considered a good "talking parrot," it has been ruthlessly stolen from the wild by poachers who cut down or climb nesting trees to remove young from the nests.

Like the White-fronted Parrot, the Yellow-naped Parrot is found only in lowland dry forests, mangrove forests, gallery forests, savannas, mixed pastures, and woodlots of Guanacaste southeast to Carara NP. Foods eaten include the wild almond (*Terminalia*), *Acacia, Tabebuia,* buttercup tree (*Cochlospermum*), *Curatella,* figs (*Ficus*), and *Erythrina.* Some cultivated crops are also eaten, including corn, mangoes, lemons, avocados, and green bananas.

This parrot has declined where it is not protected from people who poach it for use as pets. It may be seen in protected dry forests and mangrove lagoons of Las Baulas, Guanacaste, Palo Verde, Santa Rosa, and Carara NPs and Lomas Barbudal BR. Los Inocentes Lodge and La Ensenada are good places to see them.

Mealy Parrot (Mealy Amazon)

Amazona farinosa

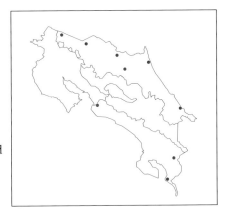

COSTA RICAN NAMES: **Lora; lora verde**.

9/15 trips; 32 sightings.

STATUS: Permanent resident.

LENGTH: 15.0–16.9 inches.

WEIGHT: 1 pound 2.9 ounces–1 pound 11.0 ounces (535–766 grams).

VOCALIZATION TAPES: B, E, T, V, Z, BB, CC.

RANGE: Southeastern Mexico to southeastern Brazil.

ELEVATIONAL RANGE: Sea level to 1,600 feet.

253

Mealy Parrot adult

The Mealy Parrot, the largest parrot in Costa Rica, is a green parrot whose identification marks are a whitish eye-ring and a narrow black cere above the bill. A bird of lowland rainforests of the Caribbean and southern Pacific slopes, the Mealy Parrot has a distribution similar to that of the Red-lored Parrot. However, the Mealy Parrot declines as an area is deforested whereas the Red-lored Parrot increases. This parrot may be encountered as pairs or in small flocks. During the rainy season, Mealy Parrots roost at night in communal flocks exceeding one hundred birds. Foods include fruits, nuts, and seeds of palms (*Euterpe*), figs (*Ficus*), *Cecropia, Brosimum, Inga, Pithecellobium,* buttercup tree (*Cochlospermum*), *Virola,* and *Casearia.*

Look for the Mealy Parrot in Tortuguero and Cahuita NPs, Selva Verde Lodge, La Selva Biological Field Station, and along the road east from Los Inocentes Lodge on the Caribbean slope. On the southern Pacific slope, this parrot can be seen at Carara NP, Rancho Casa Grande, and south to Tiskita Jungle Lodge.

CUCKOO FAMILY (Cuculidae)

Squirrel Cuckoo

Piaya cayana

Costa Rican names: *Bobo chiso; cuco ardilla.*

14/15 trips; 89 sightings.

Status: Permanent resident.

Length: 18 inches.

Weight: 3.5 ounces (98 grams).

Vocalization tapes: B, D, T, V, X, BB, CC.

Range: Northwestern Mexico to northern Argentina.

Elevational range: Sea level to 8,000 feet.

There are eleven members of the cuckoo family in Costa Rica, including two northern migrants (Black-billed and Yellow-billed Cuckoos), one endemic species on Cocos Island (Cocos Cuckoo), and eight permanent residents: Mangrove, Squirrel, Striped, and Pheasant Cuckoos; Lesser and Rufous-vented Ground-Cuckoos; and Groove-billed and Smooth-billed Anis. The Squirrel Cuckoo is a widespread, common, and conspicuous bird whose bright rufous plumage is readily sighted in treetop foliage.

Squirrel Cuckoo adult

This adaptable bird is found in dry, moist, and wet forests; gallery and mangrove forests; forest edges; woodlots; shade coffee plantations; and pastures with scattered trees. Foraging singly or in pairs, the Squirrel Cuckoo searches leaf cover for caterpillars, grasshoppers, moths, beetles, ants, katydids, small lizards, and spiders. Occasionally it will follow army ant swarms to capture escaping creatures.

The Squirrel Cuckoo is common in the forests of Tortuguero NP, along the coast from Limón to Cahuita NP, and in the forests of La Selva Biological Field Station, Selva Verde, and El Gavilán Lodge. It is very common in shade coffee plantations of the Central Plateau. The Squirrel Cuckoo may be seen throughout Guanacaste and at middle and higher elevations, including Monteverde Cloud Forest Reserve, Rara Avis, Rancho Naturalista, Rainforest Aerial Tram, Braulio Carrillo NP, and the Wilson Botanical Garden near San Vito.

Groove-billed Ani

Crotophaga sulcirostris
Costa Rican names: *Tijo;*
zopilotillo; garrapatero
piquiestriado.
14/15 trips; 102 sightings.
Status: Permanent resident.
Length: 12 inches.
Weight: 2.5–2.8 ounces (70–80 grams).
Vocalization tapes: B, D, F, O.
Range: Central Texas to northwestern Argentina.
Elevational range: Sea level to 7,500 feet.

The Groove-billed Ani is a conspicuous black bird of tropical lowlands that is not in the blackbird family (Icteridae). A cuckoo, this social bird lives in small groups that include two or three monogamous pairs and their young in a territory that may encompass 2.5 to 25 acres. All members of the flock cooperate in nesting and raising young. This ani is named for prominent grooves along the curving contour of the bill. The Costa Rican name for this bird is *tijo* and is derived from its call: "tee-ho, tee-ho, tee-ho."

The Groove-billed Ani is a common, adaptable bird of open country, roadsides, plantations, and pastures. Groups of anis forage for grasshoppers, flies, wasps, ants, cicadas, *Norops* lizards, and cockroaches. Like Cattle Egrets, anis accompany livestock and capture insects flushed by cows or horses. Some-

Groove-billed Ani adult

Adult in sunning posture

times anis will pick ticks from the skin of these animals, and they also follow army ants to catch insects flushed by them.

Anis frequently seek prey in wet foliage and subsequently dry themselves by sunning in an upright pose with outstretched wings. This sunning behavior may also help raise their body temperature in the morning, because at night their body temperature drops from 105 to 93 degrees Fahrenheit.

Nesting is a cooperative activity carried out by the entire flock of anis from June through November. All the females lay their eggs in the nest, with the most dominant female laying her eggs last, on top of the others. Those last eggs have the greatest chance of hatching. The nest eventually contains twelve to fifteen eggs. All of the males and females take part in incubation. The entire group of anis feeds the young, and the group may renest several times in one season.

Look for the Groove-billed Ani in lowland and middle elevations of the Caribbean lowlands, Guanacaste Province, the Central Plateau, and scattered locations of the southern Pacific lowlands, including Quepos, San Isidro del General, and the Wilson Botanical Garden at San Vito. At higher elevations, it occurs near Monteverde, Hotel El Pórtico at San José de la Montaña on Barva Volcano, Tapantí NP, and Rancho Naturalista.

Similar Species: Smooth-billed Ani (Crotophaga ani)

Smooth-billed Ani adult

The similar Smooth-billed Ani (11/15 trips; 26 sightings) is a recent addition to Costa Rica's avifauna. It is distinguished by a huge high-arching bill that lacks the grooves of the Groove-billed Ani. It was first recorded in the country in 1931, when it extended its range from Panama. It is now found throughout the southern Pacific lowlands and continues to extend its range into the foothills approaching the Central Plateau and southern portions of Guanacaste.

OWL FAMILY (Strigidae)

Tropical Screech-Owl

Otus choliba

Costa Rican names: *Lechucita neotropical; estucurú; sorococa.*

5/15 trips; 7 sightings.

Status: Permanent resident.

Length: 7.9–9.4 inches.

Weight: 3.4–5.6 ounces (97–160 grams).

Vocalization tapes: E, N, Z.

Range: Costa Rica to Paraguay.

Elevational range: 1,300–5,000 feet.

Four screech-owls are found in Costa Rica: the Tropical, Pacific, Vermiculated, and Bare-shanked. The Bare-shanked Screech-Owl is found at higher elevations, the Pacific and Vermiculated Screech-Owls are found at lowland elevations, and the Tropical Screech-Owl is a bird of foothills and middle elevations. The Tropical Screech-Owl is the common screech-owl of the Central Plateau and premontane forests from the Tilarán Mountains south to the Panama border. This owl has a pair of ear tufts and a call that is a long trill ending with a "toot-toot."

Tropical Screech-Owl adult

The Tropical Screech-Owl inhabits mixed woodland, open areas, farms, woodlots, plantations, orchards, second-growth forests, and urban areas. It hunts at night by perching on low tree branches and watching for insects, spiders, beetles, crickets, snakes, scorpions, rodents, and bats. Sometimes this owl will hunt near security lights to capture katydids and moths attracted to the lights.

The Tropical Screech-Owl can sometimes be attracted by playing a tape of its call or by taping and playing back its call. The use of such playbacks should be discontinued after the owl comes to the tape to avoid disrupting normal territorial behavior. This owl is regularly encountered at the Wilson Botanical Garden near San Vito, at Talari Mountain Lodge near San Isidro del General, Xandari Plantation, and in shade coffee plantations of the Central Plateau.

Similar Species: Vermiculated Screech-Owl (*Otus guatemalae*)

Vermiculated Screech-Owl adult

The Vermiculated Screech-Owl (2/15 trips; 2 sightings) occurs in wet tropical lowlands of the Caribbean slope and the southern Pacific slope to elevations of 3,300 feet, so the range does not overlap with that of the Pacific Screech-Owl. The Vermiculated Screech-Owl has relatively inconspicuous ear tufts and occurs in two color phases: grayish brown and rufous. This screech-owl does not have vertical streaking on the breast.

It hunts at night near forest openings or in tall second-growth forests. Food items include moths, beetles, and katydids. Nesting occurs from March through April in old trogon nesting cavities in dead trees. The range extends from northwestern Mexico to Bolivia. Vocalizations can be heard on tapes B, G, N, T, BB, and CC. It is present at La Selva Biological Station and is especially easy to see in the Arboretum area at night with limited use of tape recordings and spotlights.

Spectacled Owl

Pulsatrix perspicillata

Costa Rican names: ***Buho de anteojos; oropopo; olopopo.***

2/15 trips; 2 sightings.

Status: Permanent resident.

Length: 16.9–20.4 inches.

Weight: 1 pound 5 ounces–2 pounds 2 ounces (590–980 grams), male; 2 pounds 5 ounces–2 pounds 12 ounces (1,050–1,250 grams), female.

Vocalization tapes: B, E, I, N, Z, BB, CC.

Range: Southern Mexico to northern Argentina.

Elevational range: Sea level to 5,000 feet.

Spectacled Owl adult

Spectacled Owl chick

The Spectacled Owl is the largest owl in Costa Rica's forests. Adults feature white highlights around the dark brown facial disks that surround each eye, giving the owl its name. Even the downy-white young have a spectacled appearance because of their brown facial disks. In Peru, this owl has a local name meaning "the undertaker," because one of its most common calls is a muffled series of seven to nine staccato, ventriloquial notes that are likened to the sound of an undertaker pounding nails into a coffin. The notes descend slightly in pitch and accelerate in frequency toward the end of the call. Sometimes a pair of these owls will call back and forth to each other.

The Spectacled Owl inhabits dry, moist, and wet tropical forests throughout the lowlands and middle elevations of both slopes. It may be encountered in primary forest, secondary forest, gallery forest, and shade coffee plantations and along forest and stream edges. Hunting occurs mainly at night when the owl perches at mid-canopy levels and watches for the movement of grasshoppers, opossums, katydids, lizards, skunks, jays, oropendolas, bats, crabs, and mice.

This widespread owl may be found in extensive forests of Tortuguero, Corcovado, Tapantí, Guanacaste, Santa Rosa, Carara, and Palo Verde NPs. It has been observed on night boat trips along the canals of Tortuguero NP and along trails of the Sirena Biological Station. It has also been seen at Selva Verde, El Gavilán Lodge, near the entrance of the Monteverde Cloud Forest Reserve, and on the grounds of Villa Lapas near Carara NP.

Mottled Owl adult

Mottled Owl (Mottled Wood-Owl)

Ciccaba virgata

COSTA RICAN NAMES: ***Lechuza café; hu de león.***

6/15 trips; 12 sightings.

STATUS: Permanent resident.

LENGTH: 11.4–15.0 inches.

WEIGHT: 6.2–11.3 ounces (175–320 grams).

VOCALIZATION TAPES: B, D, I, J, N, S, T, AA, BB, CC.

RANGE: Northern Mexico to northern Argentina.

ELEVATIONAL RANGE: Sea level to 7,200 feet.

The Mottled Owl, a relatively widespread and common owl of Costa Rica's lowland and middle elevations, is distinguished from smaller screech-owls by its lack of ear tufts and its more heavily "mottled" breast. One of its calls is a series of about six ventriloquial-sounding notes that are each best described as "whoOOoo," with more emphasis and volume in the middle of each note.

This owl inhabits forest edges and openings, shade coffee plantations, and second growth. Hunting takes place at night. Prey includes cockroaches, grasshoppers, beetles, katydids, small rodents, bats, tree frogs, salamanders, lizards, and small snakes. It has been observed coming to lights at night to feed on insects attracted to the lights.

This bird can be found in lowland and middle elevations of the Caribbean slope and occurs regularly at Rancho Naturalista. In Guanacaste, it is found in gallery forests like those along the Río Corobicí at La Pacífica, and in moist and wet forests of the southern Pacific lowlands and middle elevations. It has been observed at the Wilson Botanical Garden and at Savegre Mountain Lodge.

POTOO FAMILY (Nyctibiidae)

Common Potoo (Gray Potoo) and Northern Potoo

Nyctibius griseus and *N. jamaicensis*

COSTA RICAN NAMES: ***Pájaro estaca; pájaro palo; nictibio común.***

5/15 trips; 5 sightings.

STATUS: Permanent resident.

LENGTH: 13.0–15.0 inches.

WEIGHT: 5.1–7.1 ounces (145–202 grams).

VOCALIZATION TAPES: E, I, P, V, Z, BB, CC.

RANGE: Nicaragua to northern Argentina.

ELEVATIONAL RANGE: Sea level to 4,100 feet.

Common Potoo adult

The Common Potoo is found across a broad range of lowland and middle-elevation habitats and has one of the most intriguing bird calls in Costa Rica. The Common Potoo (*N. griseus*) is found in the lowlands of the Caribbean slope and southern Pacific slope. The Northern Potoo (*Nyctibius jamaicensis*), which is very similar but slightly larger, is found in similar habitats from southern Mexico to the Guanacaste region of Costa Rica. The song of the Common Potoo is a mournful series of four to six descending flutelike tones. When the call of the potoo is heard amid the shadows of a tropical forest on a moonlit night, the rainforest takes on a nearly mystical quality.

For many years, this eerie "song" was attributed to sloths, because when people used lights to locate the source of the call, the potoo was overlooked and sloths were sometimes spotted in the same tree. In South America, the Common Potoo has the nickname *alma perdida,* meaning "lost soul," because its song is so melancholy.

Common and Northern Potoos are found in rainforest edges, dry and mangrove forests, open woodlands, mixed woods, pastures, plantations, savannas, and forest openings with scattered trees and fence posts that serve as perches for hunting. The potoo spends the day asleep on a branch or post, camouflaged as a wooden stump or branch. At dusk it becomes active and begins hunting. The diet comprises beetles, flying ants and termites, praying mantises, cicadas, grasshoppers, bugs, leafhoppers, and moths.

Nesting behavior is similar to that of the Great Potoo. A single egg is laid on a slight depression or within a circular branch scar on the top of an upward-sloping branch. The male incubates the egg during the day and the female incubates at night. The egg hatches after thirty-three days, and the fledgling period is forty-seven to fifty-one days. This extremely long period at the nest is the second longest known for land birds in tropical America and is exceeded only by the Black Vulture.

The Common Potoo is widespread throughout Caribbean and Pacific lowland and middle elevations, but it is not commonly seen. It can be seen and heard along the canals of Tortuguero NP on night boat trips, and it has been encountered on night drives along country roads east from Los Inocentes Lodge and in the vicinity of La Selva and at Monteverde Lodge. The Common Potoo has also been observed in the vicinity of the Wilson Botanical Garden at San Vito by Gail Hewson-Hull.

Common Potoo close-up of head

NIGHTHAWK FAMILY (Caprimulgidae)

Common Paraque

Nyctidromus albicollis

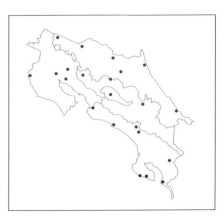

COSTA RICAN NAMES: *Cuyeo; pucuyo; tapacaminos común.*

15/15 trips; 48 sightings.

STATUS: Permanent resident.

LENGTH: 8.7–11.0 inches.

WEIGHT: 1.5–3.2 ounces (43–90 grams).

VOCALIZATION TAPES: A, B, D, F, I, P, T, V, Z, BB, CC.

RANGE: Southern Texas to northern Argentina.

ELEVATIONAL RANGE: Sea level to 5,600 feet.

One of the great sounds associated with sunset in the American tropics is the call of the Common Pauraque. The call of this tropical nighthawk resembles its local name: *cuyeo*. Other descriptions of its memorable songs are "Who-are-you?" and "hip-hip, hip-hip, hip-hip hooray." At night, the eyes reflect like glowing reddish-orange coals when a flashlight or the headlights of a car are focused on this bird as it rests on roads, lawns, or footpaths.

The pauraque inhabits second-growth forest, shade coffee plantations, forest edges, and openings and pasturelands with scattered trees and shrubs. During the day it rests on the ground amid brushy cover, where it is nearly invisible because of its cryptic markings. Sometimes it rests on branches near the ground. At dusk it flies low over the landscape to catch moths, butterflies, wasps, winged ants, beetles, and other insects. It frequently rests on roads and trails where it can be viewed. In flight, the male has a white bar visible near its wing tips, but the wings are wider than on the Lesser Nighthawk. The female has buffy wing bars. The pauraque's longer tail is rounded at the tip, while the tip of the nighthawk's narrow tail is notched.

The Common Pauraque is the most common member of the nighthawk family in the country and is readily observed or heard throughout lowland and middle elevations of the Caribbean and Pacific slopes. It can often be encountered on the grounds of rural tourism lodges and along country roads after dark.

Common Pauraque adult

Nest on ground with one egg

HUMMINGBIRD FAMILY (Trochilidae)

Bronzy Hermit

Glaucis aenea

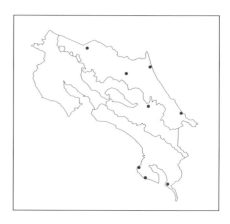

COSTA RICAN NAME: **Ermitaño bronceado.**

8/15 trips; 24 sightings.

STATUS: Permanent resident.

LENGTH: 3.5–3.9 inches.

WEIGHT: 0.11–0.23 ounce (3–6.5 grams).

RANGE: Eastern Nicaragua to Ecuador.

ELEVATIONAL RANGE: Sea level to 2,500 feet.

One of the greatest delights while exploring Costa Rica is viewing the beauty, abundance, and diversity of the hummingbirds. About twenty-three hummingbirds are known from the entire United States, but Costa Rica has fifty-two species! This high diversity is significant because hummingbirds are important flower pollinators. The Bronzy Hermit is one of six "hermit" hummingbirds. The Bronzy Hermit has a greenish back, a rufous breast and belly, a dark eye mask, and a long, moderately decurved bill.

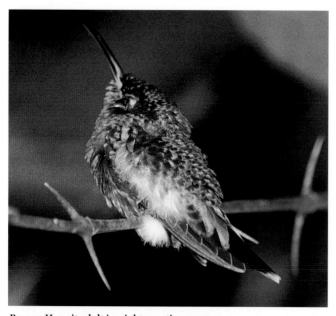

Bronzy Hermit adult in night roosting posture

The Bronzy Hermit, found in the wet lowlands of the Caribbean and southern Pacific slopes, is a bird of rainforest second growth, swamps, and forest and stream edges. As with other hermits, it feeds on the nectar of *Heliconia* and banana (*Musa*) flowers. Additional nutrition is provided by plucking small insects and spiders from leaves.

One of the best places to look for the Bronzy Hermit is at Tortuga Lodge near Tortuguero NP. It starts nesting in January under the fronds of palm trees in the courtyard. The bird has also been observed sleeping on vegetation overhanging water on night boat trips in Tortuguero NP. During the day it can be seen at other sites in the Caribbean lowlands, including Pizote Lodge near Cahuita and La Selva Biological Station. In the southern Pacific lowlands, this hummingbird can be seen at Tiskita Jungle Lodge and on the Osa Peninsula at Sirena Biological Station and Drake Bay Wilderness Resort.

Long-tailed Hermit
(Western Long-tailed Hermit)

Phaethornis superciliosus
(Phaethornis longirostris)

COSTA RICAN NAME: **Ermitaño colilargo**.

7/15 trips; 24 sightings.

STATUS: Permanent resident.

LENGTH: 5.1–6.3 inches.

WEIGHT: 0.14–0.26 ounce (4–7.5 grams).

VOCALIZATION TAPE: V, CC.

RANGE: Southern Mexico to central Brazil.

ELEVATIONAL RANGE: Sea level to 3,300 feet.

Identification of Costa Rica's fifty-two hummingbirds can be challenging, but some species are easy to identify because of obvious marks or geographical distribution that excludes similar species. The Long-tailed Hermit is a large hummingbird of wet lowlands with a very long, decurved bill, a dark eye mask, a brownish body, and very long, white-tipped central tail feathers. The Green Hermit is similar but occurs at higher elevations. A recent review of the taxonomy of this hummingbird has resulted in the recommendation that the Long-tailed Hermit be split into an eastern species (*P. superciliosus*), which occurs in Venezuela, the Guianas, and northern Brazil, and a western species (*P. longirostris*), which occurs from southern Mexico through Costa Rica to western

Long-tailed Hermit adult feeding on *Heliconia rostrata* flower; long tail is pointed to side

Ecuador and northwestern Peru. That recommendation has not yet been accepted, so it is treated here as the Long-tailed Hermit.

The Long-tailed Hermit is a rainforest species associated with sun-dappled forest edges, older second growth, and streams that pass through the forest understory where there is enough sunlight for the plants they depend on for nectar: *Heliconia pogognatha, Costus, Aphelandra,* and passionflower (*Passiflora vitifolia*). As with many other hermits, it feeds by "traplining"—repeatedly visiting the same flowers over a large area. Small insects and spiders are also gleaned from vegetation.

This hermit forms "leks," or singing assemblies. From ten to twenty-five males perch at eye level in understory vegetation and call to attract females with a note described as "sree." The call note is given at a higher pitch and then at a lower pitch with a one-note-per-second frequency. Since the long tail flicks with each call, that movement should be looked for when trying to spot this bird in the undergrowth. The leks at La Selva Biological Station are particularly well known.

In the Caribbean lowlands, the Long-tailed Hermit can be seen at Tortuguero NP, La Selva Biological Station, and on the grounds of El Pizote Lodge near Cahuita. In the southern Pacific lowlands, it occurs at Carara NP, Villa Lapas, Lapa Ríos, Corcovado Lodge Tent Camp, Tiskita Jungle Lodge, and Sirena Biological Station in Corcovado NP.

Similar Species: Green Hermit (Phaethornis guy)

The Green Hermit (11/15 trips; 35 sightings) is a dark greenish, middle-elevation species closely related to the Long-tailed Hermit. It has a long, decurved bill and a long tail like the Long-tailed Hermit, but the Long-tailed Hermit is found at lower elevations. The female has long, central white tail feathers, and the male has shorter white-tipped tail feathers. There is also a dark mask that is prominent on the lighter green female but less conspicuous on the male because of its dark green plumage. This hummingbird, which is about five inches long, is fairly common in moist and wet forests of premontane sites. Lek behavior by groups of displaying and calling males is also characteristic of the Green Hermit. The call is a monotonous single note that can be heard on vocalization tapes A, V, Y, BB, and CC.

The Green Hermit occurs in the forest understory, tall second growth, and forest edges at elevations from 1,650 to 6,500 feet along the length of the Caribbean and Pacific slopes. It feeds by "traplining" on the nectar of *Heliconia, Costus, Canna,* banana (*Musa*), *Centropogon, Pachystachys, Razisea,* and *Columnea.* This hummingbird may be observed on the Caribbean slope at Rancho Naturalista, La Virgen del Socorro, La Catarata de la Paz (Peace Waterfall), La Paz Waterfall Gardens, Rainforest Aerial Tram, and midlevels of Braulio Carrillo NP. The Green Hermit occurs in the Monteverde Cloud Forest Reserve and along the Palm and River Trails of the Wilson Botanical Garden at San Vito.

Green Hermit adult female at feeder

Little Hermit
(Stripe-throated Hermit)

Phaethornis longuemareus
(Phaethornis striigularis saturatus)

COSTA RICAN NAME: **Ermitaño enano**.

12/15 trips; 40 sightings.

STATUS: Permanent resident.

LENGTH: 3.75 inches.

WEIGHT: 0.08–0.11 ounce (2.3–3.2 grams).

VOCALIZATION TAPE: T.

RANGE: Southern Mexico to northern Brazil.

ELEVATIONAL RANGE: Sea level to 5,000 feet.

The Little Hermit is one of Costa Rica's smallest hummingbirds and is easy to identify. Identification marks include a conspicuous dark facial mask bordered above by a whitish stripe, cinnamon-brown to bronzy-green body color, a long and slightly decurved bill, and central tail feathers that are buffy white. This hermit is found in many of the same habitats and regions as the much larger Long-tailed Hermit. Recent taxonomic studies have suggested splitting the Little Hermit into two species—the Little Hermit (*Phaethornis longuemareus*) in Trinidad, northeastern Venezuela, and French Guiana, and the Stripe-throated Hermit (*Phaethornis striigularis*) from southern Mexico through Costa Rica to northern Venezuela and western Ecuador. Genetic studies show that the striped-throated species is more closely related to the Gray-chinned Hermit of Peru and northern Brazil than to the "little hermit" of Venezuela. This proposal has not yet been accepted, so this hummingbird is still referred to as the Little Hermit in Costa Rica.

The Little Hermit is found in moist and wet lowland and middle-elevation forest edges, young secondary forests, gallery forests, shade coffee plantations, flowering hedges, gardens, and parks. This bold little hummingbird is a common backyard species and will even fly into open rooms of rural homes to feed on the nectar of blooming house plants. Feeding by "traplining," it visits *Canna, Scutellaria,* shrimp plant (*Pachystachys lutea*), and other small flowers. It will also eat spiders and small insects. Large flowers are punctured at the base of the corolla to "steal" the nectar without pollinating the flower.

The Little Hermit usually forages singly, but throughout much of the year it is possible to encounter "leks," or singing assemblies, of up to twenty-five males

Little Hermit adult at Canna flower

that perch within three feet of the ground in very thick brush. One song of the males consists of a ventriloquial five-note phrase of thin, high-pitched squeaks that Slud (1964) described as "squick, squick, squick-squick-squick," with the first two notes long and the remaining three quick and descending. The long, white-tipped tail is pumped up and down as the bird sings. The ventriloquial sound makes you look higher in the foliage than the bird's actual location.

The Little Hermit can be encountered on the Caribbean slope from Tortuguero NP inland to La Selva Biological Station, Selva Verde, El Gavilán Lodge, the Rainforest Aerial Tram, lower levels of Braulio Carrillo NP, and up to the elevation of Rancho Naturalista, where it comes to the feeders and hummingbird pools. On the southern Pacific slope, this hermit can be seen at Los Cusingos, Manuel Antonio NP, Sirena Biological Station in Corcovado NP, Lapa Ríos, Corcovado Lodge Tent Camp, Tiskita Jungle Lodge, and at the Wilson Botanical Garden. A few are found in gallery forests of Guanacaste.

Violet Sabrewing

Campylopterus hemileucurus

COSTA RICAN NAME: *Ala de sable violáceo*.

8/15 trips; 12 sightings.

STATUS: Permanent resident.

LENGTH: 6 inches.

WEIGHT: 0.33–0.42 ounce (9.5–11.8 grams).

VOCALIZATION TAPE: CC.

RANGE: Southern Mexico to western Panama.

ELEVATIONAL RANGE: 3,300–8,000 feet.

Violet Sabrewing adult male

The striking Violet Sabrewing is one of the larger hummingbirds in Costa Rica and a species of foothills and middle-elevation forests. The Violet Sabrewing male is rich bluish violet on the head, back, and upper chest and has a long tail with conspicuous white spots on the outer edges. The long bill is strongly decurved. The female's back is green, the chest is gray, the gorget is blue, and the tail is similar to that of the male. The subspecies found in Costa Rica and western Panama, *Campylopterus hemileucurus mellitus,* is different from the subspecies found from southern Mexico to Nicaragua.

The Violet Sabrewing inhabits forest edges, second-growth forest, banana plantations, and flower gardens. It visits flowers of *Heliconias,* banana (*Musa*), ornamental banana (*M. coccinea*), hot lips (*Cephaelis*), and *Palicourea.* Violet Sabrewings can be regularly encountered at the Monteverde Cloud Forest Reserve, Hummingbird Gallery, and throughout the Monteverde vicinity; at Rancho Naturalista; Vista del Valle Restaurant at kilometer 119 on the PAH; and along the River Trail at the Wilson Botanical Garden. They visit nectar feeders at Monteverde, La Paz Waterfall Gardens, and Rancho Naturalista and are very aggressive in chasing other hummingbirds from the feeders.

White-necked Jacobin

Florisuga mellivora

COSTA RICAN NAME: **Jacobino nuquiblanco.**

9/15 trips; 43 sightings.

STATUS: Permanent resident.

LENGTH: 4.3–4.7 inches.

WEIGHT: 0.23–0.26 ounce (6–7.4 grams).

RANGE: Southern Mexico to Brazil.

ELEVATIONAL RANGE: Sea level to 4,000 feet.

The White-necked Jacobin, with its iridescent blue, green, and white markings, is one of the most beautiful of Costa Rica's hummingbirds. The male has a short, straight bill, a deep blue head and throat, a white breast, and a rich green back highlighted by a white collar on the back of the neck. The female lacks the blue head and white collar and has a scaly pattern on its bluish-green throat.

A resident of moist and wet tropical forests, the White-necked Jacobin pollinates flowers of *Inga, Vochysia, Symphonia, Bauhinia, Heliconia,* and *Erythrina* trees and the flowers of epiphytic plants like *Norantea* and *Columnea.* Small insects are captured on the wing.

The White-necked Jacobin inhabits lowland and middle elevations of the

White-necked Jacobin adult male

White-necked Jacobin adult female

Caribbean slope and can be seen in Tortuguero NP, La Selva Biological Station, El Gavilán Lodge, and Selva Verde; along the Caribbean coast to Cahuita; on the Rainforest Aerial Tram property; and at lower levels of Braulio Carrillo NP. It is common at Rancho Naturalista near Tuís. On the Pacific slope, it can be seen at Corcovado Lodge Tent Camp, Sirena Biological Station, Lapa Ríos, Corcovado NP, and on the grounds of Tiskita Jungle Lodge.

Green Violet-ear

Colibri thalassinus cabanidis

COSTA RICAN NAME: *Colibrí orejivioláceo verde*.

14/15 trips; 35 sightings.

STATUS: Permanent resident; endemic highland subspecies.

LENGTH: 4.2–4.5 inches.

WEIGHT: 0.17–0.20 ounce (4.8–5.7 grams).

VOCALIZATION TAPES: X, BB.

RANGE: Central Mexico to Bolivia.

ELEVATIONAL RANGE: 3,300–10,000 feet.

The Green Violet-ear is a common highland hummingbird whose name describes its markings. It is iridescent green with a bluish-violet mask that passes through the lower portion of the eye and to the "ear." The bill is straight to slightly decurved, and there is a conspicuous blue band across the tail. The most vocal of highland hummingbirds, the Green Violet-ear is often heard before it is seen—and is often heard but unseen. The call is a repetitious series of high-pitched chirps, with each phrase usually consisting of a higher note and two lower notes.

This hummingbird inhabits pasture and forest edges, second growth, and rural backyards. It visits many different flowers in mountainous areas and captures insects on the wing. Among flowers visited are *Salvia, Lobelia, Cirsium, Centropogon,* hot lips (*Cephaelis*), *Besleria, Cuphaea, Stachytarpheta, Columnea, Inga, Clusia,* and *Erythrina.*

The Green Violet-ear can be encountered at Hotel El Pórtico near San José de la Montaña on Barva Volcano, La Paz Waterfall Gardens, Monteverde Cloud Forest Reserve, Savegre Mountain Lodge near San Gerardo de Dota, and at kilometers 66, 77, 80, 86, and 96 in Cerro de la Muerte.

Green Violet-ear adult in flight

Violet-crowned Woodnymph (Crowned Woodnymph, Purple-crowned Woodnymph)

Thalurania colombica venusta

COSTA RICAN NAME: *Ninfa violeta y verde.*

9/15 trips; 48 sightings.

STATUS: Permanent resident

LENGTH: 3.3–4.3 inches.

WEIGHT: 0.14–0.16 ounce (3.9–4.6 grams).

RANGE: Central Mexico to central Panama, northern Colombia and western Venezuela.

ELEVATIONAL RANGE: Sea level to 4,000 feet.

A hummingbird that almost glows with deep iridescent tones of green and bluish violet is the Violet-crowned Woodnymph. This medium-sized hummingbird is bluish violet on the crown and over the shoulders. The huge gor-

Violet-crowned Woodnymph adult male showing extremely large green gorget

Adult female showing large white gorget

get, which extends farther down onto the chest than on most hummingbirds, is bright green on the male and white on the female.

The Violet-crowned Woodnymph inhabits wet lowland and middle-elevation rainforests, older second growth, forest edges, and light gaps in mature forest. Males forage in the upper canopy for nectar of bromeliads, *Columnea, Inga,* and plants of the blueberry family (Ericaceae). Females forage near the ground on understory flowers of *Heliconia, Costus, Hamelia, Cornutia, Besleria,* and hot lips (*Cephaelis*). Insects and spiders are captured on leaf cover, and some insects are captured in flight.

In Caribbean lowlands, this bird can be encountered at La Selva Biological Station and nearby lodges like Selva Verde and El Gavilán Lodge. Other locations include La Virgen del Socorro, Rara Avis, Rancho Naturalista, Rainforest Aerial Tram, La Paz Waterfall Gardens, and lower levels of Braulio Carrillo NP. In the southern Pacific slope, it occurs in Corcovado NP, including the Sirena Biological Station, Lapa Ríos, Corcovado Lodge Tent Camp, Tiskita Jungle Lodge, and Wilson Botanical Garden at San Vito.

Fiery-throated Hummingbird

Panterpe insignis
>
> COSTA RICAN NAME: ***Colibrí garganta de fuego***.
>
> 12/15 trips; 15 sightings.
>
> STATUS: Permanent resident; endemic highland species.
>
> LENGTH: 4.25 inches.
>
> WEIGHT: 0.2 ounce (4.9–6.2 grams).
>
> VOCALIZATION TAPE: BB.
>
> RANGE: Costa Rica to western Panama.
>
> ELEVATIONAL RANGE: 4,600–9,000 feet.

The Fiery-throated Hummingbird is one of the most stunning hummingbirds of Costa Rica's forested highlands. This medium-sized hummingbird is dark green with a blue tail, but its most striking feature is the throat, which is an intense iridescent red in the central portion, surrounded by iridescent orange. The crown is deep blue. Sexes are identical.

This aggressive hummingbird visits flowers of *Cavendishia, Macleania, Clusia, Centropogon, Tropaeolum, Gaiadendron, Vaccinium, Cestrum, Fuschia,* and *Bomarea*. It may pierce flowers that have a corolla that is too long for their bill, like *Centropogon* or *Fuschia*, or use holes that have been previously made at the

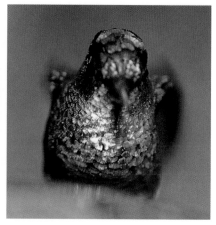

Fiery-throated Hummingbird adult, sexes similar

Close-up view of the Fiery-throated Hummingbird's gorget

base of those flowers by bumblebees or Slaty Flowerpiercers. Small insects are also eaten.

The Fiery-throated Hummingbird may be seen at Poás NP, Savegre Mountain Lodge, and birding sites in Cerro de la Muerte at kilometers 66, 86, and 96.

Rufous-tailed Hummingbird

Amazilia tzacatl

COSTA RICAN NAME: ***Amazilia rabirrufa***.

15/15 trips; 123 sightings.

STATUS: Permanent resident.

LENGTH: 3.2–4.3 inches.

WEIGHT: 0.18–0.19 ounce (5.2–5.5 grams).

VOCALIZATION TAPE: T.

RANGE: Northeastern Mexico to western Ecuador.

ELEVATIONAL RANGE: Sea level to 5,000 feet.

The Rufous-tailed Hummingbird is the most common hummingbird in Costa Rica. It is often seen visiting backyard flower gardens throughout the country. It is a medium-sized green hummingbird with a reddish bill and a rusty-colored tail.

This hummingbird inhabits disturbed forest, forest edges, meadows, pas-

Rufous-tailed Hummingbird adult male showing red bill, rufous tail, and gray belly

Adult female on nest

tures interspersed with brush, woodlots, second-growth forest, shade coffee plantations, and urban and rural backyards. The Rufous-tailed Hummingbird visits flowers that are both native and introduced, including *Hamelia, Tabebuia, Lantana, Costus,* banana (*Musa*), coffee (*Coffea arabica*), *Heliconia, Stachytarpheta,* and hot lips (*Cephaelis*). Insects and spiders are also eaten. Where abundant flowers provide a good source of nectar, this hummingbird is aggressive and chases away other hummingbirds, bees, and butterflies.

This common hummingbird can be seen throughout lowland and middle elevations of the Caribbean and Pacific slopes and throughout premontane levels, including San José and suburbs of the Central Plateau, the Turrialba region, Rancho Naturalista, and Wilson Botanical Garden. Few sightings occur above 4,000 feet in elevation. It is less common in the dry forests of Guanacaste, where it is largely replaced by the Cinnamon Hummingbird.

Snowcap

Microchera albocoronata
>   COSTA RICAN NAME: ***Copete de nieve.***
>   4/15 trips; 20 sightings.
>   STATUS: Permanent resident.
>   LENGTH: 2.4–2.6 inches.
>   WEIGHT: 0.09 ounce (2.5–2.6 grams).
>   RANGE: Honduras to western Panama.
>   ELEVATIONAL RANGE: 1,000–4,600 feet.

The Snowcap is one of the smallest of Costa Rica's fifty-two hummingbirds. Only the Scintillant Hummingbird is smaller. It is also one of the most beautiful and eagerly sought species for nature lovers visiting Central America. Like a jewel in the rainforest, its iridescent purple body and snow white cap make a first sighting a lifetime memory. Young male snowcaps molting into adult plumage exhibit a calico pattern of purplish splotches on bronzy green. The female is bronzy green above and dull white below and has a white spot behind the eye.

This unmistakable hummingbird lives in middle-elevation wet forests along the Caribbean slope. It inhabits the rainforest canopy, where it feeds on nectar of epiphytes like *Norantea, Columnea,* and *Cavendishia* and on the flowers of *Warscewiczia, Inga,* and *Pithecellobium* trees. In forest edges and openings, the Snowcap feeds near the ground on the flowers of shrubs and vines like *Hamelia,* hot lips (*Cephaelis*), *Psychotria, Besleria, Stachytarpheta,* and *Gurania.* The Snowcap is relatively rare, but it is consistently observed at Rara Avis and in the "hummingbird meadow" at Rancho Naturalista, where it visits the feeders.

Snowcap adult male

Adult female

Purple-throated Mountain-gem (Variable Mountain-gem)

Lampornis calolaema
(Lampornis castaneoventris)

COSTA RICAN NAME: *Colibrí montañés gorgimorado.*

5/15 trips; 5 sightings.

STATUS: Permanent resident; endemic highland species.

LENGTH: 3.9–4.5 inches.

WEIGHT: 0.17–0.22 ounce (4.7–6.2 grams).

RANGE: Southern Nicaragua to central Costa Rica.

ELEVATIONAL RANGE: 2,600–8,200 feet.

Purple-throated Mountain-gem adult male (adult female is identical to Gray-tailed Mountain-gem female)

Any visitor to Monteverde will quickly be attracted by the abundant and beautiful Purple-throated Mountain-gem, because it is a frequent visitor at feeders. The male has a purple gorget and a white streak behind the eye. The female has a similar white streak behind the eye, but it has a cinnamon-colored throat and breast. The female is identical to the female Gray-tailed Mountain-gem. The Purple-throated Mountain-gem is found in middle- and high-elevation forests of northern Costa Rica. It visits flowers of *Satyria* and *Cavendishia* in the blueberry family, as well as those of *Columnea, Clusia, Stachytarpheta,* and hot lips (*Cephalis*).

The Purple-throated Mountain-gem lives at middle and upper elevations of mountains from Tenorio to the Monteverde region, La Virgen del Socorro, volcanoes surrounding the Central Plateau, and at the northern end of the Talamanca Mountains at Kiri Lodge and Tapantí NP. The best place to view it is at the hummingbird feeders at the Monteverde Cloud Forest Reserve, the nearby Hummingbird Gallery, at feeders in the gardens of tourism lodges in the Monteverde community, and at the La Paz Waterfall Gardens near Vara Blanca.

Similar Species: Gray-tailed (White-throated) Mountain-gem (*Lampornis cinereicauda*)

Adult male showing white gorget

The Gray-tailed (White-throated) Mountain-gem (10/15 trips; 23 sightings) has resulted from differentiation through natural selection from a common mountain-gem ancestor that was geographically separated by the mountains in northern Costa Rica and the Talamanca Mountains of the south. The species in the north became the Purple-throated Mountain-gem, and in the Talamanca Mountains, the gray-tailed species developed a white gorget instead of a purple one. The tail is blue-black on the purple-throated species.

The white-throated species has become further differentiated between a gray-tailed species with a white throat in the Costa Rican mountains and a blue-tailed species with a white throat (*L. castaneoventris*) in the mountains of western Panama. Females are identical to the female Purple-throated Mountain-gem. An endemic highland species, this hummingbird of the montane forests is found at elevations of 5,000 to 10,000 feet. Epiphytic plants visited for nectar include *Cavendishia, Satyria, Centropogon,* and *Alloplectus.*

Although the range of this bird is extremely limited, it is regularly encountered in the San Gerardo de Dota region along the road that leads from the PAH to Savegre Mountain Lodge at kilometer 80 and on the lodge balcony at Savegre Mountain Lodge, where it visits the hummingbird feeders. It can be also observed along the private road in Cerro de la Muerte located at kilometer 66 along the PAH.

Adult male in flight showing gray tail

Adult female (identical to female Purple-throated Mountain-gem)

Green-breasted Mango

Anthracothorax prevostii

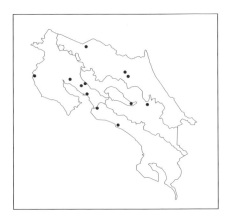

COSTA RICAN NAME: *Manguito pechiverde.*

9/15 trips; 24 sightings.

STATUS: Permanent resident.

LENGTH: 4.3–4.7 inches.

Weight: 0.24–0.25 ounce (6.8–7.2 grams).

RANGE: Northeastern Mexico to northwestern Peru.

ELEVATIONAL RANGE: Sea level to 3,200 feet.

In a country with fifty-two different hummingbirds, it is reassuring that some are so easy to identify that they cannot be confused with others. The Green-breasted Mango is such a species. The greenish female has a white breast with a

Green-breasted Mango adult male

Green-breasted Mango adult female

"blackish-green necktie" marking on the throat and center of the breast. The male is darker green and has a similar but broader "black necktie" marking on the throat and center of the breast. It has a purplish tail. The bill is long and slightly decurved on both sexes, and the dark tail is tipped with white on the female.

The Green-breasted Mango is a hummingbird of dry and moist lowland and middle-elevation grasslands; savannas; dry, gallery, and mangrove forests; older second growth; shade coffee plantations; forest edges; and fencerows planted with flowering trees and shrubs. Among flowers visited are *Inga, Bauhinia, Ceiba, Calycophyllum, Combretum, Ipomoea, Hibiscus, Erythrina,* and *Caesalpinia.* Insects are captured in flight.

The Green-breasted Mango can be seen on the Caribbean slope at La Selva Biological Station, Turrialba, and Rancho Naturalista, where it visits the nectar feeders. On the Pacific slope, it is most abundant in the Guanacaste region and the vicinity of the Palo Verde NP. It has been seen at Tamarindo, at Hacienda Solimar, at La Ensenada Lodge, along the road leading from the PAH near Río Lagarto to Monteverde, and southeast to Playa Doña Ana, Carara NP, Villa Lapas, and Tárcol Lodge.

Green-crowned Brilliant
(Green-fronted Brilliant)

Heliodoxa jacula

Costa Rican name: ***Brillante
frentiverde.***

8/15 trips; 16 sightings.

Status: Permanent resident.

Length: 4.1–5.1 inches.

Weight: 0.29–0.33 ounce (8.2–9.4
grams).

Range: Costa Rica to western
Ecuador.

Elevational range: 2,300–6,600
feet.

The Green-crowned Brilliant is a medium-sized hummingbird with a short, straight bill; a dark green body; a small purple spot on the throat; and a white spot behind the eye. The female has a green body and a white breast speckled with green. It is one of the most common hummingbirds in the cloud forests of Monteverde.

This is a hummingbird of cloud forest, premontane, and montane forests. It visits epiphytic flowers in the canopy like *Marcgravia* and plants of forest edges like *Heliconia,* hot lips (*Cephaelis*), and *Drymonia conchocalyx.* Though most hummingbirds feed while hovering in front of the flower, this bird perches on the flower or feeder while feeding.

Green-crowned Brilliant adult male

Green-crowned Brilliant adult female

The Green-crowned Brilliant is found at midlevel locations along the Caribbean slope. Among the best places to see it are along the trails at the Monteverde Cloud Forest Reserve, at feeders by the Reserve headquarters, and at the nearby Hummingbird Gallery. It can also be observed in Braulio Carrillo NP, La Paz Waterfall Gardens, Tapantí NP, and in the "hummingbird meadow" at Rancho Naturalista.

Magnificent Hummingbird (Rivoli's Hummingbird)

Eugenes fulgens

COSTA RICAN NAME:
Colibrí magnífico.

14/15 trips; 38 sightings.

STATUS: Permanent resident; endemic highland subspecies.

LENGTH: 4.7–5.5 inches.

WEIGHT: 0.30–0.35 ounce (8.5–10 grams).

VOCALIZATION TAPE: F.

RANGE: Arizona to western Panama.

ELEVATIONAL RANGE: 6,000–10,000 feet.

The Magnificent Hummingbird is the largest hummingbird of Costa Rica's mountains. It has a long, straight bill (1.2–1.5 inches long), a dark green body with a bright green gorget, a violet forehead, and a white spot behind the eye. This hummingbird is found from Arizona to western Panama. The subspecies found in Costa Rica and western Panama (*E. fulgens spectabilis*) is endemic to that region and is larger and lighter than the subspecies found from Arizona to Nicaragua.

A bird of montane forests, the Magnificent Hummingbird visits epiphytes in oak trees (*Satyria* and *Cavendishia*), passionflowers (*Passiflora*), and flowers of forest openings, roadsides, pastures, and disturbed sites like giant thistle (*Cirsium*), *Penstemon, Bomarea costaricensis, Fuschia, Centropogon, Erythrina, Lobelia*, and *Cestrum*. The Magnificent Hummingbird will aggressively defend nectar sources like giant thistles from other hummingbirds and has been known to grab large bumblebees from these thistles and toss them from the flowers.

The Magnificent Hummingbird occurs in the mountains from the Monteverde Cloud Forest Reserve and La Virgen del Socorro southward through the volcanoes surrounding the Central Plateau and the Talamanca Mountains

Magnificent Hummingbird adult male showing long, straight bill and white spot behind eye

Magnificent Hummingbird adult female

to the Panama border. Among the best places to view it are Poás NP and along the PAH in Cerro de la Muerte, including locations at kilometers 66, 80, 86, and 96. It also comes to the hummingbird feeders at Savegre Mountain Lodge.

Volcano Hummingbird

Selasphorus flammula

COSTA RICAN NAMES: *Chispitas; chispita volcanera; colibrí mosca.*

10/15 trips; 37 sightings.

STATUS: Permanent resident; endemic highland species.

LENGTH: 3.0–3.1 inches.

WEIGHT: 0.09–0.10 ounce (2.5–2.8 grams).

RANGE: Costa Rica to western Panama.

ELEVATIONAL RANGE: 6,000–10,000 feet.

The Volcano Hummingbird is an endemic bird that is found only on the volcanoes of the Central Plateau (Irazú, Poás, and Barva) and south through the Talamanca Mountains to Barú Volcano in western Panama.

The tiny Volcano Hummingbird is one of the most attractive hummingbirds in the mountains. The colorful gorget is flared at the lower sides and features different colors in different regions. Males living on Poás and Barva Volcanoes have rosy-red gorgets; males of the Talamanca Mountains have

Volcano Hummingbird adult male near flowers of *Monochaetum volcanicum*

lavender or purplish-gray gorgets; and males living on the Irazú and Turrialba Volcanoes have dull-purple gorgets. The female has a white breast and a speckled throat, and the outer three tail feathers on each side of the tail have white to buffy tips.

A resident of montane forests, paramo, and stunted forests of high elevations near the treeline, the Volcano Hummingbird visits flowers of *Fuschia*, *Salvia*, *Bomarea*, foxglove (*Digitalis*), Indian paintbrush (*Castilleja*), blueberry (*Vaccinium*), blackberry (*Rubus*), and *Miconia*. It feeds through holes at the base of *Centropogon* flowers that have been pierced by Slaty Flowerpiercers. The Volcano Hummingbird is common at the summit of the Irazú, Poás, and Barva Volcanoes and at Amistad NP; it can be observed along the PAH in Cerro de la Muerte at kilometers 66, 80, 86, and 96 and at Savegre Mountain Lodge.

Similar Species:
Scintillant Hummingbird
(*Selasphorus scintilla*)

The Scintillant Hummingbird (11/15 trips; 33 sightings) is the smallest hummingbird in Costa Rica. Similar in appearance to the Volcano Hummingbird (2.6–2.8 inches in length; 2.1 grams), it is found in premontane forests at lower elevations (3,000 feet) up to montane forests (8,000 feet). It is not as abundant in higher paramo habitats. The gorget flares at the lower sides like that of the Volcano Hummingbird, but it is orangish red. The breast, sides, and belly are rufous, and there is much rufous color in the tail.

The female is similar in size and profile to the Volcano Hummingbird, but it also shows more rufous on the breast, sides, and tail than the female Volcano Hummingbird. Since it has such a short bill, it visits small flowers of *Salvia*, *Lantana*, *Hyptis*, blackberry (*Rubus*), and *Stachytarpheta*.

Like the Volcano Hummingbird, this bird is endemic to Costa Rica and western Panama. It may be observed on Barva, Irazú, and Poás Volcanoes; in the Monteverde Cloud Forest Reserve; in the vicinity of Hotel El Pórtico at San José de la Montaña; and along the PAH in Cerro de la Muerte at kilometers 66, 80, and 96. The Scintillant Hummingbird regularly visits nectar feeders and flowers on the grounds of Savegre Mountain Lodge.

Scintillant Hummingbird adult male visiting flowers of *Fuschia*

Scintillant Hummingbird adult female visiting flowers of *Fuschia*

TROGON FAMILY (Trogonidae)

Resplendent Quetzal

Pharomachrus mocinno

COSTA RICAN NAME: *Quetzal.*

14/15 trips; 38 sightings.

STATUS: Permanent resident; endemic highland subspecies.

LENGTH: 14 inches (plus 18.7–32.2-inch tail on males).

WEIGHT: 7.2–8.3 ounces (206–236 grams).

VOCALIZATION TAPES: O, S, AA, BB.

RANGE: Southern Mexico to western Panama.

ELEVATIONAL RANGE: 3,900–9,800 feet.

The Resplendent Quetzal (pronounced "ket-sál") is one of the most stunning and beautiful birds in the world. The iridescent green body, fluffy-looking crown, cherry-red breast, and shimmering two-foot or longer green tail provide a vision of tropical beauty that most people will never forget. The long green tail on the male consists of four upper tail covert feathers that grow from above the base of the real tail. The "real" tail is much shorter—about seven to eight inches long—and is white when viewed from below. The male quetzal is also adorned with elongated green, satinlike wing covert feathers that drape over the sides.

The quetzal is the national bird of Guatemala and is featured as the standard of currency there, but it is very rare in that country. The Resplendent Quetzal of Costa Rica is a different subspecies (*Pharomachrus m. costaricensis*) and is found only in the mountains of Costa Rica and western Panama.

The quetzal is one of ten trogons found in Costa Rica, but it is the only one with a long "tail." It is a bird of cloud forests in the Monteverde area and montane forests surrounding the Central Plateau and Talamanca Mountains. A quetzal will sit quietly in an upright posture on a horizontal branch for long periods, watching for a blackberry, fig, wild avocado, or small lizard. The food item is frequently plucked from its stem or perch as the bird hovers, and then the quetzal returns to its perch.

Because the iridescent green or blue of this bird is a structural color caused by refraction of light on the feathers, the plumage is dull and hard to spot in the shade—and spectacular when viewed in sunlight. When flushed, the male quetzal drops backward off its perch to avoid damage to its tail feathers.

Resplendent Quetzal adult male

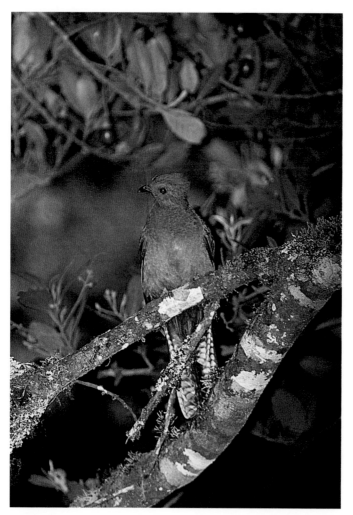

Resplendent Quetzal adult female

Nesting occurs from March through June. A cavity or abandoned woodpecker hole is selected in a dead, rotten tree. The male defends an area with a radius of about 1,100 feet around the nesting tree. The young are fed Golden Beetles (*Plusiotis resplendens*), fruits, lizards, snails, and caterpillars.

The Resplendent Quetzal may be observed in the Monteverde Cloud Forest Reserve and vicinity and in the montane forests of Poás NP and Barva Volcano. It is also found in the San Gerardo de Dota region, including Savegre Mountain Lodge. Along the PAH in Cerro de la Muerte, the quetzal may sometimes be seen, with permission and for a fee, along the private road at kilometer 66 and at other private reserves that advertise along the highway.

Slaty-tailed Trogon

Trogon massena

COSTA RICAN NAME:
Trogón coliplomizo.

11/15 trips; 33 sightings.

STATUS: Permanent resident.

LENGTH: 12–14 inches.

WEIGHT: 5.1 ounces (145 grams).

VOCALIZATION TAPES: B, D, O, S, T,
BB, CC.

RANGE: Southeastern Mexico to
northwestern Ecuador.

ELEVATIONAL RANGE: Sea level to
4,000 feet.

The Slaty-tailed Trogon is a large, colorful member of the trogon family. Trogons often sit quietly on horizontal branches in the lower canopy. To distinguish trogons, look carefully at the color of the breast, the presence or absence of a white band between the throat and breast, the pattern on the underside of the tail, and the color of the eye-ring. The Slaty-tailed Trogon has a red breast but no white upper breast band; the underside of the tail is dark gray with no

Slaty-tailed Trogon adult male

Slaty-tailed Trogon adult female

white markings; and the bill and eye-ring are orange. This trogon is often heard before it is seen, because it makes a repetitive call of the same note, repeated about once or twice per second: "Kuow-kuow-kuow-kuow."

This trogon inhabits mature forest, second growth, and forest edges. It is diurnal and usually solitary except during the nesting season. Like other trogons, it sits quietly and watches for fruit, katydids, caterpillars, or lizards. Once food is spotted, it flies from its perch, hovers momentarily as it snatches the food item, and then returns to the perch. Fruits eaten include small palm fruits, *Coussarea, Hamelia, Virola, Didymopanax,* and *Guatteria.* This trogon may also follow troops of monkeys and capture insects flushed by them.

A resident of moist and wet lowland forests of Caribbean and southern Pacific slopes, the Slaty-tailed Trogon can be seen along the canals of Tortuguero NP, on the grounds of Tortuga Lodge, and at La Selva Biological Station. In the southern Pacific lowlands, it can be encountered at Carara NP, Villa Lapas, Wilson Botanical Garden, Lapa Ríos, Corcovado Lodge Tent Camp, Tiskita Jungle Lodge, and Sirena Biological Station within Corcovado NP.

Violaceous Trogon

Trogon violaceus

Costa Rican name:
Trogón violáceo.

11/15 trips; 43 sightings.

Status: Permanent resident.

Length: 9 inches.

Weight: 2.0–2.3 ounces (56–66 grams).

Vocalization tapes: A, B, D, E, J, O, T, V, BB, CC.

Range: Southern Mexico to northern Bolivia and western Brazil.

Elevational range: Sea level to 4,000 feet.

The Violaceous Trogon, the most common and widespread trogon in Costa Rica, is one of three yellow-breasted trogons in the country. It has a violet-blue head and is the only yellow-breasted trogon with a yellow eye-ring. The others have gray eye-rings. The male has fine barring on the tail, with broader white tips on the underside of the tail feathers. The female is gray with a yellow breast and has an incomplete white eye-ring. The call is a series of about forty to fifty strong, thrushlike chirps at about the same pitch, given at a frequency of about two per second.

Violaceous Trogon adult male

This adaptable and widespread trogon is found in the Guanacaste dry forest, especially in riparian forests. It is also found in moist and wet forests of lower and middle elevations throughout the Caribbean and southern Pacific slopes. This trogon frequents moist and wet forest edges, second-growth forest, and openings with scattered trees. It usually sits quietly on a horizontal branch high in the canopy. From its perch it will fly out to pluck a fruit, insect, or lizard while hovering. It is also known to perch near wasp nests and fly out to capture wasps on the wing. Nests are excavated within wasp nests.

On the Caribbean slope, look for this trogon at La Selva Biological Station, along the coast from Limón to Cahuita, and at Rancho Naturalista, Rainforest Aerial Tram, and lower levels of Braulio Carrillo NP. In Guanacaste, the Violaceous Trogon can be seen in Palo Verde and Santa Rosa NPs, Lomas Barbudal BR, La Pacífica, La Ensenada Lodge, Villa Lapas, Carara NP, and at Playa Doña Ana south of Puntarenas. On the southern Pacific slope, it is present at the Wilson Botanical Garden, Manuel Antonio NP, Rancho Casa Grande, Corcovado Lodge Tent Camp, and Tiskita Jungle Lodge.

Collared Trogon

Trogon collaris

>Costa Rican names: ***Trogón collarejo; viuda roja; quetzal macho.***
>
>7/15 trips; 19 sightings.
>
>Status: Permanent resident.
>
>Length: 10 inches.
>
>Weight: 2.2–2.5 ounces (63.4–78.6 grams).
>
>Vocalization tapes: D, J, O, T, W, Y.
>
>Range: Southern Mexico to northern Bolivia and southeastern Brazil.
>
>Elevational range: 2,300–8,200 feet.

Although upstaged in beauty by the Resplendent Quetzal, the colorful Collared Trogon is one of the spectacular sights in Costa Rica's highlands. The male has a cherry-red breast that is edged above by a white line; an iridescent green back, head, and upper chest; no eye-ring; and a black face and black

Collared Trogon adult male

Collared Trogon adult female

throat. The tail has narrow black-and-white barring, with the tip featuring a slightly wider white bar. The bill is yellow. The attractive female has a reddish-orange breast, narrow white bar above the breast, medium-brown head and shoulders, black upper chest and face, and no eye-ring. The tail has no barring. It is grayish-rufous, with feather tips that have narrow black and white bars. The bill of the female is bright yellow with a black stripe along the top edge.

The Collared Trogon is a bird of mature cloud forests and montane forests. It sits quietly in the understory or at forest edges, watching for insects and fruits. Most prey consists of caterpillars, bugs, beetles, and other insects. This trogon may accompany mixed flocks and capture insects as they try to escape.

Look for the Collared Trogon in highland forests at Tapantí NP, La Virgen del Socorro, Rancho Naturalista, and the Wilson Botanical Garden near San Vito; along the trail at kilometer 66 of the PAH in Cerro de la Muerte; at kilometer 80 of the PAH along the road that descends from the PAH to Savegre Mountain Lodge; and on the grounds of Savegre Mountain Lodge.

Black-throated Trogon

Trogon rufus

COSTA RICAN NAME: ***Trogón cabeciverde***.

11/15 trips; 19 sightings.

STATUS: Permanent resident.

LENGTH: 9 inches.

WEIGHT: 2.0 ounces (57 grams).

VOCALIZATION TAPES: O, U, BB, CC.

RANGE: Honduras to northeastern Argentina.

ELEVATIONAL RANGE: Sea level to 3,300 feet.

The Black-throated Trogon is a yellow-breasted trogon with a green head, yellow bill, and bluish-gray eye-ring. Barring on the tail is similar to that of the Violaceous Trogon. The female is brown with a yellow breast. The call is a series of three to four identical notes, which each drop in pitch and sound like "e-oo, e-oo, e-oo, e-oo." The notes are given at a rate of about one per second.

In contrast to the Violaceous Trogon, which inhabits the upper canopy of disturbed forests, the Black-throated Trogon inhabits the shaded lower canopy of mature lowland rainforest. It will sit quietly on a horizontal branch for long periods and occasionally fly out to snatch an insect or fruit while on the wing. Nesting occurs from February through June. A pair of trogons excavate the nest cavity in the base of a rotten tree stump with their bills and share incubation duties.

Black-throated Trogon adult male

Black-throated Trogon adult female

In the Caribbean lowlands, the Black-throated Trogon can be observed in rainforests at Tortuga Lodge, La Selva Biological Station, and Rancho Naturalista. In the southern Pacific lowlands, it occurs at Dr. Skutch's reserve (Los Cusingos), Wilson Botanical Garden, and Corcovado NP, including Sirena Biological Station, Lapa Ríos, Corcovado Lodge Tent Camp, and Tiskita Jungle Lodge.

KINGFISHER FAMILY (Alcedinidae)

Ringed Kingfisher

Ceryle torquata

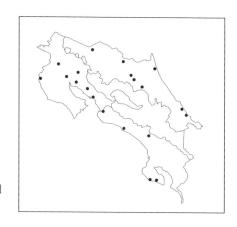

COSTA RICAN NAME: **Martín pescador collarejo**.

14/15 trips; 63 sightings.

STATUS: Permanent resident.

LENGTH: 16 inches.

WEIGHT: 10.2 ounces (290 grams).

VOCALIZATION TAPES: D, F, T, V.

RANGE: Southern Texas to Tierra del Fuego.

ELEVATIONAL RANGE: Sea level to 3,000 feet.

The Ringed Kingfisher is the largest kingfisher in the Americas. The male has a thick, bushy crest, large bill, white collar, bluish head, bluish back, and rufous breast and belly. The female has a blue band across the upper chest. It is much larger than the Belted Kingfisher, which has white on the belly.

This kingfisher can be observed perching on dead trees, branches, or power lines adjacent to or over rivers, lakes, lagoons, mangrove swamps, and flooded tidal marshes. Often it will perch fifteen to thirty-five feet above the water, which is higher than other kingfishers usually perch. When prey is sighted, it dives headfirst into the water and captures small fish, frogs, and small snakes. It

Ringed Kingfisher adult male

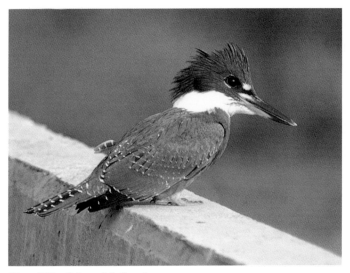

Ringed Kingfisher adult female

does not hover above the water to spot prey as Belted and Amazon Kingfishers do.

The Ringed Kingfisher nests from January through March. A burrow is excavated in the cut bank of a river, road bank, or eroded hillside. The horizontal burrow is six inches high, four inches wide, and six to eight feet deep. The young fledge after five weeks and continue to be fed by the parents for several weeks after leaving the burrow. This kingfisher is common and can be found along watercourse edges throughout the length of the Caribbean and Pacific lowlands, including Guanacaste. One of the best places to see it is along the canals of Tortuguero NP.

Amazon Kingfisher

Chloroceryle amazona

    Costa Rican name: ***Martín pescador amazónico***.

    14/15 trips; 32 sightings.

    Status: Permanent resident.

    Length: 11.5 inches.

    Weight: 3.9 ounces (110 grams).

    Vocalization tapes: V, W.

    Range: Southern Mexico to northern Argentina.

    Elevational range: Sea level to 3,000 feet.

Six kingfishers are found in the Americas, and all six are found in Costa Rica. Almost a foot long, the Amazon Kingfisher is the largest of the dark green kingfishers and has an extremely long, thick bill. The male has a wide, rufous band across the chest and a white belly. The female has a white throat and breast that is speckled with green on the sides. The Amazon Kingfisher inhabits the edges of both fast-flowing and slow-moving streams and rivers, mangrove lagoons, and lake shores where the forest canopy is not closed over the water. It perches or hovers above the water to spot its quarry and dives head-first to capture fish.

The Amazon Kingfisher can be found along the length of the Caribbean and Pacific slopes. It can be seen in Tortuguero and Cahuita NPs and along rivers and estuaries between Limón and Cahuita. On the Pacific slope, this kingfisher occurs in mangrove lagoons near Tamarindo, Punta Morales, La Ensenada Lodge, and the lagoons at Puntarenas; along the Río Tárcoles; at Villa Lapas; in the General Valley; at Los Cusingos; along the Río Térraba; in Quepos; and near the Sirena Biological Station in Corcovado NP.

Amazon Kingfisher adult male with rufous breast band; female lacks rufous breast band

Similar Species: Green Kingfisher (*Chloroceryle americana*)

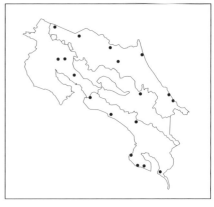

The Green Kingfisher (12/15 trips; 52 sightings) resembles a miniature Amazon Kingfisher. The male is dark green with a white collar and a rufous breast band. The female has a white throat and white belly that are highlighted with two incomplete, speckled green breast bands and green speckles on the sides. The wings of both sexes have white speckles, which are absent on the Amazon. The bill is not as thick as that of the Amazon Kingfisher. This bird is only seven inches long compared to nearly a foot for the Amazon Kingfisher.

The Green Kingfisher inhabits the edges of quiet or slow-moving woodland streams, pools, and canals. It perches on wires, rocks, or overhanging twigs one to fifteen feet above the water and dives headfirst to capture small fishes and aquatic invertebrates. Its "rattling" call can be heard on vocalization tapes F and T.

Nesting occurs from February through April when the monogamous pair of kingfishers excavate a burrow into a cut bank along a stream or river. The burrow is two to three feet deep into the bank, and the entrance is concealed by vines or roots. The Green Kingfisher is found from sea level to 4,000 feet along river and wetland edges throughout lowland and middle elevations of the Caribbean and Pacific slopes. It is one of the most common kingfishers in Costa Rica.

Green Kingfisher adult male with rufous breast band; female has two indistinct green breast bands

American Pygmy Kingfisher

Chloroceryle aenea

COSTA RICAN NAME: **Martín pescador enano**.

7/15 trips; 14 sightings.

STATUS: Permanent resident.

LENGTH: 5 inches.

WEIGHT: 0.6 ounce (18 grams).

RANGE: Southern Mexico to central Brazil.

ELEVATIONAL RANGE: Sea level to 2,000 feet.

The American Pygmy Kingfisher is the smallest kingfisher in the Americas— only about five inches long. It appears to be a miniature version of the Green- and-rufous Kingfisher. The male is iri- descent green above and rufous below, but it has a white belly. The belly of the Green-and-rufous Kingfisher is ru- fous. The female has a green breast band with fine white speckles. In Spanish, it is called *martín pescador enano,* meaning the "dwarf kingfisher."

This tiny kingfisher inhabits shal- low forested wetlands, including backwater ponds, pools, puddles, and mangrove lagoons. It is extremely dif- ficult to see because it frequently sits

American Pygmy Kingfisher adult male with rufous breast; female has green chest band above the rufous breast

in thick, shady, streamside brush as it watches for small fish and insects. It may dive headfirst for its prey or fly out to capture insects, like damselflies, on the wing. Nesting occurs from March through April. Three to four young are raised in a one-foot-deep burrow in a dirt bank or within the overturned root mass of a fallen tree.

The best place to see this kingfisher is in Tortuguero NP. It can be seen along the canals during the day or on night boat tours as it roosts among fo- liage on the edges of backwater canals like Caño Harold. Other places where it has been observed include small streams in Carara NP and in mangrove forests at the estuary of the Río Tárcoles near Tárcol Lodge.

MOTMOT FAMILY (Momotidae)

Turquoise-browed Motmot

Eumomota superciliosa

COSTA RICAN NAMES: ***Pájaro bobo; momoto cejiceleste***.

7/15 trips; 13 sightings.

STATUS: Permanent resident.

LENGTH: 13–15 inches.

WEIGHT: 2.3 ounces (65 grams).

VOCALIZATION TAPES: D, BB.

RANGE: Southeastern Mexico to northwestern Costa Rica.

ELEVATIONAL RANGE: Sea level to 2,600 feet.

Turquoise-browed Motmot adult

One of the most delightful experiences for tourists exploring Costa Rica's wildlands is encountering birds unlike anything ever seen before. Motmots are such birds. They leave the observer with lasting memories of their form, beauty, and rich colors. The Turquoise-browed Motmot is one of six motmots in the country. Others are the Tody, Broad-billed, Keel-billed, Rufous, and Blue-crowned Motmots. The Turquoise-browed Motmot has a slender greenish and turquoise body, with a rufous back and breast, a black mask and bill, a black throat patch edged by turquoise, bright iridescent turquoise stripes over the eyes, and a long, slender tail with bare central veins above "racquet tips" on the two central tail feathers. When alarmed, the motmot twitches its tail back and forth like a pendulum.

The Turquoise-browed Motmot lives in dry forests of Guanacaste. Sitting quietly in the cover of brushy thickets and small trees, it watches for small lizards, snakes, beetles, spiders, grasshoppers, katydids, butterflies, dragonflies, and bees. When prey is spotted, the motmot flies out and snatches the creature from its perch or in flight. The motmot flies back to its perch, thrashes the creature against the perch to dispatch it, and subsequently swallows it. Its call is a series of single notes, spaced at intervals of five to ten seconds, that have the quality of a coarse, brief, distant train whistle.

Motmots are closely related to kingfishers, and their reproductive behavior is similar. They are monogamous and nest in burrows in dirt banks from May through June. The burrows may penetrate four to five feet into the bank. The young are fed insects and small lizards for about four weeks before they fledge.

The Turquoise-browed Motmot is found throughout forests of Guanacaste, including Palo Verde, Guanacaste, Santa Rosa, and Carara NPs and Lomas Barbudal BR. It can be seen at La Pacífica, Hacienda Solimar, La Ensenada Lodge, and in other dry forest habitats. The "trick" to spotting this motmot is to look into dry forest thickets and small trees, four to eight feet above the ground, and watch for the movement of the pendulum-like tail feathers.

Blue-crowned Motmot
(Blue-diademed Motmot)

Momotus momota

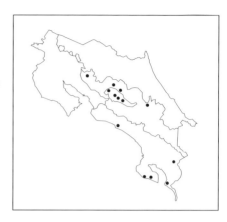

COSTA RICAN NAMES: ***Pájaro bobo;
momoto común.***

13/15 trips; 67 sightings.

STATUS: Permanent resident.

LENGTH: 15–17 inches.

WEIGHT: 4.2 ounces (120 grams).

VOCALIZATION TAPES: A, B, D, I, S,
T, Y, BB.

RANGE: Northeastern Mexico to
northern Argentina.

ELEVATIONAL RANGE: Sea level to
7,000 feet.

The Blue-crowned Motmot is one of the most beautiful and widespread of Costa Rica's motmots. It inhabits backyards and gardens throughout the country. Early in the morning, its deep, ventriloquial "whoot-whoot" call is one of the country's most memorable bird sounds. Since the top of the head is crowned with an iridescent pale blue circle, Dr. Alexander Skutch calls this bird the Blue-diademed Motmot. The long, racquet-tipped tail often swings from side to side as the bird quietly sits in the shady understory.

This motmot is found in riparian forests in Guanacaste, moist and wet forests of low and middle elevations, second growth, shade coffee plantations, mixed woodland, pastures, wooded ravines, wooded backyards, and residential areas of the Central Plateau. The Blue-crowned Motmot sits quietly on horizontal branches in the understory, where it watches for small lizards, beetles, walking sticks, cicadas, katydids, spiders, nestling birds, and small snakes. Once prey is spotted, the motmot flies out, captures the creature, and returns to a perch. This motmot may follow army ants to capture prey flushed by the ants. Fruits are occasionally eaten, and sometimes it visits bird feeders to eat bananas, papayas, and watermelon.

Nesting occurs from March through May in burrows that are excavated in cut banks along creeks or rivers, roadsides, or steep hillsides. The burrow may be five to fourteen feet back from the entrance and have three to four eggs inside. Both parents incubate the eggs and care for the young.

The Blue-crowned Motmot's unusual distribution includes the Central Plateau and surrounding suburbs of San José, Monteverde Cloud Forest Reserve, Hotel El Pórtico at San José de la Montaña, Poás NP, and Rancho Naturalista. It inhabits gallery forests of Guanacaste but is absent in the Caribbean lowlands. In the southern Pacific lowlands, it occurs at Manuel Antonio and Corcovado NPs, Sirena Biological Station, Lapa Ríos, Rancho Casa Grande, Corcovado Lodge Tent Camp, and Tiskita Jungle Lodge. Among the best places to see this motmot are the Wilson Botanical Garden and Rancho Naturalista, where it visits bird feeders, and on the grounds of Xandari Plantation Hotel at Alajuela. Since this bird is difficult to spot, walk slowly, stop frequently, and scan the low horizontal branches. One will frequently materialize before your eyes.

Blue-crowned Motmot adult

JACAMAR FAMILY (Galbulidae)

Rufous-tailed Jacamar

Galbula ruficauda

Costa Rican names: ***Gorrión de montaña; jacamar rabirrufo***.

10/15 trips; 18 sightings.

Status: Permanent resident.

Length: 9 inches.

Weight: 1.0 ounce (27 grams).

Vocalization tapes: B, D, T, BB, CC.

Range: Southern Mexico to north-eastern Argentina.

Elevational range: Sea level to 4,000 feet.

Rufous-tailed Jacamar adult female, with buffy throat patch; male throat patch is white

A large number of Costa Rican birds have stunning iridescent colors. Trogons, hummingbirds, and motmots provide vibrant and colorful rainforest memories, but if you ever see a Rufous-tailed Jacamar in full sunlight, you will have seen the magic of iridescence at its finest. The metallic green back and throat band nearly glow and at times take on shimmering bronzy to coppery tones. The iridescent effect is not caused by pigment in the feathers, which are actually dull brown to gray. The structure of the feathers refracts sunlight like a prism to create the colors you see. The throat of the male is white and that of the female is buffy. Jacamars look like enormous hummingbirds with long, straight bills held at an upturned angle. Because of the unusual position of the eyes, when the bill is upturned the bird is actually looking forward.

The Rufous-tailed Jacamar is a bird of the forest edge, second growth, streamsides, and forests with an open understory. A jacamar will sit quietly on a favorite perch within two to fifteen feet of the ground and watch for passing butterflies, dragonflies, bees, and beetles. When one is spotted, the jacamar flies out from its perch and grasps the insect in flight with its long bill. It then returns to its perch, removes the insect's wings, and eats it. A well-used perch will have many butterfly wings on the ground below. Jacamars are partial to perches that overlook a muddy or sandy streamside bank that is visited by butterflies or to perches overlooking rotten, fallen fruit that is attracting butterflies.

The reproductive behavior of jacamars is similar to motmots and kingfishers. Both parents excavate a burrow into a cut bank or termitary and share the duties of incubation. On observing the emergence of young jacamars from an earthen burrow, Dr. Alexander Skutch wrote: "They were truly gems from the earth, as scintillating as any diamond, emerald, or other precious stone."

The Rufous-tailed Jacamar inhabits moist and wet lowlands and foothills of the Caribbean and southern Pacific slopes. On the Caribbean slope, it occurs at La Selva Biological Station, Rara Avis, and Rancho Naturalista. On the southern Pacific slope, this jacamar can be encountered along trails at Carara NP, Villa Lapas, Sirena Biological Station in Corcovado NP, and the Wilson Botanical Garden. One of the best ways to find this bird is to learn its calls: single, high-pitched squeaks that sound like a baby's "squeaky toy"; a series of about twelve to fifteen high-pitched squeaks at the same pitch given in rapid succession; and a high-pitched trill that descends in pitch over a several-second duration.

PUFFBIRD FAMILY (Bucconidae)

White-necked Puffbird

Notharchus macrorhynchos

COSTA RICAN NAME: **Buco collarejo**.

10/15 trips; 14 sightings.

STATUS: Permanent resident.

LENGTH: 9.5–10 inches.

WEIGHT: 3.7 ounces (105 grams).

VOCALIZATION TAPE: U.

RANGE: Southern Mexico to northeastern Argentina.

ELEVATIONAL RANGE: Sea level to
2,000 feet.

Puffbirds are like motmots and jacamars in their perching and hunting behavior, but they lack iridescent colors. Five puffbirds occur in Costa Rica: the White-necked, Pied, and White-whiskered Puffbirds; the Lanceolated Monklet, and the White-fronted Nunbird. The White-necked Puffbird is easily identified by its short, rounded body; thick, straight bill; and bold black-and-white markings that include a black cap and a black bar across the chest.

The White-necked Puffbird inhabits dry to wet forests in the lowlands of both slopes. It is usually found at forest edges and in forest clearings where scattered tall trees or power lines provide hunting perches. This bird perches in the open and sits quietly for long periods as it scans the surrounding area for

White-necked Puffbird adult

insects and small lizards. With its large keen eyes, it can spot small insects up to sixty feet away. After prey is captured, the puffbird returns to its perch and beats it against the branch to dispatch it before eating it.

In the Caribbean lowlands, the White-necked Puffbird may be seen along the canals of Tortuguero NP and on the grounds of tourism lodges adjacent to mature forest—like Tortuga Lodge and Pizote Lodge. On the Pacific slope, this puffbird can be encountered in Guanacaste, Palo Verde, Santa Rosa, and Manuel Antonio NPs and Lomas Barbudal BR.

Emerald Toucanet adult

TOUCAN FAMILY (Ramphastidae)

Emerald Toucanet
(Blue-throated Toucanet)

Aulacorhynchus prasinus

> COSTA RICAN NAMES: *Curré;*
> *tucancillo verde.*
>
> 14/15 trips; 49 sightings.
>
> STATUS: Permanent resident; endemic
> highland subspecies.
>
> LENGTH: 12.5–14.5 inches.
>
> WEIGHT: 6.3 ounces (180 grams).
>
> VOCALIZATION TAPES: B, D, X, AA,
> BB, CC.
>
> RANGE: Southern Mexico to eastern
> Peru.
>
> ELEVATIONAL RANGE: 2,600–8,000
> feet.

Among the favorite birds of Costa Rica's forests are toucans. Their bright and varied colors, interesting calls, and "outrageous" bill design always steal the show during a rainforest outing. Toucan family members include Keel-billed

315

and Chestnut-mandibled Toucans and four smaller species: Emerald and Yellow-eared Toucanets and Collared and Fiery-billed Aracaris. The Emerald Toucanet is easily distinguished by its bright green plumage. Only about a foot long, it is the smallest toucan in the country and is found only at middle and higher elevations. In contrast, others occupy lowland and middle elevations. In the highlands of Costa Rica and western Panama, this toucanet is geographically isolated and has a blue throat. It is a separate subspecies (*A. p. caeruleogularis*) from Emerald Toucanets in Mexico, which have a white throat.

The Emerald Toucanet is found in cloud forests, montane forests, second growth, forest edges, mixed pastures, and woodlands. It is frequently encountered in small flocks of six to eight that roam the forest in search of fruiting trees, lizards, and insects. This toucanet is frequently mobbed and scolded by songbirds because it eats eggs and young from other birds' nests. The call is a low-pitched chirp that resembles the bark of a small dog.

In northern regions, look for the Emerald Toucanet in the Monteverde Cloud Forest Reserve and surrounding lands, La Virgen del Socorro, Hotel El Pórtico near San José de la Montaña on Barva Volcano, and in Poás NP. In the Cerro de la Muerte and Talamanca Mountains, the Emerald Toucanet can be seen at Savegre Mountain Lodge and in the San Gerardo de Dota area. It can also be seen in forests along the PAH at kilometers 66 and 96. It is sometimes found at the Wilson Botanical Garden and visits bird feeders there to eat bananas.

Collared Aracari

Pteroglossus torquatus

> Costa Rican names: ***Cusingo; tití; félix; tucancillo collarejo***.
>
> 11/14 trips; 52 sightings.
>
> Status: Permanent resident.
>
> Length: 15–17 inches.
>
> Weight: 8.1 ounces (230 grams).
>
> Vocalization tapes: B, D, T, BB, CC.
>
> Range: Southern Mexico to western Ecuador.
>
> Elevational range: Sea level to 3,900 feet.

Aracaris (pronounced "ara-sorry") are the most colorful members of the toucan family in Costa Rica. It is suspected that the two aracaris in this country have a common ancestor. However, geographic isolation caused by the country's mountain ranges has separated the birds for so long that natural selection has resulted in the development of two separate species. The one in the Caribbean lowlands, the Collared Aracari, is black over the back and tail and has a colorful pattern of yellow, red, and black on the breast. The call is a shrill, two-note "cheep-eep" in which the second note is higher than the first.

The Collared Aracari travels in small flocks of six to fifteen in second growth, forest edges, and openings with scattered trees. The additional sun-light in these areas stimulates fruiting of trees and shrubs that provide foods, including fruits of *Protium,* palms, and *Cecropia.* These birds roost at night as family groups in tree cavities.

Look for this bird at Tortuguero NP, Tortuga Lodge, La Selva Biological Sta-tion, El Gavilán Lodge, and in the Caribbean lowlands east from Los Inocentes Lodge to Guacimo, Guapiles, Limón, and south along the coast to Cahuita NP. At Rancho Naturalista they regularly visit the feeders to eat bananas. Some sightings occur in Guanacaste, and they can be seen in eastern portions of Santa Rosa NP.

Collared Aracari adult

Fiery-billed Aracari

Pteroglossus frantzii

COSTA RICAN NAMES: ***Cusingo;
tucancillo piquianaranjado***.

12/15 trips; 32 sightings.

STATUS: Permanent resident; endemic
southern Pacific lowland species.

LENGTH: 15–17 inches.

WEIGHT: 8.8 ounces (250 grams).

RANGE: Southwestern Costa Rica and
western Panama.

ELEVATIONAL RANGE: Sea level to
5,000 feet.

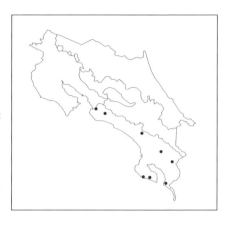

The Fiery-billed Aracari has a stunning orangish-red, yellow, and black bill that leaves little doubt about its identity. The bright yellow breast is highlighted by reddish smudges, a red breast band edged with black, and a black central spot. The call is similar to the two-note call of the Collared Aracari. The Fiery-billed Aracari is found only in Costa Rica's Pacific southern lowlands and adjacent areas of western Panama.

This colorful member of the toucan family inhabits the upper canopy of mature forests, forest edges, and pastures with scattered trees. It travels through the forest in flocks of about six to ten birds. Among fruits eaten are those of *Protium, Dipterodendron, Lacistema, Souroubea,* and pokeweed (*Phytolacca*). The aracari's long bill aids in reaching ripe fruits. This bird also raids

the nests of other birds and eats the eggs and young. At night, families of aracaris roost in the same tree cavity.

The Fiery-billed Aracari may be encountered in Carara, Corcovado, and Manuel Antonio NPs and Drake Bay Wilderness Resort, Rancho Casa Grande, Lapa Ríos, Villa Lapas, Corcovado Lodge Tent Camp, and Tiskita Jungle Lodge. Other locations include the San Isidro del General area and Dr. Alexander Skutch's forest reserve, Los Cusingos, which is named after the Fiery-billed Aracari. It also occurs at middle elevations like at San Vito and the Wilson Botanical Garden.

Fiery-billed Aracari adult

Keel-billed Toucan

Keel-billed Toucan

Ramphastos sulfuratus

COSTA RICAN NAMES: **Curré negro; tucán pico iris.**

12/15 trips; 47 sightings.

STATUS: Permanent resident.

LENGTH: 20–23 inches.

WEIGHT: 1 pound 1.6 ounces (500 grams).

VOCALIZATION TAPES: B, D, S, T, BB, CC.

RANGE: Southern Mexico to Colombia and Venezuela.

ELEVATIONAL RANGE: Sea level to 4,000 feet.

319

Keel-billed Toucan view from above showing slender bill profile

The large and beautiful Keel-billed Toucan is one of the most memorable birds in Costa Rica. Referred to as the Rainbow-billed Toucan by the ornithologist Alexander Skutch, this toucan has a huge bill that is a fascinating blend of yellow, orange, lime green, and pastel blue with a cherry-red tip. Although the bill looks thick and clumsy, it has a slender profile when viewed from above and is used with great precision when plucking ripe fruits. The call is a series of shrill, ascending trilled chirps that sound more like the call of a giant cricket than a bird.

This toucan inhabits Caribbean lowland and middle-elevation forests, including older second growth and pastures interspersed with mature trees. The Keel-billed Toucan travels through the canopy in small flocks of up to six birds. The diet includes fruits of *Virola, Protium, Alchornea,* figs (*Ficus*), *Cupania, Cnestidium, Didymopanax,* and palm fruits (*Astrocaryum* and *Iriartea*). Small lizards, spiders, snakes, insects, and the eggs and nestlings of small birds are also eaten.

The Keel-billed Toucan is regularly encountered in the Caribbean lowlands, including Tortuguero and Cahuita NPs, La Selva Biological Station, and the region east of Los Inocentes Lodge. At higher elevations, it is common in the Monteverde area and at Rancho Naturalista.

Chestnut-mandibled Toucan (Swainson's Toucan)

Ramphastos swainsonii

> COSTA RICAN NAMES: *Quioro; Dios-te-dé; gran curré negro; tucán de Swainson.*
>
> 12/15 trips; 76 sightings.
>
> STATUS: Permanent resident.
>
> LENGTH: 22 inches.
>
> WEIGHT: 1 pound 10.4 ounces (750 grams).
>
> VOCALIZATION TAPES: BB, CC.
>
> RANGE: Eastern Honduras to northern Colombia.
>
> ELEVATIONAL RANGE: Sea level to 6,000 feet.

Chestnut-mandibled Toucan adult

The Chestnut-mandibled Toucan is the largest toucan in Costa Rica. It is easily distinguished from the Keel-billed Toucan by the large bill that is chestnut brown below and bright yellow above. The call is a repetitious series of ascending squeals, each followed by two ascending squeaks.

The habits of this toucan are similar to those of the Keel-billed Toucan. Small flocks roam the canopy of mature forest searching for fruiting trees, insects, small vertebrates, and occasional eggs and nestlings of small birds. This toucan can often be seen calling from the tops of canopy trees.

This bird is found in many of the same Caribbean lowland sites as the Keel-billed Toucan, including Tortuguero and Cahuita NPs, La Selva Biological Station, and lowlands east of Los Inocentes Lodge. However, it also occurs in the southern Pacific lowlands. It may be encountered at Carara and Corcovado NPs, Sirena Biological Station, Lapa Ríos, Rancho Casa Grande, Villa Lapas, Corcovado Lodge Tent Camp, and Tiskita Jungle Lodge. Other sites include the Talari Mountain Lodge near San Isidro del General and the Wilson Botanical Garden.

WOODPECKER FAMILY (Picidae)

Acorn Woodpecker

Melanerpes formicivorus

Costa Rican name: ***Carpintero careto***.

10/15 trips; 32 sightings.

Status: Permanent resident.

Length: 8.3–9.3 inches.

Weight: 3.0 ounces (85 grams).

Vocalization tapes: D, F, BB.

Range: Western United States to Colombia.

Elevational range: 5,000–10,000 feet.

High in the montane forests of Cerro de la Muerte and the Talamanca Mountains is a boldly marked woodpecker well known for its ecological relationship to oaks—the Acorn Woodpecker. The clownlike facial markings of black, white, yellow, and red are unique among Costa Rica's woodpeckers. Only three other woodpeckers are known in the highlands: a local nonmigratory subspecies of Hairy Woodpecker, the Golden-olive Woodpecker, and the uncommon, migratory Yellow-bellied Sapsucker.

Acorn Woodpecker adult

Acorn Woodpecker adult at nest

Cache of acorns in fence post near Savegre Mountain Lodge

The Acorn Woodpecker inhabits high-elevation oak woodlands and adjacent pastures where there are scattered trees. Acorns and insects are the most common foods. It excavates small holes in tree bark, power poles, or even in fence posts as caches for those acorns. Holes are also drilled into the bark of live trees so it can feed on the sap that drains from those holes. This woodpecker also flies out to capture insects on the wing. A social species, it lives in groups of three to eight individuals that include offspring from previous nestings.

Nesting is an extended-family activity that occurs from April through August. A pair of woodpeckers excavate a hole high in a dead tree or a telephone pole. Nests usually contain three to five eggs, but sometimes more than one female in the family group lays eggs, so up to thirteen have been recorded. Both parents incubate the eggs. The young are cared for by the parents and by young from the previous one or two years' broods.

The Acorn Woodpecker can be observed in forests and pastures with scattered oak trees in Cerro de la Muerte and the Talamanca Mountains. Along the PAH, it can be encountered at kilometers 66 and 80 and on the grounds of Savegre Mountain Lodge.

Golden-naped Woodpecker

Melanerpes chrysauchen

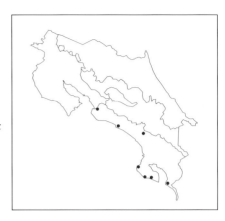

CostaRican name: ***Carpintero nuquidorado.***

12/15 trips; 22 sightings.

Status: Permanent resident; endemic southern Pacific lowland species.

Length: 7 inches.

Weight: 2.1 ounces (60 grams).

Range: Costa Rica and western Panama.

Elevational range: Sea level to 500 feet.

The Golden-naped Woodpecker is one of several "pairs" of rainforest species that have one counterpart in the Caribbean lowlands and one in the southern Pacific lowlands. They have a common ancestor and have been geographically separated by the country's mountains for so long that they have developed through natural selection into separate species. The corresponding Caribbean lowland species is the Black-cheeked Woodpecker. Both birds have a black stripe through the eye, a creamy-buff breast, a horizontal yellow bar across the face above the bill, a reddish-orange belly, and a red cap. However, the back of the Golden-naped Woodpecker's head (the nape) is bright yellowish gold. The back is black with white down the center, and the tertial feathers are tipped with white.

Living in family groups of three to six, this bird occupies the upper and middle canopy of moist and wet forests in the southern Pacific lowlands. It also occurs in adjacent forest openings and pastures that have scattered trees. The Golden-naped Woodpecker's diet includes insect larvae and beetles that live under the bark and in the wood of rainforest trees. A variety of fruits are also eaten, including *Cecropia* and bananas.

Nesting occurs from March through June in the trunk of a tall dead tree. This is one of the few birds whose nesting habit is for both parents to spend the night together on the nest. After fledging, the young stay with the parents until the following year's nesting season. They all sleep together in a tree cavity or in the nesting tree. Sometimes this woodpecker nests twice in the same breeding season. When it does, the four-month-old females from the first brood help care for the second brood.

The Golden-naped Woodpecker, endemic to southwestern Costa Rica and western Panama, inhabits Carara, Manuel Antonio, and Corcovado NPs. It can be seen at Sirena Biological Station within Corcovado NP and at Lapa Ríos,

Rancho Casa Grande, Villa Lapas, Drake Bay Wilderness Resort, Corcovado Lodge Tent Camp, and Tiskita Jungle Lodge. In the San Isidro del General area, this woodpecker can be observed in Dr. Alexander Skutch's forest reserve, Los Cusingos, and at the Wilson Botanical Garden.

Golden-naped Woodpecker adult

Adult in palm-tree nest cavity, Corcovado Lodge Tent Camp

Black-cheeked Woodpecker

Melanerpes pucherani

COSTA RICAN NAME: **Carpintero carinegro.**

10/15 trips; 34 sightings.

Status: Permanent resident.

LENGTH: 7.0–7.5 inches.

WEIGHT: 2.2 ounces (63 grams).

VOCALIZATION TAPES: S, T, CC.

RANGE: Southeastern Mexico to western Ecuador.

ELEVATIONAL RANGE: Sea level to 3,900 feet.

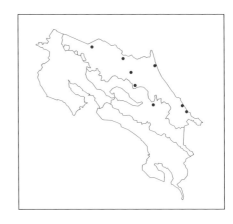

The Black-cheeked Woodpecker is the common rainforest species of the Caribbean slope that is closely related to the Golden-naped Woodpecker of the southern Pacific lowland forests. It has a black stripe through the eye and cheek area, a yellow bar in front of the eyes, a creamy-buff breast, and a reddish-orange belly. It differs from the Golden-naped Woodpecker in having a red crown that extends all the way down the back of the head. The back has a ladder pattern of white lines on a black background.

This woodpecker inhabits all levels of mature moist and wet forests, older second growth, and adjacent pastures that have scattered live or dead trees. It explores dead wood, epiphytes, and tree trunks for insect larvae, beetles, ter-

Black-cheeked Woodpecker adult at feeder

mites, and ants. Flying insects are also spotted from a perch and captured on the wing. The diverse diet includes nectar from Balsa (*Ochroma*) and kapok (*Ceiba*) flowers, fruits, berries, and *Cecropia* fruits. At the bird feeders of Rancho Naturalista, this bird is attracted to cooked rice, and at the Tilajari Resort Hotel it comes to the feeders for papayas.

The Black-cheeked Woodpecker, found only on the Caribbean slope, can be seen in Tortuguero NP and southeast along the Caribbean coast to Cahuita NP. Farther inland it occurs at La Selva Biological Station, the surrounding Puerto Viejo en Sarapiquí area, Rainforest Aerial Tram, and lower levels of Braulio Carrillo NP. This bird regularly occurs at Rancho Naturalista.

Hoffmann's Woodpecker

Melanerpes hoffmannii

> Costa Rican name: ***Carpintero de Hoffmann.***
>
> 14/15 trips; 55 sightings.
>
> Status: Permanent resident.
>
> Length: 7.5–8.0 inches.
>
> Weight: 2.4 ounces (68 grams).
>
> Vocalization tape: BB.
>
> Range: Southern Honduras to Costa Rica.
>
> Elevational range: Sea level to 7,000 feet.

Hoffmann's Woodpecker male, with red on crown.

Hoffmann's Woodpecker, the most common woodpecker of Guanacaste and the Central Plateau, resembles the Red-bellied Woodpecker of the eastern United States, except that the nape is yellow. The crown is red, the black back has a ladder pattern, the breast is creamy tan, and the belly is yellowish. The female lacks the red crown. Hoffmann's Woodpecker is closely related to the Red-crowned Woodpecker of the southern Pacific slope. In Carara NP and Villa Lapas, the ranges of the two species overlap, so in that area it is possible to see woodpeckers intermediate in characteristics between the two species.

Hoffmann's Woodpecker occurs in tropical dry forest and surrounding woodlands that have been cleared as pastures, shade coffee plantations, ranches, backyards, and gardens. It explores dead wood and bark for insect larvae, ants, and beetles. Fruits, bananas, berries, and *Cecropia* fruits are eaten, as well as the nectar of balsa (*Ochroma*) and African tulip tree (*Spathodea campanulata*) flowers.

The distribution of Hoffmann's Woodpecker encompasses almost all of the Guanacaste region, including ranches, resorts, NPs, and BRs. It also occurs in the Monteverde area, throughout the Central Plateau, south to Carara NP, and east to the Turrialba area and Rancho Naturalista. This woodpecker is readily attracted to a tape recording of the Ferruginous Pygmy-Owl.

Lineated Woodpecker

Dryocopus lineatus

COSTA RICAN NAMES: *Carpintero lineado; picamadero barbirrayado*.
14/15 trips; 38 sightings.
STATUS: Permanent resident.
LENGTH: 12.5–13.5 inches.
WEIGHT: 6.9 ounces (197 grams).
VOCALIZATION TAPES: B, D, S, V, BB, CC.
RANGE: Northern Mexico to northern Argentina.
ELEVATIONAL RANGE: Sea level to 3,900 feet.

The two largest woodpeckers in Costa Rica are the Lineated and the Pale-billed. Some obvious differences make these large-crested birds easy to distinguish. The bright red area includes the top of the Lineated Woodpecker's head but does not surround the eyes. The areas around the eyes are black. The Pale-billed Woodpecker has a crested head on which the bright red area surrounds the eyes and extends to the throat. The Lineated Woodpecker also has a white stripe on each side of the neck that extends across the face to the base of the bill. The Pale-billed Woodpecker has no such facial stripes. Finally, the white lines on the upper back do not meet to form a V on the Lineated Woodpecker, but they do meet to form a V on the back of the Pale-billed Woodpecker.

The loud, resonant pecking of the Lineated Woodpecker consists of a rapid-fire burst of pecks given during a two- to three-second interval. In contrast, the pecking of the Pale-billed Woodpecker is a sharp "double-peck" that gives that species one of its nicknames in Spanish: *dos golpes*, meaning "two blows."

The Lineated Woodpecker occurs at forest edges and in gallery forests, second growth, mixed woodlands, pastures, wooded plantations, and gardens. Food items include insect larvae, beetles, ants, and *Heliconia* fruits. It may open the trunks of *Cecropia* trees and eat the *Azteca* ants within. Lineated Woodpeckers live as mated pairs but sleep separately in different tree cavities. This woodpecker is found in gallery forests of Guanacaste and lowland moist and wet forests along the length of both Caribbean and Pacific slopes.

Adult female Lineated Woodpecker. The red of the crest does not include the eyes. On the male, the red of the crest extends forward to the back edge of the upper bill.

Adult male Pale-billed Woodpecker. Notice that the red of the crest includes the eyes. On the female, the front edge of the crest is black.

WOODCREEPER FAMILY (Dendrocolaptidae)

Wedge-billed Woodcreeper

Glyphorhynchus spirurus

COSTA RICAN NAME: ***Trepadorcito pico de cuña***.

9/15 trips; 25 sightings.

STATUS: Permanent resident.

LENGTH: 5.5–6.0 inches.

WEIGHT: 0.6 ounce (16.5 grams).

VOCALIZATION TAPES: R, T, W, CC.

RANGE: Southern Mexico to central Brazil.

ELEVATIONAL RANGE: Sea level to 5,000 feet.

Wedge-billed Woodcreeper adult in night roosting cavity on side of tree stump

The Wedge-billed Woodcreeper is a small bird with a plain olive-gray head and a rich cinnamon-rufous back and tail. Sexes are identical. The bill is short, with a straight, wedge-shaped profile. The throat is buffy, and there is a buff-colored stripe over the eye. The upper chest has fine buffy vertical streaking. This is one of the most common woodcreepers in the country. The Wedge-billed Woodcreeper has a fast, high-pitched warbling trill that consists of about seven interconnected notes.

This woodcreeper inhabits lowland moist and wet forests, older second forest, forest edges, and partially cleared forest openings. It forages for small insects and spiders by hopping upward on thick tree trunks. It feeds by using its wedge-shaped bill to pry up pieces of bark, moss, and lichen to expose prey underneath. At night this woodcreeper sleeps in vertical cracks in tree stumps just a few feet above the ground.

This woodcreeper occurs in Caribbean and southern Pacific lowlands. On the Caribbean slope, it is regularly encountered at La Selva Biological Station, Rancho Naturalista, and lower levels of Braulio Carrillo NP. On the Pacific slope, it can be observed at Carara NP, Wilson Botanical Garden, and Corcovado NP, including Sirena Biological Station, Lapa Ríos, Villa Lapas, Corcovado Lodge Tent Camp, and Tiskita Jungle Lodge.

Spot-crowned Woodcreeper (Spotted-crowned Woodcreeper)

Lepidocolaptes affinis

COSTA RICAN NAME: ***Trepador cabecipunteado***.

10/15 trips; 21 sightings.

STATUS: Permanent resident.

LENGTH: 8.0–8.5 inches.

WEIGHT: 1.2 ounces (35 grams).

VOCALIZATION TAPES: R, BB.

RANGE: Central Mexico to northern Bolivia.

ELEVATIONAL RANGE: 3,300–10,000 feet.

Spot-crowned Woodcreeper adult

Most woodcreepers live in tropical lowlands, but the Spot-crowned Wood-creeper is the exception, as it is the only one found primarily from 5,000 feet to the timberline. The crown of this chestnut-cinnamon woodcreeper has small, oval buffy spots that become elongated buffy streaks on the back of the head and the sides of the face, neck, and upper breast. The bill is pale, the throat is pale buffy, and the call is a high-pitched trill.

This woodcreeper lives in the same montane forests as the Acorn Wood-pecker. It climbs trees in forests and forest edges as well as scattered trees in adjacent pastures. The long, slightly decurved bill is used to probe bark, lichens, mosses, and epiphytes for insects and insect larvae. Sometimes this bird joins "mixed flocks" of Common or Sooty-capped Bush-Tanagers and other birds as they forage in the canopy.

The most dependable sites to see this bird are on the private trail at kilometer 66 of the PAH in Cerro de la Muerte, in San Gerardo de Dota from the PAH at kilometer 80 along the road descending to Savegre Mountain Lodge, and on the grounds of Savegre Mountain Lodge.

ANTBIRD FAMILY (Thamnophilidae)

Barred Antshrike

Thamnophilus doliatus

COSTA RICAN NAME:
Batara barreteado.

10/14 trips; 16 sightings.

STATUS: Permanent resident.

LENGTH: 6.5–7.0 inches.

WEIGHT: 1.0 ounce (28 grams).

VOCALIZATION TAPES: B, D, S, T, W, Y, BB.

RANGE: Northeastern Mexico to northeastern Argentina.

ELEVATIONAL RANGE: Sea level to 4,600 feet.

Antbirds include about 250 species in the American tropics. There are 23 in Costa Rica. These are generally secretive rainforest birds of earth-tone colors that live in the shaded obscurity of the forest floor. Depending on their size, shape, and habitat niche, birds in this family include antwrens, antvireos, antbirds, and antshrikes. These birds do not command attention like toucans, macaws, and quetzals do, but they provide a vital essence to the spirit and diversity of the rainforest. Members of this family are referred to as antbirds because some follow swarms of army ants and capture insects and other invertebrates as they attempt to escape from the ants. They do not eat the ants.

The Barred Antshrike is one of the most easily identified members of this family. The male has a pronounced bushy crest and fine zebra-striped barring over the entire body. The female has a prominent rufous crest and is rufous over the wings, tail, and back. The breast of the female is pale cinnamon, and the sides of the face and back of the neck have fine black stripes. The call is one of the great sounds of the rainforest. It is an accelerating series of staccato nasal notes, given over a five-second period, that increase in frequency as they are given and end with a higher-pitched squeak.

The Barred Antshrike inhabits brushy thickets and second growth of humid lowland forests and gallery forests in Guanacaste. It eats beetles, caterpillars, spiders, and other insects. Sometimes it follows army ant swarms.

This antshrike can be encountered in gallery forests of Guanacaste and at Carara NP, Los Cusingos, Villa Lapas, Tiskita Jungle Lodge, and Lomas Barbudal BR. It occurs in the Caribbean lowlands at La Selva Biological Station and EARTH University near Guapiles. It is usually necessary to record and play back the call of this antbird in order to get it to briefly emerge from thick underbrush so it can be seen. Some Costa Rican naturalist guides carry a tape recorder and directional microphone in order to attract and provide viewing opportunities for these seldom-seen birds.

Barred Antshrike adult male

Bicolored Antbird

Gymnopithys leucaspis
> Costa Rican name: ***Hormiguero bicolor.***
> 1/15 trips; 1 sighting.
> Status: Permanent resident.
> Length: 5.5–5.8 inches.
> Weight: 1.1 ounces (30 grams).
> Vocalization tapes: W, BB, CC.
> Range: Northern Honduras to western Brazil.
> Elevational range: Sea level to 5,600 feet.

Easily identified, the Bicolored Antbird is the only small antbird with a pure-white breast. The back is dark brown, and it has the "blue goggles" that also characterize Chestnut-backed and Immaculate Antbirds. This antbird follows swarms of army ants, often in the company of Tawny-winged Woodcreepers. This bird moves ahead of advancing ants, perching on low twigs and exposed roots. When a small creature tries to escape, the antbird flies down to snatch the insect or spider. It does not eat the ants.

The Bicolored Antbird inhabits moist and wet lowland and middle-elevation forests. It occurs in mature forest, second growth, and adjacent openings. The call is a good one for an avid birder to learn because it usually indicates that a swarm of army ants is nearby, and that may provide the opportunity to see other rarely seen rainforest birds following the ants. The call is a loud, brief, churry, buzzing note.

This antbird nests from April through September and usually places its nest in the hollow center of a dead tree or a palm stump near the ground. The distribution includes the Caribbean and southern Pacific lowlands and middle elevations. It has been observed at the Wilson Botanical Garden and on the hillside forest trail behind Corcovado Lodge Tent Camp.

Bicolored Antbird male

TITYRA FAMILY (Tityridae)

Black-crowned Tityra

Tityra inquisitor

COSTA RICAN NAME:
Tityra coroninegra.
9/15 trips; 16 sightings.
STATUS: Permanent resident.
LENGTH: 7.25 inches.
WEIGHT: 1.8 ounces (50 grams).
RANGE: Central Mexico to north-eastern Argentina.
ELEVATIONAL RANGE: Sea level to 4,000 feet.

The two tityras in Costa Rica are easy to identify: they are medium-sized birds with thick gray or pink bills, grayish-white bodies, black wings, and broad black bars across the tails. The Masked Tityra is named for the pink mask across its face and eyes. The Black-crowned Tityra is named for its black cap. Each has a short, rounded profile and a relatively short tail.

Habitat includes forest edges and clearings with scattered trees, from which the tityra scans the surrounding terrain for insects or fruit. When a food item is sighted, the tityra flies out and snatches it while on the wing. This bird is usually sighted in pairs or as family groups and is often in the company of Masked Tityras.

The Black-crowned Tityra can be observed in both the Caribbean and Pacific lowlands up to premontane levels. Among good locations to see it are Cahuita and Tortuguero NPs, La Selva Biological Field Station, and Rancho Naturalista on the Caribbean slope, and Hacienda Solimar, Carara and Manuel Antonio NPs, Talari Mountain Lodge, and the Wilson Botanical Garden on the Pacific slope.

Black-crowned Tityra adult

MANAKIN FAMILY (Pipridae)

Long-tailed Manakin

Chiroxiphia linearis

COSTA RICAN NAMES: ***Toledo; saltarín toledo; saltanix colilargo.***

4/15 trips; 8 sightings.

STATUS: Permanent resident.

LENGTH: 4.5 inches (plus two 4- to 6-inch tail feathers on the male).

WEIGHT: 0.7 ounce (19 grams).

VOCALIZATION TAPE: BB.

RANGE: Southern Mexico to Costa Rica.

ELEVATIONAL RANGE: Sea level to 5,000 feet.

One of the most stunning birds in Costa Rica is the ornately marked Long-tailed Manakin. It is one of ten manakins in the country. The others are the Red-capped, Blue-crowned, White-crowned, Lance-tailed, White-ruffed, Orange-collared, and White-collared Manakins; Gray-headed Piprites; and Thrush-like Schiffornis. Manakins are well known for their lek behavior during the breeding season.

The male Long-tailed Manakin has a small, rounded black body highlighted by a red crest, a powder-blue back, bright orange legs, and two long, slender black tail feathers. The female is olive green above with paler greenish hues below. Young males resemble the females and do not acquire their adult plumage until about four years of age. The three-note call, referred to as "to-le-do," rises from the original note to a higher pitch and then drops back to the original pitch. This whistled call, given synchronously by two males displaying on a lek, has a rich resonance and a harmonic or echolike quality that sounds like the bird is whistling from the bottom of a well.

While most manakins are characteristic of lowland rainforests, the Long-tailed Manakin is found primarily in dry forests and gallery forests of Guanacaste and western portions of the Central Plateau. It also occurs in second-growth and mangrove forests, where these birds watch for small fruits, which they pluck while on the wing. Preferred fruits include *Ardisia revoluta, Cecropia peltata, Cocoloba caracasana, Trichilia cuneata, Trema micrantha, Muntingia calabura,* and *Psychotria* spp.

Mating season extends from March through September. The courtship ritual is incredible and bizarre! Pairs of bonded males associate with each other throughout the year, although no mating is involved. When mating season ar-

rives, leks form that are multiple "arenas," each occupied by a pair, or sometimes a trio, of displaying males. The pairs of males give synchronous "toledo"
vocalizations until a female arrives. With both males facing the female, they alternately jump into the air in an acrobatic display that may include a hundred
alternating jumps! The dominant of the two males eventually mates with the
female. Then the female leaves to build the nest, lay the eggs, and raise the
young by herself while the two males continue their life together.

Look for the Long-tailed Manakin in gallery forests in Santa Rosa, Guanacaste, Palo Verde, and Carara NPs and Lomas Barbudal BR; near Monteverde
at the Ecological Farm and Children's Rainforest; along the Río Corobicí trail
at La Pacífica; and at Hacienda Solimar and La Ensenada Lodge. It will typically be observed low in thick shrubbery and at mid-levels of the forest canopy.
In the Central Plateau, it can be encountered at La Universidad de la Paz in El
Rodeo near Ciudad Colón and on the grounds of Xandari Plantation.

Long-tailed Manakin adult male

Long-tailed Manakin subadult male, similar to female

White-collared Manakin

Manacus candei

> Costa Rican names: ***Bailarín;
> saltarín cuelliblanco***.
>
> 9/15 trips; 30 sightings.
>
> Status: Permanent resident.
>
> Length: 4.25 inches.
>
> Weight: 0.7 ounce (18.5 grams).
>
> Vocalization tapes: T, BB, CC.
>
> Range: Southeastern Mexico to
> western Panama.
>
> Elevational range: Sea level to
> 3,200 feet.

The White-collared Manakin adds a spritelike presence to Caribbean lowland rainforests—even when it is not seen. The male has a black cap; a white throat, neck, and shoulder area; black wings; a yellow belly; and bright orange legs. When the male is displaying, the throat feathers of its neck are extended so far forward that the bill almost disappears amid the throat feathers. The female is greenish with a yellow belly and orange legs.

In the southern Pacific lowlands is a geographically isolated species closely related to the White-collared Manakin: the Orange-collared Manakin. These two birds appear to have had a common ancestor. Habitat for the White-collared Manakin includes primary and secondary rainforest understory, thick forest margins, and stream edges. Preferred foods consist of small fruits like *Hamelia* and insects. These foods are plucked while the bird is on the wing.

White-collared Manakin adult male

This manakin nests from April through August. Several males display in leks in thick understory. Each male establishes a display area and clears all debris from the ground in a four-foot-diameter plot that has several vertical saplings. As each male leaps back and forth from one stem to the other, the throat feathers are extended forward and the wings snap loudly with each jump. When a female enters the display area, the pair jumps simultaneously, passing in mid-jump. When the males are on a lek, they produce a sharp, loud snapping sound with their wings that travels far through the forest understory. It sounds like the loud snapping of fingers.

Among the best places to observe the White-collared Manakin are along the nature trail behind Tortuga Lodge, at Tortuguero and Cahuita NPs, along the Río Sarapiquí at Selva Verde Lodge, at La Selva Biological Field Station, and in the forests at Rancho Naturalista.

FLYCATCHER FAMILY (Tyrannidae)

Black Phoebe

Sayornis nigricans

    Costa Rican name: ***Mosquero de agua***.

    14/15 trips; 40 sightings.

    Status: Permanent resident.

    Length: 6 inches.

    Weight: 0.7 ounce (21 grams).

    Vocalization tapes: F, X.

    Range: Southwestern United States to northwestern Argentina.

    Elevational range: 2,000–7,200 feet.

Costa Rica's avifauna includes seventy-nine flycatchers, many of which can be difficult to identify. The Black Phoebe, however, is distinctive by its markings, behavior, and habitat. This medium-sized flycatcher is black with white in the lower central portion of the belly. Its tail-bobbing behavior and tendency to perch along wetland edges resembles characteristics of the Eastern Phoebe in North America. It is typically found along stream edges, where it sallies from perches to capture insects.

Black Phoebe adult

The Black Phoebe is found at middle and higher elevations along boulder-strewn streams. It is frequently found perching on buildings and power lines among homesteads and towns along streams. Food items include flies, wasps, bees, beetles, crickets, caterpillars, grasshoppers, and an occasional small fish.

In Caribbean lowlands and foothills, the Black Phoebe can be seen along the main highway to Limón on the Río Roca, the Río Blanco, and at the Río Sucio bridge on the road from Guacimo to La Selva Biological Station. In the southern Pacific region, it can be seen along the Río Chirripó Pacífico from the bridge between San Isidro del General and Dr. Skutch's reserve. At higher Pacific slope elevations, the Black Phoebe can be seen along the Río Grande de Orosí in Tapantí NP and along the Río Savegre at Savegre Mountain Lodge in San Gerardo de Dota.

Long-tailed Tyrant

Colonia colonus

> Costa Rican name: ***Mosquero coludo***.
>
> 8/15 trips; 20 sightings.
>
> Status: Permanent resident.
>
> Length: 5 inches, plus 4- to 4.75-inch-long tail feathers.
>
> Weight: 0.5 ounce (15 grams).
>
> Vocalization tape: CC.
>
> Range: Northeastern Honduras to northeastern Argentina.
>
> Elevational range: Sea level to 2,000 feet.

The Long-tailed Tyrant is another easily identified flycatcher. Small and black, it has a grayish cap that extends to the nape and merges into a whitish stripe down the back. A white horizontal stripe extends from above the bill past the eye. The male has two long, stringlike feathers that extend four to five inches beyond the tail. The female is similar but does not have the long tail feathers. The Long-tailed Tyrant perches in an upright posture so the tail feathers hang straight down. The profile is unique and conspicuous even at a distance.

An inhabitant of tropical lowlands, this flycatcher sits conspicuously on the highest branches of dead trees and on power lines in forest openings, meadows, plantations, stream edges, and in recently cleared forest lands. It flies out to capture flies, bees, and other insects on the wing and then returns to its perch. With the two long tail feathers streaming behind, it is a delight to watch. Pairs are often observed perching together. Stingless bees (*Trigona* sp.) and flying termites are common food items.

The Long-tailed Tyrant may be observed in Cahuita NP and the surrounding communities of Cahuita and Puerto Viejo, in the Limón region, along the canals of Tortuguero NP, and at La Selva Biological Field Station, Puerto Viejo en Sarapiquí, Rara Avis, and lower levels of Braulio Carrillo NP.

Long-tailed Tyrant adult

Tropical Kingbird

Tyrannus melancholicus

COSTA RICAN NAMES:
Tirano tropical; pecho amarillo.
15/15 trips; 165 sightings.
STATUS: Permanent resident.
LENGTH: 8.25 inches.
WEIGHT: 1.4 ounces (40 grams).
VOCALIZATION TAPES: A, B, D, F, V, X.
RANGE: Southeastern Arizona to central Argentina.
ELEVATIONAL RANGE: Sea level to 8,000 feet.

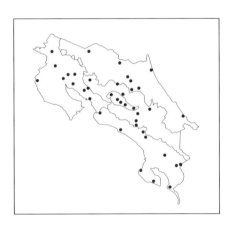

The ever present Tropical Kingbird, or "TK" as it is often called by birders, is one of the most common birds in Costa Rica. Its bright yellow breast and its tendency to sit on prominent perches in open areas make it easy to observe. Since there are several other flycatchers with yellow breasts that also sit in open areas, care should be taken to distinguish them from Tropical Kingbirds. Among the most common are the Great Kiskadee, Boat-billed Flycatcher, Social Flycatcher, and Gray-capped Flycatcher. The Boat-billed Flycatcher and Great Kiskadee have distinctive calls; they are larger and they have a black mask with a white stripe above the eyes. The Tropical Kingbird does not. The Social Flycatcher is smaller and has a proportionally smaller head. It has a gray stripe through the eyes and a white stripe above each eye. The Gray-capped Flycatcher is similar to the Social Flycatcher but has a white forehead and lacks the white stripe above the eye. The Tropical Kingbird also has a deeply notched tail.

The Tropical Kingbird is present in all regions of Costa Rica and adapts well to cities, farms, backyards, river edges, and cleared lands. The "TK" may fly out from its favorite perch to catch bees, dragonflies, beetles, wasps, and moths on the wing and then return to its perch. Several prey items may be captured on a single flight. The Tropical Kingbird may perch near flowers or mud puddles to capture butterflies. It has also been observed capturing prey from the surface of water and flying to the ground to capture insects or spiders. Wherever you stay in Costa Rica, there will probably be a Tropical Kingbird nearby. It is probably the easiest of all birds to encounter.

Tropical Kingbird adult

Great Kiskadee

Pitangus sulphuratus

COSTA RICAN NAMES: ***Bienteveo grande; cristofué; pechoamarillo***.

15/15 trips; 139 sightings.

STATUS: Permanent resident.

LENGTH: 9 inches.

WEIGHT: 2.4 ounces (68 grams).

VOCALIZATION TAPES: D, S, V, Y, BB, CC.

RANGE: Southern Texas to central Argentina.

ELEVATIONAL RANGE: Sea level to 5,000 feet.

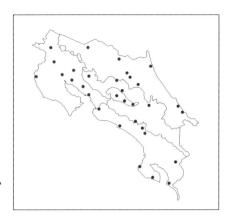

Like the Tropical Kingbird, the Great Kiskadee is one of the most common birds in Costa Rica. It is also one of the most vocal, announcing its presence from prominent perches with a loud "kis-ka-dee" call. This bird is easy to identify because it tells you its name! The bold markings include a bright yellow breast, a black mask, a white stripe above the eyes that extends to the back of the head, a black cap that usually conceals a yellow crown-patch, and an olive-

Great Kiskadee adult

brownish body. Distinguishing marks include rufous edges on the primary and secondary wing feathers and rufous tail feathers. The similar Boat-billed Flycatcher has a broader bill and lacks rufous markings on the wing and tail feathers. Its call is also very different from the Great Kiskadee's call. The Boat-billed Flycatcher has a call that sounds like an extended series of squeaks on an infant's "squeaky toy."

The Great Kiskadee is found in pastures, agricultural lands, forest edges, cities, suburban backyards, woodlands, and wetland edges. With its large size and formidable bill, it may sally from a perch to catch insects on the wing or fly to the ground to catch lizards, small snakes, mice, earthworms, spiders, grasshoppers, and beetles. It may plunge into shallow water to capture frogs, tadpoles, insects, and small fish. Fruit may be eaten from a perch or on the wing, and at feeders it will eat bananas. The Great Kiskadee may raid the nests of smaller birds and eat their eggs or young. Although the Great Kiskadee will commonly catch insects at ground level, the similar Boat-billed Flycatcher catches its insect prey at middle to higher levels of the forest canopy and rarely comes to the ground to catch insects.

From lowland to middle elevations of both slopes, the Great Kiskadee is present on the grounds and courtyards of most hotels, roadside restaurants, and wilderness lodges. Just listen for their "kis-ka-dee" call.

Yellowish Flycatcher

Empidonax flavescens
 Costa Rican name: ***Mosquerito amarillento***.
 6/15 trips; 12 sightings.
 Status: Permanent resident.
 Length: 5 inches.
 Weight: 0.4 ounce (12 grams).
 Vocalization tape: AA.
 Range: Southeastern Mexico to western Panama.
 Elevational range: 2,600–8,000 feet.

Most small flycatchers of the genus *Empidonax* are difficult to identify, but the "friendly" Yellowish Flycatcher of Costa Rica's mountains is easily approached. It has the most conspicuous whitish-yellow eye-ring of all *Empidonax* flycatchers. The back is yellowish olive, the breast is yellow, and there are two prominent yellowish wing bars.

The Yellowish Flycatcher inhabits montane forests, mountain pastures, and forest edges. Amid relatively open understory, it sits on perches that are sometimes no more than two feet from the ground. It flies out to pluck insects from foliage and on the ground. Small berries are sometimes eaten.

This bird occurs in mountainous regions through the length of the country. It has been observed at Hotel El Pórtico at San José de la Montaña and Tapantí NP, and it is regularly observed in wooded pastures adjacent to the cabins and trails at Savegre Mountain Lodge.

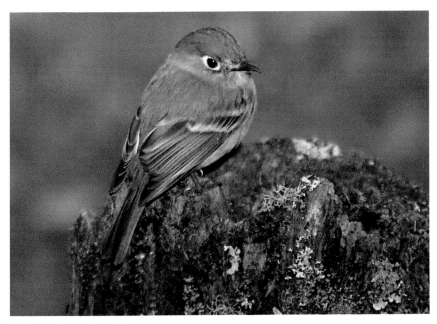

Yellowish Flycatcher adult

Black-capped Flycatcher

Empidonax atriceps

COSTA RICAN NAME: ***Mosquerito cabecinegro.***

11/15 trips; 22 sightings.

STATUS: Permanent resident; endemic highland species.

LENGTH: 4.5 inches.

WEIGHT: 0.3 ounce (9 grams).

RANGE: Costa Rica to western Panama.

ELEVATIONAL RANGE: 6,000–11,000 feet.

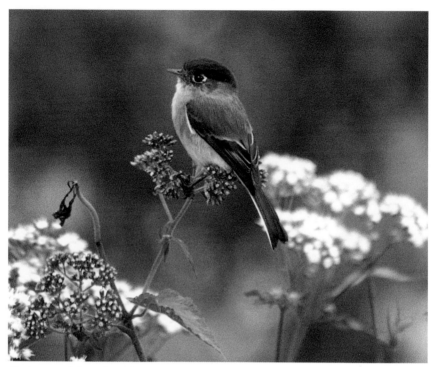

Black-capped Flycatcher adult

Three small, easily identified flycatchers are found at higher elevations and are unusual in their tolerance of humans: the Yellowish Flycatcher, Black-capped Flycatcher, and Tufted Flycatcher. Each can be approached closely. As the name implies, the Black-capped Flycatcher has a black cap, as well as a dark brown back and wings, brownish-tan chest, yellowish belly, and two brownish wing bars. The only other flycatcher with an obvious black cap is the Torrent Tyrannulet, which is silvery gray with dark wings and tail. The Torrent Tyrannulet is found primarily along mountain streams.

The Black-capped Flycatcher, often observed in pairs, is characteristic of montane forests, pastures, trails, and clearings. It perches on posts and branches where it has a view of the surrounding area. When an insect is sighted, it flies out to capture it on the wing and then returns to the same perch. Beetles, flies, and butterflies are among the prey eaten.

Endemic to the mountains surrounding the Central Plateau through the Talamanca Mountains to western Panama, this flycatcher can be observed in Poás and Irazú NPs and at higher elevations of Cerro de la Muerte. Along the PAH, it can be observed at kilometers 66, 77, 80, and 86. The Black-capped Flycatcher is regularly seen on the grounds and trails of Savegre Mountain Lodge.

Tufted Flycatcher

Mitrephanes phaeocercus

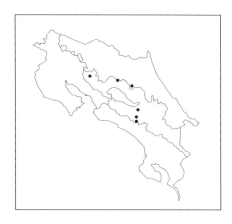

COSTA RICAN NAME: *Mosquerito moñudo*.

12/15 trips; 26 sightings.

STATUS: Permanent resident.

LENGTH: 4.75 inches.

WEIGHT: 0.3 ounce (8.5 grams).

VOCALIZATION TAPES: BB, CC.

RANGE: Northwestern Mexico to eastern Bolivia.

ELEVATIONAL RANGE: 2,300–10,000 feet.

The Tufted Flycatcher is the third of the three "friendly" flycatchers that can be observed in Costa Rica's mountains. The other two are the Yellowish Flycatcher and the Black-capped Flycatcher. These small birds are easily approached. The prominent crest and ochraceous color make this bird easy to identify.

In montane forests, this flycatcher occurs at forest edges, in pastures, and in light gaps within the forest. The Tufted Flycatcher watches the surrounding area from a favorite perch on a tree or shrub. When an insect passes, the bird flies out, captures it on the wing, and returns to its perch.

Tufted Flycatcher adult

The Tufted Flycatcher occurs along the foothills and higher elevations of both slopes. It can be seen along the road at La Virgen del Socorro and Braulio Carrillo and Tapantí NPs on the Caribbean slope. It also occurs at Monteverde Cloud Forest Reserve, in Cerro de la Muerte at kilometers 66 and 80, and at Savegre Mountain Lodge.

Common Tody-Flycatcher

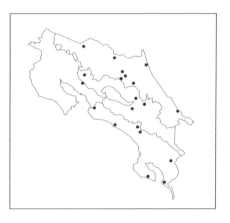

Todirostrum cinereum

COSTA RICAN NAMES: *Espatulilla común; pechita; tontilla.*

14/15 trips; 51 sightings.

STATUS: Permanent resident.

LENGTH: 3.75 inches.

WEIGHT: 0.2 ounce (6.5 grams).

VOCALIZATION TAPES: A, BB.

RANGE: Mexico to southern Brazil.

ELEVATIONAL RANGE: Sea level to 5,000 feet.

One of the smallest flycatchers in Costa Rica is the Common Tody-Flycatcher. Less than four inches long, it is identified by the black hood that extends over pale yellowish eyes, giving it a sinister hooded appearance. It also has a dark gray back, black tail, and bright yellow throat, breast, and belly. The black wing feathers have yellowish edges. Unique behaviors include constantly flipping the tail upward and walking sideways along branches while looking for prey.

Common Tody-Flycatcher adult

The Common Tody-Flycatcher is regularly encountered in backyards, courtyards, forest and wetland edges, and ornamental shrubbery of urban and rural homes. It occurs in second-growth lowland forests, plantations, and gallery and mangrove forests. This tody-flycatcher feeds by making extremely quick flights from its perch to trap flies, beetles, ants, wasps, and other insects against the foliage they are resting on. The relatively large, wide bill is an effective tool for such a hunting technique.

A bird of moist and wet lowland and middle-elevation habitats, the Common Tody-Flycatcher is found on both Caribbean and southern Pacific slopes. In the Caribbean region, it can be found in Cahuita and Tortuguero NPs, in Limón, and at the Tilajari Resort Hotel, the Guapiles and Guacimo area, La Selva Biological Station, Puerto Viejo en Sarapiquí vicinity, Rara Avis, and Rancho Naturalista. In the Pacific lowlands, it occurs at Carara and Manuel Antonio NPs, San Isidro del General, Wilson Botanical Garden, Quepos, Lapa Ríos, Villa Lapas, Rancho Casa Grande, Corcovado Lodge Tent Camp, and Tiskita Jungle Lodge.

Torrent Tyrannulet

Serpophaga cinerea

Costa Rican name: *Mosquerito guardarríos*.
13/15 trips; 27 sightings.
Status: Permanent resident.
Length: 4 inches.
Weight: 0.3 ounce (8 grams).
Vocalization tape: X.
Range: Costa Rica to northern Bolivia.
Elevational range: 800–6,500 feet.

Three birds are typically associated with the streams of Costa Rica's foothills and mountains: the Black Phoebe, the Torrent Tyrannulet, and the American Dipper. The Torrent Tyrannulet is a small, slender, pearly-gray flycatcher with a black cap, black wings, and black tail. It lives along fast-flowing, boulder-strewn streams, where it perches on rocks or on branches that extend over the water. From these perches, it sallies out to capture insects such as flies, damselflies, and stoneflies that may be in flight or perched on streamside vegetation.

The Torrent Tyrannulet is found in foothills and higher elevations along streams of both the Caribbean and Pacific slopes. It can be seen on the Caribbean slope from the bridge at La Virgen del Socorro and at the bridge

Torrent Tyrannulet adult

Torrent Tyrannulet nest on side of boulder; note whitewash below nest

crossing by the Catarata de la Paz (Peace Waterfall). On the Pacific slope, it can be observed along the Río Macho and Río Grande de Orosí in Tapantí NP and along the Río Savegre at Savegre Mountain Lodge.

Ochre-bellied Flycatcher

Mionectes oleagineus

> COSTA RICAN NAME: ***Mosquerito***
> ***aceitunado***.
>
> 9/15 trips; 15 sightings.
>
> STATUS: Permanent resident.
>
> LENGTH: 5 inches.
>
> WEIGHT: 0.5 ounce (13 grams).
>
> VOCALIZATION TAPES: G, T, U, BB,
> CC.
>
> RANGE: Mexico to central Brazil,
> Trinidad, and Tobago.
>
> ELEVATIONAL RANGE: Sea level to
> 4,000 feet.

Ochre-bellied Flycatcher adult feeding on fruits of *Heliconia rostrata*

The Ochre-bellied Flycatcher is interesting among flycatchers because its diet comprises mainly fruits and berries—not insects. The body is grayish olive-green without any stripes or wing bars. The belly has an "ochraceous" color that also is apparent under the wings when the bird is in flight.

355

Habitat includes lowland wet forest, second growth, courtyard areas, and clearings adjacent to forests. This incredibly agile flycatcher flies from a perch and plucks fruits from *Heliconia, Clusia, Faramea, Alchornea, Siparuna, Zanthoxylum,* mistletoe (*Gaiadendron*), palms, and members of the family Araceae. A few insects are also taken. Sometimes this bird forages as part of a mixed flock.

The reproductive behavior is quite different from most flycatchers. The males are promiscuous and do not form pair bonds. They form a leklike assembly of up to half a dozen males that are spaced in the mid-canopy about 50 to 160 feet apart. They sing and display by alternately raising each wing to display "their armpits"—the ochre colors of the underwing. This "wing-flipping" behavior takes place up to seven months of the year. After mating, the female leaves the male and raises two to three young in an elaborate pendulous sac-shaped nest that is about a foot high and four inches wide.

In the Caribbean lowlands, the Ochre-bellied Flycatcher can be observed in Cahuita NP, La Selva Biological Station, Selva Verde Lodge, and Rancho Naturalista. In the southern Pacific lowlands, this bird can be seen at Manuel Antonio and Corcovado NPs, Lapa Ríos, Villa Lapas, Rancho Casa Grande, Corcovado Lodge Tent Camp, Tiskita Jungle Lodge, Sirena Biological Station, and the Wilson Botanical Garden.

SWALLOW FAMILY (Hirundinidae)

Blue-and-white Swallow

Notiochelidon cyanoleuca

COSTA RICAN NAME: **Golondrina azul y blanco.**

15/15 trips; 94 sightings.

STATUS: Permanent resident; some southern migrants.

LENGTH: 4.25 inches.

WEIGHT: 0.4 ounce (10 grams).

RANGE: Nicaragua to Tierra del Fuego.

ELEVATIONAL RANGE: Sea level to 10,000 feet.

The most common swallow in Costa Rica is the Blue-and-white Swallow. The breast is snow white, and the top half of the head, the back, and the tail are deep glossy blue. This swallow is commonly seen resting on power lines and telephone wires outside homes and buildings at middle and higher elevations. Most are permanent residents, but from May through September some South American migrants are present.

In natural habitats, the Blue-and-white Swallow may be seen "flycatching"

Pair of adult Blue-and-white Swallows

over openings and wetlands in montane and premontane forests. It is far more abundant, however, in settled areas and around buildings. Among insects that are caught on the wing are beetles, flies, and wasps.

This monogamous swallow raises two broods of young from March through June. After fledging, the young return to the nest each night to sleep with the parents until they are two months old. The Blue-and-white Swallow is widespread in middle and higher elevations but uncommon on the Caribbean coast and Pacific coastal lowlands. There are some records at sea level at the outlet of the Río Barú at Playa Dominical.

Mangrove Swallow

Tachycineta albilinea

COSTA RICAN NAME: ***Golondrina lomiblanca.***

14/15 trips; 40 sightings.

STATUS: Permanent resident.

LENGTH: 5 inches.

WEIGHT: 0.1 ounce (14 grams).

RANGE: Northern Mexico to eastern Panama; coastal areas of northern Peru.

ELEVATIONAL RANGE: Sea level to 3,900 feet.

Mangrove Swallow adult

Complementing the distribution of the Blue-and-white Swallow, the Mangrove Swallow inhabits Caribbean and Pacific lowlands. This swallow is dark iridescent green above and snow white on the throat, chest, and belly. It has a white rump patch and a slender white line above each eye.

The Mangrove Swallow inhabits lowland canals, lakes, marshes, and mangrove lagoons, where it frequently perches in large groups on dead trees and stumps that project from the water. It forages over water and captures flies and other insects on the wing.

In the Caribbean lowlands, the mangrove swallow can be seen along the canals of Tortuguero NP, in wetlands of the Puerto Viejo en Sarapiquí area, at La Selva Biological Station, and from Limón to Cahuita. On the Pacific slope, it is widespread in wetlands of Guanacaste, along the entire coast, and inland to the Río Térraba valley. It is present in Carara, Palo Verde, Corcovado, Santa Rosa, Guanacaste, and Manuel Antonio NPs.

JAY FAMILY (Corvidae)

White-throated Magpie-Jay

Calocitta formosa

    COSTA RICAN NAMES:
    Urraca copetona; urraca; piapia azul.
    9/15 trips; 42 sightings.
    STATUS: Permanent resident.
    LENGTH: 18 inches.
    WEIGHT: 7.2 ounces (205 grams).
    VOCALIZATION TAPES: D, BB.
    RANGE: Central Mexico to Costa Rica.
    ELEVATIONAL RANGE: Sea level to
    4,000 feet.

One of the largest and most conspicuous songbirds in Guanacaste is the White-throated Magpie-Jay. This social and vocal bird is normally seen in family groups of five to ten birds and is quite attractive. The blue body, white breast, exceptionally long blue tail, and tall, forward-curving topknot feathers on its head make it unmistakable. A closely related species is found in Mexico: the Black-throated Magpie-Jay.

White-throated Magpie-Jay adult

The White-throated Magpie-Jay is found in savannas, dry forests, gallery forests, farmsteads, ranches, backyards, and woodlots. Roaming in family groups, these intelligent and omnivorous jays search for small lizards, caterpillars, frogs, beetles, grasshoppers, katydids, and cockroaches. Other foods include fruits, corn, eggs, the young of other birds, and nectar of balsa (*Ochroma*) flowers. At La Ensenada Lodge, they enter the open-air restaurant to pick up fallen food scraps.

Nesting season occurs from February through July. While incubating, the female is visited by several family members and the male, who all take turns feeding her. The young are fed by the parents and by young from previous broods.

White-throated Magpie-Jay close-up of head

The White-throated Magpie-Jay can be found in Guanacaste's NPs—Guanacaste, Palo Verde, Santa Rosa, and Las Baulas—and in the Lomas Barbudal BR. It can also be seen at Sugar Beach, Tamarindo, Los Inocentes Lodge, Hacienda Solimar, La Ensenada Lodge, Playa Doña Ana, La Pacífica, and southeast to Tárcol Lodge at the mouth of the Río Tárcoles.

Brown Jay

Cyanocorax morio

Costa Rican names: ***Urraca parda; piapia.***

15/15 trips; 56 sightings.

Status: Permanent resident.

Length: 15.5 inches.

Weight: 8.3 ounces (235 grams).

Vocalization tapes: B, D, S, T, BB.

Range: Southern Texas to western Panama.

Elevational range: Sea level to 8,200 feet.

The Brown Jay is the most common and widespread jay in Costa Rica. It is found from lowland to high elevations—often in disturbed and developed habitats. Other jays in this country are tied to more specific habitats: the White-throated Magpie-Jay in the Guanacaste dry forest, the Black-chested Jay in the lowlands and foothills of the southeastern Caribbean slope, the Azure-hooded Jay in cloud forests and wet mountain forests, and the rare Silvery-throated Jay in high mountain forests. Costa Rica's other jays are quite colorful,

Brown Jay adult

but the Brown Jay is a plain dark brown above and white below. Immature jays have varying amounts of yellow on their bills, and the bills of adults are dark brown.

Habitats occupied by the Brown Jay include natural forests, second-growth forests, shade coffee and banana plantations, ranches, pastures, urban wood-lots, and wooded backyards. An omnivorous bird, the Brown Jay's diet includes small lizards, frogs, insects, spiders, dragonflies, *Cecropia,* corn, balsa (*Ochroma*) and banana (*Musa*) flowers, and eggs and nestlings of smaller birds. It comes to bird feeders for cooked rice.

The Brown Jay lives in family groups of six to ten birds throughout the year. Some groups of over twenty are occasionally encountered and may represent two family groups. Nesting begins in January and extends to June. The oldest birds in the family group build a nest in an isolated tree. More than one female may lay eggs, so the clutch size may vary from two to seven. Up to five females may take turns incubating the eggs. While on the nest, the female, and nearby females, give a loud "whining" call to beg other family members to feed them. After hatching, the young are fed by up to ten family members.

In the Caribbean lowlands, the Brown Jay may be observed in the Guacimo and Guapiles areas, Puerto Viejo en Sarapiquí near La Selva, La Virgen del Socorro, Turrialba, and Rancho Naturalista. In Guanacaste, it occurs on the properties of La Pacífica and Hacienda Solimar and in Palo Verde, Guanacaste, Santa Rosa, and Carara NPs. The Brown Jay is mostly absent from the southern Pacific lowlands south of Manuel Antonio NP. At higher elevations, the Brown Jay is common at Monteverde Cloud Forest Reserve, Hotel El Pórtico at San José de la Montaña, the Central Plateau, and volcanoes surrounding the Central Plateau.

DIPPER FAMILY (Cinclidae)

American Dipper (Water Ouzel)

Cinclus mexicanus

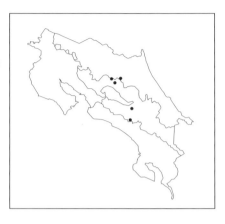

COSTA RICAN NAME: **Mirlo acuático plomizo.**

8/15 trips; 11 sightings.

STATUS: Permanent resident.

LENGTH: 5.52–7.87 inches.

WEIGHT: 1.6 ounces (46 grams).

VOCALIZATION TAPE: F.

RANGE: Northern Alaska to western Panama.

ELEVATIONAL RANGE: 2,000–8,200 feet.

The dipper is a fascinating dark gray bird found in fast-flowing, boulder-strewn streams in Costa Rica's mountains and foothills. The American Dipper has a small, rounded body, short tail, and relatively long legs. It is one of three birds to look for along boulder-strewn streams. The other two are the Torrent Tyrannulet and the Black Phoebe. The name "dipper" is derived from the bird's behavior of "dipping" up and down as it hops and flies from rock to rock.

In Costa Rica, the American Dipper is found along mountain streams. It typically will fly downstream and proceed to hop, climb, and fly upstream

American Dipper adult

from boulder to boulder while periodically submerging to capture larvae of mayflies, midges, mosquitoes, craneflies, dragonflies, beetles, and sometimes small fish.

From February through May, two to four eggs are laid in a well-camouflaged nest along the side of a stream. Look for the American Dipper from the bridge at La Virgen del Socorro, at the Peace Waterfall (Catarata de la Paz), along the Río Savegre at Savegre Mountain Lodge, and from the bridges over the Río Grande de Orosí and its tributaries in Tapantí NP.

WREN FAMILY (Troglodytidae)

Rufous-naped Wren

Campylorhynchus rufinucha

COSTA RICAN NAMES: ***Soterrey nuquirrufo; chico piojo; salta piñuela; soterrey matraquero.***

11/15 trips; 42 sightings.

STATUS: Permanent resident.

LENGTH: 6.75 inches.

WEIGHT: 1.3 ounces (36 grams).

VOCALIZATION TAPES: D, L, BB.

RANGE: Central Mexico to Costa Rica.

ELEVATIONAL RANGE: Sea level to 2,600 feet.

The wren family is well represented in Costa Rica's avifauna, with twenty-three species present. They live in habitats ranging from tropical dry forests to lowland wet forests and montane forests at timberline. The largest wren is the seven-inch-long Rufous-naped Wren. This songbird of the Guanacaste dry forest is easily seen and readily identified because family groups of three or more individuals continuously call to each other as they boldly explore garden shrubs and vines for food. The bright rufous colors over the back of the neck, the rufous-checked back, the white breast, and the cream-colored eyestripe are distinctive.

Rufous-naped Wren adult with twig in bill for nest construction

Rufous-naped Wren nest in bullhorn acacia

A close relative of the Cactus Wren in the southwestern United States, the Rufous-naped Wren inhabits Guanacaste's dry forests, savannas, gallery forests, second-growth forests, small woodlots, backyards, and gardens. Each group of wrens includes a mated pair and young from the previous year. They eat beetles, cockroaches, crickets, and other invertebrates like spiders.

A pair of Rufous-naped Wrens defends a territory throughout the year and maintains a globe-shaped nest made of grasses and plant fibers. This nest is most frequently in a bullhorn acacia (*Acacia collinsi*). The thorns provide protection from predators. The bullhorn acacia ants (*Pseudomyrmex*) attack any creatures that approach the nest. The young are cared for by both parents. After fledging, young stay with the parents until the subsequent breeding season.

The Rufous-naped Wren is found throughout Guanacaste from the Nicaragua border southeast to Carara NP, Alajuela, Xandari Plantation, and the grounds of Zoo Ave at La Garita, which is west of the Juan Santamaría International Airport.

House Wren
(Southern House Wren)

Troglodytes aedon (T. musculus)
> Costa Rican names: **Soterrey cucarachero; soterrey; zoterré; cucarachero; ratonerita.**
> 15/15 trips; 101 sightings.
> Status: Permanent resident.
> Length: 4 inches.
> Weight: 0.4 ounce (12 grams).
> Vocalization tapes: A, D, L, T.

RANGE: Southern Canada to Tierra del
Fuego.

ELEVATIONAL RANGE: Sea level to
9,000 feet.

The ubiquitous House Wren is found around homes and backyards throughout Costa Rica. Taxonomists consider this the same species throughout North
and South America, although previously House Wrens from southern Mexico
through Tierra del Fuego were considered a separate species: the Southern
House Wren. The bubbling, musical song of the wren adds a warm sense of fa-
miliarity to birders from North America.

The House Wren inhabits brushy areas, plantations, farm woodlots, ornamental tree and shrub plantings, weedy pastures, river edges, and backyards.
They are constantly singing to defend their territories from other wrens. They
are easily noticed as they search for small insects and invertebrates. This wren
sleeps in tree cavities, nest boxes, or other "nooks and crannies" in natural vegetation and buildings.

Although the northern race of House Wren is migratory and often polyga-
mous, the southern race or subspecies of House Wren is nonmigratory and
monogamous. Both parents care for the young. They renest to raise a second
and third brood in the same season. The young may stay in the territory to
help care for the young of the subsequent brood. House Wrens can be found
around lodges, farm buildings, backyards, and resorts throughout the country.

House Wren at nest cavity in tree stump, Savegre Mountain Lodge

Gray-breasted Wood-Wren

Henicorhina leucophrys

> Costa Rican name: ***Soterrey de selva pechigrís.***
>
> 15/15 trips; 33 sightings.
>
> Status: Permanent resident.
>
> Length: 4.25 inches.
>
> Weight: 0.6 ounce (18 grams).
>
> Vocalization tapes: A, D, L, X, AA, BB, CC.
>
> Range: Central Mexico to northern Bolivia.
>
> Elevational range: 2,600–10,000 feet.

Gray-breasted Wood-Wren adult

The Gray-breasted Wood-Wren, found at middle and high elevations ranging from 2,600 to 10,000 feet, has a gray breast, a striped throat, and a tail that is typically cocked upright. It is found in mountain forests, where it inhabits thick undergrowth, including bamboo thickets, brushy thickets, and fallen plant debris. There it searches for small insects and other invertebrates. Timberline and Ochraceous Wrens are found in similar habitats, thus it is worth reviewing tapes with the songs of these three wrens when birding in montane forests so you can distinguish them. Tape L has all three high-elevation species. The Gray-breasted Wood-Wren is a close relative of the White-breasted Wood-Wren, which is associated more with Costa Rica's lowland forests and foothills.

On the Caribbean slope, the Gray-breasted Wood-Wren can be encountered at La Virgen del Socorro, Braulio Carrillo and Tapantí NPs, the Peace Waterfall (Catarata de la Paz), and the Monteverde Cloud Forest Reserve. On the Pacific slope, it occurs along the PAH in Cerro de la Muerte at kilometers 66, 80, and 96, at Savegre Mountain Lodge, and along the River Trail at the Wilson Botanical Garden. As with most wrens, this bird is usually very tape-responsive when a recording of its song is played. Tape recordings should be used briefly and with discretion to avoid disrupting the normal behavior of this bird.

THRUSH and ROBIN FAMILY (Turdidae)

Clay-colored Robin
(Costa Rica's national bird)

Turdus grayi

> Costa Rican names: *Yigüirro; mirlo pardo.*
>
> 15/15 trips; 127 sightings.
>
> Status: Permanent resident.
>
> Length: 9.25 inches.
>
> Weight: 2.7 ounces (76 grams).
>
> Vocalization tapes: D, S, T, BB, CC.
>
> Range: Southern Texas to northern Colombia.
>
> Elevational range: Sea level to 8,000 feet.

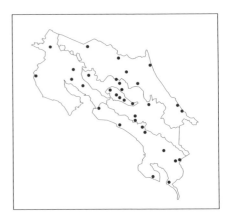

There are fifteen members of the thrush family in Costa Rica, including five robins: White-throated, Clay-colored, Pale-vented, Mountain, and Sooty. The Clay-colored Robin is the most abundant and widely distributed. It also has the distinction of being Costa Rica's national bird. In a nation that has so many colorful and spectacular birds, it seems unusual that such a drab bird was selected as the national bird. However, the *yigüirro* is an ever-present backyard

Clay-colored Robin adult

bird with a varied musical repertoire that has won the hearts of Costa Ricans. It is their constant companion as they work in their yards and gardens.

The Clay-colored Robin is largely silent until the breeding season begins. Then it begins a rich and melodious serenade that coincides with the beginning of the annual rainy season. It is therefore considered that this robin "calls the rains" each year. This is the main robin found at lowland elevations, but it also occurs up to the highlands, where it shares habitats with other robins.

This bird's name describes its markings: Clay-colored. The bill is yellowish; the iris is reddish brown in adults and brown in first-year birds. The male and female are similar. The Pale-vented Robin, on the Caribbean slope, is slightly darker brown, with a white belly and vent area. The White-throated Robin, primarily on the Pacific slope, has a white throat patch with fine black striping above the throat patch and a conspicuous yellow eye-ring and bill.

The Clay-colored Robin eats fruits, berries, worms, snails, lizards, and insects. It visits bird feeders to eat bananas and papayas. This widespread robin is found in the yards and gardens of hotels, tourism lodges, ranches, farms, shade coffee plantations, and private homes throughout the country. It inhabits settled places in lowland areas ranging from dry forests of Guanacaste to wet forests of Tortuguero and high elevations like the courtyard of Savegre Mountain Lodge in Cerro de la Muerte at 7,200 feet.

Similar Species: Mountain Robin (*Turdus plebejus*)

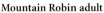
Mountain Robin adult

The Mountain Robin (14/15 trips; 49 sightings) is a high-elevation thrush associated with natural montane forests. It is known locally as the *mirlo montañero,* or *yigüirro de montaña.* Darker than the Clay-colored Robin, it is grayish brown, with an olive-green cast over the back, dark gray eyes, a black bill, and black legs. The male and female are identical and are similar in size to the Clay-colored Robin (9.5 inches). Its song is a rather monotonous series of shrill chirps (vocalization tapes BB, CC).

This robin inhabits mountain forests and forest edges where there are fruit-bearing shrubs and trees covered with epiphytes and mosses. These produce fruits and harbor insects and other invertebrates that constitute its diet.

The Mountain Robin ranges from southern Mexico to western Panama. Within Costa Rica, it is found at elevations from 3,000 to 10,000 feet. It can be observed at the Monteverde Cloud Forest Reserve, Hotel El Pórtico at San José de la Montaña, Poás and Tapantí NPs, and along the PAH in Cerro de la Muerte at kilometers 66, 80, 86, and 96.

Sooty Robin

Turdus nigrescens

COSTA RICAN NAMES: *Escarchado; escarchero; mirlo negruzco.*

13/15 trips; 30 sightings.

STATUS: Permanent resident; endemic highland species.

LENGTH: 10 inches.

WEIGHT: 3.4 ounces (96 grams).

VOCALIZATION TAPES: BB.

RANGE: Costa Rica and western Panama.

ELEVATIONAL RANGE: 7,000–11,000 feet.

The coal-black Sooty Robin is the largest thrush in Costa Rica and is an endemic songbird found only at the highest elevations from central Costa Rica to western Panama. Its black body is highlighted by an orange bill and eye-ring, orange legs, and pale bluish-gray irises. The iris is conspicuously lighter than that of the Mountain Robin. The Slaty-backed Nightingale-Thrush is similar in plumage to the Sooty Robin, but it is much smaller (only 6.75 inches long) and is found at lower elevations and in different habitats than the Sooty Robin.

The Sooty Robin is a bird of pastures, gardens, open areas near the summit of volcanoes, paramo shrublands above timberline, and parklands in montane forest. It eats fruits from the blueberry family (Ericaceae), blackberries (*Rubus*), melastome fruits, and small insects. The Sooty Robin should be looked for at

Sooty Robin adult

upper elevations of Poás and Irazú NPs and in Cerro de la Muerte along the PAH at kilometers 66, 80, 86, and 96.

Black-faced Solitaire

Myadestes melanops

COSTA RICAN NAMES: *Jiguero; solitario carinegro.*

13/15 trips; 28 sightings.

STATUS: Permanent resident; endemic highland species.

LENGTH: 6.75 inches.

WEIGHT: 1.2 ounces (33 grams).

VOCALIZATION TAPES: A, AA, BB, CC.

RANGE: Costa Rica and western Panama.

ELEVATIONAL RANGE: 3,000–9,000 feet.

One of the most magical sounds in Costa Rica's mountain forests is the ethereal, flutelike song of the Black-faced Solitaire. It fills the epiphyte-laden cloud forest with melodious one-, two-, and three-note phrases. This small slate-gray thrush has a black face highlighted by an orange bill, an orange eye-ring, and orange legs. Sexes are similar.

Black-faced Solitaire adult

Habitats utilized by the endemic Black-faced Solitaire include mature cloud forest, montane forest, bamboo thickets, shrubby understory, brushy areas, and pastures. This solitaire forages for small fruits, berries, and a few insects.

The Black-faced Solitaire is found at middle and higher elevations of both Caribbean and Pacific slopes along the length of Costa Rica into western Panama. This thrush is heard more often than seen because its habitat is often very thick with epiphytes. The Black-faced Solitaire can be seen — and heard—at the Monteverde Cloud Forest Reserve, La Virgen del Socorro, and Rara Avis; at Braulio Carrillo, Poás, Tapantí, and Amistad NPs; along the road that descends from kilometer 80 on the PAH to Savegre Mountain Lodge; and in the forests of Savegre Mountain Lodge.

Orange-billed Nightingale-Thrush

Catharus aurantiirostris

> COSTA RICAN NAMES: **Jilguerillo; inglesito; zorzal piquianaranja**.
>
> 4/15 trips; 10 sightings.
>
> STATUS: Permanent resident.
>
> LENGTH: 6.25 inches.
>
> WEIGHT: 1.0 ounce (27 grams).
>
> VOCALIZATION TAPE: D.
>
> RANGE: Southern Mexico to Venezuela.
>
> ELEVATIONAL RANGE: 2,000–7,500 feet.

Four nightingale-thrushes occur in Costa Rica: the Black-billed, Slaty-backed, Ruddy-capped, and Orange-billed. Nightingale-thrushes look like miniature robins as they hop around on the ground in thick underbrush. The bill, eye-rings, and legs are orange on the Orange-billed Nightingale-Thrush. The wings and tail are brownish olive, and the head and breast are gray in the southern Pacific lowlands. In northwestern parts of its range, this bird has a grayish-olive head. The southern Pacific lowland gray-headed race of Orange-billed Nightingale-Thrush is considered by some taxonomists to be a separate species—*Catharus griseiceps*.

This nightingale-thrush is a second-growth species found in thick, shrubby habitats and the edges of forests, shade coffee plantations, and rural gardens. It forages for small insects, spiders, other invertebrates, small fruits, and berries. It frequently flips its wings upward and raises and lowers its tail in a manner similar to that of the Black-billed Nightingale-Thrush.

The Orange-billed Nightingale-Thrush is a middle-elevation species found in Caribbean forests at Tapantí NP and Rancho Naturalista. It is also found in Pacific premontane and lower montane forests, and in the Central Plateau east to Turrialba, where the higher-elevation distribution of the Black-billed Nightingale-Thrush begins. It also occurs at higher elevations in hilly terrain of the Nicoya Peninsula. The best places to look for the Orange-billed Nightingale-Thrush are at the Wilson Botanical Garden, in Monteverde, and in shade coffee plantations near the entrance to Tapantí NP.

Orange-billed Nightingale-Thrush adult

SILKY-FLYCATCHER FAMILY (Ptilogonatidae)

Long-tailed Silky-flycatcher

Ptilogonys caudatus

COSTA RICAN NAMES: ***Timbre; pitorreal; capulinero colilargo.***

11/15 trips; 28 sightings.

STATUS: Permanent resident; endemic highland species.

LENGTH: 9.5 inches.

WEIGHT: 1.3 ounces (37 grams).

VOCALIZATION TAPE: BB.

RANGE: Costa Rica and western Panama.

ELEVATIONAL RANGE: 4,000–10,000 feet.

Long-tailed Silky-flycatcher adult female

The Long-tailed Silky-flycatcher, a distinctive and beautiful songbird of the Talamanca Mountains, is an endemic bird found only from those mountains to western Panama. The plumage is elegant. The body and breast are medium gray highlighted by a yellow head, yellow throat, and white crest. The belly and vent are yellow, and the wings and long tail are black. The female has a darker gray forehead, a more olive-green body, a whitish belly, and a shorter tail than that of the male. On the wing, they are distinctive for their long-tail profile and because they have an undulating flight pattern.

This silky-flycatcher is typically encountered in small flocks in montane forests, along forest edges, and in solitary trees of mountain pastures. It feeds on small fruits and berries, including mistletoe (*Gaiadendron*), *Fuschia,* and *Solanum* sp. From a perch at the top of a tree, it sallies to capture insects on the wing.

The Long-tailed Silky-flycatcher is usually found above 6,000 feet elevation from Poás and Irazú NPs southeast to the Talamanca Mountains, Cerro de la Muerte, and Amistad NP. Look for it along the PAH, including kilometers 66, 80, and on the grounds of Savegre Mountain Lodge.

Bananaquit adult

BANANAQUIT FAMILY (Coerebidae)

Bananaquit

Coereba flaveola

COSTA RICAN NAMES: ***Pinchaflor;*** ***picaflor; cazadorcita; santa marta;*** ***reinita mielera.***

15/15 trips; 55 sightings.

STATUS: Permanent resident.

LENGTH: 3.5 inches.

WEIGHT: 0.3 ounce (9.5 grams).

VOCALIZATION TAPES: Y, CC.

RANGE: Southern Mexico to southern Brazil.

ELEVATIONAL RANGE: Sea level to 5,000 feet.

The Bananaquit, widespread throughout tropical America, is ever busy as it explores flowers in forests and gardens. Over thirty races are recognized throughout the American tropics. Distinguishing marks are a black cap, black eye mask, and white stripe above the eye. The throat is gray, and the breast and belly are yellow. The back is dark grayish, and the dark gray wings have a small white patch at the base of the primaries. The female is paler than the male. The slender bill is slightly decurved. At higher elevations, the Bananaquit may be found in mixed flocks with tanagers and warblers.

In lowland and middle-elevation moist and wet forests, the Bananaquit visits flowers of the forest canopy, understory, forest edges, clearings, plantations, hedges, parks, and gardens. It hangs from the stems of plants as it punctures the base of flowers to reach the nectar. On small flowers like *Stachytarpheta* the Bananaquit apparently pollinates the flowers, but on larger flowers it takes the nectar without pollinating the plants. Among flowers visited are *Erythrina, Symphonia, Hibiscus,* and *Allamanda.* It also eats the protein bodies on *Cecropia* trees known as "Müllerian bodies." Additional food items include fruit pulp, bananas, caterpillars, butterflies, beetles, wasps, and spiders.

This prolific little bird nests all year and may produce two or three broods annually. Throughout the year, male and female Bananaquits maintain separate sleeping quarters in globe-shaped nests similar to those used for nesting. The Bananaquit is common throughout lowland and middle elevations of the Caribbean slope and in the southern Pacific lowlands and middle elevations, including the Wilson Botanical Garden at San Vito.

Bananaquit adult female in nest

WARBLER FAMILY (Parulidae)

Tennessee Warbler

Vermivora peregrina

> COSTA RICAN NAME: ***Reinita verdilla***.
>
> 15/15 trips; 84 sightings.
>
> STATUS: Northern migrant.
>
> LENGTH: 4.5 inches.
>
> WEIGHT: 0.3 ounce (8.5 grams).
>
> VOCALIZATION TAPES: C, F.
>
> RANGE: Alaska to northern United States; winters from southern United States to Colombia and Venezuela.
>
> ELEVATIONAL RANGE: Sea level to 10,000 feet.

The Tennessee Warbler is the second most commonly sighted migrant warbler in Costa Rica. The number of sightings is exceeded only by the Chestnut-sided Warbler. This bird has a straight, slender, pointed bill and an olive-gray body. The head is grayish on the male, with a subtle whitish line over the eye. On the female, the body is similar, but the head is olive gray and the stripe over the eye is yellowish. After arriving in Costa Rica in mid-September, the Tennessee

Tennessee Warbler adult male, winter plumage

Warbler remains until early May. It spends twice as many months on its wintering grounds as on its breeding grounds.

The Tennessee Warbler is adapted to dry, moist, and wet disturbed forests, early second growth, backyards, gardens, shade coffee plantations, and forest edges. During the breeding season, this warbler is insectivorous, but on the wintering grounds it eats insects and fruits. Often traveling in small flocks, these warblers search outer twigs, branches, and leaves for small insects, spiders, insect eggs, cocoons, and larvae. Small fruits eaten include *Didymopanax, Miconia, Xylopia, Hamelia, Trema, Urera,* mistletoe (*Gaiadendron*), and protein bodies on *Cecropia* trees. The Tennessee Warbler also drinks nectar at flowers of *Aphelandra sinclairiana, Inga, Calliandra,* banana (*Musa*), *Eucalyptus, Callistemon, Combretum,* poró (*Erythrina poeppigiana*), *Erythrina lanceolata* (a living fence-post species), and *Grevillea* (a shade tree in coffee plantations). This warbler regularly visits bird feeders to eat bananas and cooked rice.

Your birding skills may be put to the test in Guanacaste by Tennessee Warblers that have been feeding on bright orange *Combretum* flowers. The bright orange pollen creates a unique "orange-faced warbler" that you will not find in field guides.

On the Caribbean slope, the Tennessee Warbler may be encountered at La Selva Biological Station, La Virgen del Socorro, Rancho Naturalista, and Cahuita NP. It is regularly encountered in the Central Plateau and throughout Guanacaste. In the highlands, it occurs at Poás, Irazú, Tapantí, and Amistad NPs; Hotel El Pórtico near San José de la Montaña; Monteverde Cloud Forest Reserve; Cerro de la Muerte at Savegre Mountain Lodge; and along the PAH at kilometers 66 and 80. It is common throughout the southern Pacific lowlands.

Chestnut-sided Warbler

Dendroica pensylvanica

COSTA RICAN NAME:
Reinita de costillas castañas.

14/15 trips; 106 sightings.

STATUS: Northern migrant.

LENGTH: 4.5 inches.

WEIGHT: 0.2–0.3 ounce (6.8–9.1 grams).

VOCALIZATION TAPES: C, F.

RANGE: Southern Canada to eastern United States; winters from southern Mexico to eastern Panama.

ELEVATIONAL RANGE: Sea level to 6,000 feet.

Chestnut-sided Warbler adult, winter
plumage and characteristic posture:
raised tail and drooped wings

The Chestnut-sided Warbler is the most commonly observed neotropical migrant warbler. Most neotropical migrant warblers spend much of the winter in breeding plumage, but the Chestnut-sided Warbler lacks its familiar "chestnut-sided" markings until it molts into breeding plumage in late January to March. In winter plumage, it has a vireolike appearance: the head and back are bright lime green to olive green. It has a white eye-ring, a white throat and belly, a gray tail, and grayish wings with two pale yellowish wing bars. A distinctive feature is its foraging posture of slightly drooped wings and the tail cocked in an upright position like a wren or gnatwren.

Feeding occurs in second-growth forests, shrubby areas, forest edges, shade coffee plantations, and gardens. It feeds primarily by gleaning insects, caterpillars, and spiders from the underside of leaves. A small percentage of the diet is made up of berries like *Miconia* and *Lindackeria*. This warbler maintains wintering territories of 2.4–4.0 acres. Individuals join mixed flocks of Golden-crowned Warblers and Checker-throated and Dot-winged Antwrens that forage within their territory. Arriving in September, the Chestnut-sided Warbler winters in moist and wet forests throughout the Caribbean and southern Pacific lowlands and adjacent middle elevations. It returns north from mid-April to mid-May.

Gray-crowned Yellowthroat

Geothlypis poliocephala

> Costa Rican name: ***Antifacito coronigrís***.
>
> 8/15 trips; 11 sightings.
>
> Status: Permanent resident.
>
> Length: 5.25 inches.
>
> Weight: 0.5 ounce (15.5 grams).
>
> Vocalization tapes: D, BB, CC.
>
> Range: Northern Mexico to western Panama.
>
> Elevational range: Sea level to 5,000 feet.

Gray-crowned Yellowthroat adult; note that the black mask ends behind the eyes

There are four yellowthroat warblers in Costa Rica: the Common, Olive-crowned, Masked, and Gray-crowned Yellowthroats. The Common Yellowthroat, a neotropical migrant, is distinguished by a buffy-white belly. The male has a white border along the top edge of the facial mask. The Olive-crowned Yellowthroat is olive above with a yellow belly, and the male has a black mask that extends to the back of the head. There is no whitish edging above the black mask. It is found only in the Caribbean lowlands.

The Masked Yellowthroat is found only in the San Vito area in the southern Pacific lowlands. The male has a black mask that extends to the back of the head and is bordered by gray along its top edge. The Masked Yellowthroat is disjunct from other populations of the same species in South America and may eventually be designated as a separate species—the Chiriquí Yellowthroat (*Geothlypis chiriquensis*). The male Gray-crowned Yellowthroat has a black mask that ends behind the eyes. Unlike other yellowthroats that have black bills, the Gray-crowned Yellowthroat has a bicolored bill that is black above and yellow below. It has an eye-ring with a gap at the front and back edges of the eye.

The Gray-crowned Yellowthroat is found in pastures, sugarcane plantations, and cleared forest land in grassy stages of early succession. It gleans caterpillars, beetles, bugs, spiders, and other insects from low vegetation. Insects may be caught in flight. Some berries are also eaten.

This yellowthroat is found throughout the lowlands of both slopes, including dry, moist, and wet forests. This warbler may be seen at the Guapiles airport, El Gavilán Lodge, Puerto Viejo en Sarapiquí area, Rara Avis, Palo Verde NP, La Pacífica, Talari Mountain Lodge, and Corcovado Lodge Tent Camp.

Wilson's Warbler

Wilsonia pusilla

COSTA RICAN NAME: ***Reinita gorrinegra***.

15/15 trips; 71 sightings.

STATUS: Northern migrant.

LENGTH: 4.25 inches.

WEIGHT: 0.4 ounce (11 grams).

VOCALIZATION TAPES: C, F.

RANGE: Alaska to southwestern and northeastern United States; winters from southern United States to central Panama.

ELEVATIONAL RANGE: 3,000–12,000 feet.

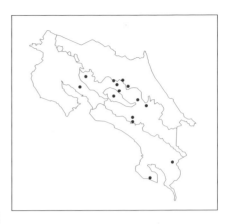

One of the most easily identified neotropical migrant warblers is the Wilson's Warbler. The male has a yellow body and black cap. The female is less distinctive because the cap is absent or gray instead of black. The migrant Yellow Warbler resembles the Wilson's Warbler but lacks the black cap, and frequently the breast shows longitudinal chestnut streaking. The Yellow Warbler also typically winters at lower elevations than the Wilson's Warbler.

Wilson's Warbler adult male gleaning insects from leaves

The Wilson's Warbler inhabits moist and wet forests, second-growth forest, forest edges, shrubby fields, shade coffee plantations, and backyards. Most foraging occurs within ten feet of the ground and consists of gleaning insects, caterpillars, beetles, aphids, and wasps from the surface of leaves. This agile warbler may hover to pick insects from the undersurface of leaves and catch insects in flight. The diet includes some berries and protein bodies of *Cecropia*.

As with the Chestnut-sided Warbler, the Wilson's Warbler defends a winter territory as its feeding area. It may feed by itself or join mixed flocks or pairs of Rufous-capped Warblers that are foraging within its territory. It is present in Costa Rica from mid-September to mid-May.

The Wilson's Warbler, primarily found at middle and higher elevations, is the only migrant warbler regularly encountered in paramo shrubs above timberline. It can be seen in Poás, Braulio Carrillo, Tapantí, Amistad, and Irazú NPs and Barva Volcano (Hotel El Pórtico). On the Caribbean slope, it winters at La Virgen del Socorro, Rara Avis, and Rancho Naturalista. On the Pacific slope, it occurs at Savegre Mountain Lodge and in Cerro de la Muerte along the PAH at kilometers 66, 77, 80, 86, 96, and at the Wilson Botanical Garden.

Slate-throated Redstart (Slate-throated Whitestart)

Myioborus miniatus

COSTA RICAN NAME: *Candelita pechinegra*.

15/15 trips; 37 sightings.

STATUS: Permanent resident.

LENGTH: 4.75 inches.

WEIGHT: 10 grams.

VOCALIZATION TAPES: A, D, J, X, BB, CC.

RANGE: Northern Mexico to Peru.

ELEVATIONAL RANGE: 2,500 to 7,000 feet.

The Slate-throated Redstart (now called Slate-collared Whitestart by some taxonomists) is the most widely distributed redstart in the Americas. The name "Whitestart" refers to white highlights on the sides of the tail that flash conspicuously as the bird forages. There are twelve subspecies, or races, that range from northern Mexico to Peru. The northernmost subspecies has a cherry-red breast, and the southernmost subspecies has a lemon-yellow breast. Two subspecies occur in Costa Rica: *Myioborus m. comptus* in northern and central Costa Rica (including Monteverde) and *Myioborus m. aurantiacus* in southeastern Costa Rica. Both have dark gray faces, throats, and backs; dark rufous caps; yellowish-orange breasts and bellies; and gray tails with white edging.

The Slate-throated Redstart inhabits cloud forests, upper premontane forests, and lower montane forests throughout the length of the country. Ranging from the upper canopy to the understory, this inquisitive warbler explores vegetation and tree trunks while drooping its wings and "flashing" its tail open and closed. This behavior may help flush insects so they can be caught and eaten. This redstart also eats the protein bodies of *Cecropia* and may accompany mixed foraging flocks of other warblers and tanagers. Pairs remain together throughout the year.

This warbler may be encountered at La Virgen del Socorro, Catarata de la Paz (Peace Waterfall), La Paz Waterfall Gardens, Braulio Carrillo NP, and Rancho Naturalista. Two of the best places to see it are in the Monteverde vicinity and along the River Trail at the Wilson Botanical Garden.

Slate-throated Redstart adult

Collared Redstart
(Collared Whitestart)

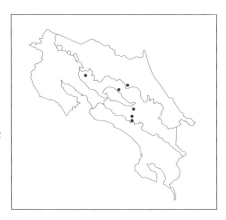

Myioborus torquatus

> Costa Rican names: ***Amigo del hombre; candelita collareja.***
>
> 14/15 trips; 36 sightings.
>
> Status: Permanent resident; endemic highland species.
>
> Length: 5.0 inches.
>
> Weight: 0.4 ounce (11 grams).
>
> Vocalization tape: AA.
>
> Range: Costa Rica and western Panama.
>
> Elevational range: 5,000 to 10,000 feet.

One of the most delightful songbirds in Costa Rica is the spritely Collared Redstart. A nonmigratory highland warbler, this curious bird frequently comes out of the undergrowth to check out human visitors. It appears so "friendly" that it is locally referred to as *amigo del hombre,* or "friend of man." From only a few feet away it is possible to see its colorful markings: yellow face

Collared Redstart adult

and throat, gray throat band, yellow breast, rufous crown, and gray back. The gray tail is edged with white. In fact, some taxonomists now call redstarts "whitestarts" because of the distinctive white outer-tail-feather markings that can be seen as the bird frequently droops its wings and spreads its tail while foraging.

The Collared Redstart lives in moist and wet montane forests, second growth, and brushy edges of forests and pastures where it forages within ten to fifteen feet of the ground. It may catch flying insects by sallying from perches. This warbler will also join mixed flocks or follow cattle or horses in mountain pastures to catch insects flushed by livestock. Pairs remain together throughout the year.

The Collared Redstart is found in Costa Rica's mountains throughout the length of the country from the Tilarán Mountains to Panama. It is regularly encountered at Monteverde, on volcanoes of the Central Cordillera, and in Braulio Carrillo, Tapantí, and Amistad NPs. It also occurs in the Talamanca Mountains and on mountains of Cerro de la Muerte along the PAH at kilometers 66 and 80 and at Savegre Mountain Lodge.

Chestnut-headed Oropendola adult male

BLACKBIRD and ORIOLE FAMILY (Icteridae)

Chestnut-headed Oropendola

Psarocolius wagleri

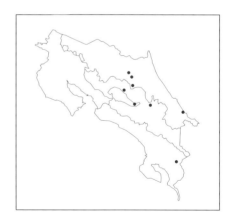

COSTA RICAN NAME: *Oropéndola cabecicastaña.*

9/15 trips; 28 sightings.

STATUS: Permanent resident.

LENGTH: 13.8 inches, male; 10.6 inches, female.

WEIGHT: 7.5 ounces (212 grams), male; 3.9 ounces (110 grams), female.

VOCALIZATION TAPES: BB, CC.

RANGE: Southern Mexico to north-western Ecuador.

ELEVATIONAL RANGE: Sea level to 5,500 feet.

The blackbird family, well represented in Costa Rica, includes twenty-two oropendolas, caciques, grackles, cowbirds, meadowlarks, and orioles. The largest members of this family are the Chestnut-headed, Montezuma, and

Crested Oropendolas. They nest in colonies and are conspicuous because of their size, noisy behavior, and clusters of large pendulous nests that may exceed three feet in length. The Chestnut-headed Oropendola is crow-sized, with a black body, a chestnut-colored head, a black tail with yellow edges, pale blue eyes, and a huge yellowish-ivory bill. The upper bill extends to the top of the head in a bizarre "casque" configuration that may give extra resonance to its unusual call, which sounds like several drops of water falling into a pool. Males are twice as large as females.

The Chestnut-headed Oropendola lives in lowland and middle-elevation forests of the Caribbean slope and in the southern Pacific region near the Panama border. It inhabits mature forest, forest edges, and clearings where tall, solitary trees provide secure nesting sites. A colony usually includes thirty to forty pairs. Flocks of oropendolas roam the forest searching for ripe fruits, bananas, *Cecropia* fruits, nectar, and invertebrates.

At the onset of the nesting season (April), the female weaves an intricate pendulous nest at the end of a tree branch. Each female lays two to three eggs. Some nesting colonies are built in the presence of wasp nests or Stingless Bee colonies (*Trigona*). These insects attack and kill parasitic botfly larvae (*Philornis*) that infest the skin of newly hatched oropendolas. In colonies not protected by bees or wasps, oropendolas tolerate visits by giant cowbirds, which lay eggs in their nests. Baby cowbirds pluck botfly larvae off oropendola chicks and eat the larvae, which helps oropendolas survive. This long-lived species may live and reproduce for more than twenty-six years.

Look for Chestnut-headed Oropendolas on the Caribbean slope near Cahuita, on the grounds of El Pizote Lodge, at La Selva Biological Station, and in the Guapiles lowlands approaching the lower levels of Braulio Carrillo NP. They occasionally visit the feeders at Rancho Naturalista to eat bananas and are a common breeder at Tapantí NP. On the Pacific slope, they occur at the Wilson Botanical Garden. Look for the Crested Oropendola in the San Vito area near the Wilson Botanical Garden. That species was discovered nesting for the first time in Costa Rica in 2000 near Sabalito, which is close to the Panama border.

Montezuma Oropendola

Psarocolius montezuma

Costa Rican name: ***Oropéndola de Moctezuma***.

13/15 trips; 93 sightings.

Status: Permanent resident.

Length: 20 inches, male; 15 inches, female.

Weight: 1 pound 2.3 ounces (520 grams), male; 8.1 ounces (230 grams), female.

Vocalization tapes: B, D, S, T, BB, CC.

Range: Southern Mexico to central Panama.

Elevational range: Sea level to 5,000 feet.

The imposing—and noisy—Montezuma Oropendola is twice as large as the Chestnut-headed Oropendola. Its colorful facial markings include pale blue fleshy areas on its "cheeks," pinkish to orange fleshy wattles under the cheeks, and a black bill tipped with reddish orange. The body is chestnut brown with a black head and chest. The central two tail feathers are black, and the remainder of the tail feathers are yellow.

Montezuma Oropendola adult male

Montezuma Oropendola adult male display posture. Photographed with permission, courtesy of G. A. Septon, Milwaukee Public Museum.

Oropendola nesting colony

The calls of the Montezuma Oropendola are among the most impressive sounds of the rainforest. As a male perches on a horizontal branch, it gives its distinctive call. A resonant gurgling, bubbling series of ascending notes are made as it tips upside down and flops out its wings. The call resembles the sound of bubbles rising in a water cooler, but the tones are more metallic. This impressive display attracts females in a promiscuous colony where the females outnumber males by three to one.

This oropendola inhabits lowland and middle elevations of the Caribbean slope and eastern portions of the Guanacaste region. It occurs in forested and semiforested habitats where tall, solitary trees in open areas provide ideal sites for nesting colonies. These colonies may contain thirty to sixty pendulous nests that hang from the end of slender branches that are too small to support the weight of approaching predators. Flocks range through moist and wet forests in search of ripe fruits, bananas, *Cecropia* fruits, nectar of banana and balsa (*Ochroma*) flowers, small vertebrates, and invertebrates.

Nesting behavior is similar to that of the Chestnut-headed Oropendola. The female does all the nest building, incubation, and care of the young. The finely woven pendulous nests are slightly longer than Chestnut-headed Oropendola nests—from three to six feet long.

The Montezuma Oropendola is common throughout the Caribbean lowlands. At middle elevations it can be seen at Rancho Naturalista and near Turrialba. In the Central Plateau and surrounding area, it occurs at the Cachí Reservoir area and Curridabat. In Guanacaste it is less common east of Cañas, Tilarán, Río Lagarto, and along the road from the PAH to Monteverde.

Great-tailed Grackle

Quiscalus mexicanus

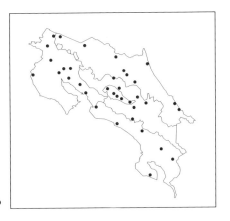

COSTA RICAN NAMES: *Sanate; zanate; zanate grande; clarinero.*

15/15 trips; 127 sightings.

STATUS: Permanent resident.

LENGTH: 17 inches.

WEIGHT: 8.1 ounces (230 grams), male; 4.4 ounces (125 grams), female.

VOCALIZATION TAPES: B, D, F, S, T.

RANGE: Southwestern United States to northwestern Peru.

ELEVATIONAL RANGE: Sea level to 5,000 feet.

Like grackles everywhere, the Great-tailed Grackle is widely distributed and little appreciated. It is common around farms, towns, and cities, where it adapts to all the nesting sites and food sources that humans inadvertently provide them. In bright sunlight, the black male grackle has some very interesting purple, greenish, and blue iridescent highlights. It is twice the size of the female, which has more subdued brown to grayish-black plumage. This grackle makes its presence known by a wide variety of assorted chirps, clucks, squeaks, and metallic toots and whistles.

Grackles occur in open, cleared, and settled areas in lowland and middle elevations of both slopes. Early in the twentieth century it was found only along the Pacific coast, but it spread to the Caribbean slope by the 1960s and into the Central Plateau by the 1970s. It is generally regarded as a pest, because it eats the eggs and young of songbirds as well as fruits, berries, and grain on farms and plantations. This omnivorous bird eats lizards, dragonflies, millipedes, snails, mice, toads, grasshoppers, carrion, food scraps, small fish, spiders, crayfish, salamanders, frogs, and snakes.

The Great-tailed Grackle nests from January through July in "loose aggregations" or colonies. Both males and females are promiscuous. The young stay with the female for up to ten weeks after fledging. Large groups frequently become a nuisance when they roost together at night in yards, parks, or gardens. This abundant bird is found throughout most settled areas of Costa Rica and is scarce only in large areas of unbroken forest and at montane levels.

Great-tailed Grackle adult male

Baltimore Oriole (Northern Oriole)

Icterus galbula

Costa Rican names: ***Cacicón; cacique veranero; bolsero norteño.***

15/15 trips; 124 sightings.

Status: Northern migrant.

Length: 7 inches.

Weight: 1.2 ounces (34 grams).

Vocalization tapes: C, F.

Range: Southeastern Canada to eastern United States; winters from central Mexico to northern South America.

Elevational range: Sea level to 7,200 feet.

One of the most common neotropical migrants in Costa Rica is the Baltimore Oriole. Formerly known as the Northern Oriole, it has a black head and shoulder area with a bright orange breast, belly, and rump. The wings are black with single white wing bars and white edging on the primaries. The female is yellowish orange with black wings and single white wing bars.

The Baltimore Oriole inhabits the canopy of dry, moist, and wet forests and is especially abundant in trees of farm woodlots, living fencerows, shade coffee plantations, orchards, and backyard gardens. This songbird has benefited from the extensive use of *Inga, Erythrina, Calliandra,* bananas (*Musa*), and citrus trees by humans. They eat flowers, nectar, and fruits from those plants. Other foods include nectar of *Combretum* vines, balsa (*Ochroma*), *Ceiba,* and *Norantea* flowers.

One of the most delightful birding experiences in Costa Rica is watching an *Erythrina* or *Inga* tree in full bloom, alive with a "feeding frenzy" of Baltimore Orioles, Tennessee Warblers, Rufous-tailed Hummingbirds, Clay-colored Robins, Hoffmann's Woodpeckers, and Palm and Blue-gray Tanagers. Additional foods taken by Baltimore Orioles include insects and spiders. They come to bird feeders for orange halves, bananas, grape jelly, sugar water (four parts water to one part cane sugar), and grape water (half grape jelly and half water).

This migratory oriole is present from early September to early May. It winters on both slopes at lowland and middle elevations and sporadically at higher elevations. The greatest abundance is in Guanacaste and the Central Plateau.

Baltimore Oriole adult male

TANAGER FAMILY (Thraupidae)

Golden-browed Chlorophonia

Chlorophonia callophrys

COSTA RICAN NAMES: ***Ruadlo;
clorofonia cejidorada.***

10/15 trips; 11 sightings.

STATUS: Permanent resident; endemic
highland species.

LENGTH: 5 inches.

WEIGHT: 0.9 ounce (25 grams).

VOCALIZATION TAPES: AA, BB.

RANGE: Costa Rica and western
Panama.

ELEVATIONAL RANGE: 3,000 to
10,000 feet.

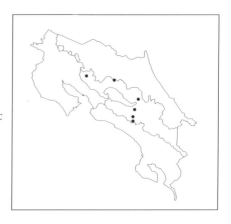

Golden-browed Chlorophonia adult male

Golden-browed Chlorophonia adult female

A total of fifty-three tanagers, euphonias, honeycreepers, and one chlorophonia add greatly to the beauty of Costa Rica's forests. Their spectacular and varied colors make the tanager family an avian treat for North American travelers who come from areas that support no more than one or two tanager species. The Golden-browed Chlorophonia is one such beauty that will provide lifetime memories. Rather chunky in profile, this tanager is endowed with a vivid green body, powder-blue nape and crown, yellow eyebrow marking, and yellow belly. The female is duller green overall and lacks the yellow eyebrow marking.

The Golden-browed Chlorophonia inhabits moist and wet high-elevation forests, where it lives among mossy, epiphyte-laden branches that provide food and nesting sites. Preferred habitat includes mature forest, forest edges, shrubby areas adjacent to forest openings, and pastures where sunshine stimulates greater fruiting. Outside the breeding season, flocks of ten to twelve chlorophonias forage for small fruits and berries of mistletoes (*Gaiadendron* and *Psittacanthus*), melastomes, fruits of the blueberry family (*Satyria* and *Psammisia*), and figs. They also glean foliage and twigs for small insects and spiders.

The Golden-browed Chlorophonia can be observed at Monteverde Cloud Forest Reserve, Catarata de la Paz (Peace Waterfall), Turrialba, Tapantí NP, and in Cerro de la Muerte along the PAH at kilometers 66 and 80 and at Savegre Mountain Lodge.

Thick-billed Euphonia adult male

Thick-billed Euphonia

Euphonia laniirostris

Costa Rican names: *Agüío; eufonia piquigruesa*.

10/15 trips; 24 sightings.

Status: Permanent resident.

Length: 4.25 inches.

Weight: 0.5 ounce (15 grams).

Vocalization tape: U.

Range: Costa Rica to eastern Brazil.

Elevational range: Sea level to 4,000 feet.

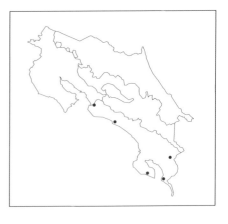

Euphonias are short, "chunky" tanagers with small bills that have green or "gunmetal-blue" backs and yellow bellies. They have varying patterns of yellow, powder blue, or rufous on the foreheads, crowns, and throats. There are nine euphonias in Costa Rica: the Yellow-crowned, Yellow-throated, Spot-crowned, Tawny-capped, Elegant (Blue-hooded), Olive-backed, Scrub, White-vented, and Thick-billed. Look at the patterns of yellow on the foreheads and throats to distinguish them. The Thick-billed Euphonia is yellow on the forehead and crown, and the throat is yellow.

The Yellow-throated Euphonia is similar but has yellow only on the forehead (not on the crown) and the vent is white, whereas the vent is yellow on the Thick-billed Euphonia. The female Thick-billed Euphonia is greenish olive above and yellowish olive below. A subadult male is similar to the female but has a yellow forehead and black face mask that extends from the bill to the eye and upper cheek area.

The Thick-billed Euphonia forages in small groups in second growth, forest edges, gardens, and pastures where shrubs provide fruits and small berries from melastomes and mistletoes. They also come to feeders for bananas. Sometimes this euphonia forages with mixed flocks of tanagers and honey-creepers.

This monogamous bird nests from March through September. Two to three broods may be raised each season. This is the only euphonia whose young of the previous year apparently help the parents care for the young hatched the following year. When a predator threatens a nest, this euphonia mimics the distress call of other birds, which attracts additional birds to help drive away the predator.

The Thick-billed Euphonia is only found in southern Pacific lowland and middle-elevation forests near the Panama border. It occurs at Corcovado NP, Corcovado Lodge Tent Camp, and Tiskita Jungle Lodge. The best place to see it is at the Wilson Botanical Garden at San Vito, where it regularly visits the bird feeders to eat bananas.

Thick-billed Euphonia adult female

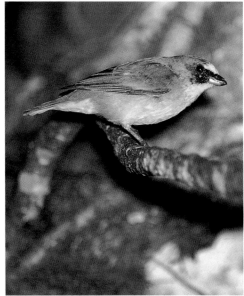

Thick-billed Euphonia subadult male

Spot-crowned Euphonia
(Spotted-crowned Euphonia)

Euphonia imitans

COSTA RICAN NAMES: ***Agüío
barranquillo; eufonia vientrirrojiza***.

5/15 trips; 20 sightings.

STATUS: Permanent resident;
Southern Pacific lowland endemic
species.

LENGTH: 4.0 inches.

WEIGHT: 0.5 ounce (14 grams).

VOCALIZATION TAPE: BB.

RANGE: Costa Rica and western
Panama.

ELEVATIONAL RANGE: Sea level to
4,500 feet.

The Spot-crowned Euphonia is an endemic bird found only in Costa Rica's
southern Pacific lowland and middle elevations and adjacent areas of Panama.
This euphonia, in addition to having a dark blue body and yellow breast, has a
dark blue throat. The yellow forehead and crown form a cap that covers the top
front of the head. Speckles of dark blue in the yellow crown are barely visible
but give this euphonia its name. The female is easy to identify. Its body is
greenish yellow, the forehead and breast are rufous, and it has the short, thick
bill characteristic of euphonias.

An inhabitant of moist and wet forests at lowland and middle elevations,
the Spot-crowned Euphonia usually forages singly or as pairs for ripe fruits
and small berries. Occasionally it visits forest edges and scattered trees and

Spot-crowned Euphonia adult male

Spot-crowned Euphonia adult female

shrubs in open areas. It eats flesh from guavas (*Psidium guajava*), melastome berries, epiphytes, and the upright fruiting stalks of *Piper* plants. Some insects and caterpillars are also eaten.

This euphonia occurs rarely as far north as Carara NP but is more commonly encountered in Corcovado NP, Corcovado Lodge Tent Camp, Lapa Ríos, and Tiskita Jungle Lodge. The best place to see it is at the Wilson Botanical Garden, where it can be seen along the River Trail and regularly visits the bird feeders there to eat bananas.

Speckled Tanager adult

Speckled Tanager

Tangara guttata

> Costa Rican names: *Zebra; tangara moteada*.
>
> 11/15 trips; 30 sightings.
>
> Status: Permanent resident.
>
> Length: 5 inches.
>
> Weight: 0.7 ounce (20 grams).
>
> Range: Costa Rica to northern Brazil; Trinidad.
>
> Elevational range: 1,000 to 4,600 feet.

The beautiful Speckled Tanager is a "foothill" species because it is found along the middle elevations of Costa Rica's mountains. The plumage has an intricate pattern of black feathers edged with lime green over the back and wings. Black feathers over the head are edged with golden yellow. Black feathers on the throat and breast are edged with white. The belly is white and the flanks are lime-yellow. The overall speckled effect is unique among Costa Rican tanagers.

This tanager travels through the canopy of mature and second-growth forests in groups of three to six birds and may sometimes join flocks of Silver-throated Tanagers, Golden-hooded Tanagers, and Green Honeycreepers. Forest-edge habitats, shrubby areas in forest openings, pastures, and shade coffee plantations are also visited. Foods include bananas and small fruits of *Miconia, Souroubea guianensis, Lantana,* and *Dipterodendron elegans.* Small insects, caterpillars, and spiders are gleaned from twigs and leaves.

On the foothills of the Caribbean slope, the Speckled Tanager can be seen at La Virgen del Socorro, Rainforest Aerial Tram, lower levels of Braulio Carrillo NP (Quebrada González Trail), and at Rancho Naturalista. On the foothills of the Pacific slope, this attractive tanager may be seen at Los Cusingos near San Isidro del General, Vista del Valle Restaurant at kilometer 119 on the PAH, and at the Wilson Botanical Garden. It comes to the bird feeders for bananas at all three locations.

Silver-throated Tanager

Tangara icterocephala
 COSTA RICAN NAMES: **Juanita;**
 tangara dorada.
 13/15 trips; 43 sightings.
 STATUS: Permanent resident.
 LENGTH: 5.0 inches.
 WEIGHT: 0.7 ounce (21 grams).
 VOCALIZATION TAPES: BB, CC.
 RANGE: Costa Rica to western
 Ecuador.
 ELEVATIONAL RANGE: Sea level to
 5,500 feet.

Like the Speckled Tanager, the Silver-throated Tanager is another jewel of Costa Rica's foothills and middle-elevation forests. The bird's name is derived from the glistening, silvery-white throat. When viewed from the front when the bird is all fluffed up, the throat appears as a silver necklace against a background of golden yellow. The back and wings show similarities to the Speckled Tanager because the feathers are black with bright lime-yellow edgings.

Silver-throated Tanager adult

This tanager inhabits moist and wet forests of Costa Rica's foothills, including mature and second-growth forests and cloud forests where the vegetation is heavily laden with epiphytes, vines, and mossy growth. It also occurs along forest edges and in brushy second growth of forest openings and pastures. Foraging as pairs or in groups of up to a dozen individuals, the Silver-throated Tanager is often in the company of tanagers, warblers, and honeycreepers. Preferred foods include fruits of *Miconia,* figs (*Ficus*), *Souroubea, Cecropia,* insects, caterpillars, and spiders. It searches for food by hopping along a branch, looking all directions, and leaning diagonally or hanging down to view the underside of branches and leaves.

In the Caribbean foothills and middle elevations, the Silver-throated Tanager can be seen at La Virgen del Socorro, Monteverde Cloud Forest Reserve, Rara Avis, Rainforest Aerial Tram, lower levels of Braulio Carrillo NP, Tapantí NP, and Rancho Naturalista. The best places to see it are along the trails and at the feeders of the Wilson Botanical Garden at San Vito and at the Vista del Valle Restaurant feeders at kilometer 119 on the PAH. This bird can occasionally be seen during the postbreeding season at Corcovado Lodge Tent Camp in January and February.

Golden-hooded Tanager

Tangara larvata

COSTA RICAN NAMES: ***Siete colores; mariposa; tangara capuchidorada***.

14/15 trips; 82 sightings.

STATUS: Permanent resident.

LENGTH: 5.0 inches.

WEIGHT: 0.7 ounce (19 grams).

VOCALIZATION TAPE: T.

RANGE: Southern Mexico to western Ecuador.

ELEVATIONAL RANGE: Sea level to 5,000 feet.

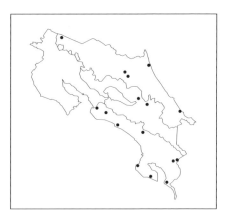

One of the most beautifully marked songbirds in Costa Rica is the Golden-hooded Tanager. A golden hood covers the head and is set off by a black face mask that has turquoise and blue highlights on the forehead and cheeks. The upper chest and back are black, the belly is white, and the sides and rump are turquoise. The black wing feathers are edged with gold. When viewed in good light, the Golden-hooded Tanager is one of the most memorable avian gems of the American tropics. In poor light, this species can be difficult to identify. Young have a greenish-yellow head, a grayish-black back, a pale grayish to olive breast, and a yellowish-green throat.

Golden-hooded Tanager adult

The Golden-hooded Tanager forages in the upper canopy of mature moist and wet forests in tropical lowlands and middle elevations. It occurs in secondary forests, shade coffee plantations, forest edges, in forest openings, and in backyards and gardens landscaped with fruiting trees and shrubs. This social species occurs in pairs, as groups of three or four, and occasionally in flocks of up to twenty-five or thirty individuals. Sometimes it occurs with other tanagers, warblers, and honeycreepers. It feeds on fruits of melastomes (*Miconia*), *Cecropia*, figs (*Ficus*), mistletoe, *Piper,* and bananas (*Musa*). Most fruits are eaten while perched, but fruits are sometimes plucked while hovering and insects are frequently caught in flight as this agile tanager sallies from perches.

Two, and sometimes three, broods are produced during an extended nesting season from February through September. The young are fed by both parents and by tanagers in adult plumage that may be offspring from the previous year. Young from the first brood also help feed the second brood.

This attractive tanager may be encountered along the Caribbean coast from Tortuguero NP through Limón to Cahuita NP; inland to La Selva Biological Station at Puerto Viejo en Sarapiquí, Guapiles, Turrialba, and Rancho Naturalista; and northwest to the Río Frío region east of Los Inocentes Lodge. In southern Pacific lowland and middle elevations, the Golden-hooded Tanager can be observed at Carara NP, Vista del Valle Restaurant feeders at kilometer 119 on the PAH, San Isidro del General, Los Cusingos, Talari Mountain Lodge, the Wilson Botanical Garden, Hotel del Sur, Manuel Antonio and Corcovado NPs, Rancho Casa Grande, Lapa Ríos, Corcovado Lodge Tent Camp, and Tiskita Jungle Lodge.

Bay-headed Tanager

Tangara gyrola

COSTA RICAN NAME: ***Tangara cabecicastaña***.

12/15 trips; 36 sightings.

STATUS: Permanent resident.

LENGTH: 5.25 inches.

WEIGHT: 0.8 ounce (23 grams).

RANGE: Costa Rica to eastern Brazil and Trinidad.

ELEVATIONAL RANGE: 330 to 5,000 feet.

Another of Costa Rica's colorful tanagers is the Bay-headed Tanager. It has a bright reddish-chestnut (bay-colored) head. The back, wings, and tail are lime green. The throat, chest, and rump are sky blue, the shoulders are golden yel-

Bay-headed Tanager adult

low, and the thighs are tan. There is a golden-yellow edging on the nape between the head and the back. This tanager demonstrates interesting differences in plumage over its range in Central and South America and the Caribbean. In Trinidad, northeastern Colombia, and northern Venezuela, the throat and chest are bright green instead of sky blue.

The Bay-headed Tanager inhabits mature moist and wet forests, second-growth forest, shade coffee plantations, and clearings and pastures with scattered tall trees. It travels as pairs or in family groups year-round, and it is frequently observed in the company of other tanagers and honeycreepers. Preferred foods include fruits and berries of *Miconia,* figs (*Ficus*), *Lycianthes synanthera, Souroubea guianensis, Cecropia,* protein bodies on *Cecropia* leaves, and small insects.

On the Caribbean slope, the Bay-headed Tanager is a foothill species found from elevations of 2,000 to 5,000 feet. It occurs at lower levels of Braulio Carrillo NP, Rainforest Aerial Tram, Turrialba, and Rancho Naturalista. On the Pacific slope, this tanager occurs from lowland elevations in Corcovado NP, Lapa Ríos, Corcovado Lodge Tent Camp, and Tiskita Jungle Lodge to inland sites like Dr. Skutch's farm (Los Cusingos), Talari Mountain Lodge, and up to middle elevations like the Wilson Botanical Garden near San Vito.

Green Honeycreeper

Chlorophanes spiza

> COSTA RICAN NAMES: *Rey de trepadores; mielero verde*.
>
> 13/15 trips; 52 sightings.
>
> STATUS: Permanent resident.
>
> LENGTH: 5 inches.
>
> WEIGHT: 0.7 ounce (19 grams).
>
> RANGE: Southern Mexico to south-eastern Brazil.
>
> ELEVATIONAL RANGE: Sea level to 4,000 feet.

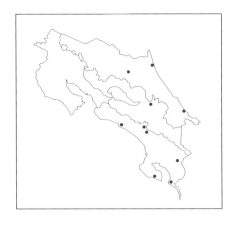

The name "Green Honeycreeper" applies best to the female of this tanager. It is lime green above and lighter lime green on the belly. The male has a bright yellow bill, which is black along the top edge. There is a black hood over the front half of the head, and the remainder of the male's body is a beautiful turquoise hue.

The Green Honeycreeper inhabits lower and middle elevations of moist and wet mature forests, second growth, forest edges, scattered trees and shrubs in open areas, shade coffee plantations, and gardens. Usually traveling as pairs or in family groups, this honeycreeper often accompanies mixed flocks of tanagers, warblers, and other songbirds. Preferred foods include fruits of *Miconia, Clusia,* bananas (*Musa*), *Cecropia,* and insects caught on the wing.

Green Honeycreeper adult male

On the Caribbean slope, the Green Honeycreeper is found from Tortuguero NP through Limón to Cahuita NP, inland to La Selva Biological Station, Tilajari Resort Hotel, and Rancho Naturalista. In the southern Pacific lowlands, it occurs at Manuel Antonio NP and inland to San Isidro del General, where it can be seen at the bird feeders eating bananas at Los Cusingos and at Talari Mountain Lodge. Other locations include Corcovado Lodge Tent Camp, Tiskita Jungle Lodge, Lapa Ríos, and the Wilson Botanical Garden. It is a common visitor at the banana feeders at the Wilson Garden.

Green Honeycreeper adult female

Red-legged Honeycreeper

Cyanerpes cyaneus

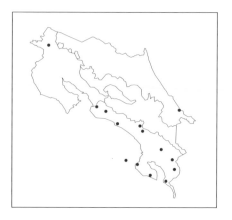

Costa Rican names: *Picudo; tucuso; trepador; mielero patirrojo*.

13/15 trips; 36 sightings.

Status: Permanent resident.

Length: 4.5 inches.

Weight: 0.5 ounce (13.5 grams).

Vocalization tapes: D, T.

Range: Northern Mexico to eastern Brazil.

Elevational range: Sea level to 4,000 feet.

Red-legged Honeycreeper adult male

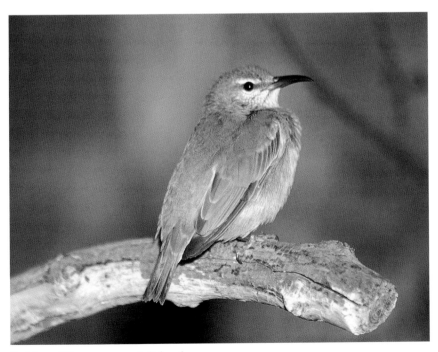

Red-legged Honeycreeper adult female

The Red-legged Honeycreeper is one of the most beautiful members of the tanager family. The male is richly patterned with royal blue and coal black over the back, and the breast is deep blue. It has a black mask; a slender, decurved bill; and a pale turquoise forehead. The wings and tail are black, and the legs are bright red. The female is pale mint green and resembles the female Green Honeycreeper, but the female of that species is brighter lime green. Also, the female Red-legged Honeycreeper shows pale vertical green streaking on the breast.

This stunning honeycreeper travels through the canopy of dry, moist, and wet mature forests of Costa Rica's lowlands. It is one of the few tanagers well adapted to the tropical dry forests of the Guanacaste region. In addition to foraging in mature forest, pairs and small flocks of five to fifteen members inhabit shade coffee plantations, gallery forests in drier regions, savanna forests, and gardens in settled areas. It may join mixed flocks of other songbirds in search of flowering or fruiting trees.

Flower nectar is an important food of this honeycreeper, which explains why this bird adapts well in Guanacaste, where there are numerous flowering trees during the dry season. Nectar sources include *Inga, Calliandra, Erythrina,* and *Genipa.* While hovering or hanging upside down, this honeycreeper uses its long, slender bill to reach into the cracks of newly opening tropical fruit pods for brightly colored seeds, like *Clusia,* before other tanagers can access them. Other foods are berries of *Miconia,* bananas, and the pulp of oranges. It also gleans small insects and spiders from foliage.

On the Caribbean slope, the Red-legged Honeycreeper occurs at Cahuita NP and in the Cahuita vicinity. It inhabits the Río Frío region near the Nicaragua border. On the Pacific slope, this honeycreeper occurs in Guanacaste, Palo Verde, and Santa Rosa NPs, but it is most common from Carara NP southeast to the Panama border, including San Isidro del General, Talari Mountain Lodge, Los Cusingos, Wilson Botanical Garden, Manuel Antonio and Corcovado NPs, Rancho Casa Grande, Lapa Ríos, Drake Bay Wilderness Resort, Corcovado Lodge Tent Camp, and Tiskita Jungle Lodge. It is also abundant on the Isla del Caño BR in the Pacific Ocean.

Blue-gray Tanager

Thraupis episcopus

COSTA RICAN NAMES: ***Viuda;
tangara azuleja.***

15/15 trips; 143 sightings.

STATUS: Permanent resident.

LENGTH: 6 inches.

WEIGHT: 1.0–1.6 ounces (27–45 grams).

VOCALIZATION TAPES: D, X.

RANGE: Central Mexico to central Brazil.

ELEVATIONAL RANGE: Sea level to 7,200 feet.

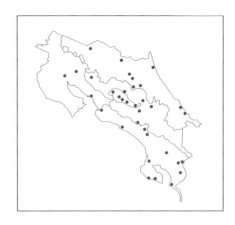

The Blue-gray Tanager is one of the best known and most common songbirds in the country. It is known to Costa Ricans as *viuda*, meaning "widow," but the reason for that name is unclear, because this tanager occurs in pairs throughout the year. The Blue-gray Tanager has a gray body with bluish-turquoise wings and wing coverts. The tail is bluish, and the bill is relatively short and thick. Their calls are a series of bubbling, twittering squeaks.

This abundant tanager is common in parks, gardens, backyards, forest edges, hedges, shade coffee plantations, and second-growth forests. Occurring in small flocks or as pairs, the Blue-gray Tanager forages for fruits of figs (*Ficus*), Mico-

Blue-gray Tanager adult

nia, Didymopanax, Cecropia, Piper, bananas (*Musa*), and papayas. Other foods include nectar of balsa (*Ochroma lagopus*) and *Erythrina*. This is one of the only tanagers known to eat leaves and flowers. It regularly visits bird feeders to eat bananas. Insects are gleaned from leaves and twigs and caught in flight.

Nesting occurs from March through July. Both parents usually build a cup-shaped nest, but in some cases they take over the nest of another tanager and incubate the eggs of the other tanager as well as their own.

On the Caribbean slope, the Blue-gray Tanager inhabits lowlands from Nicaragua to Panama and inland to Puerto Viejo en Sarapiquí, La Selva Biological Station, Turrialba, and Rancho Naturalista. It is uncommon in Guanacaste, but it is common throughout the southern Pacific lowlands, at Wilson Botanical Garden, and in the Central Plateau. Some are found in the highlands at Monteverde, Hotel El Pórtico on Barva Volcano, and Savegre Mountain Lodge.

Palm Tanager

Thraupis palmarum

Costa Rican name: ***Tangara palmera***.

14/15 trips; 92 sightings.

Status: Permanent resident.

Length: 6.25 inches.

Weight: 1.0–1.7 ounces (27–48 grams).

Vocalization tape: U.

Range: Eastern Honduras to southern Brazil.

Elevational range: Sea level to 5,000 feet.

Palm Tanager adult under lighting showing greenish-olive color

Palm Tanager adult under lighting showing bluish color

The Palm Tanager is the most widespread tanager in Latin America. It is found from Honduras to southern Brazil. On a cloudy day, the plumage is plain and almost colorless, but in sunlight, the Palm Tanager's body may appear iridescent grayish olive or grayish blue. The head and face are greenish olive. True to its name, this tanager often perches and nests in the top of palms.

The Palm Tanager is the most common of three "nondescript tanagers" in Costa Rica. The others are the Plain-colored Tanager and Olive Tanager. The Plain-colored Tanager is medium gray with a lighter belly and bluish "shoulders." The Olive Tanager, found in the Caribbean lowlands, is more olive green than the olive-gray Palm Tanager. The wings of the Olive Tanager are the same color as the back. The wings are blackish on the Palm Tanager.

This common tanager inhabits moist and wet tropical lowlands and is especially abundant in plantations of coconut, African oil palm, *pejivalle* palm, or ornamental palms. Common in backyards, gardens, and parks, it travels in pairs. Preferred foods include figs (*Ficus*), *Cecropia, Didymopanax, Miconia,* papaya, and banana (*Musa*). It gleans insects from palm, *Cecropia,* and banana leaves in an acrobatic manner that frequently involves hanging upside down to catch its prey. The Palm Tanager will also sally to catch flying insects.

The Palm Tanager is found throughout the Caribbean lowlands from Nicaragua to the Panama border and inland to Puerto Viejo en Sarapiquí, La Selva Biological Station, Rancho Naturalista, and Rara Avis. It is extremely abundant at Tortuguero and Cahuita NPs. In the southern Pacific lowlands, its distribution extends along the coast from Puntarenas and Carara NP to Panama and inland to San Isidro del General and the Wilson Botanical Garden at San Vito. It is common at Manuel Antonio and Corcovado NPs, Rancho Casa Grande, Lapa Ríos, Corcovado Lodge Tent Camp, Drake Bay Wilderness Resort, and Tiskita Jungle Lodge.

Cherrie's Tanager

Ramphocelus costaricensis

COSTA RICAN NAMES: ***Sargento; rabadilla tinta; terciopelo; sangre de toro; tangara lomiescarlata.***

13/15 trips; 78 sightings.

STATUS: Permanent resident; southern Pacific lowland endemic species.

LENGTH: 6.25 inches.

WEIGHT: 0.9–1.3 ounces (25.5–37 grams).

VOCALIZATION TAPES: A, D (listed under Scarlet-rumped Tanager).

RANGE: Southwestern Costa Rica and western Panama.

ELEVATIONAL RANGE: Sea level to 5,500 feet.

Among the most distinctive, beautiful, and memorable tanagers in Costa Rica is the bird formerly known as the Scarlet-rumped Tanager. The Scarlet-rumped Tanager was found in both the Caribbean and southern Pacific lowlands, but it has been geographically separated so long that the species became genetically different through natural selection. This bird has been split into Passerini's Tanager in the Caribbean lowlands and Cherrie's Tanager in the Pacific lowlands. The males on both slopes are identical, with a brilliant scarlet back and rump patch, a thick bluish-white bill with a black tip, and a coal-black body.

The females are different. The female Passerini's Tanager, in the Caribbean lowlands, has a gray head, an olive-yellow back, and a dull-yellow breast. In the Pacific lowlands, the Cherrie's Tanager female has a similar gray head and yellow belly, but the upper breast and rump are bright peach colored. Immature males look like females. When they molt into adult plumage they take on a "dappled" look, with black feathers on their female-looking plumage. Cherrie's Tanager is more vocal. Among its most common calls is a burst of squeaky, irregular chirps.

Cherrie's tanager is found in second-growth forests, forest edges, shrubby pastures, shade coffee plantations, gardens, backyards with fruiting shrubs, and at bird feeders stocked with bananas. It is often seen in open areas perched on fences, vines, or shrubs. Pairs and small flocks may join mixed flocks of tanagers, warblers, and saltators in search of *Cecropia* and *Piper* fruits, small berries, bananas (*Musa*), and insects.

Found only in southern Pacific lowland and middle elevations, Cherrie's

Cherrie's Tanager adult male

Cherrie's Tanager molting subadult male

Cherrie's Tanager adult female showing peach-colored upper chest area

413

Tanager occurs along the coast at Carara, Manuel Antonio, and Corcovado NPs; Rancho Casa Grande; Villa Lapas; Lapa Ríos; Quepos; Drake Bay Wilderness Resort; Corcovado Lodge Tent Camp; and Tiskita Jungle Lodge. Farther inland it is common at Vista Del Valle Restaurant feeders at kilometer 119 on the PAH, San Isidro del General, Los Cusingos, Talari Mountain Lodge, Parrita, and the Wilson Botanical Garden.

Similar Species: Passerini's Tanager (*Ramphocelus passerinii*)

Passerini's Tanager adult female showing dull yellowish upper chest area

The Passerini's Tanager (12/15 trips; 62 sightings) is a common resident of the Caribbean lowlands and is found from southern Mexico to Costa Rica. As mentioned in the previous account, this bird was formerly known as the Scarlet-rumped Tanager until it was split from the Cherrie's Tanager. The males are identical to the Cherrie's Tanager, but the females have a uniform dull-yellow breast and rump without the peach-colored upper chest and rump of the female Cherrie's Tanager. Other details of its description and natural history are similar to those of the Cherrie's Tanager. It is less vocal than the previous tanager (Vocalization tapes A, D—listed under Scarlet-rumped Tanager).

Found only in Caribbean lowland and middle elevations, Passerini's Tanager occurs in coastal areas from Tortuguero NP through Limón to the Panama border. It is found inland to Guapiles and Puerto Viejo en Sarapiquí, Tilajari Resort Hotel, La Selva Biological Station, Selva Verde Lodge, El Gavilán Lodge, Rara Avis, Turrialba, Rancho Naturalista, Rainforest Aerial Tram, lower levels of Braulio Carrillo NP, and west to Kiri Lodge near the entrance to Tapantí NP.

White-lined Tanager

Tachyphonus rufus

COSTA RICAN NAMES: **Fraile;**
tangara forriblanca.

9/15 trips; 27 sightings.

STATUS: Permanent resident.

LENGTH: 6.75 inches.

WEIGHT: 0.9–1.4 ounces (25.7–40
grams).

RANGE: Costa Rica to southeastern
Brazil; Trinidad.

ELEVATIONAL RANGE: Sea level to
4,600 feet.

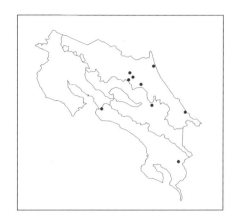

In contrast to the stunning colors of most tanagers, the male White-lined Tanager is coal black. The reference to "white-lined" comes from inconspicuous white linings on the edge of the wings and white on the scapular feathers of the shoulder area. These white feathers are usually concealed when the bird is at rest. The bicolored bill is black above and white below, with a black tip. The similar White-shouldered Tanager is also black, but is distinguished by a conspicuous white wing patch. The female White-lined Tanager is uniform rufous and could be confused with the similar Cinnamon Becard, Rufous Mourner, or Rufous Piha. However, the female is usually in the company of the black male and has a typical straight, thick tanager bill. The female White-shouldered Tanager is olive colored above and yellowish below. The White-lined Tanager commonly visits feeders for bananas. The other "rufous songbirds" do not visit feeders and are associated with more mature forests.

White-lined Tanager adult male showing bicolored bill

The White-lined Tanager is an adaptable bird of forest second growth, forest edges, shrubby areas, hedges, gardens, and backyards. This bird travels in pairs throughout the year, and family groups can be observed together following the nesting season. Among fruits eaten are guavas (*Psidium guajava*), bananas (*Musa*), oranges, *Miconia* berries, *Cecropia,* and bromeliad fruits. Insects, including ants, beetles, bugs, flies, and spiders, are captured in flight or caught while concealed on ground cover.

The White-lined Tanager is most abundant in Caribbean lowland and middle elevations. It can be seen in the Tortuguero and Cahuita areas and inland to Guapiles and Puerto Viejo en Sarapiquí. It occurs at La Selva Biological Station and at higher elevations like Rara Avis, Turrialba, and Rancho Naturalista. It regularly comes to the feeders at Rancho Naturalista for bananas. In the southern Pacific lowlands, it is less common but can sometimes be seen at Carara NP and the Wilson Botanical Garden at San Vito.

White-lined Tanager adult female; note thick tanager bill

Common Bush-Tanager

Chlorospingus ophthalmicus

Costa Rican name: ***Tangara de monte ojeruda.***

10/15 trips; 34 sightings.

Status: Permanent resident.

Length: 5.25 inches.

Weight: 0.7 ounce (20 grams).

Vocalization tapes: A, X, AA, BB, CC.

Range: Central Mexico to northwestern Argentina.

Elevational range: 1,300 to 7,500 feet.

Common Bush-Tanager adult

The Common Bush-Tanager is a widely distributed bird of cloud forests. It also occurs in wet and rainforests in the foothills and middle elevations of Costa Rica's mountains. It is typically seen exploring epiphyte-covered branches of trees in search of flower nectar, small fruits, insects, and spiders. This tanager has a small, rounded body characterized by a grayish-brown head, a conspicuous white mark behind each eye, an olive back, yellowish sides, and a white belly. The Common Bush-Tanager usually travels in mixed flocks of up to a dozen bush-tanagers, woodcreepers, tanagers, antwrens, and antvireos. The body shape and active, inquisitive foraging behavior resemble that of the Black-capped Chickadee of North America.

On the Caribbean slope, the Common Bush-Tanager frequents cloud forests at the Monteverde Cloud Forest Reserve and may also be encountered at La Virgen del Socorro, Peace Waterfall (Catarata de la Paz), La Paz Waterfall Gardens, and middle elevations of Braulio Carrillo and Tapantí NPs. At the Hummingbird Gallery at Monteverde, this bird regularly visits the nectar feeders. On the Pacific slope, it can be found from the Skutch farm up to Savegre Mountain Lodge, but it is most frequently seen at the Wilson Botanical Garden at San Vito, where it also visits the feeders to eat bananas.

Sooty-capped Bush-Tanager

Chlorospingus pileatus

> Costa Rican name: ***Tangara de monte cejiblanca.***
>
> 14/15 trips; 37 sightings.
>
> Status: Permanent resident; endemic highland species.
>
> Length: 5.25 inches.
>
> Weight: 0.7 ounce (20 grams).
>
> Vocalization tape: BB.
>
> Range: Costa Rica and western Panama.
>
> Elevational range: 6,500 to 10,000 feet.

The Sooty-capped Bush-Tanager is another high-elevation endemic that makes Costa Rica a special destination for birding. This tanager is characterized by a compact, rounded body that is yellowish on the upper chest and sides, olive above, white on the belly, and highlighted by a black head that has a wide white blaze extending from above the eyes to the back of the head. The black extends over the top of the head and as a mask through the eyes to the back of the head. As with Common Bush-Tanagers, it travels in mixed flocks of

Sooty-capped Bush-Tanager adult feeding on Cavendishia fruits

over a dozen Sooty-capped Bush-Tanagers, warblers, and Ruddy Treerunners. It is typically found at higher elevations than the Common Bush-Tanager.

This tanager inhabits montane wet and rainforests, older second growth, and forest edges where it searches thick, epiphytic vegetation for insects, spiders, and fruits. Preferred foods include small waxy berries of the blueberry family (Ericaceae), like *Cavendishia, Psammisia,* and *Satyria*. Other foods include blackberries (*Rubus*) and berries of *Miconia* and *Fuschia*.

Among the best places to look for the Sooty-capped Bush-Tanager are the Monteverde Cloud Forest Reserve, Poás NP, Savegre Mountain Lodge, and sites along the PAH in Cerro de la Muerte at kilometers 66, 80, 86, and 96.

SALTATOR, GROSBEAK, and FINCH FAMILY
(Emberizidae)

Buff-throated Saltator

Saltator maximus

Costa Rican names: ***Sinsonte verde; saltator gorgianteado.***

15/15 trips; 79 sightings.

Status: Permanent resident.

Length: 8 inches.

Weight: 1.8 ounces (50 grams).

Vocalization tapes: D, U, BB, CC.

Range: Southeastern Mexico to southeastern Brazil.

Elevational range: Sea level to 5,000 feet.

Within the family Emberizidae are two subfamilies: Cardinalidae and Emberizinae. The first subfamily includes grosbeaks and saltators. The second includes finches, seedeaters, flowerpiercers, and sparrows. The first subfamily contains four saltators: Black-headed, Buff-throated, Grayish, and Streaked. The Buff-throated Saltator is the most common. It has a small white chin patch with a conspicuous bib that is buffy and edged with black. The head is gray with a slender white line above each eye. The back is olive green, and the breast and belly are light grayish brown. This is one of the larger, heavier-bodied songbirds, and it has a long, thick bill, which is characteristic of saltators. Sexes are identical. The song is a series of chirps and warbles reminiscent of a thrush.

The Buff-throated Saltator inhabits forest edges, shade coffee plantations, second growth, and gardens. It seeks out fruits, insects, and soft plant materials like flowers and buds. Traveling in pairs, this bird sometimes accompanies Cherrie's or Passerini's Tanagers. It will follow army ants to catch escaping insects and visits backyard bird feeders to eat bananas.

This saltator lives in moist and wet lowland and middle-elevation habitats. Along the Caribbean slope it occurs from Tortuguero NP to Cahuita NP, and inland to Guapiles, Puerto Viejo en Sarapiquí, and Turrialba. It is common at La Selva Biological Station, Selva Verde, and El Gavilán Lodge. It regularly visits the feeders at Rancho Naturalista and Tilajari Resort Hotel. In the southern Pacific lowlands, the Buff-throated Saltator is found from Carara NP through Quepos and Manuel Antonio NP to Corcovado NP, Villa Lapas, Rancho Casa Grande, Lapa Ríos, Corcovado Lodge Tent Camp, and Tiskita Jungle Lodge. Inland it is common at San Isidro del General, at Los Cusingos, and on the grounds of Talari Mountain Lodge. It visits the feeders at Los Cusingos, Talari Mountain Lodge, and the Wilson Botanical Garden.

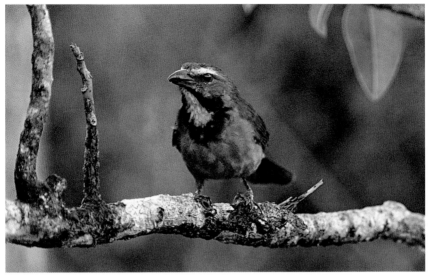

Buff-throated Saltator adult showing buffy bib surrounded by black edging

Similar Species: Black-headed Saltator (*Saltator atriceps*)

The largest saltator in Costa Rica, the Black-headed Saltator (7/15 trips; 28 sightings), is 9.5 inches long. The back and tail are yellowish olive, the top of the head is black, and the sides of the face and head are gray. There is a white line above each eye. The large bib marking on the upper chest is white edged with black on the sides. The bill is long and extremely thick at the base. The habitat preferences and foods are similar to those of the Buff-throated Saltator, but the Black-headed Saltator may have a stronger affinity for being near water. It travels in family groups but often is difficult to see. A quite vocal species, its repertoire includes a unique "smacking" note and a bubbling phrase of about eight notes that sounds quite wrenlike (Vocalization tapes: B, D, T, CC).

This distinctive saltator, which ranges from central Mexico to eastern Panama, is primarily a bird of Caribbean lowland and middle elevations to about 4,000 feet. It occurs from Limón to Cahuita, and inland it is regularly encountered at La Selva Biological Station, Turrialba, and on the grounds of Rancho Naturalista and Tilajari Resort Hotel, where it comes to the feeders for bananas and papayas.

Black-headed Saltator adult showing white throat, black on sides of bib marking

Grayish Saltator

Saltator coerulescens

Costa Rican names: *Sensontle; sinsonte; saltator grisáceo.*

7/15 trips; 10 sightings.

Status: Permanent resident.

Length: 8 inches.

Weight: 1.8 ounces (52 grams).

Vocalization tapes: D, E, V, W, Z, CC.

Range: Northwestern Mexico to eastern Brazil.

Elevational range: Sea level to 6,000 feet.

Like other saltators, the Grayish Saltator has an "oversized" bill that is long, straight, and very thick at the base. The body is uniformly gray, with buffy areas near the flanks. There is a white line above the eye, a small white spot under the lower eyelid, and a small white throat patch edged by a short black stripe on each side. The throat patch does not have the "bib" appearance of the Buff-throated and Black-headed Saltators. Sexes are identical.

This saltator inhabits forest edges, brushy fields, second growth, shade coffee plantations, and backyard gardens with hedges—even in San José. Pairs stay together throughout the year and search for fruits, flowers, leaf buds and new leaves, vine tendrils, and insects. This songbird will visit feeders for bananas.

Grayish Saltator adult showing small white bib with black on sides

This saltator has an unusual distribution that includes the Central Plateau, Sarchí, San José, and brushy pastures and second growth of middle elevation slopes of Barva, Poás, and probably Irazú Volcanoes up to about 6,000 feet. It is also found in the Río Frío/Caño Negro region, Tilajari Resort Hotel, eastward from the Central Plateau to La Selva Biological Station, Turrialba, and near the Panama border at the Wilson Botanical Garden at San Vito.

Streaked Saltator

Saltator albicollis

    Costa Rican name: ***Saltator listado***.

    8/15 trips; 19 sightings.

    Status: Permanent resident.

    Length: 7.25 inches.

    Weight: 1.4 ounces (40 grams).

    Range: Costa Rica to Peru; Lesser Antilles.

    Elevational range: Sea level to 6,000 feet.

The Streaked Saltator is the only saltator with a streaked pattern of brownish stripes on a white breast. The bill has a typical saltator profile—with an extremely thick base. The back is yellowish olive, the tail is grayish, and the gray head has a white stripe above each eye. Sexes are identical.

    Inhabitants of forest edges, shrubby thickets, second growth, brushy pastures, and backyard gardens, Streaked Saltators live as pairs. Foods include

Streaked Saltator adult

fruits, flower petals, young leaf buds, ants, beetles, and other slow-moving insects.

The Streaked Saltator is only found in the southern Pacific lowlands. It can be seen at Los Cusingos, Talari Mountain Lodge, in brushy woodlots and hedges near San Isidro del General, Lapa Ríos, Corcovado Lodge Tent Camp, and Tiskita Jungle Lodge. It is regularly encountered at the Wilson Botanical Garden at San Vito.

Yellow-faced Grassquit

Tiaris olivacea

Costa Rican names: *Gallito; semillerito cariamarillo.*

15/15 trips; 53 sightings.

Status: Permanent resident.

Length: 4 inches.

Weight: 0.4 ounce (10 grams).

Vocalization tape: CC.

Range: Central Mexico to north-western Venezuela; Greater Antilles.

Elevational range: Sea level to 7,200 feet.

Within the subfamily Emberizinae are grassquits, seedeaters, finches, seed-finches, flowerpiercers, and sparrows. This subfamily includes thirty-nine species in Costa Rica. Many inhabit grasslands, pastures, roadside ditches, and forest openings, where they feed on small grass seeds and insects. One easily identified bird is the Yellow-faced Grassquit. When viewed from the front, the male appears to have a bright yellow X across its black face. The head, face, and upper chest are black; the back is yellowish olive; and the belly is grayish olive. The female is paler olive green, and the X pattern on the face is pale yellow.

The Yellow-faced Grassquit is common in open grassy habitats and shrubby edges. Traveling in small flocks or as singles or pairs, it strips seeds from grass or eats it from the ground. Small berries are plucked from trees and shrubs, and insects are gleaned from foliage. It may occur with Variable or White-collared Seedeaters.

On the Caribbean slope, the Yellow-faced Grassquit lives in lowlands from Puerto Viejo en Sarapiquí and Guapiles to Cahuita and inland to La Selva Biological Station. It lives at middle elevations at Turrialba and Rancho Naturalista. In the highlands, it occurs at Vara Blanca, Monteverde, and Savegre Mountain Lodge. In southern Pacific lowland and middle elevations, it occurs at Quepos, San Isidro del General, Rancho Casa Grande, Talari Mountain Lodge, Los Cusingos, Lapa Ríos, Corcovado Lodge Tent Camp, Tiskita Jungle Lodge, and the Wilson Botanical Garden.

Yellow-faced Grassquit adult

Variable Seedeater

Sporophila aurita

> Costa Rican names: ***Espiguero variable; setillero de laguna.***
>
> 15/15 trips; 96 sightings.
>
> Status: Permanent resident.
>
> Length: 4 inches.
>
> Weight: 0.4 ounce (10–12 grams).
>
> Vocalization tapes: V, CC.
>
> Range: Southern Mexico to north-western Peru.
>
> Elevational range: Sea level to 5,000 feet.

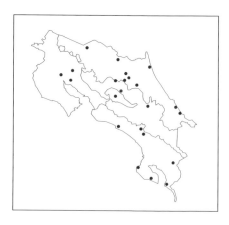

The Variable Seedeater is the most common of six seedeaters in Costa Rica. A lowland bird of grassy areas, this seedeater occurs in two color phases. The male of the Caribbean slope race (*S. a. corvina*) is black with a white spot (not a wing bar) on the primaries. The male in the Pacific lowlands (*S. a. aurita*) has a white rump; a white lower breast and belly; a white wing spot; a narrow, incomplete neck collar; and a black throat.

The White-collared Seedeater differs from the Pacific race of the Variable Seedeater by having two white wing bars, a white throat, and a complete white

Variable Seedeater adult, Caribbean race

Variable Seedeater adult, Pacific race

collar around the neck. The females of both races are dark olive above and paler below. The Pacific race female has more yellowish white on the belly.

The similar Blue-black Grassquit is all black with no white wing spots and has a more pointed bill than the Variable Seedeater. The Blue Seedeater lives in the highlands. The Thick-billed Seed-Finch has an extremely thick, deep convex bill that is much larger than that of the Variable Seedeater.

The Variable Seedeater inhabits forest edges, roadsides, grassy fields, pastures, gardens, and small patches of forest. It lives in pairs and travels in small, single-species flocks or with seedeaters, seed-finches, and grassquits. Preferred foods include seeds, berries, and insects. The Variable Seedeater is found throughout grassy habitats in the lowlands of both the Caribbean and Pacific slopes.

Slaty Flowerpiercer

Diglossa plumbea

    COSTA RICAN NAME: **Pinchaflor plomizo.**

    12/15 trips; 35 sightings.

    STATUS: Permanent resident; endemic highland species.

    LENGTH: 4 inches.

    WEIGHT: 0.3 ounce (9 grams).

    VOCALIZATION TAPE: AA.

    RANGE: Costa Rica and western Panama.

    ELEVATIONAL RANGE: 4,000 to 10,000 feet.

One of the most fascinating birds in Costa Rica's highlands is the Slaty Flowerpiercer. Both the slate-gray male and the tan-colored female have sharp pointed bills with a distinctive "kink" near the tip like the end of a can opener. This unique tip facilitates puncturing the base of flowers so it is possible to "steal" nectar without pollinating the flowers. Bananaquits do the same thing with flowers in the lowlands. The Slaty Flowerpiercer is a member of the flowerpiercer genus

Slaty Flowerpiercer adult male

Slaty Flowerpiercer adult female

Diglossa that includes at least eighteen species in mountainous areas from southern Mexico to the Andes of South America.

The Slaty Flowerpiercer frequents highland meadows, roadsides, forest edges, shrubby clearings, backyard gardens, and montane forest canopy. Small insects are also caught in flight. This highland endemic can be observed visiting flowers at the Monteverde Cloud Forest Reserve, on Poás, Barva, and Irazú Volcanoes, at Savegre Mountain Lodge (visiting flowers and hummingbird feeders in the courtyard), and along the PAH in Cerro de la Muerte at kilometers 66, 77, 80, 86, and 96.

Yellow-thighed Finch

Pselliophorus tibialis

COSTA RICAN NAME: *Saltón de muslos amarillos.*

14/15 trips; 25 sightings.

STATUS: Permanent resident; endemic highland species.

LENGTH: 7.25 inches.

Weight: 1.1 ounces (31 grams).

RANGE: Costa Rica and western Panama.

ELEVATIONAL RANGE: 4,000 to 10,000 feet.

The Yellow-thighed Finch is a large, dark-gray highland endemic finch with a black head and bright yellow thighs. Traveling as mated pairs or in small family groups, this finch ranges through montane forests and is especially common in forest edges, thickets, brushy ravines, bamboo clumps, and thick, shrubby areas near pastures. Sometimes they join mixed flocks of tanagers and warblers in search of berries, nectar, insects, and spiders.

Look for this highland bird near the summit and picnic area in Poás NP, in Tapantí NP, at Savegre Mountain Lodge, and along the PAH in Cerro de la Muerte at kilometers 66, 77, 80, and 96.

Yellow-thighed Finch adult showing yellow thighs

Orange-billed Sparrow

Arremon aurantiirostris

COSTA RICAN NAME: **Pinzón piquinaranja**.

9/15 trips; 19 sightings.

STATUS: Permanent resident.

LENGTH: 6 inches.

WEIGHT: 1.2 ounces (35 grams).

VOCALIZATION TAPES: BB, CC.

RANGE: Southern Mexico to northwestern Ecuador.

ELEVATIONAL RANGE: Sea level to 4,000 feet.

The Orange-billed Sparrow is a lowland rainforest bird whose name describes its most conspicuous feature: an orange bill. This brightly marked sparrow has a black facial mask and contrasting white throat, a narrow black band across the upper chest, yellow shoulders, and a white lower chest and belly. The crown is black, and there is a slender grayish-white line above each eye. Sexes are identical. The song—a thin, high-pitched whistled twittering phrase—is usually given while perched in thick underbrush. The bill of the immature is black, not orange.

An inhabitant of mature wet forest and older second-growth forest, this sparrow lives in thick understory vegetation. Occurring as pairs or in family groups, this sparrow forages on the ground and in low shrubs in search of small fruits, berries, and insects. It will sometimes attend army ant swarms to capture escaping insects.

Orange-billed Sparrow adult

The subspecies of Orange-billed Sparrow found in the Caribbean lowlands (*A. a. ruficorsalis*) occurs to 3,200 feet elevation and can be encountered along the loop trail at Tortuga Lodge, in the Arboretum and along Sendero Tres Ríos at La Selva Biological Station, and on the grounds of Rancho Naturalista. The Pacific slope subspecies (*A. a. aurantiirostris*) can be seen from Carara NP southeast to Manuel Antonio and Corcovado NPs; at Villa Lapas, Rancho Casa Grande, Lapa Ríos, Drake Bay Wilderness Resort, and Tiskita Jungle Lodge; and along the River Trail at the Wilson Botanical Garden.

Black-striped Sparrow

Arremonops conirostris

COSTA RICAN NAME: *Pinzón cabecilistado*.

12/15 trips; 71 sightings.

STATUS: Permanent resident.

LENGTH: 6.5 inches.

WEIGHT: 1.3 ounces (37.5 grams).

VOCALIZATION TAPES: A, BB.

RANGE: Northern Honduras to northern Brazil.

ELEVATIONAL RANGE: Sea level to 5,000 feet.

Black-striped Sparrow adult

Though not brightly marked like the Orange-billed Sparrow, the Black-striped Sparrow adds a special touch to lowland and middle-elevation forests with its distinctive song—an accelerating series of about two dozen chirps that start slowly and continue with increasing frequency to a trill at the end. It gives the impression of a bird "trying to start its motor." This attractive sparrow has a gray head with two black stripes on top of the head, a black stripe through each eye, a black bill, and olive-yellow back, tail, and wings. The sides are light gray fading to white on the belly, and there are yellow highlights on the outer edges of the wing feathers. Sexes are identical.

The Black-striped Sparrow lives in moist and wet forest edges, thickets, young second growth, weed patches, gardens, shade coffee plantations, and banana plantations. Living as pairs or in family groups, this sparrow explores short trees, shrubs, and ground cover for insects, small frogs, lizards, bananas, corn, berries, and small seeds.

On the Caribbean slope, this sparrow can be seen, and heard, at Tortuguero and Cahuita NPs, Tortuga Lodge, El Pizote Lodge, La Selva Biological Station, Selva Verde, El Gavilán Lodge, Rara Avis, and Rancho Naturalista. On the Pacific slope, the Black-striped Sparrow inhabits Carara, Manuel Antonio, and Corcovado NPs; San Isidro del General; Los Cusingos; Villa Lapas; Rancho Casa Grande; Talari Mountain Lodge; Lapa Ríos; Corcovado Lodge Tent Camp; Tiskita Jungle Lodge; and the Wilson Botanical Garden, where it visits the feeders for bananas.

Rufous-collared Sparrow

Zonotrichia capensis

> Costa Rican names: ***Comemaíz;***
> ***pirrís; chingolo.***
> 15/15 trips; 103 sightings.
> Status: Permanent resident.
> Length: 5.25 inches.
> Weight: 0.7 ounce (20 grams).
> Vocalization tapes: A, D, X.
> Range: Southeastern Mexico to Tierra
> del Fuego; Hispaniola.
> Elevational range: 2,000 to
> 10,000 feet.

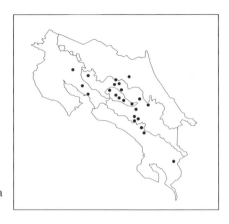

Well known throughout Costa Rica, the Rufous-collared Sparrow has a broad distribution that ranges from middle elevations to 10,000 feet. Known as *come maíz* to Ticos, the nickname means "corn eater." This attractive sparrow has a short black crest and a gray face. Two black stripes extend from the back corner of each eye and the lower mandible. The chin and throat are white. Black

Rufous-collared Sparrow adult

spots on each side of the throat create a "bow-tie" look. The most conspicuous marking is the rufous collar over the back of the neck. The back and wings have a streaked pattern of brown, rufous, and black. Sexes are similar. Young birds have a streaked breast, indistinct collar, and no "bow-tie." The distinctive song is a three-note slurred whistle with a thin, high tone, a lower tone, and a third note that slurs from a higher to lower note. It has been described as a "drink-your-tea" phrase and is reminiscent of the whistled song of an Eastern Meadowlark.

Mated pairs remain together on their territory all year and nest throughout the year. Their territories include backyards, gardens, shade coffee plantations, croplands, pastures, and shrubby forest edges. This abundant sparrow hops on the ground in search of fallen weed seeds and insects. It will come to feeders for cooked rice.

The adaptable Rufous-collared Sparrow is a common "backyard bird" that can be found at middle and high elevations throughout the length of Costa Rica, including the Central Plateau and downtown San José. The males' tendency to sing from high perches makes them easy to see.

Amadon, Dean. 1983. Great Curassow (*Crax rubra*). In *Costa Rican Natural History,* ed. Daniel H. Janzen, 569–570. Chicago: Univ. of Chicago Press. 816 pp.

Ammon, Elizabeth M., and William M. Gilbert. 1999. Wilson's Warbler (*Wilsonia pusilla*). In *The Birds of North America,* no. 478, ed. Alan Poole and Frank Gill. Philadelphia, Pa.: Academy of Natural Sciences; Washington, D.C.: American Ornithologists' Union. 28 pp.

Arnold, Keith A. 1983. Great-tailed Grackle (*Quiscalus mexicanus*). In *Costa Rican Natural History,* ed. Daniel H. Janzen, 601–603. Chicago: Univ. of Chicago Press. 816 pp.

Brown, Leslie, and Dean Amadon. 1989. *Eagles, Hawks, and Falcons of the World.* Vols. 1 and 2. Secaucus, N.J.: Wellfleet Press. 945 pp.

Buckley, Neil J. 1999. Black Vulture (*Coragyps atratus*). In *The Birds of North America,* no. 411, ed. Alan Poole and Frank Gill. Philadelphia, Pa.: Academy of Natural Sciences; Washington, D.C.: American Ornithologists' Union. 24 pp.

Burton, John A., ed. 1973. *Owls of the World.* New York: E. P. Dutton. 216 pp.

Byers, Clive, Jon Curson, and Urban Olsson. 1995. *Sparrows and Buntings: A Guide to the Sparrows and Buntings of North America and the World.* Boston, Mass.: Houghton Mifflin. 334 pp.

Coulter, Malcolm C., James A. Rodgers, John C. Odgen, and F. Chris Depkin. 1999. Wood Stork (*Mycteria americana*). In *The Birds of North America,* no. 409, ed. Alan Poole and Frank Gill. Philadelphia, Pa.: Academy of Natural Sciences; Washington, D.C.: American Ornithologists' Union. 28 pp.

Curson, Jon, David Quinn, and David Beadle. 1994. *Warblers of the Americas.* Boston, Mass.: Houghton Mifflin. 252 pp.

Davis. William E., Jr., and James A. Kushlan. 1994. Green Heron (*Butorides virescens*). In *The Birds of North America,* no. 129, ed. Alan Poole and Frank Gill. Philadelphia, Pa.: Academy of Natural Sciences; Washington, D.C.: American Ornithologists' Union. 24 pp.

Dumas, Jeannette V. 2000. Roseate Spoonbill (*Ajaia ajaja*). In *The Birds of North America,* no. 490, ed. Alan Poole and Frank Gill. Philadelphia, Pa.: Academy of Natural Sciences; Washington, D.C.: American Ornithologists' Union. 32 pp.

Fitzpatrick, John W. 1983. Tropical Kingbird (*Tyrannus melancholicus*). In *Costa Rican Natural History,* ed. Daniel H. Janzen, 611–613. Chicago: Univ. of Chicago Press. 816 pp.

Foster, Mercedes S. 1983. Long-tailed Manakin (*Chiroxiphia linearis*). In *Costa Rican Natural History,* ed. Daniel H. Janzen, 563–564. Chicago: Univ. of Chicago Press. 816 pp.

Frederick, Peter C., and Douglas Siegal-Causey. 2000. Anhinga (*Anhinga anhinga*). In *The Birds of North America,* no. 522, ed. Alan Poole and Frank Gill. Philadelphia, Pa.: Academy of Natural Sciences; Washington, D.C.: American Ornithologists' Union. 24 pp.

Gladstone, Douglas E. 1983. Cattle Egret (*Bubulcus ibis*). In *Costa Rican Natural History,* ed. Daniel H. Janzen, 550–551. Chicago: Univ. of Chicago Press. 816 pp.

Goodrich, Laurie J., Scott C. Crocoll, and Stanley E. Senner. 1996. Broad-winged Hawk (*Buteo platypterus*). In *The Birds of North America,* no. 218, ed. Alan Poole and Frank Gill. Philadelphia, Pa.: Academy of Natural Sciences; Washington, D.C.: American Ornithologists' Union. 28 pp.

Hogan, Kelly M. 1999. White-tipped Dove (*Leptotila verreauxi*). In *The Birds of North America,* no. 436, ed. Alan Poole and Frank Gill. Philadelphia, Pa.: Academy of Natural Sciences; Washington, D.C.: American Ornithologists' Union. 16 pp.

Howe, Hank F. 1983. Chestnut-mandibled Toucan (*Ramphastos swainsonii*). In *Costa Rican Natural History,* ed. Daniel H. Janzen, 603–604. Chicago: Univ. of Chicago Press. 816 pp.

Howell, Steven N. G., and Sophie Webb. 1995. *The Birds of Mexico and Northern Central America.* New York: Oxford Univ. Press. 851 pp.

Hoyo, Josep del, Andrew Elliott, and Jordi Sargatal. 1992. *Handbook of the Birds of the World.* Vols. 1–5. Barcelona, Spain: Lynx Edicions. Vol. 1, 696 pp.; Vol. 2, 638 pp.; Vol. 3, 821 pp.; Vol. 4, 679 pp.; Vol. 5, 759 pp., and Vol. 6, 589 pp.

Isler, Morton, and Phyllis Isler. 1999. *The Tanagers: Natural History, Distribution, and Identification.* Washington, D.C.: Smithsonian Institution Press. 406 pp.

Janzen, Daniel H. 1983a. *Costa Rican Natural History.* Chicago: Univ. of Chicago Press. 816 p.

_____. 1983b. Scarlet Macaw (*Ara macao*). In *Costa Rican Natural History,* ed. Daniel H. Janzen, 547–548. Chicago: Univ. of Chicago Press. 816 pp.

_____. 1983c. Orange-chinned Parakeet (*Brotogeris jugularis*). In *Costa Rican Natural History,* ed. Daniel H. Janzen, 548–550. Chicago: Univ. of Chicago Press. 816 pp.

Jenni, Donald A. 1983. Northern Jacana (*Jacana spinosa*). In *Costa Rican Natural History,* ed. Daniel H. Janzen, 584–586. Chicago: Univ. of Chicago Press. 816 pp.

Jenni, Donald A., and Terrence R. Mace. 1999. Northern Jacana (*Jacana spinosa*). In *The Birds of North America,* no. 467, ed. Alan Poole and Frank Gill. Philadelphia, Pa.: Academy of Natural Sciences; Washington, D.C.: American Ornithologists' Union. 20 pp.

Johnsgard, Paul A. 2000. *Trogons and Quetzals of the World.* Washington, D.C.: Smithsonian Institution Press. 223 pp.

Johnson, L. Scott. 1998. House Wren (*Troglodytes aedon*). In *The Birds of North America,* no. 380, ed. Alan Poole and Frank Gill. Philadelphia, Pa.: Academy of Natural Sciences; Washington, D.C.: American Ornithologists' Union. 32 pp.

Kaufmann, Ken. 1996. *Lives of North American Birds.* Boston, Mass.: Houghton Mifflin. 675 pp.

Keppie, Daniel M., and Clait E. Braun. Band-tailed Pigeon (*Columba fasciata*). In *The Birds of North America,* no. 530, ed. Alan Poole and Frank Gill. Philadelphia, Pa.: Academy of Natural Sciences; Washington, D.C.: American Ornithologists' Union. 28 pp.

Kingery, Hugh E. 1966. American Dipper (*Cinclus mexicanus*). In *The Birds of North America,* no. 229, ed. Alan Poole and Frank Gill. Philadelphia, Pa.: Academy of Natural Sciences; Washington, D.C.: American Ornithologists' Union. 28 pp.

Kirk, David A., and Michael J. Mossman. 1998. Turkey Vulture (*Cathartes aura*). In *The Birds of North America,* no. 339, ed. Alan Poole and Frank Gill. Philadelphia, Pa.: Academy of Natural Sciences; Washington, D.C.: American Ornithologists' Union. 32 pp.

Koenig, Walter D., Peter B. Stacey, Mark T. Stanback, and Ronald L. Mumme. 1995. Acorn Woodpecker (*Melanerpes formicivorus*). In *The Birds of North America,* no. 194, ed. Alan Poole and Frank Gill. Philadelphia, Pa.: Academy of Natural Sciences; Washington, D.C.: American Ornithologists' Union. 24 pp.

Kushlan, James A., and Keith L. Bildstein. 1992. White Ibis (*Eudocimus albus*). In *The Birds of North America,* no. 9, ed. A. Poole, P. Stettenheim, and F. Gill. Philadelphia, Pa.: Academy of Natural Sciences; Washington, D.C.: American Ornithologists' Union. 20 pp.

La Bastille, Anne. 1983. Resplendent Quetzal (*Pharomachrus mocinno*). In *Costa Rican Natural History,* ed. Daniel H. Janzen, 599–601. Chicago: Univ. of Chicago Press. 816 pp.

Latta, Steven C., and Christine A. Howell. 1999. Common Pauraque (*Nyctidromus albicollis*). In *The Birds of North America,* no. 429, ed. Alan Poole and Frank Gill. Philadelphia, Pa.: Academy of Natural Sciences; Washington, D.C.: American Ornithologists' Union. 16 pp.

Lawton, Marcy F. 1983. Brown Jay (*Cyanocorax morio*). In *Costa Rican Natural History,* ed. Daniel H. Janzen, 573–574. Chicago: Univ. of Chicago Press. 816 pp.

Leck, Charles F. 1983. Bananaquit (*Coereba flaveola*). In *Costa Rican Natural History,* ed. Daniel H. Janzen, 567–568. Chicago: Univ. of Chicago Press. 816 pp.

McDonald, David B., and Wayne K. Potts. 1994. Cooperative Display and Relatedness among Males in a Lek-Mating Bird. *Science* 266: 1030–1032.

Meyer, Kenneth D. 1995. Swallow-tailed Kite (*Elanoides forficatus*). In *The Birds of North America,* no. 138, ed. Alan Poole and Frank Gill. Philadelphia, Pa.: Academy of Natural Sciences; Washington, D.C.: American Ornithologists' Union. 24 pp.

Meyer de Schauensee, Rodolphe, and William H. Phelps, Jr. 1978. *A Guide to the Birds of Venezuela.* Princeton, N.J.: Princeton University Press. 424 pp.

Mock, Douglas W. 1983. Boat-billed Heron (*Cochlearius cochlearius*). In *Costa Rican Natural History,* ed. Daniel H. Janzen, 565–567. Chicago: Univ. of Chicago Press. 816 pp.

Morton, Ed S. 1983. Clay-colored Robin (*Turdus grayi*). In *Costa Rican Natural History,* ed. Daniel H. Janzen, 610–611. Chicago: Univ. of Chicago Press. 816 pp.

Mueller, Allan J. 1992. Inca Dove (*Columbina inca*). In *The Birds of North America,* no. 28, ed. Alan Poole and Frank Gill. Philadelphia, Pa.: Academy of Natural Sciences; Washington, D.C.: American Ornithologists' Union. 12 pp.

Nettleship, David N. 2000. Ruddy Turnstone (*Arenaria interpres*). *The Birds of North America,* no. 537, ed. Alan Poole and Frank Gill. Philadelphia, Pa.: Academy of Natural Sciences; Washington, D.C.: American Ornithologists' Union. 32 pp.

Nol, Erica, and Michele S. Blanken. 1999. Semipalmated Plover (*Charadrius semipalmatus*). In *The Birds of North America,* no. 444, ed. Alan Poole and Frank Gill. Philadelphia, Pa.: Academy of Natural Sciences; Washington, D.C.: American Ornithologists' Union. 24 pp.

Nol, Erica, and Robert C. Murphy. 1994. American Oystercatcher (*Haematopus palliatus*). In *The Birds of North America,* no. 82, ed. Alan Poole and Frank Gill. Philadelphia, Pa.: Academy of Natural Sciences; Washington, D.C.: American Ornithologists' Union. 24 pp.

Oring, Lewis W., Elizabeth M. Gray, and J. Michael Reed. 1997. Spotted Sandpiper (*Acti-*

tis macularia). In *The Birds of North America,* no. 289, ed. Alan Poole and Frank Gill. Philadelphia, Pa.: Academy of Natural Sciences; Washington, D.C.: American Ornithologists' Union. 32 pp.

Parsons, Katharine C., and Terry L. Master. 2000. Snowy Egret (*Egretta thula*). *The Birds of North America,* no. 489, ed. Alan Poole and Frank Gill. Philadelphia, Pa.: Academy of Natural Sciences; Washington, D.C.: American Ornithologists' Union. 24 pp.

Powers, Donald R. 1996. Magnificent Hummingbird (*Eugenes fulgens*). In *The Birds of North America,* no. 221, ed. Alan Poole and Frank Gill. Philadelphia, Pa.: Academy of Natural Sciences; Washington, D.C.: American Ornithologists' Union. 20 pp.

Quinn, James S., and Jennifer M. Startek-Foote. 2000. Smooth-billed Ani (*Crotophaga ani*). *The Birds of North America,* no. 539, ed. Alan Poole and Frank Gill. Philadelphia, Pa.: Academy of Natural Sciences; Washington, D.C.: American Ornithologists' Union. 16 pp.

Remsen, Jr., J. Van. 1983. Green Kingfisher (*Chloroceryle americana*). In *Costa Rican Natural History,* ed. Daniel H. Janzen, 564–565. Chicago: Univ. of Chicago Press. 816 pp.

Richardson, Michael, and Daniel W. Brauning. 1995. Chestnut-sided Warbler (*Dendroica pensylvanica*). In *The Birds of North America,* no. 190, ed. Alan Poole and Frank Gill. Philadelphia, Pa.: Academy of Natural Sciences; Washington, D.C.: American Ornithologists' Union. 20 pp.

Rimmer, Christopher C., and Kent P. McFarland. 1998. Tennessee Warbler (*Vermivora peregrina*). In *The Birds of North America,* no. 350, ed. Alan Poole and Frank Gill. Philadelphia, Pa.: Academy of Natural Sciences; Washington, D.C.: American Ornithologists' Union. 24 pp.

Rising, James D., and Nancy J. Flood. 1998. Baltimore Oriole (*Icterus galbula*). In *The Birds of North America,* no. 384, ed. Alan Poole and Frank Gill. Philadelphia, Pa.: Academy of Natural Sciences; Washington, D.C.: American Ornithologists' Union. 32 pp.

Robinson, Julie A., J. Michael Reed, Joseph P. Skorupa, and Lewis W. Oring. 1999. Black-necked Stilt (*Himantopus mexicanus*). *The Birds of North America,* no. 449, ed. Alan Poole and Frank Gill. Philadelphia, Pa.: Academy of Natural Sciences; Washington, D.C.: American Ornithologists' Union. 32 pp.

Rodgers, James A., Jr., and Henry T. Smith. 1995. Little Blue Heron (*Egretta caerulea*). In *The Birds of North America,* no. 145, ed. Alan Poole and Frank Gill. Philadelphia, Pa.: Academy of Natural Sciences; Washington, D.C.: American Ornithologists' Union. 32 pp.

Schreiber, Ralph W. 1983. Magnificent Frigatebird (*Fregata magnificens*). In *Costa Rican Natural History,* ed. Daniel H. Janzen, 577–579. Chicago: Univ. of Chicago Press. 816 pp.

Schreiber, Ralph W., and Michael B. McCoy. 1983. Brown Pelican (*Pelecanus occidentalis*). In *Costa Rican Natural History,* ed. Daniel H. Janzen, 594–597. Chicago: Univ. of Chicago Press. 816 pp.

Shealer, David. 1999. Sandwich Tern (*Sterna sandvicensis*). In *The Birds of North America,* no. 405, ed. Alan Poole and Frank Gill. Philadelphia, Pa.: Academy of Natural Sciences; Washington, D.C.: American Ornithologists' Union. 28 pp.

Sherry, Tom W. 1983a. Rufous-tailed Jacamar (*Galbula ruficauda*). In *Costa Rican Natural History*, ed. Daniel H. Janzen, 579–581. Chicago: Univ. of Chicago Press. 816 pp.

———. 1983b. Ochre-bellied Flycatcher (*Mionectes oleaginea*). In *Costa Rican Natural History*, ed. Daniel H. Janzen, 586–587. Chicago: Univ. of Chicago Press. 816 pp.

———. 1983c. Common Tody-flycatcher (*Todirostrum cinereum*). In *Costa Rican Natural History*, ed. Daniel H. Janzen, 608–610. Chicago: Univ. of Chicago Press. 816 pp.

Skeel, Margaret A., and Elizabeth P. Mallory. 1996. Whimbrel (*Numenius phaeopus*). In *The Birds of North America*, no. 219, ed. Alan Poole and Frank Gill. Philadelphia, Pa.: Academy of Natural Sciences; Washington, D.C.: American Ornithologists' Union. 28 pp.

Skutch, Alexander F. 1977. *Aves de Costa Rica*. San José, Costa Rica: Editorial Costa Rica. 148 pp.

———. 1983a. *Birds of Tropical America*. Austin: Univ. of Texas Press. 305 pp.

———. 1983b. Ruddy Ground-Dove (*Columbina talpacoti*). In *Costa Rican Natural History*, ed. Daniel H. Janzen, 568–569. Chicago: Univ. of Chicago Press. 816 pp.

———. 1983c. Laughing Falcon (*Herpetotheres cachinnans*). In *Costa Rican Natural History*, ed. Daniel H. Janzen, 582–583. Chicago: Univ. of Chicago Press. 816 pp.

———. 1987. *Helpers at Birds' Nests: A Worldwide Survey of Cooperative Breeding and Related Behavior*. Iowa City: Univ. of Iowa Press. 298 pp.

———. 1996. *Orioles, Blackbirds and Their Kin: A Natural History*. Tucson: Univ. of Arizona Press. 291 pp.

———. 1997. *Life of the Flycatcher*. Norman: Univ. of Oklahoma Press. 162 pp.

Slud, Paul. 1964. *The Birds of Costa Rica: Distribution and Ecology*. Vol. 128. New York: Bulletin of the American Museum of Natural History. 430 pp.

Smith, Susan M. 1983a. Turquoise-browed Motmot (*Eumomota superciliosa*). In *Costa Rican Natural History*, ed. Daniel H. Janzen, 577. Chicago: Univ. of Chicago Press. 816 pp.

———. 1983b. Tropical Screech-Owl (*Otus choliba*). In *Costa Rican Natural History*, ed. Daniel H. Janzen, 592. Chicago: Univ. of Chicago Press. 816 pp.

———. 1983c. Rufous-collared Sparrow (*Zonotrichia capensis*). In *Costa Rican Natural History*, ed. Daniel H. Janzen, 618. Chicago: Univ. of Chicago Press. 816 pp.

Stiles, F. Gary. 1983a. Green Heron (*Butorides virescens*). In *Costa Rican Natural History*, ed. Daniel H. Janzen, 552–554. Chicago: Univ. of Chicago Press. 816 pp.

———. 1983b. Long-tailed Hermit (*Phaethornis superciliosus*). In *Costa Rican Natural History*, ed. Daniel H. Janzen, 597–599. Chicago: Univ. of Chicago Press. 816 pp.

———. 1983c. Variable Seedeater (*Sporophila aurita*). In *Costa Rican Natural History*, ed. Daniel H. Janzen, 604–605. Chicago: Univ. of Chicago Press. 816 pp.

———. 1983d. Tennessee Warbler (*Vermivora peregrina*). In *Costa Rican Natural History*, ed. Daniel H. Janzen, 613–614. Chicago: Univ. of Chicago Press. 816 pp.

Stiles, F. Gary, and Daniel H. Janzen. 1983a. Turkey Vulture (*Cathartes aura*). In *Costa Rican Natural History*, ed. Daniel H. Janzen, 560–562. Chicago: Univ. of Chicago Press. 816 pp.

———. 1983b. Roadside Hawk (*Buteo magnirostris*). In *Costa Rican Natural History*, ed. Daniel H. Janzen, 551–552. Chicago: Univ. of Chicago Press. 816 pp.

Stiles, F. Gary, and Alexander F. Skutch. 1989. *A Guide to the Birds of Costa Rica*. Ithaca, N.Y.: Cornell Univ. Press. 511 pp.

Stouffer, Philip C., and R. Terry Chesser. 1998. Tropical Kingbird (*Tyrannus melancholicus*). In *The Birds of North America,* no. 358, ed. Alan Poole and Frank Gill. Philadelphia, Pa.: Academy of Natural Sciences; Washington, D.C.: American Ornithologists' Union. 20 pp.

Strauch, Jr., Joe G. 1983. Spotted Sandpiper (*Actitis macularia*). In *Costa Rican Natural History,* ed. Daniel H. Janzen, 544. Chicago: Univ. of Chicago Press. 816 pp.

Telfair, Raymond C. II. 1994. Cattle Egret (*Bubulcus ibis*). In *The Birds of North America,* no. 113, ed. Alan Poole and Frank Gill. Philadelphia, Pa.: Academy of Natural Sciences; Washington, D.C.: American Ornithologists' Union. 32 pp.

Telfair, Raymond C. II, and Michael L. Morrison. 1995. Neotropic Cormorant (*Phalacrocorax brasilianus*). In *The Birds of North America,* no. 137, ed. Alan Poole and Frank Gill. Philadelphia, Pa.: Academy of Natural Sciences; Washington, D.C.: American Ornithologists' Union. 24 pp.

Watts, Bryan D. 1995. Yellow-crowned Night-Heron (*Nyctanassa violacea*). In *The Birds of North America,* no. 161, ed. Alan Poole and Frank Gill. Philadelphia, Pa.: Academy of Natural Sciences; Washington, D.C.: American Ornithologists' Union. 24 pp.

Wiley, R. Haven. 1983. Rufous-naped Wren (*Campylorhynchus rufinucha*). In *Costa Rican Natural History,* ed. Daniel H. Janzen, 558–560. Chicago: Univ. of Chicago Press. 816 pp.

Wolf, Blair O. 1997. Black Phoebe (*Sayornis nigricans*). In *The Birds of North America,* no. 268, ed. Alan Poole and Frank Gill. Philadelphia, Pa.: Academy of Natural Sciences; Washington, D.C.: American Ornithologists' Union. 20 pp.

Mammals

The fauna of Costa Rica includes at least 228 mammals. Considering the small size of the country, this represents a greater diversity of mammals than occurs in more northern temperate climates. For example, Minnesota is four times larger than Costa Rica and has just 80 mammal species.

A review of the mammals provides some revealing insights, such as that half are bats! In northern environments, few bats are present and all are insect eaters, but in tropical regions, bats fill many habitat niches and have diverse food habits. They eat insects, nectar, fruits, fish, and blood. Many bats are essential to the survival of tropical plants because they pollinate flowers or disperse the seeds.

Additionally, because the complex tropical forest canopy provides numerous habitat niches, many mammals are adapted to living and traveling through the treetops to seek food, dens, and safety. These species include bats, opossums, monkeys, squirrels, sloths, small wild cats, and large members of the weasel family like Tayras.

Costa Rican mammals represent an unusual mix of species that have temperate North American or tropical South American origins. These factors are explained in the chapter on biogeography.

From a tourism and viewing standpoint, mammals can be difficult to see. Most are either crepuscular (active at dawn or dusk) or nocturnal. Many live in the dense forest and are difficult to spot. The most conspicuous mammals are monkeys, sloths, squirrels, and an occasional White-tailed Deer or Agouti. The best chances of seeing mammals exist while hiking early or late in the day or when taking escorted day or night drives, hikes, or boat tours with naturalist guides. When hoping to see the more elusive wild mammals, it is important to walk silently, stand or sit quietly for extended periods, and refrain from talking. In protected reserves like Corcovado NP, it is possible to see rare mammals like tapirs and peccaries because they tend to be more active during the day. This is also true for mammals in other national parks and at La Selva Biological Field Station, where Agoutis and herds of Collared Peccaries roam during the day.

Costa Rican mammals make an incredible array of sounds that can bring life, suspense, and excitement to a tropical forest. There is an excellent CD from the Library of Natural Sounds at the Cornell Laboratory of Ornithology by Louise H. Emmons et al. (1997, Vocalization tape H) called *Sounds of Neotropical Rainforest Mammals: An Audio Field Guide*. The roar of a Jaguar, howling of howler monkeys, tooth clacking of peccaries, and birdlike whistle of a tapir are among the fascinating sounds included. The sounds of many of the mammals described in this book are recorded on that CD.

Thirty-one mammals have been selected for species accounts. They represent some of the most conspicuous and abundant mammals as well as some of the more unique and seldom-seen species that add a sense of wonder, mystery, and excitement to Costa Rica's tropical forests. Even if they are unseen, they are probably there watching you.

Mantled howler monkey peeking out of canopy

OPOSSUM FAMILY (Didelphidae)

Common Opossum

Didelphis marsupialis

COSTA RICAN NAMES: *Zarigüella; raposa; zorro pelón; zorra mochila.*

6/15 trips; 12 sightings.

TOTAL LENGTH: 25.4–40.0 inches, including 10.0–21.1-inch tail.

WEIGHT: 1 pound 7 ounces–4 pounds 10 ounces (665–2,090 grams).

RANGE: Southern Texas to northern Argentina.

ELEVATIONAL RANGE: Sea level to 4,900 feet, with some records up to 7,300 feet.

The Common Opossum is the largest of nine opossums in Costa Rica. Primarily nocturnal, this marsupial occurs in pristine rainforests, coffee plantations, farms, cities, and gardens. Its range includes Caribbean lowlands, dry forests of Guanacaste, and southern Pacific lowland forests near the Panama border.

The size of a large house cat, the Common Opossum has grizzled gray or black fur. The cheeks are black in contrast to the white cheeks of the Virginia Opossum (*D. virginianus*), which also occurs in Guanacaste. Foods include natural and cultivated fruits, seeds, insects, crayfish, snails, mice, snakes, lizards, eggs, small birds, and even fish.

Females bear about six young twice per year, primarily in February and July. The young remain in the female's pouch for about sixty days after being born. When approached, this opossum growls, hisses, and bites an attacker rather than "play possum" like the Virginia Opossum does. Predators include Coyotes,

feral dogs, Boa Constrictors, Tayras, Ocelots, Cougars, and Jaguars. They are reported immune to the bites of venomous snakes.

This opossum may be seen with the aid of spotlights on night excursions in farm or ranch groves in Guanacaste, La Selva Biological Field Station, Manuel Antonio NP, or in the San Isidro del General area.

Common Opossum adult

Gray Four-eyed Opossum

Philander opossum

    Costa Rican name:
    Zorro de cuatro ojos.

    3/15 trips; 3 sightings.

    Total length: 21.0–24.0 inches, including 11.1–11.8-inch tail.

    Weight: 9.8 ounces–3 pounds 1 ounce (263–1,400 grams).

    Range: Tamaulipas, Mexico, to northeastern Argentina.

    Elevational range: Sea level to 4,800 feet.

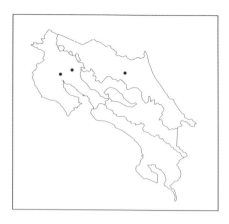

The Gray Four-eyed Opossum gets its name from two white spots above its eyes, giving it a "four-eyed" appearance. The size of a small house cat, this marsupial has short grayish fur that is not as grizzled as the fur of Common or Virginia Opossums. The very long tail is dark and furred at the base and light and bare toward the tip. The similar Brown Four-eyed Opossum (*Metachirus nudicaudatus*) can be distinguished by a buff spot over each eye, brownish color over the back, and a longer tail than that of the Gray Four-eyed Opossum.

Gray Four-eyed Opossum adult

This opossum produces an average litter of 4.2 to 4.6 young twice each year. Kits stay attached to the teats of the female for at least sixty days. The young reach sexual maturity at seven months of age.

This marsupial lives in dry and moist lowland forests of both the Caribbean and Pacific slopes near streams and swampy areas. It may be encountered at night in trees or on the ground at La Pacífica, La Selva Biological Field Station, Tortuguero NP, or Selva Verde in the Caribbean lowlands. The diet consists of wild fruits, nectar, fish, crabs, frogs, mice, and insects. It is also encountered on farms, where it eats fruits and grains. Predators include Jaguars, Cougars, Ocelots, Tayras, and Boa Constrictors.

PORCUPINE FAMILY (Erethizontidae)

Prehensile-tailed Porcupine (Mexican Prehensile-tailed Porcupine)

Coendu mexicanus

COSTA RICAN NAME: **Puerco espín.**

2/15 trips; 2 sightings.

TOTAL LENGTH: 31.3–39.4 inches, including 17.1–19.1-inch tail.

WEIGHT: 3 pounds 1 ounce–5 pounds 12 ounces (1,400–2,600 grams).

RANGE: Mexico to Panama.

ELEVATIONAL RANGE: Sea level to 9,800 feet.

Prehensile-tailed Porcupine adult

445

This tropical porcupine is an agile and intelligent mammal that shares a feature with opossums: a prehensile tail. Although the North American Porcupine has a short tail thickly covered with quills, this porcupine has a long prehensile tail that is bare at the tip. It can hang from tree branches as it reaches for fruits, blossoms, young leaves, seeds, and nuts. While eating, this porcupine holds fruits and seeds in its paws like a squirrel. One interesting adaptation is that when this porcupine is in the treetops, the fur and spines lie parallel to the contours of the body. When the porcupine descends to the ground, it fluffs out the fur and spines so they are perpendicular to the contours of the body. This makes the animal look larger and more intimidating to potential predators (Winnie Hallwachs, personal communication 2001).

Although widespread, this porcupine is seldom seen. In Guanacaste it is more conspicuous in the deciduous trees because of the sparse foliage. It occurs up to middle and high elevations like at the Monteverde Cloud Forest Reserve and to 8,500 feet in Cerro de la Muerte. It lives in dry, moist, and wet forests of both Caribbean and Pacific slopes. This porcupine can regularly be encountered on night drives along the road that descends from kilometer 80 on the PAH to Savegre Mountain Lodge. Prehensile-tailed Porcupines sleep in hollow trees during the day and are sometimes found with spotlights at night as they cross roads or feed in the treetops.

Sac-wing Bat adult

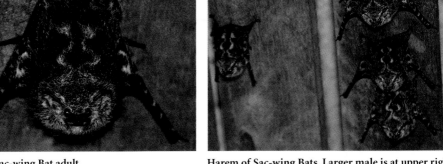

Harem of Sac-wing Bats. Larger male is at upper right.

SHEATH-TAILED BAT FAMILY (Emballonuridae)

Sac-wing Bat
(Greater White-lined Bat)

Saccopteryx bilineata

Costa Rican names: ***Murciélago de saco; murciélago de listas.***

4/15 trips; 4 sightings.

Total length: 2.1–2.2 inches, including 0.8-inch tail.

Weight: 0.22–0.33 ounce (6.2–9.3 grams).

Vocalization tape: H.

Range: Colima, Mexico, to Brazil and Trinidad and Tobago.

Elevational range: Sea level to 1,650 feet.

The Sac-wing Bat is a common insect-eating bat in Pacific and Caribbean lowland forests, including dry forests of Guanacaste. Often more conspicuous than other bats, it roosts during the day on the buttresses of large trees like strangler figs (*Ficus*) and kapok (*Ceiba*) trees. Roosts may also be encountered under large tree limbs and under the eaves of porch roofs. As they roost upside down, their heads are uplifted at a sharp angle that is characteristic of this genus. This bat is nocturnal and insectivorous. It usually forages near streams, moist habitats, and forest clearings.

This bat has short dark brown to black fur and two unbroken wavy white lines along the back. It occurs in "harems" of one to nine females and a male.

The name "Sac-wing" comes from scent glands under the wings that the male uses to attract females and to intimidate male bats. A male will hover in front of his harem while chirping to them and wafting his "bat scent" toward them. Females produce one young per year. Young can fly when only two weeks of age, but continue nursing for several months.

This bat may be observed under thatched eaves at Selva Verde Lodge, in abandoned settlers' cabins at La Selva Biological Station, in historic buildings at Santa Rosa NP, and at the Sirena Biological Station in Corcovado NP.

Similar Species: Brazilian Long-nosed Bat (*Rhynchonycteris naso*)

Colony of Brazilian Long-nosed Bats at typical daytime roosting site on palm tree by water's edge

A similar insectivorous species, the Brazilian Long-nosed Bat (1/15 trips; 2 sightings), has two broken wavy white lines on its back and is typically seen hanging upside down in vertical rows on the trunks of palm trees or tree limbs overhanging watercourses in tropical lowlands from southern Veracruz, Mexico, to southeastern Brazil. Sightings can be made on palm trunks along the water's edge on the Río Frío, in the Caño Negro NWR, and at La Laguna del Lagarto Lodge and Tortuguero NP. It is slightly smaller than the Sac-wing Bat and weighs about 0.13 ounce (3.8 to 3.9 grams). Colonies include ten to twenty-four individuals and several larger males among smaller females. They do not form harems as do Sac-wing Bats. Feeding is done over water.

LEAF-NOSED BAT FAMILY (Phyllostomidae)

Tent-making Bat

Uroderma bilobatum
> Costa Rican name: ***Murciélago***.
> 2/15 trips; 3 sightings.
> Total length: 2.4 inches.
> Weight: 0.46–0.70 ounce (13.0–20.0 grams).
> Range: Southern Mexico to southeastern Brazil.
> Elevational range: Sea level to 4,300 feet.

Tent-making Bats get their name from the way they bite the main veins of long leaves like *Heliconia* or palm leaves so that the leaves droop to create a tentlike waterproof shelter. This protects them from rain in areas that receive up to two hundred inches of precipitation per year. These bats sleep in their leaf shelters in tightly packed colonies ranging from two to fifty-nine individuals. Each bat is characterized by two prominent white stripes on the face and a "leaf-nose." Females roost in separate colonies when they bear their young. Each female gives birth to two young. Pups are believed to be born from January through April. They stay with the female for one month.

The Tent-making Bat is found in moist and wet Caribbean and Pacific lowlands. Although primarily a fruit-eating species, it also eats insects. Foods include fruits of figs and piper. This bat may be encountered at Tortuga Lodge, Villa Lapas, and in the vicinity of La Selva.

Colony of Tent-making Bats

Heliconia leaf being used by colony of Tent-making Bats

NEW WORLD MONKEY FAMILY (Cebidae)

Mantled Howler (Howling) Monkey

Allouata palliata

COSTA RICAN NAMES: ***Congo; mono negro.***

13/15 trips; 70 sightings.

TOTAL LENGTH: 41.1–50.4 inches, including a 21.5–25.8-inch tail.

WEIGHT: 6 pounds 13 ounces– 21 pounds 10 ounces (3,100–9,800 grams).

VOCALIZATION TAPE: H.

RANGE: Veracruz, Mexico, to western Colombia and Ecuador.

ELEVATIONAL RANGE: Sea level to 7,100 feet.

Male Mantled Howler Monkey howling

Female Mantled Howler Monkey with young

The Mantled Howler Monkey is the most conspicuous of four wild primates in Costa Rica's forests because of its lionlike roars. The sound can be heard up to a mile away. Adults have prehensile tails that aid in traveling through the tree-tops. They also provide a secure grip as the monkey reaches for the leaves, fruits, and flowers that make up its diet. The black fur is highlighted by a fringe of long copper-colored hair on the sides and lower back, which gives this howler its "mantled" name.

Howlers live in troops of two to forty-four individuals, averaging about thirteen. At La Pacífica in Guanacaste, densities approach one troop per 75 acres. Young monkeys reach sexual maturity at three to three-and-a-half years of age. The youngest sexually mature male and female in a troop are the so-cially dominant leaders. They maintain their dominance for thirteen to forty-eight months before being displaced by younger individuals. Only about 30 percent of young howler monkeys survive their first year, but some individuals may live up to twenty-five years. The gestation period is about 180 days and young stay with the mother for twelve to fifteen months.

This monkey lives in mangrove, dry, and wet forests from sea level up to montane cloud forests. Tolerant of humans, it occupies second-growth forests and even ranch woodlots. Many tropical forest wildlife species feed on nutri-

Field Guide to the Wildlife of Costa Rica

tious fruits or seeds, but the Mantled Howler Monkey primarily eats "roughage"—young leaves of a wide variety of tropical trees and vines that are low in nutrition but available in great abundance. A few fruits and flowers are also eaten. Many tropical plants contain toxins like alkaloids, cyanide, or strychnine, so howler monkeys learn to select plants with low concentrations of such chemicals. Some trees increase the concentrations of these toxins in response to feeding by the monkeys, so the monkeys need to keep changing their diet to find plants low in toxins.

Howlers are readily seen at close range in the dry forests of Guanacaste. This includes Santa Rosa, Guanacaste, and Palo Verde NPs; Lomas Barbudal BR; La Ensenada Lodge; La Pacífica; Hacienda Solimar; and forests near Tamarindo, Brasilito, and Sugar Beach. There is also viewing from boats in the canals at Tortuguero NP and in moist and wet forests of the Pacific slope, including Carara NP, Sirena Biological Station, private lodges in the vicinity of Corcovado NP, and at Tiskita Jungle Lodge. They are often heard but seldom seen in the cloud forests of Monteverde. While watching howler monkeys, keep an eye on the males. They may circle around you, get overhead, and urinate on you! This is a defense against predators.

Central American Spider Monkey (Black-handed Spider Monkey)

Ateles geoffroyi

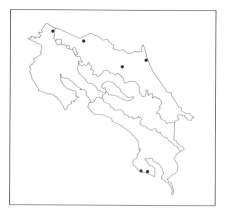

COSTA RICAN NAMES: *Mono araña; mono colorado.*

10/15 trips; 24 sightings.

TOTAL LENGTH: 37.0–57.9 inches, including 25.0–33.1-inch tail.

WEIGHT: 13 pounds 3.5 ounces–19 pounds 13.2 ounces (6,000–9,000 grams).

VOCALIZATION TAPE: H.

RANGE: Veracruz, Mexico, to southeastern Panama.

ELEVATIONAL RANGE: Sea level to 7,200 feet.

The long, slender arms and prehensile tail of this endangered primate contribute to its common name: spider monkey. This monkey has become endangered throughout its range because of habitat loss and killing of adults so the young can be captured for the pet trade. Adults weigh about the same as a howler monkey, but the stocky build of howler monkeys makes them appear

Adult spider monkey holding upper branch with its tail

Female spider monkey with young

heavier. Black-handed Spider Monkeys have blond to reddish-brown fur over their backs and sides. As the name implies, the hands and feet are black.

Spider monkeys, active throughout the day, move gracefully through treetops in search of ripe fruits. They also eat seeds, flowers, leaves, buds, and some small animals. Although a troop may consist of more than twenty individuals,

the monkeys separate into several foraging groups during the day. At dusk, the monkeys gather to sleep. The home territory of spider monkeys ranges from 153 to 284 acres.

After maturing at the age of four to five, spider monkeys may live up to twenty-seven years. Females produce their first young at five to seven years, and give birth to one young thereafter at seventeen- to forty-five-month intervals. Infant monkeys are cared for by the mother for over a year.

Spider monkeys are found throughout Costa Rica's lowlands, including dry forests of Guanacaste and moist and wet lowland forests of the Caribbean and southern Pacific slopes. Look for spider monkeys along the canals of Tortuguero NP, La Selva Biological Station, and Santa Rosa and Corcovado NPs, including the Sirena Biological Station.

White-faced Capuchin (White-throated Capuchin)

Cebus capucinus

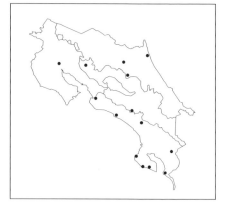

COSTA RICAN NAMES: *Mono cariblanco; mono cara blanca; mico.*

15/15 trips; 31 sightings.

TOTAL LENGTH: 27–39.5 inches, including 13.8–21.7-inch tail.

WEIGHT: 5 pounds 14.4 ounces–8 pounds 8.3 ounces (2,666–3,868 grams).

VOCALIZATION TAPE: H.

RANGE: Belize to northern and western Colombia.

ELEVATIONAL RANGE: Sea level to 8,200 feet.

Most people recognize this primate as the "organ-grinder's monkey." However, as with other neotropical primates, this monkey belongs in the forest, not at the end of someone's leash. White-faced Capuchins have prehensile tails and are smaller than howler and spider monkeys. They are characterized by black bodies with a white to yellowish face, throat, and shoulder region.

White-faced monkeys are found in forests ranging from dry and mangrove forests in Guanacaste to moist and wet lowland forests of the Caribbean and southern Pacific coasts. They even occur up to the level of montane forests in the Talamanca Mountains. Capuchins are diurnal and feed on fruits, nuts, shoots, buds, flowers, caterpillars, cicadas, beetles, and ants. In contrast to spider monkeys, which feed primarily in treetops, this monkey forages from ground level to the upper canopy. White-faced monkeys reach sexual maturity at three years of age and may live more than forty years. Females have a single young at approximately nineteen-month intervals. Infants are weaned at one year of age. This monkey lives in groups of five to thirty-six individuals that defend home ranges of 79–210 acres. White-faced Capuchins benefit forests by pollinating flowers and dispersing seeds in their droppings.

Capuchins are easily seen in most lowland forests of Costa Rica, including Santa Rosa, Guanacaste, Palo Verde, Tortuguero, Corcovado, Braulio Carrillo, Manuel Antonio, and Carara NPs. They can be seen in cloud forests of Monteverde (the Ecological Farm property), in the montane forests of Savegre Mountain Lodge, and even in the mangrove lagoon forests near Quepos.

White-faced Capuchin adult

White-faced Capuchin; close-up of face

Red-backed Squirrel Monkey

Saimiri oerstedii oerstedii
and S. o. citrinellus

> Costa Rican names:
> ***Tití; mono tití.***
>
> 6/15 trips; 15 sightings.
>
> Status: Permanent resident; southern Pacific lowland endemic species.
>
> Total length: 24.9 inches, including 14.3-inch tail.
>
> Weight: 1 pound 5.1 ounces–2 pounds 1.5 ounces (600–950 grams).
>
> Vocalization tape: H.
>
> Range: Southern Pacific coast of Costa Rica and adjacent Panama lowlands.
>
> Elevational range: Sea level to 1,545 feet.

The beautiful Red-backed Squirrel Monkey is the smallest and rarest primate in Costa Rica. Its body is about the size of a large North American Fox Squirrel. It is the only monkey in this country without a prehensile tail. It also poses a great distributional puzzle. The range of this monkey is separated from South American squirrel monkeys by the Andes Mountains in Colombia. It is suspected that pre-Columbian Indians from South America had trade routes along the Pacific Coast and brought monkeys as pets to native tribes in Central America. Some squirrel monkeys apparently escaped and adapted through natural selection over thousands of years until they became a separate species.

There are two subspecies in Costa Rica that are distinctive and geographically separate. Those of the Osa/Golfo Dulce/Tiskita region near Panama (*Saimiri oerstedii oerstedii*) have black caps and are reddish over their backs, shoulders, and flanks. Squirrel monkeys of Quepos and the Manuel Antonio NP region (*Saimiri oerstedii citrinellus*) have gray caps and reddish "saddles" over their backs and are grayish on their shoulders and flanks.

These monkeys move through treetops with long, graceful leaps as they search for fruit, seeds, leaves, birds' eggs, and insects. Their habitat includes moist and wet Pacific lowland forests from Manuel Antonio NP to the Osa Peninsula, including Corcovado NP and lowlands east of Golfo Dulce into western Panama.

This diurnal monkey is easily viewed as groups of ten to sixty-five individuals in the treetops. The home range varies from 42 to 99 acres. Red-backed Squirrel Monkeys mate in January and February and have young after 170

Red-backed Squirrel Monkey; race found on Osa Peninsula and at Tiskita Jungle Lodge (*S. o. oerstedii*). Note black cap and red over shoulders and back.

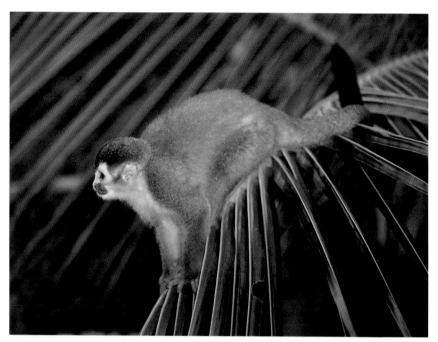

Red-backed Squirrel Monkey; race found at Manuel Antonio National Park and vicinity (*S. o. citrinellus*). Note gray cap and pale rusty back.

Squirrel monkey in mid-leap at Tiskita Jungle Lodge

days. Females have their first young at two years and produce one young about every thirteen to fourteen months thereafter. Squirrel monkeys can live up to twenty-one years. Predators include Boa Constrictors, Tayras, and Collared Forest-Falcons.

This endangered primate is present in Corcovado NP, including the Sirena Biological Station. The best place to view this monkey is near the cabins at Tiskita Jungle Lodge, at Rancho Casa Grande, and at Manuel Antonio NP. As with howler monkeys, beware when observing them at close range. They may get overhead and defecate on you! The author can verify that they have uncanny accuracy!

ANTEATER FAMILY (Myrmecophagidae)

Tamandua (Lesser, Banded, or Collared Anteater)

Tamandua mexicana

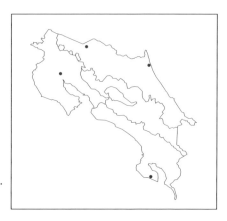

Costa Rican names: ***Tamandua; oso jaceta; hormiguero.***

2/15 trips; 2 sightings.

Total length: Up to 44.6 inches, including 21.4-inch tail.

Weight: 7 pounds 1 ounce–18 pounds 11 ounces (3,200–8,500 grams).

Vocalization tape: H.

Range: Veracruz, Mexico, to Peru.

Elevational range: Sea level to 4,900 feet.

The size of a raccoon, the Tamandua is the most common of three anteaters in Costa Rica. When approached by a dog or other predator, this mammal stands on its hind legs, balancing with its long prehensile tail and holding its muscular forelegs in a "boxer-like" pose. If an animal approaches too closely, the Tamandua will slash downward with its long, sharp claws.

The head and body are tan to light brown, with black over the back and a black stripe extending forward over each shoulder. The forelegs have well-developed claws that are used to tear open nests of ants and termites. The slender snout and long, sticky tongue are used to probe for the ants, termites, and occasional bees that constitute its diet.

The Tamandua lives in dry, moist, and wet forests of the Caribbean and Pacific slopes. Some live in trees and their diet comprises mostly ants. Others forage primarily for termites on the ground. Some are active in daytime and others forage at night. Tamanduas are solitary and occupy a territory of about 185 acres.

One young at a time is born to an adult female each year, and the young stays with the female until it is about half grown. When moving from one location to another, the young rides on the back of the mother. It dismounts to feed when the mother locates ants or termites.

The low frequency of Tamandua sightings is partially a reflection of how difficult it is to spot small mammals in the rainforest canopy. It is much easier to see them in the sparse foliage of the dry forests in Guanacaste. It may be encountered at Palo Verde, Guanacaste, Tortuguero, Corcovado, and Santa Rosa NPs; Caño Negro NWR; La Selva Biological Field Station; and in the Osa Peninsula, including the Corcovado Lodge Tent Camp and along the nearby trail to the Río Madrigal.

Tamandua adult feeding on ants in bullhorn acacia

SLOTH FAMILY (Bradypodidae)

Three-toed Sloth (Brown-throated Three-toed Sloth)

Bradypus variegatus

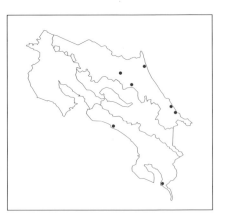

COSTA RICAN NAME: ***Perezoso de tres dedos.***

8/15 trips; 19 sightings.

TOTAL LENGTH: 22.4–26.0 inches, including 2.6–2.8-inch tail.

WEIGHT: 5 pounds 1 ounce–12 pounds 2 ounces (2,300–5,500 grams).

RANGE: Honduras to northern Argentina.

ELEVATIONAL RANGE: Sea level to 1,800 feet.

The Three-toed Sloth is one of the most distinctive and abundant rainforest mammals. Each foreleg has three long, curved claws that help grasp branches as it climbs. It has coarse pale brown to grayish hair that often has a greenish tinge caused by algae. The face is white with a dark stripe extending into each

Young Three-toed Sloth

Three-toed Sloth adult female climbing tree with young on belly

eye. There is often a light patch on the throat and chest. In a way, sloths are "cold-blooded." Their body temperature drops as much as twelve degrees at night to conserve energy. Each morning they climb to treetops to warm up in the sun.

There is a myth that sloths only eat *Cecropia* leaves, but they actually eat leaves from at least ninety-six trees and vines. Since sloths are often in dense foliage, they are not usually seen except in sparsely branched trees like *Cecropia*. Each sloth eats leaves from a unique combination of about forty tree species. Bacteria in the sloth's stomach are adapted to digesting those leaves—much like bacteria digest grass in the stomach of a cow. The combination of tree species needed is different for each sloth, so they can live at higher densities than if they all depended on the same plants. Densities may be as great as three sloths per acre but are usually about one per acre.

A sloth reaches sexual maturity at three years of age and may live twenty to thirty years. An infant clings to the mother for its first six months of life. During that time the young learns which leaves to eat from the female. The mother chews the leaves and passes them to the young so that the bacteria necessary for digestion are transferred to the young. Then the female leaves the young sloth alone in her territory for six months so it can learn to survive on its own. When the young sloth reaches one year of age, the female returns and forces the young to find its own territory.

Three-toed Sloths are most abundant in the Caribbean lowlands, especially in Cahuita NP and the nearby Cahuita vicinity. They can be seen along canals of Tortuguero NP, in *Cecropia* trees just east of Guapiles along the main highway from Guapiles to Limón, in the Central Park at Limón, and along the highway from Limón to Cahuita. They are also found at La Selva Biological Field Station and on the Pacific slope near Quepos, Manuel Antonio NP (along Perezoso Trail), Corcovado NP, and Tiskita Jungle Lodge.

Two-toed Sloth

Choloepus hoffmanni

> Costa Rican name: ***Perezoso de dos dedos***.
>
> 6/15 trips; 11 sightings.
>
> Total length: 21.3–27.6 inches; no tail.
>
> Weight: 8 pounds 13 ounces–17 pounds 7 ounces (4,000–8,000 grams).
>
> Range: Nicaragua to Colombia.
>
> Elevational range: Sea level to 9,200 feet.

The Two-toed Sloth is distinguished from the Three-toed Sloth by its long yellowish-brown to gray fur that gives the appearance of a "cheap faded blond wig." The short, somewhat piglike snout is also different from the less pronounced nose of the Three-toed Sloth. Each foreleg has two long, curved claws. The Three-toed Sloth is found only in lowlands, but this sloth is also found up to middle elevations and cloud forests.

Two-toed Sloths are more nocturnal and include more fruit in their diet than Three-toed Sloths. They can be very difficult to see when curled asleep in the treetops. They occur at a lower density than Three-toed Sloths—about one animal per five to seven acres.

Both sloths together account for about 70 percent of the combined weight of all rainforest mammals. Their densities greatly exceed those of monkeys. In one square mile of forest, there might be over 1,900 sloths and 190 howler

Two-toed Sloth adult on weekly trip to ground to defecate at Limón Central Park

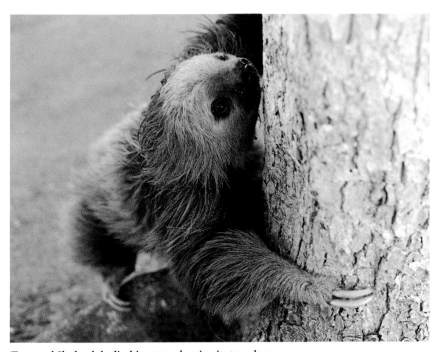
Two-toed Sloth adult climbing tree, showing its two claws

monkeys. However, howler monkeys are more conspicuous because they are so noisy and active.

Once a week each sloth descends to the base of the tree on which it has been feeding—and defecates. This refertilizes the tree with nutrients from the leaves that were eaten by the sloth. Sloth Moths fly from the hair of the sloth and lay eggs on the feces. After hatching, Sloth Moth larvae use sloth droppings as food. After the larvae develop into adult moths, they return to the forest canopy to locate a sloth. These moths feed on algae that grows within grooves of the sloth's hair. These insects are among many moths, beetles, mites, and ticks that live only on the bodies of sloths. As many as 900 insects may live on a single sloth!

The best place to see Two-toed Sloths is in the Central Park at Limón. There has been a population of sloths in this urban park for at least thirty years. This sloth can also be observed in trees along the highway from Limón south to Puerto Viejo, in Cahuita NP, and along the canals of Tortuguero NP. They occur in the moist and wet forests of the Osa Peninsula, including Corcovado NP and Tiskita Jungle Lodge. Sometimes they can be spotted in middle-elevation cloud forests of the Monteverde Cloud Forest Reserve, at Monteverde's Ecological Farm, in the central city park in Orotina, and in the Turrialba region.

ARMADILLO FAMILY (Dasypodidae)

Nine-banded Armadillo

Dasypus novemcinctus

> Costa Rican names: ***Cusuco;
> armado.***
>
> 4/15 trips; 4 sightings.
>
> Total length: 27.0–40.3 inches,
> including 11.4–17.7-inch tail.
>
> Weight: 7 pounds 1 ounce–
> 15 pounds 7 ounces (3,200–7,000
> grams).
>
> Vocalization tape: H.
>
> Range: Southwestern Missouri to
> northeastern Argentina.
>
> Elevational range: Sea level to at
> least 8,000 feet.

The armored appearance, pointed snout, and long, bare tail of the armadillo leave little doubt about its identity. This mammal evolved in South America and has steadily spread northward through Central America and into the United States. Armadillos are in an order of mammals called Edentata— meaning mammals without teeth. Actually, Nine-banded Armadillos have tiny

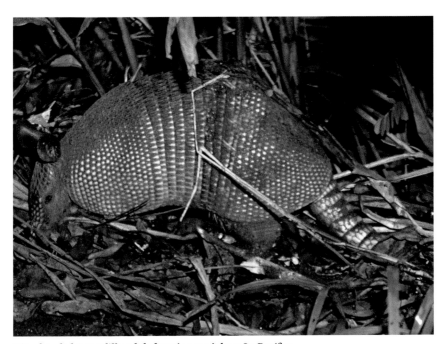

Nine-banded Armadillo adult foraging at night at La Pacífica

peglike teeth that help in eating ants, termites, caterpillars, beetles, slugs, earthworms, centipedes, fruits, and small invertebrates.

The bony plates on the body provide protection from most predators except Jaguars, Cougars, large dogs, and Coyotes. The nine "bands" around the central portion of the body provide flexibility. The number of bands may vary from seven to ten, but the usual number is nine. The shell of the armadillo suggests that it is slow-moving like a turtle, but it is as agile as a rabbit and can rapidly escape from a predator by running away, by leaping straight upward, or by quickly digging a hole with its well-developed claws.

Nine-banded Armadillos reach sexual maturity at one year of age. After mating, the fertilized egg undergoes "delayed implantation," whereby embryo development is delayed for up to 170 days. Then the egg divides into four separate and identical eggs. This results in identical quadruplets, which are born about 70 days later. Armadillos have an average life span of four years.

Armadillos live in the dry forests of Guanacaste, lowland moist and wet forests of the Caribbean and southern Pacific regions, middle elevations, and cloud forests. They can be common around farms, yards, and gardens as well as pristine forests. The best time to look for armadillos is at night with a flashlight as they explore yards and gardens. During the daytime they usually sleep in underground burrows, but they can occasionally be encountered early or late in the day. Sightings have been made on the grounds of La Pacífica, Palo Verde NP, and at CATIE near Turrialba.

SQUIRREL FAMILY (Sciuridae)

Variegated Squirrel

Sciurus variegatoides

Costa Rican name: ***Ardilla.***
10/15 trips; 20 sightings.

Total length: 20.1–22.0 inches, including 9.4–12.0-inch tail.

Weight: 1.0 pound 0.1 ounce–2 pounds 0.1 ounce (450–909 grams).

Vocalization tape: H.

Range: Chiapas, Mexico, to central Panama.

Elevational range: Sea level to 5,700 feet.

The Variegated Squirrel is the largest squirrel in Costa Rica. Color patterns range from coal black and grizzled black to rufous and light gray. The sides are frequently silvery gray above and rufous below. The belly is white to cinnamon, and the tail may be black above with rufous, tawny, and white hairs below. This squirrel is in the same genus as Fox and Gray Squirrels of the United States.

Variegated Squirrel

Its diet comprises acorns, nuts, fruits, buds, green plant parts, insects, bird eggs, and small reptiles. Breeding occurs primarily from January through June. Litters of four to eight young are born after a gestation period of forty-five days. The young are raised in tree cavities or leaf nests.

A resident throughout the country except for highlands and the Pacific lowlands south of Manuel Antonio NP, this squirrel is most conspicuous and abundant in Guanacaste. Active during the day, the Variegated Squirrel may be encountered in tropical dry forests of Palo Verde, Guanacaste, and Santa Rosa NPs, farm groves, riparian forests, and scattered woodlots. Other sightings may be expected in the Caribbean lowlands from La Selva southeast to Cahuita and on the Pacific coast at Carara NP, Manuel Antonio NP, and in the Central Plateau, including the grounds of the Parque Bolívar Zoo.

Red-tailed Squirrel
(Neotropical Red Squirrel)

Sciurus granatensis

COSTA RICAN NAMES: *Ardilla roja; ardilla chisa; chiza*.

6/15 trips; 14 sightings.

TOTAL LENGTH: 13.0–20.5 inches, including 5.5–11.0-inch tail.

WEIGHT: 8.0 ounces–1 pound 2.3 ounces (228–520 grams).

VOCALIZATION TAPE: H.

RANGE: Northwestern Costa Rica to Ecuador, Colombia, and Venezuela.

ELEVATIONAL RANGE: Sea level to 9,000 feet.

Red-tailed Squirrel adult

The Red-tailed Squirrel is smaller, darker, and more uniform in color than the Variegated Squirrel. It ranges from black to rusty brown above and light yellowish to rufous brown below. Although scarce in Guanacaste, it is more common than the Variegated Squirrel in Costa Rica's moist and wet lowland and middle-elevation forests. It is active throughout the day.

Where people put out bananas to feed birds, like at the Wilson Botanical Garden, this squirrel regularly visits the feeders. Large fruits, palm fruits, legumes, mushrooms, young leaves, flowers, and tree bark make up much of the diet. Red-tailed Squirrels forage on the ground and in trees.

This squirrel produces two or three litters per year, and each litter averages two young. Mating activity is especially apparent during the dry season. Four to eight males pursue a female through the treetops for several hours prior to mating. Young are born after forty-four days and are cared for by the female for eight to ten weeks. Red-tailed Squirrels occur at densities up to four per acre. The average home range is about 1.5 acres for females and 3.7 acres for males.

Tepescuintle adult

CAVY FAMILY (Dasyproctidae)

Tepescuintle (Paca)

Agouti paca

COSTA RICAN NAME: *Tepezcuintle*.

1/15 trips; 2 sightings.

TOTAL LENGTH: 29.1 inches, including 0.9-inch tail.

WEIGHT: 8 pounds 13 ounces–26 pounds 7 ounces (5,810–12,000 grams).

VOCALIZATION TAPE: H.

RANGE: Southern Mexico to south-eastern Brazil.

ELEVATIONAL RANGE: Sea level to 6,600 feet.

The cocker spaniel–sized Tepescuintle, or Paca, is the largest rodent in Costa Rica. It is a member of the cavy family, which includes guinea pigs, Agoutis, and chinchillas. The rows of whitish spots along the sides provide camouflage and suggest the pattern of a White-tailed Deer fawn. Enlarged, hollow cheek areas of the skull serve as resonating chambers to amplify the loud and ominous roar it makes when fighting or defending itself. Intensive hunting pressure has made the Tepescuintle rare in many areas because it is highly regarded for the quality of its meat.

The Tepescuintle is nocturnal and solitary except for females accompanied by young. A female has only one young in May or June after a gestation period of 115 days. It spends daytime hours in a shallow burrow under tree roots or in a hollow log—often near water. At night it searches for fallen fruits, seeds, leaves, stems, and roots. It will also eat fallen mangoes or avocados in orchards and may visit gardens to eat corn, watermelons, or squash. If pursued, a Tepescuintle has two escape strategies: it will either run a short distance and stand motionless for up to 45 minutes, or it will leap into a marsh or stream and submerge for many minutes with only the eyes and nostrils exposed.

Habitat ranges from riparian forests in Guanacaste to moist and wet rainforests of the Caribbean and southern Pacific regions. This species can survive in forest fragments, farmland, and edges of cities where thickets provide adequate hiding places.

Agouti

Dasyprocta punctata

COSTA RICAN NAMES: ***Guatusa; guatuza; cherenga***.

8/15 trips; 12 sightings.

TOTAL LENGTH: 16.3–24.4 inches, including 0.4–1.0-inch tail.

WEIGHT: 5 pounds–8 pounds 13 ounces (2,270–4,000 grams).

VOCALIZATION TAPE: H.

RANGE: Mexico to northern Argentina.

ELEVATIONAL RANGE: Sea level to 7,900 feet.

The Agouti is a medium-sized mammal in the cavy family that looks like a short-eared, chestnut-brown rabbit with a tiny, hairless tail. It gives the appear-

Agouti adult

ance of walking on its tiptoes and sits upright to eat seeds in its paws like a squirrel. The Agouti is prey for Jaguars, Cougars, Ocelots, Margays, Tayras, coatis, Boa Constrictors, and large raptors. If approached, an Agouti will erect the long hairs on its rump and thump its hind feet on the ground. If that is not successful in deterring a predator, it will race through the underbrush while making high-pitched barks.

Habitat ranges from dry forests in Guanacaste to moist and wet forests of the Caribbean and Pacific lowlands. In areas protected from hunting, the Agouti is active in daytime. With constant hunting pressure, it adapts to a more nocturnal existence. Hollow logs or burrows are used as dens.

The Agouti is an important disperser of forest seeds. Seeds such as those of *almendro* (*Dipteryx panamensis*), *pejivalle* (*Bactris gasipes*), and *caobilla* (*Carapa guiansis*) are collected and buried in times of seed abundance and retrieved in times of food scarcity. Seeds not eaten may eventually germinate and grow.

A pair of Agoutis occupies a home range of 5 to 9.6 acres. The male has an unusual habit of spraying the female with urine during its courtship ritual to attract her attention! The subsequent gestation period is 44 days, and the litter size is usually one or two. After the young are born, the female places them in tiny burrows that are too small for her to enter. This provides protection from predators. She calls them out to nurse.

One of the best places to see Agoutis is during the day at La Selva Biological Station. Look for them on the lawn among the cabins across the Stone suspension bridge from the headquarters and along the Tres Ríos trail. They can also be seen crossing trails at Carara, Santa Rosa, and Manuel Antonio NPs; at Corcovado Lodge Tent Camp; and on the grounds of the Wilson Botanical Garden.

Agouti adult female nursing young

WEASEL FAMILY (Mustelidae)

Tayra

Eira barbara

> Costa Rican names: ***Tolumuco;***
> ***gato de monte; cholumuco; tejón;***
> ***cabeza de viejo.***
>
> 5/15 trips; 5 sightings.
>
> Total length: 38.5–45.2 inches, including 15.0–18.5-inch tail.
>
> Weight: 8 pounds 13 ounces– 13 pounds 4 ounces (4,000–6,000 grams).
>
> Vocalization tape: H.
>
> Range: Central Mexico to northern Argentina.
>
> Elevational range: Sea level to 7,400 feet.

The Tayra, a dark brown to black fox-sized mammal, is typically glimpsed as it runs up and down tree trunks and along tree branches in search of prey. The tail is long and bushy, and the head may be black, dark brown, or light grayish in contrast to the dark brown body. This gives rise to the Spanish name *cabeza de viejo,* meaning "old man's head." Most Tayras in Costa Rica have a dark head. The Tayra appears to fill an ecological niche as a predator similar to that of the Fisher, an arboreal fox-sized member of the weasel family in boreal forests of the northern United States and Canada.

The Tayra is active throughout the day. Its relentless hunting behavior occurs on the ground and in trees. Prey includes just about anything smaller than a White-tailed Deer—figs, fruits, domestic poultry, sloths, squirrels, Agoutis, Tepescuintles, mice, rats, lizards, wild birds, and eggs. This mammal is usually solitary. Occasionally Tayras are encountered as pairs or females with young. They may even hunt in groups of up to twenty animals.

Habitats occupied by the Tayra range from dry and riparian forests of Guanacaste to wet lowland forests of the Caribbean and southern Pacific slopes. It also occurs at higher elevations throughout the mountains of Costa Rica. Habitat includes farms, plantations, and undisturbed forest.

The Tayra makes its den in a hollow tree, hollow log, or sheltered burrow. It has one to three young after a gestation period of sixty-five to seventy days. When the young are two months old, the female teaches them to hunt. The Tayra may be seen along the canals of Tortuguero NP, in the forests of La Selva Biological Field Station, and in Santa Rosa or Guanacaste NPs.

Tayra adult

RACCOON FAMILY (Procyonidae)

Kinkajou

Potos flavus

COSTA RICAN NAMES: *Marta; martilla; oso mielero.*

4/15 trips; 9 sightings.

TOTAL LENGTH: 34.8–41.3 inches, including 18.1– 21.1-inch tail.

WEIGHT: 4 pounds 6 ounces– 10 pounds 2 ounces (2,000–4,600 grams).

VOCALIZATION TAPE: H.

RANGE: Southern Mexico to southern Brazil.

ELEVATIONAL RANGE: Sea level to 6,800 feet.

The Kinkajou is sometimes called "honey bear" because of its habit of inserting its long tongue into bee hives so it can lick the honey. Although it is nocturnal and seldom seen, its appealing face, soft gray fur, and prehensile tail have made it a well-known tropical mammal.

Habitat varies from riparian forests of Guanacaste to lowland wet forests in the Caribbean and southern Pacific slopes, cloud forests, and montane forests.

Kinkajou adult

It lives in treetop environments where its diet comprises insects, grubs, small mammals, birds, bird eggs, honey, bananas, and wild fruits. Fruits eaten include guava (*Psidium*), inga (*Inga coruscans*), jobo (*Spondias mombin*), palm (*Welfia georgia*), and nectar of balsa (*Ochroma pyramidale*) flowers. The Kinkajou is ecologically important because it disperses fruit seeds in its droppings. When a tree is full of fruits, from seven to eight Kinkajous may gather at night to feed. They make their presence known with noisy barks, whistles, and shrill screams that can be heard up to a mile away. In good habitat, this mammal can reach a density of three to four animals per acre.

The Kinkajou usually has one young after a gestation period of 90 days. The den is typically in a hollow tree. In the past it has been hunted to capture the young ones as pets. However, since it sleeps during the day and makes noise all night, it makes a very poor pet. The nocturnal Kinkajou is rarely seen except during night hikes using spotlights. This species can be seen along the canals of Tortuguero NP and at La Virgen del Socorro, La Selva Biological Field Station, the Ecological Farm at Monteverde, La Pacífica, and the Sirena Biological Station.

White-nosed Coati (Coatimundi)

Nasua narica (Nasua nasua)

COSTA RICAN NAMES: **Pizote; coatimundi.**

6/15 trips; 8 sightings.

TOTAL LENGTH: 33.5–54.3 inches, including 16.5–26.8-inch tail.

WEIGHT: 6 pounds 10 ounces–15 pounds 7 ounces (3,000–7,000 grams).

VOCALIZATION TAPE: H.

RANGE: Texas, New Mexico, and Arizona to northwestern Colombia.

ELEVATIONAL RANGE: Sea level to 6,900 feet.

The Coatimundi is the largest and most conspicuous member of the raccoon family in Costa Rica. A social mammal, it is active throughout the day and is usually seen in family groups of fifteen to twenty. Groups may occasionally exceed thirty individuals. These groups consist of young males, females, and young. Old males are typically loners. Distinctive features are the long, dark, furry tail, which is held upright as it forages on the ground, and the highly flexible nose, which is used to sniff for food.

White-nosed Coati adult male foraging at Monteverde Cloud Forest Reserve

The coati is at home on the ground or in trees. Its omnivorous diet includes fruit, nuts, figs, insects, lizards, small mammals, birds, bird eggs, snails, worms, crabs, insect larvae, carrion, turtle eggs, and snakes. At night a group of coatis sleeps in the treetops. If a group of coatis is attacked, or perhaps shot at, the entire troop drops out of the treetop in a bewildering array of falling bodies that confuses the predator. Then all the coatis race off to safety. Coatis can fight fiercely as a group, so they have few predators. Jaguars, Cougars, Tayras, hawk-eagles, and Boa Constrictors will occasionally prey on a Coatimundi. White-faced Capuchins will sometimes prey on baby coatis in their nests.

A band of coatis led by adult females may occupy a home range of 75 to 125 acres. During the breeding season, a solitary male will briefly join a band of coatis for mating. From two to four young are born in a leafy treetop nest platform after a gestation period of 70 to 77 days. Young stay in the nest for about five weeks. In Guanacaste they may reproduce twice each year.

This mammal is found in habitats ranging from dry forests in Guanacaste to moist and wet forests of the Caribbean and southern Pacific slopes. The coati is most conspicuous, however, in Guanacaste, where family groups are frequently encountered crossing roads and trails in Palo Verde, Guanacaste, and Santa Rosa NPs and in Lomas Barbudal BR. This species is also commonly encountered at Hacienda Solimar, Corcovado Lodge Tent Camp, Wilson Botanical Garden, and in the Monteverde vicinity at the Ecological Farm, Monteverde Lodge, Hummingbird Gallery, and the Cloud Forest Reserve headquarters.

CAT FAMILY (Felidae)

Ocelot

Leopardus pardalis

Costa Rican names: *Manigordo; ocelote.*

1/15 trips; 1 sighting.

Total length: 38.5–51.2 inches, including 11.0–15.7-inch tail.

Weight: 17 pounds 10 ounces–33 pounds 2 ounces (8,000–15,000 grams).

Range: Southern Texas to northern Argentina.

Elevational range: Sea level to 8,600 feet, with records over 10,000 feet.

Although rarely seen, wild cats evoke a great sense of anticipation and excitement among rainforest travelers who hope to glimpse one. There are six wild cats in Costa Rica: Jaguar, Cougar, Jaguarundi, Ocelot, Margay, and Little Spotted Cat. Human demand for the spotted pelt of the Ocelot has caused populations to be greatly persecuted in the past, but protection as an endangered species is helping restore its numbers.

Ocelot adult

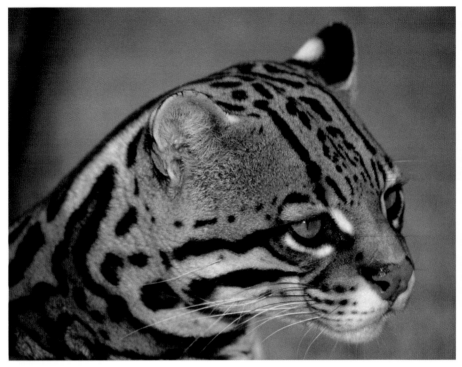

Ocelot; close-up of head

The Ocelot is a medium-sized cat adapted to riparian and dry forests of Guanacaste, moist and wet forests of the Caribbean and southern Pacific slopes, and montane forests of Braulio Carrillo and La Amistad NPs. It occupies undisturbed forests, second-growth forests, and agricultural areas.

The Ocelot is nocturnal but also hunts at dawn and dusk. Prey includes Spiny Rats, Agoutis, birds, lizards, opossums, snakes, and amphibians. It usually hunts on the ground, but it can also climb trees. A female Ocelot maintains a territory of 250 to 3,360 acres, which it defends from other females, and the male maintains a territory of 800 to 4,080 acres, which it defends against other males. The male's territory may include the territories of several females.

Females reach reproductive age at eighteen to twenty-two months, and they may produce young every other year to the age of thirteen. One to two young are born after a gestation period of seventy to eighty days. Cubs stay with the female for up to a year. The Ocelot is rarely seen, but it can be encountered on night excursions with the aid of spotlights or from boats at night along the canals of Tortuguero NP.

Jaguarundi

Herpailurus yaguarondi

COSTA RICAN NAMES: *Yaguarundi; león breñero; león miquero.*

2/15 trips; 2 sightings.

TOTAL LENGTH: 39.8–54.7 inches, including a 10.0–19.9-inch tail.

WEIGHT: 8 pounds 13 ounces–19 pounds 13 ounces (4,000–9,000 grams).

VOCALIZATION TAPE: H.

RANGE: Southern Texas to northern Argentina.

ELEVATIONAL RANGE: Sea level to 6,600 feet.

One of the most unusual and poorly known wild cats is the Jaguarundi. It has a house cat–like head; a long body; a long, slender tail; and short legs. There is a resemblance to the Tayra, but the tail is not as bushy. This cat occurs in reddish and grayish-black color morphs.

The Jaguarundi inhabits riparian forests in Guanacaste, lowland moist and wet forests, ranches, farms, and montane forests. Extremely agile and an

Jaguarundi adult, red color phase

Jaguarundi adult, gray color phase

excellent hunter, the Jaguarundi hunts primarily on the ground. It eats quail, wood-quail, tinamous, small rodents, armadillos, lizards, and insects. It also pursues prey in trees.

The Jaguarundi is the most vocal of Costa Rica's wild cats. It makes thirteen vocalizations, including birdlike chirps. One to four young are born in a hollow tree or den after a sixty- to seventy-five-day gestation period. The average litter size is two. This cat is more active during the day than other cats. Sightings have been made in the vicinity of La Selva and at Savegre Mountain Lodge. Most sightings are likely to be a quick glimpse of the animal bounding across a forest road or trail.

Similar Species: Cougar (*Puma concolor, Felis concolor*)

The Cougar resembles a very large, heavy-bodied version of the red-phase Jaguarundi. Although subspecies from the American Rockies can reach a length of almost nine feet and weigh over two hundred pounds, Cougars of Costa Rica's forests are smaller and more slender. Most probably do not exceed sixty to seventy pounds (27.25–31.80 kilograms). The Cougar occurs in dry and wet forests from sea level to

Cougar adult, Costa Rican subspecies

10,000 feet but is seldom seen. The sounds made by the Cougar are recorded on vocalization tape H. It preys on White-tailed Deer, Brocket Deer, Tepescuintles, Agoutis, armadillos, monkeys, Tamanduas, iguanas, raccoons, and, occasionally, cattle and horses. Good populations exist in Tortuguero and Corcovado NPs. Tracks are regularly encountered at the Sirena Biological Station.

Jaguar

Panthera onca

COSTA RICAN NAME: *Tigre*.

0/15 trips; 0 sightings.

TOTAL LENGTH: 87–120 inches, including 20.5–26.0-inch tail.

WEIGHT: 132–348 pounds (59.9–158.0 kilograms).

VOCALIZATION TAPE: H.

RANGE: Southern Arizona to northern Argentina.

ELEVATIONAL RANGE: Sea level to 6,600 feet, with some records up to 10,000 feet.

The awesome but endangered Jaguar is the largest carnivore in the Americas. Its massive and muscular body enables it to overwhelm prey up to the size of a tapir and kill by puncturing the prey's skull with large canines. A Jaguar's body

483

is highlighted by black rosettes on a golden-brown background. Some Jaguars are a melanistic black phase in which black rosettes are visible like black velvet against a plain black background. The Jaguar has become a symbol of rainforest preservation, because its survival depends on the protection of large tracts of forest.

The Jaguar lives in dry and riparian forests in Santa Rosa and Guanacaste NPs, cloud forests, montane forests, and moist and wet forests in Caribbean and southern Pacific lowlands. The best population in Costa Rica is on the Osa Peninsula in Corcovado NP, where Jaguars frequent areas near rivers, lagoons, and beaches.

This cat hunts during the day and night in protected areas where it is not exposed to hunting. It hunts by stalking its prey or by lying in ambush. Prey includes peccaries, White-tailed and Brocket Deer, White-faced Capuchins, tapirs, Agoutis, sloths, birds, caimans, fish, iguanas, snakes, and domestic livestock. It is reported to hunt sea turtles at night along the beach near Sirena Biological Station on the Osa Peninsula. Jaguars occupy territories that they defend against other Jaguars of the same sex. Males occupy home ranges up to 5,800 acres.

Jaguar adult

Jaguar track (forepaw) compared to a 2-inch-diameter camera lens cap near Sirena Biological Station

The Jaguar matures at three years of age and may live up to eleven years in the wild. Mating may occur at any time of year and is accompanied by very noisy roaring, grunting, and "caterwauling." When a female is receptive, a pair may mate up to a hundred times in a day. The gestation period is 90 to 111 days. There are usually one or two cubs in a litter, with some records of three or four. The cubs accompany the female for eighteen to twenty-four months.

Chances of seeing a Jaguar in the wild are very low, but one of the best concentrations of these great cats is at Sirena Biological Station in Corcovado NP. Tracks can be observed on the beach, along trails, on sandy banks of the Río Pavo, and along the banks of nearby Río Llorona. A Jaguar track is wider than it is long, and forefoot prints are larger than hindfoot prints. A forefoot print can be six inches wide across the toes!

White-lipped Peccary adult

PECCARY FAMILY (Tayassuidae)

White-lipped Peccary

Tayassu pecari (Dicotyles pecari)

Costa Rican name: ***Cariblanco***.

2/15 trips; 2 sightings.

Total length: 45.3–49.2 inches, including 2.0-inch tail.

Weight: 55 pounds 2 ounces– 75 pounds (25.0–34.0 kilograms).

Vocalization tape: H.

Range: Southern Mexico to northern Argentina.

Elevational range: Sea level to 4,900 feet.

Like the tapir and Jaguar, the endangered White-lipped Peccary is an indicator of wilderness rainforest habitat. Where large rainforest tracts exist, this wild pig occurs in roving herds of up to a couple hundred individuals. Early rainforest explorers feared encounters with this peccary because of its aggressive behavior. In spite of its ability to defend itself from other predators, this peccary is one of the first species to disappear when rainforest habitat is opened up with roads and subjected to poaching.

The White-lipped Peccary roams the forest in search of palm nuts, fruits, roots, tubers, and invertebrates. It can eat very hard palm nuts by using its massive molars. The tusks are effective in defense against Jaguars and Cougars.

When threatened, these peccaries make loud clacking noises with their tusks, and the long hairs of the back are erected to make the hogs look more intimidating. They also emit a powerful musky odor from scent glands on the back.

The peccary is active throughout the day. The approach of a herd can be ominous: There is a clattering noise from the tusks and the rustling of many feet through the forest litter. A strong, musky odor fills the air and remains long after the animals have passed. If approached by peccaries, one's best escape strategy is to climb a tree. Since peccaries can't jump, it is only necessary to climb about three feet to get above them.

Female peccaries mature at eighteen months of age, and they usually have two young 156 days after mating. The precocious young follow the mother soon after birth. The best remaining populations of White-lipped Peccaries in Costa Rica are in Corcovado NP.

Skull of White-lipped Peccary adult showing molars used to crush seeds and canines used for defense

Collared Peccary

Tayassu tajacu

Costa Rican names: **Saíno; zahíno; chancho de Monte; saíno de collar.**

2/15 trips; 5 sightings.

Total length: 34.3–37.0 inches, including 0.8–2.2-inch tail.

Weight: 30 pounds 14 ounces–55 pounds 2 ounces (14–25 kilograms).

Vocalization tape: H.

Range: Arizona, New Mexico, and Texas to northern Argentina.

Elevational range: Sea level to 9,800 feet.

While the White-lipped Peccary is dark with a whitish muzzle, this smaller peccary is marked by a faint whitish collar over the shoulders. It is adapted to a much greater range of habitats and is found to higher elevations. Because of intensive hunting pressure, this mammal has been greatly reduced outside national parks and protected reserves.

The Collared Peccary is found in Guanacaste's dry forests, moist and wet lowland rainforests of the Caribbean and Pacific slopes, and montane forests. It can exist in disturbed rainforest from which White-lipped Peccaries have disappeared.

Reproductive details are similar to those of the White-lipped Peccary. Though the Collared Peccary is not often seen, the musk hangs heavy along forest trails where a herd has recently passed. Their presence is also indicated by disturbed soil where they have rooted for tubers, roots, snakes, and insect larvae. Many mammals in tropical forests assist in dispersing seeds that have passed through their digestive tracts, but the peccary is an exception. It chews seeds with its molars before swallowing them, so they are "seed destroyers." This is a survival problem for many plants, but not for the rainforest yam.

The rainforest yam (*Dioscorea*) contains diosgenin, which is a type of "pig progesterone"—birth control for peccaries. If peccaries eat this yam, they stop having young and the "yam eaters" die out! It is a natural form of selective peccary birth control that helps the yam survive in a forest full of peccaries. The yam extract was known by native Americans in Mexico and used for birth control, because pig progesterone is similar to human progesterone. It was reported that once a month they gave a drink with the yam extract to young unmarried girls in their villages to prevent them from having babies before they married. A Penn State University chemist, Russell Marker, checked out this rumor in 1940 and identified the source of this medicine. He formed a company named Syntex, and in 1951 one of their chemists, Carl Djerassi, developed the first human birth control pills from the rainforest yam!

The Collared Peccary may occur in herds of up to thirty, but a typical herd is from two to fifteen. It is not as aggressive as the White-lipped Peccary, but observers should keep their distance. The best place to see this species is along the trails of La Selva Biological Field Station, where protection from poaching has allowed it to become abundant. Researchers there appreciate the peccaries because they are predators of snakes, including venomous snakes like the Bushmaster.

Collared Peccary adult

Rainforest yam (*Dioscorea*), which contains "pig progesterone" to prevent destruction of seeds by peccaries

DEER FAMILY (Cervidae)

White-tailed Deer

Odocoileus virginianus

COSTA RICAN NAMES: **Venado; venado cola blanca**.

4/15 trips; 5 sightings.

TOTAL LENGTH: 59.1–86.6 inches, including 3.9–9.8-inch tail.

WEIGHT: 50–80 pounds (22.7–36.3 kilograms).

VOCALIZATION TAPE: H.

RANGE: Southern Canada to northern Brazil.

ELEVATIONAL RANGE: Sea level to at least 7,200 feet.

It may seem surprising to encounter White-tailed Deer in tropical Costa Rica. This deer originated in North America and dispersed through Mexico and Central America to South America. Like raccoons and Cougars, the White-tailed Deer demonstrates "Bergman's Rule." Deer near the equator have a smaller body than the same species in colder northern temperate climates. This adaptation helps preserve body heat for larger northern deer during cold weather, and smaller body size helps in dissipating heat for smaller deer in the tropics.

White-tailed Deer adult doe

The White-tailed Deer is found in lowland and middle-elevation habitats where land clearing and agriculture have improved edge habitats, and where young successional stages of vegetation provide twigs, leaves, fallen fruits, and nuts as food. They are not a species of undisturbed rainforest.

Bucks are in rut in Guanacaste from approximately July through November, and one or two fawns are born after a gestation period of 205 to 215 days. The antlers of bucks are usually no more than ten inches long along main beams that curve upward in an arching pattern. There are usually no more than two or three short tines along the beams.

This deer has been hunted so intensively in most regions that it is rarely seen except in protected dry forest habitats of Guanacaste. It is common in Palo Verde, Santa Rosa, and Guanacaste NPs, and some may be observed in the vicinity of La Selva Biological Station.

TAPIR FAMILY (Tapiridae)

Baird's Tapir

Tapirus bairdii

COSTA RICAN NAMES: **Danta;
danto**.

1/15 trips; 1 sighting.

TOTAL LENGTH: 79.5 inches, with a
2.8-inch tail.

WEIGHT: 330–660 pounds (150–
300 kilograms).

VOCALIZATION TAPE: H.

RANGE: Veracruz, Mexico, to the
western Andes in Ecuador.

ELEVATIONAL RANGE: Sea level to
11,500 feet.

The endangered Baird's Tapir is the largest mammal in Costa Rica and the largest of three tapirs in the Americas. Although it resembles a large pig, the tapir's closest relatives are horses and rhinoceroses. The tapir has well-developed incisor teeth like a horse and can bite viciously if attacked. Tapirs evolved in Asia and North America and spread southward into Central and northern South America after the creation of the Central American land bridge between North and South America three to four million years ago.

Adult tapirs are brown to blackish, with white tips on their ears. The tapir is

Baird's Tapir adult female with young near Sirena Biological Station

Baird's Tapir close-up of face

incredibly adaptable and is found in habitats ranging from dry and riparian forests in Guanacaste to rainforests in the southern Pacific and Caribbean lowlands, cloud forests of Monteverde, and montane forests in the Talamanca Mountains. A "creature of habit," it repeatedly uses the same trails, defecation sites, stream-crossing sites, mud wallows, and feeding sites. This predictability makes it very vulnerable to poaching.

Active in the daytime and at night, the tapir is usually found near water and is an excellent swimmer. The diet consists of leaves, twigs, fruits, and seeds. The highly flexible snout aids in grasping and breaking off leaves and twigs while feeding. Since some seeds pass through the digestive tract undamaged, the tapir is an important seed disperser for tropical plants.

A single young tapir, "camouflaged" by patterns of white lines and white spots, is born after a gestation period of 390–400 days. The young stays with the female for up to a year, and the female bears young once every seventeen months.

Although the Baird's Tapir is found throughout much of Costa Rica's national park system, it is rarely seen. The best place to look for it is at mud wallows, tide pools, and river banks in the vicinity of Sirena Biological Station in Corcovado NP on the Osa Peninsula.

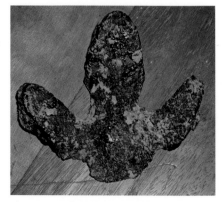

Plaster cast of tapir footprint. Note the three-toed arrangement of the foot.

BALEEN WHALE FAMILY (Balaenopteridae)

Hump-backed Whale

Megaptera novaeangliae
 COSTA RICAN NAME: ***Ballena**.*
 1/15 trips; 1 sighting.
 TOTAL LENGTH: 36–50 feet.
 WEIGHT: 20–44 tons (18,200–40,000 kilograms).
 RANGE: All oceans of the world.

Hump-backed Whale adult observed offshore from Drake Bay Wilderness Resort en route to Caño Island

The magnificent Hump-backed Whale is a migratory mammal that feeds in polar regions in summer and returns to warmer waters in winter. The pectoral fins are long and distinctive, and the dorsal fin is relatively small. White marks on the underside of the tail allow identification of individual whales. The back of the whale is black, and the throat and chest are white. Hump-backed Whales live in pods of up to twelve individuals. Migratory groups may include up to 150 whales.

In polar areas, humpbacks feed on krill and other planktonic varieties of crustaceans. They also eat cod, capelin, and herring. The humpback is well known for the highly developed vocalizations by which it communicates with others of its own species. A single young is born after a gestation period of eleven months, and the interval between births is usually two years. This whale reaches sexual maturity at the age of ten years.

Until recently, Costa Rica was not known for whale watching. However, Hump-backed Whales can be seen in the Pacific Ocean between the Drake Bay Wilderness Resort and Marenco Wilderness Camp on the Osa Peninsula and the Caño Island BR during January and February. Those whales are migrants from the California population, and the females apparently come to Costa Rica for calving. Whales also winter in the Golfo Dulce area east of the Osa Peninsula. Watch for them while flying to or from Tiskita Jungle Lodge on the eastern shore of the Golfo Dulce. Other whale habitats include the Uvita National Marine Park south of Dominical and the Islas Ballenas Marine Park on the Pacific coast, where whales winter from December through April. For more information about whales, whale conservation, and whale watching in Costa Rica, contact the conservation group "Promar" at 011-506-227-5856.

Adult whale diving offshore from Drake Bay Wilderness Resort

Banfield, A. W. F. 1974. *The Mammals of Canada*. Toronto, Ont.: Univ. of Toronto Press for the National Museum of Natural Sciences. 438 pp.

Bergman, Charles. 1999. The Peaceful Primate. *Smithsonian* 30(3): 78–86.

Boinski, Sue, K. Jack, C. Lamarsh, and J. Coltrane. 1988. Squirrel Monkeys in Costa Rica: Drifting to extinction. *Oryx* 32(1): 45–48.

Borrero H., José Ignacio. 1967. *Mamíferos Neotropicales*. Cali, Colombia: Univ. del Valle. 108 pp.

Carrillo, Eduardo, Grace Wong, and Joel C. Sáenz. 1999. *Mamíferos de Costa Rica*. Santo Domingo de Heredia, Costa Rica: Instituto Nacional de Biodiversidad. 250 pp.

de la Rosa, Carlos L., and Claudia C. Nocke. 2000. *A Guide to the Carnivores of Central America*. Austin: Univ. of Texas Press. 244 pp.

Eisenberg, John F. 1989. *Mammals of the Neotropics*. Vol. 1, *The Northern Neotropics*. Chicago: Univ. of Chicago Press. 449 pp.

Emmons, Katherine M., et al. 1996. *Cockscomb Basin Wildlife Sanctuary: Its History, Flora, and Fauna for Visitors, Teachers, and Scientists*. Caye Caulker, Belize: Producciones de la Hamaca; and Gays Mills, Wis.: Orang-utan Press. 334 pp.

Emmons, Louise. 1997. *Neotropical Rainforest Mammals: A Field Guide*. 2d ed. Chicago: Univ. of Chicago Press. 307 pp.

Glander, Kenneth E. 1996. *The Howling Monkeys of La Pacífica*. Durham, N.C.: Duke Univ. Primate Center. 31 pp.

Hall, E. Raymond. 1981. *The Mammals of North America*. Vols. 1 and 2. New York: John Wiley & Sons. 1181 pp.

Heaney, Larry R. 1983. Red-tailed Squirrel (*Sciurus granatensis*). In *Costa Rican Natural History*, ed. Daniel H. Janzen, 489–490. Chicago: Univ. of Chicago Press. 816 pp.

Henderson, Carrol L. 1970. Fish and Wildlife Resources in Costa Rica, with Notes on Human Influences. Master of Forest Resources thesis, Univ. Of Georgia, Athens. 340 pp.

Horwich, Robert H., and Jonathan Lyon. 1990. *A Belizean Rain Forest: The Community Baboon Sanctuary*. Gays Mills, Wis.: Orang-utan Press. 420 pp.

Janzen, Daniel H. 1983. White-tailed Deer (*Odocoileus virginianus*). In *Costa Rican Natural History*, ed. Daniel H. Janzen, 481–483. Chicago: Univ. of Chicago Press. 816 pp.

———, ed. 1983. *Costa Rican Natural History*. Chicago: Univ. of Chicago Press. 816 pp.

Joyce, Christopher. 1994. *Earthly Goods: Medicine-hunting in the Rainforest*. Boston: Little Brown. 304 pp.

Kaufmann, John H. 1983. White-nosed Coati (*Nasua narica*). In *Costa Rican Natural History*, ed. Daniel H. Janzen, 478–480. Chicago: Univ. of Chicago Press. 816 pp.

Leopold, Aldo S. 1959. *Wildlife of Mexico: The Game Birds and Mammals*. Berkeley: Univ. of California Press. 568 pp.

Lubin, Yael D. 1983. Tamandua (*Tamandua mexicana*). In *Costa Rican Natural History*, ed. Daniel H. Janzen, 494–496. Chicago: Univ. of Chicago Press. 816 pp.

Macdonald, David, ed. 1984. *All the World's Animals: Primates*. New York: Torstar Books. 160 pp.

Meña Moya, R. A. 1978. *Fauna y caza en Costa Rica*. San José, Costa Rica: Litografía e Imprenta LIL. 255 pp.

Pariser, Harry S. 1996. *Adventure Guide to Costa Rica*. 3rd ed. Edison, N.J.: Hunter. 546 pp.

Rowe, Noel. 1996. *The Pictorial Guide to the Living Primates*. East Hampton, N.Y.: Pogonias Press. 263 pp.

Sowls, L. K. 1983. Collared Peccary (*Tayassu tajacu*). In *Costa Rican Natural History*, ed. Daniel H. Janzen, 497–498. Chicago: Univ. of Chicago Press. 816 pp.

Sunquist, Fiona. 1986. The Secret Energy of the Sloth. *International Wildlife* 16(1): 4–11.

Timm, Robert M., et al. 1989. *Mammals of the La Selva–Braulio Carrillo Complex, Costa Rica*. North American Fauna Series, Number 75. Washington, D.C.: U.S. Dept. of Interior, Fish and Wildlife Service. 162 pp.

GLOSSARY

Altricial: Helpless at hatching or birth and requiring extensive parental care before fledging or becoming independent.

Aposematic markings: Bright markings—usually orange, yellow, blue, or red—on a creature like a frog or a butterfly that serve as warning coloration to potential predators that it contains bad-tasting or toxic chemicals that can make the predator extremely sick.

Arboreal: Reference to a creature's lifestyle and adaptations that involve living in trees. Ex.: Squirrels and monkeys are arboreal.

Arribada: A massive and synchronized arrival of sea turtles onto a beach for nesting purposes.

Arthropod: A member of the phylum Arthropoda, including segmented invertebrates like insects, spiders, and crustaceans.

Avifauna: A broad term for bird life.

Basking: The behavior of resting in the sun as a means of raising body temperature, commonly practiced by turtles, lizards, caimans, and other cold-blooded reptiles.

Batesian mimicry: A type of mimicry in which one creature, like a butterfly, that has no toxic chemicals in its body to deter predation resembles another species with toxic chemicals that deter predation so closely that predators avoid the edible species. Ex.: The Viceroy Butterfly is a Batesian mimic of the Monarch Butterfly.

Bird of prey: A bird that eats other birds and animals and typically has strong claws and a sharp beak for catching, killing, and tearing open prey species. Examples are kites, hawks, falcons, vultures, and owls. Synonym = raptor.

BR: Biological Reserve.

Brood: A family of newly hatched young birds from the same nest.

Cache (v.): The activity of storing food for later use, as practiced by species like Acorn Woodpeckers that store acorns in holes in trees for later meals. (n.): The supply of food, such as acorns, that has been stored for later use by a species like the Acorn Woodpecker.

Canopy: A layer within the overall structure of a forest. *Lower canopy* refers to the shrub and short tree layer; *midcanopy* refers to middle levels of foliage and structure among trees; *upper canopy* refers to the foliage and vegetative structure in the tops of the trees; and *supercanopy* refers to trees like *Ceiba* that project above the upper canopy.

Carapace: The upper (dorsal) shell of a turtle.

Caribbean slope: The northern and eastern portion of Costa Rica from the continental divide in the mountains eastward to the lowlands that drain toward the Caribbean.

Cere: The fleshy portion on some birds' faces located between the upper bill and the feathered portion of the face. Ex.: The male Great Curassow has a cere.

Clutch: The eggs laid in a single bird's nest, usually by a single female. (After hatching, the young are collectively referred to as a *brood*.)

Color morph: A color variety within a species that deviates from normal coloration. Ex.: There are black color morphs of Jaguars and Jaguarundis and dark or black morphs among some birds of prey.

Commensalism: A type of symbiosis in which both species involved benefit from their relationship to each other; also called *mutualism*.

Crepuscular: Appearing or being active at dawn and dusk.

Crop: The enlarged portion of the gullet at the base of a bird's throat. It is used for temporary storage of food prior to entering the gizzard or for later regurgitation to young.

Crustacean: A type of arthropod that typically has a hard shell or crust covering the body, such as lobsters, shrimp, and crabs.

Cryptic: Reference to a type of coloration that serves to camouflage a creature.

Cut bank: An exposed vertical bank of dirt, like along a road or river, that is used as a site for the nesting burrows of birds like motmots, kingfishers, and jacamars.

Decurved bill: A bird's bill that bends downward; opposite of *recurved*. Ex.: The Whimbrel has a decurved bill.

Dewlap: A fold of fleshy skin that hangs down from the chin and throat area, as on a Crested Guan or a male Green Iguana.

Diurnal: Being active during daylight hours; opposite of *nocturnal*.

Dry forest: A forest in which the total annual rainfall ranges from 40 to 80 inches per year. The dry forest in Costa Rica is found primarily in Guanacaste Province and is a tropical deciduous forest with distinctive wet and dry seasons.

Dry season: That portion of the year in which less rainfall occurs in some regions. In Costa Rica, the dry season occurs from December through March.

Ectoparasite: A parasite that lives on the skin, feathers, or fur of an animal.

Endemic: Occurring only within a limited geographic area and nowhere else in the world, such as a species that is found only in the mountains of Costa Rica and western Panama, in the lowlands of southern Costa Rica and adjacent Panama, or on Cocos Island.

Epiphyte: A plant that grows above the ground on the surface of another plant and depends on that plant for physical support. Examples include some bromeliads and orchids.

Fledge: To leave the nest (on the part of young birds).

Fledging period: The time elapsed from a bird's hatching to its leaving the nest.

Foothills: Hilly terrain at the base of mountains with elevations of about 2,000 to 4,900 feet; approximately the same as the premontane or subtropical zone. The distribution of some species is limited to foothills and not to either lowlands or highlands.

Gallery forest: A forest adjacent to a stream or river; same as riparian forest.

Gestation period: The amount of time from breeding to the birth of young.

Gorget: The iridescent area of a hummingbird's throat.

Highlands: For the purposes of this book, regions from 5,000 to 11,000 feet in elevation, including moist, wet, and rain forests and paramo. They are characterized by 40–200 inches of rainfall per year.

Host plant: The plant species that a butterfly or moth caterpillar eats prior to forming its cocoon.

Incubation period: For birds, the amount of time between when a bird begins to sit on its eggs and when the eggs hatch. For reptiles and amphibians, it is the amount of time between the laying and hatching of eggs.

Lowlands: The relatively flat terrain between foothills and the coast. It is in the elevation range from sea level to about 2,000 feet and includes dry, moist, and wet forests.

Melanistic: Having excess pigmentation, causing an individual to be very dark or black.

Metamorphosis: The process by which a creature like an insect or amphibian changes its form from an egg to a caterpillar to a cocoon to a moth or butterfly; from an egg to a nymph to an adult; or from an egg to a tadpole to a frog.

Middle elevations: Elevations from about 2,000 feet to 4,900 feet known as subtropical or premontane; also generally referred to as "foothills." This may include moist, wet, and rain forest habitats. The Central Plateau and San José are at middle elevations.

Mimicry: The phenomenon by which one creature derives a survival advantage by resembling another creature that has special defenses against predation.

Moist forest: A forest in tropical lowlands that receives from 80 to 160 inches of rainfall per year. In contrast, a "wet forest" receives from 160 to 320 inches of rainfall per year in tropical lowlands. At premontane and lower montane levels, moist forest receives 40 to 80 inches of rainfall.

Mollusks: Invertebrates that have one or two external shells that protect all or part of the body. Exs.: snails, clams, squid, and octopus.

Monogamy: A reproductive strategy by which a single male and female create a pair bond with each other and do not have multiple mates.

Montane forest: A highland wet forest (40–80 inches of rainfall per year) or rainforest (80–160 inches of rainfall per year) between 8,200 feet and 10,500 feet in elevation.

Müllerian mimicry: A phenomenon by which two different species share an undesirable characteristic like odor or toxic chemicals *and* similar identification marks that cause predators to avoid both species; opposite of *Batesian mimicry*. A famous example is the pair of passionflower butterflies *Heliconius erato* and *Heliconius melpomene*.

Nape: The back of the neck on a bird.

Nocturnal: Active at night; opposite of *diurnal*.

NP/NPs: National Park/National Parks.

NWR: National Wildlife Refuge.

Pacific slope: That portion of the Costa Rican landscape that drains from the continental divide in the mountains west and south to the Pacific Ocean, including Guanacaste and the southern Pacific lowlands.

PA H: Pan American Highway.

Paramo: A highland elevational zone above the montane zone, ranging from about 10,500 feet to the peaks of Costa Rica's highest mountains. This zone is above the tree line and is characterized by stunted shrubs, bamboo, and many composites.

Plastron: The lower (ventral) shell of a turtle.

Polyandry: A reproductive strategy of birds (like the Great Tinamou and Northern Jacana) in which the female defends a territory and mates with multiple males. The males incubate the eggs and raise the young within the female's territory.

Precocial: Active from birth or hatching and needing little parental care. It refers, for example, to newly hatched birds that are so well developed that they can leave the nest within a day or two of hatching.

Premontane: The elevational zone between approximately 2,000 and 4,900 feet; also often referred to as foothills, subtropics, or middle elevations. It includes moist, wet, and rain forests at those elevations.

Primary feathers: The outermost nine or ten flight feathers of a bird's wing. These feathers are attached to the "hand bones" of the wing and provide forward thrust on the downstroke of the wing.

Primary forest: A mature forest that has not been cut in recent times.

Rainy season: That portion of the year in which most rain falls. In Costa Rica, this refers to the period from April to December, except in the Caribbean lowlands, which experience rain throughout the year.

Raptor: A bird of prey. Examples include kites, hawks, falcons, owls, or vultures.

Riparian forest: A forest along a stream or river; same as *gallery forest*.

Sally (v.): To fly out from a perch to catch an insect or other creature or to pick a fruit while on the wing.

Savanna: An arid habitat of northwestern Costa Rica, near the Nicaragua border, characterized by open grassy ground cover and scattered short trees like *Byrsonima* and *Curatella*. It is an arid extreme of tropical dry forest maintained by fire.

Scapular feathers: Feathers that lie along the contour of the shoulder of a bird and cover the upper portions of the folded wing.

Secondary feathers: The inner medium-length flight feathers that trail on the back portion of a bird's wing. They are attached to the ulna bone and generate lift in flight.

Secondary forest: A forest that has grown back after a disturbance like burning or cutting.

Sp./Spp.: "Sp." refers to an undesignated or unidentified species within a given genus, and "spp." is a reference to multiple species within a genus. For example, "*Norops* sp." refers to a lizard that has been identified to genus, but the particular species is undetermined. "*Norops* spp." refers to multiple species of *Norops* lizards without designating individual species.

Stoop: a falconry term describing the action of a bird of prey, like a falcon, when it dives at high speed to strike and kill a bird in flight.

Symbiosis: The interdependent relationship between two species in which each species benefits from the presence and lifestyle of the other; same as *mutualism*.

Taxonomist: A person who specializes in the classification and naming of species.

Termitary: A gray globelike or elliptical nest of termites, usually located on a tree or fence post. Some birds like trogons and parakeets excavate their nest within a termitary.

Terrestrial: Living on the ground.

Tertial feathers: The tract of feathers on the wing of a bird, closest to the body, that lies over the contour of the back and covers the back of the wing when it is closed.

Tico/a: A person from Costa Rica: Tico (male); Tica (female).

Traplining: Hummingbird behavior in which an individual hummingbird repeatedly visits the same flowers for nectar over a large area in a predictable order, as in visiting traps on a trapline.

Tympanum: The round, eardrum-type area immediately behind and slightly below the eye on a frog or lizard.

Understory: Smaller trees, shrubs, and other vegetation that are generally under 25 feet in height within a taller forest.

Undertail coverts: Those bird feathers that are underneath the base of the tail.

Wading bird: A bird with long legs that wades in shallow water in order to locate its food, such as small fishes. Examples include herons and egrets.

Wet forest: A forest in tropical lowlands that receives from 160 to 320 inches of rainfall per year. At premontane and lower montane levels, wet forest receives 80 to 160 inches of rainfall per year.

Wet season: The season when most rainfall occurs; same as *rainy season*. In Costa Rica, it is the period from April to December. In some areas like the northeastern Caribbean lowlands, the wet season extends through most of the year.

APPENDIX A
Costa Rica Conservation Organizations and Field Stations

Alliance for the Monteverde Institute: Pennsylvania Audubon. Telephone: 717-213-6880; e-mail: grusso@mvinstitute.org. This organization is fundraising to buy one of the two remnant forests used by Three-wattled Bellbirds near Monteverde in the postbreeding season—an excellent project for a very rare bird.

Asociación Ornitológica de Costa Rica: www.zeledonia.org. Newsletter: *Zeledonia.*

Association for the Conservation of Nature (ASCONA): Apartado 83790-1000, San José, Costa Rica. Telephone: 506-296-5000.

Birding Club of Costa Rica: Contact at costaricabirding@hotmail.com.

Caribbean Conservation Corporation: 4424 NW 13th St., Suite #A1, Gainesville, FL 32609. Telephone: 1-800-678-7853 or 352-373-6441. Web site: www.cccturtle.org. In Costa Rica, telephone: 506-224-9215; fax: 506-234-1061; address: Apartado 246-2050, San Pedro, Costa Rica. They produce a monthly newsletter called *El Ecologista.* Through this organization it is possible to participate in citizen science research projects on Leatherback and Green Turtles at Tortuguero.

Costa Rica–Minnesota Foundation: 2424 Territorial Road, St. Paul, MN 55114. Telephone: 651-645-4103; fax: 651-645-4684. This foundation sponsors medical, cultural, and conservation exchanges between participants in Costa Rica and Minnesota. It also sponsored the first successful program for exchanges of Boy Scouts to assist Costa Rican Scouts to protect sea turtle nesting beaches from poachers on the Pacific coast.

Guanacaste Dry Forest Conservation Fund: Major efforts are under way to acquire the Rincón Rainforest and provide management funding for the Guanacaste Conservation Area. As of November 2003, $4,292,474 has been raised and used to purchase 12,328 acres, but the goal necessary to preserve this vital tropical forest is another $68,000. Tax-deductible checks should be made out to the "Guanacaste Dry Forest Conservation Fund" and sent to Professor Dan Janzen, Dept. of Biology, University of Pennsylvania, Philadelphia, PA 19104. E-mail: djanzen@sas.upenn.edu.

International Children's Rainforest: Apartado 10581-1000, San José, Costa Rica. Telephone: 506-645-5003; fax: 506-645-5104; e-mail: acmmcl@racsa.co.cr.

La Selva Biological Station, OTS: Apartado 53-3069, Puerto Viejo en Sarapiquí, Heredia, Costa Rica. Telephone: 506-766-6565; fax: 506-766-6535; e-mail: laselva@sloth.ots.ac.cr.

Las Cruces Biological Station and Wilson Botanical Garden, OTS: Apartado 73, 8257 San Vito, Coto Brus, Costa Rica. Telephone: 506-773-4370; fax: 506-773-3665; e-mail: lascruces@hortus.ots.ac.cr.

Monteverde Conservation League: Apartado 10165-1000, San José, Costa Rica. This organization is dedicated to preservation of the Monteverde Cloud Forest Reserve and associated lands.

National Biodiversity Institute (INBIO): 3100 Santo Domingo, Heredia, Costa Rica. Telephone: 506-507-8100; fax: 506-36-42-69.

National Parks Foundation (Fundación de Parques Nacionales): Apartado 236-1002, San José, Costa Rica. Telephone: 506-257-2239 or 506-257-8563.

The Nature Conservancy, International Program: 1815 North Lynn St., Arlington, VA 22209-2003. Telephone: 703-841-5300; fax: 703-841-1283; web site: www.nature.org.

Organization for Tropical Studies, Inc.: North American Headquarters: Box 90630, Durham, NC 27708-0630. Web site: www.ots.duke.edu. Costa Rican office: Apartado 676, 2050 San Pedro de Montes de Oca, San José, Costa Rica. Telephone: 506-240-6696; fax: 506-240-6783; e-mail: oet@cro.ots.ac.cr; web site: www.ots.ac.cr.

Rainforest Action Network: 221 Pine Street, Suite 500, San Francisco, CA 94104. Telephone: 415-398-4404; fax 415-398-2732; Web site: www.ran.org.

Tirimbina Rainforest Center: Milwaukee Public Museum, 2114 East Kinsington Blvd., Milwaukee, WI 53211. Telephone: 414-906-9080. Web site: www.tirimbina.org or contact webmaster@tirimbina.org. This 750-acre reserve is operated by the Milwaukee Public Museum and the Riveredge Nature Center. In Costa Rica, it is possible to contact the center in Sarapiquí at 506-761-1004. E-mail can be directed to magistra@racsa.co.cr.

World Wildlife Fund: 1250 Twenty-fourth St. NW, Washington, DC 20037. Telephone: 1-800-CALLWWF.

Wildlife Tourism Sites and Field Stations
Referred to in the Distribution Maps

Figure 11. Wildlife tourism sites referred to in the text and on species distribution maps

Each dot on the distribution maps represents one or more sightings for a species in that area by Henderson Birding Trip groups from 1987 through 2000. Sightings are also included for the Caño Negro BR for species reported as "common" or "abundant" by naturalist guide Jim Lewis. Sightings for La Laguna del Lagarto Lodge include species reported as "common" or "abundant" by lodge owner Vinzenz Schmack.

GUANACASTE REGION

G-1: Los Inocentes Lodge: Tropical moist forest. Elev.: 750'. Lat. 11°03.45' N, long. 85°50.35' W. Address: P.O. Box 228-3000, Heredia, Costa Rica. Telephone: 506-679-9190; fax: 506-265-4385; e-mail: orosina@racsa.co.cr; web site: www.arweb.com/orosi. An excellent wildlife lodge with a wide variety of wildlife on the property; a good place to stay when visiting Santa Rosa NP.

G-2: Santa Rosa NP: Tropical dry forest/premontane moist forest. Elev.: 1,350'. Lat. 10°51.50' N, long. 85°36.50' W. This park contains 122,352 acres and is an excellent example of tropical dry forest and premontane moist forest, as well as gallery forest. The famous Olive Ridley Turtle nesting beaches of Nancite are located within this park. Telephone: 506-666-5051.

G-3: Road from Liberia to Tamarindo: Tropical dry forest. Elev.: 100'. From lat. 10°37.50' N, long. 85°27.00' W to lat. 10°18.60' N, long. 85°55.00' W. Many species of the tropical dry forest can be spotted along this road en route to see the Leatherback Turtles at Tamarindo.

G-4: Tamarindo, Hotel Tamarindo Diriá, Hotel Villa Baula, Playa Grande, Las Baulas NP, and Sugar Beach: Tropical dry forest. Elev.: Sea level. Lat. 10°18.60' N, long. 85°55.00' W. Las Baulas NP, which covers 1,364 acres, protects the nesting beaches of the Leatherback Turtle at Playa Grande. Mangrove lagoons and beaches in the vicinity are important wintering sites for shorebirds, wading birds, and local wildlife. Tropical dry forests of the area provide opportunities for viewing howler monkeys and other upland wildlife. Hotel Tamarindo Diriá and Hotel Villa Baula are both convenient places to stay when going to see Leatherback Turtles. Hotel Tamarindo Diriá: Telephone: 506-653-0031; fax: 506-653-0208; e-mail: tnodiria@racsa.co.cr. Hotel Villa Baula: Telephone: 506-653-0650 and 506-653-0493; fax: 506-653-0459.

G-5: Lomas Barbudal Biological Reserve: Tropical dry forest. Elev.: 100'. Lat. 10°26.20' N, long. 85°16.00' W. Lomas Barbudal is a reserve of 5,631 acres that provides an excellent example of riparian forest within the Guanacaste region. Elegant Trogons, Scrub Euphonias, and Long-tailed Manakins are among the featured wildlife there.

G-6: Palo Verde National Park: Tropical dry forest. Elev.: 30'. Lat. 10°22.21' N, long. 85°11.84' W. Palo Verde National Park is an example of both dry forest and tropical wetlands that provide vital wintering grounds for migratory and resident waterfowl. This NP includes the area that was formerly designated as the Dr. Rafael Lucas Rodríguez Caballero NWR. The NP comprises 32,267 acres of tropical dry forest, riparian forest, and marshes. It is an important wintering site for migratory waterfowl and local Black-bellied Whistling-Ducks and Muscovy Ducks. It is also home to Jabiru storks, Scarlet Macaws, and Snail Kites. This park serves as an important research and education site for the Organization for Tropical Studies (OTS) and for the National Biodiversity Institute (INBIO). Palo Verde Biological Station: Telephone: 506-284-6105; e-mail: oet@ots.ac.cr; web site: www.ots.ac.cr.

G-7: La Pacífica (Centro Ecológico La Pacífica/Finca La Pacífica), Las Pumas, and Cañas: Tropical dry forest. Elev.: 150'. Lat. 10°27.21' N, long. 85°07.68' W. A 3,300-acre ranch and private forest reserve; formerly Finca La Pacífica. Address: Apartado 8, 5700 Cañas, Guanacaste, Costa Rica. Lodging is available to researchers only, but the restaurant is open to the public and the grounds are available for birding. Telephone: 506-669-0050; fax: 506-669-0555. Adjacent to this property is Las Pumas, the farm of Werner and Lily Hagnauer, which is operated as a wild cat rescue and rehabilitation center. All six of Costa Rica's wild cats can be observed there. Donations are appreciated.

G-8: Estancia Jiménez Núñez and lagoons: Tropical dry forest. Elev.: 250'. Lat. 10°20.55' N, long. 85°08.69' W. Private ranch with large human-made lagoons that provide habitat for many waterbirds; good raptor viewing on the road from the PAH west to this ranch. Obtain permission from the guard at the entrance to see the lagoons.

G-9: Hacienda Solimar and La Ensenada Lodge: Tropical dry forest. Hacienda Solimar: Elev.: 100'. Lat. 10°15.58' N, long. 85°09.40' W. Excellent example of dry forest and riparian forest and exceptional viewing of wetland wildlife at Estero Madrigal, including Roseate Spoonbills, Boat-billed Herons, Bare-throated Tiger-Herons, and crocodiles in the surrounding lagoon. Owner has made significant improvements to this 5,000-acre ranch to accommodate wildlife tourism since 1998. Telephone: 506-298-4292; e-mail: solimar@racsa.co.cr; web site: birdcostarica.com. La Ensenada Lodge: Elev.: Sea level to 200'. Lat. 10°08.30' N, long. 85°02.39' W. An 840-acre privately owned national wildlife refuge that provides exceptional opportunities to see wetland wildlife, mangrove lagoons, and wildlife of the dry forest. This is one of the best places in Costa Rica to see Three-wattled Bellbirds during the dry season. Telephone: 506-289-6653 or 506-228-6653; fax: 506-289-5281; e-mail: letresa@racsa.co.cr.

G-10: Río Lagarto bridge and farm lagoon: Premontane moist forest. Elev.: 140'. Lat. 10°09.76' N, long. 84°54.93' W. This is a farm pond at Ganadera Avancari just off the PAH near the bridge over the Río Lagarto. Black-bellied Whistling-Ducks, Least Grebes, Purple Gallinules, and Northern Jacanas are regularly observed there.

G-11: Pulpería La Pita and lowlands to Monteverde: Tropical moist forest. Elev.: 700'. From lat. 10°10.09' N, long. 84°54.38' W to lat. 10°18.00' N, long.

84°49.20' W. This is the road at the turnoff from the PAH by Río Lagarto, past a small store known as Pulpería La Pita, and through mixed pasture and woodland en route to Monteverde. Wildlife includes species of the Guanacaste dry forest like White-throated Magpie-Jays, Spot-bellied Bobwhites, Rufous-naped Wrens, and Long-tailed Manakins.

G-12: Puntarenas, Hotel Tioga, and Playa Doña Ana: Premontane wet forest. Elev.: Sea level. Lat. 9°58.46' N, long. 84°50.34' W. The lagoons and beaches of Puntarenas and nearby Playa Doña Ana provide excellent areas to observe shorebirds, wading birds, White-winged Doves, frigatebirds, cormorants, Black Skimmers, Anhingas, terns, and gulls. Hotel Tioga, with its downtown beachfront location, provides easy access to the beach and nearby birding sites like Carara NP. Address: P.O. Box 96-5400, Puntarenas, Costa Rica. Telephone: 506-661-0271; fax: 506-661-0127; e-mail: tiogacr@racsa.co.cr; web site: www.cmnet.co.cr/tioga.

SOUTHERN PACIFIC LOWLANDS

S-1: Carara NP, Río Tárcoles estuary, Villa Lapas, and Tárcol Lodge: Premontane moist forest. Elev.: Sea level to 100'. Lat. 9°47.72' N, long. 84°36.16' W. An excellent reserve that has wildlife of both the Guanacaste tropical dry forest and tropical wet forests of southern Pacific lowlands. One of the best places in the country to observe Scarlet Macaws and crocodiles. The Río Tárcoles estuary and surrounding forests at Hotel Villa Lapas and at Tárcol Lodge provide opportunities to see King Vultures, White Hawks, Ospreys, forest wildlife, shorebirds, and wading birds. Hotel Villa Lapas: Telephone: 506-293-4104 or 506-637-0232; fax: 506-293-4101 or 506-637-0227; e-mail: hvlapas@racsa.co.cr; web site: www.villalapas.co.cr. Tárcol Lodge address: P.O. Box 96-5400, Puntarenas, Costa Rica. Telephone: 506-430-0400 or toll-free in U.S. 1-800-593-3305; e-mail: mark@ranchonaturalista.com; web site: www. ranchonaturalista.com.

S-2: Road from Orotina to lowlands approaching Carara: Tropical moist forest. Elev.: Approx. 500'. Lat. 9°51.80' N, long. 84°34.00' W.

S-3: Road from Parrita to Puriscal: Tropical moist forest. Site 1: Elev.: 1,600'. Lat. 9°42.46' N, long. 84°24.22' W. Site 2: Elev.: 2,000'. Lat. 9°43.90' N, long. 84.23.64' W.

S-4: Manuel Antonio NP, Rancho Casa Grande, Cabinas Eclipse, and Quepos area: Premontane wet forest. Elev.: Sea level. Lat. 9°22.94' N, long. 84°08.62' W. Manuel Antonio NP is small, only 4,448 acres, but it provides excellent opportunities to see squirrel monkeys, Agoutis, White-faced Capuchins, Ctenosaurs, butterflies, and many other species of the southern Pacific lowlands. Boat

rides are available in Quepos to explore the mangrove lagoons. For information on mangrove lagoon boat tours, contact Iguana Tours at: Telephone:
506-777-1262; e-mail: iguana@iguanatours.com; web site:
www.iguanatours.com. Rancho Casa Grande is an excellent nature lodge to
use in the Quepos area. There are many squirrel monkeys on the property.
Telephone: 506-777-1646.

S-5: Talari Mountain Lodge near San Isidro del General: Premontane wet forest.
Elev.: 2,800'. Lat. 9°24.18' N, long. 83°40.07' W. Address: Rivas, San Isidro,
Apartado 517-8000, Pérez Zeledon, Costa Rica. Telephone: 506-771-0341;
e-mail: talaripz@racsa.co.cr. This rustic lodge in the country near San Isidro
has excellent wildlife viewing opportunities on the grounds. It is easy to
observe seventy species in a morning of birding there. An excellent place to
see the Slaty Spinetail and Red-legged Honeycreeper. Many birds come to the
feeders. A good place to stay if visiting Los Cusingos.

S-6: La Junta de Pacuares resort on Río General: Tropical moist forest. Elev.:
2,200'. Lat. 9°16.51' N, long. 83°38.33' W. A variety of wildlife can be seen along
the river at this site, including Gray-headed Chachalacas.

**S-7: San Isidro del General, City Lagoons, Hotel del Sur, and Los Cusingos/Skutch
farm:** Tropical moist forest. San Isidro del General: Elev.: 2,200'. Lat.
9°20.40'N, long. 83°28.00' W. City sewage lagoons: Elev.: 2,000'. Lat. 9°22.25'
N, long. 83°41.80' W. Los Cusingos: Elev.: 2,500'. Lat. 9°19.10' N, long. 83°36.75'
W. Los Cusingos is owned by Dr. Alexander Skutch and managed by the
Tropical Science Center. Make reservations for visits with the Tropical Science
Center, Apartado 8-3870-1000, San José, Costa Rica. Telephone:
506-645-5122; fax: 506-645-5034. Los Cusingos is an excellent remnant forest
reserve and is named for the Fiery-billed Aracaris that occur there. Hotel del
Sur provides a convenient place to stay in the San Isidro area. Telephone:
506-771-3033; fax: 506-234-7681; e-mail: htlsur@racsa.co.cr; web site:
www.ecotourism.co.cr/ Hotel Del Sur/.

S-8: Río Térraba bridge crossing: Tropical moist forest. Elev.: 200'. Bridge over
Río Térraba: Lat. 9°00.28' N, long. 83°13.43' W. Crocodiles are regularly
observed from this bridge.

S-9: Las Cruces/Wilson Botanical Garden at San Vito; OTS field station:
Premontane rainforest. Elev.: 3,900'. Botanical gardens: Lat. 8°47.15' N, long.
82°57.58' W. Address: Apartado 73-8257, San Vito de Java, Coto Brus, Costa
Rica, or main OTS address at Apartado 676-2050, San Pedro de Montes de
Oca, Costa Rica. Telephone: 506-773-4370 or main OTS number in San José at
506-240-6696; fax: 506-773-3665 or main OTS fax at 506-240-6783; e-mail:
lascruces@hortus.ots.ac.cr; web site: lascruces@hortus.ots.oc.cr. This OTS

field station is an exceptional example of premontane rainforest and has an excellent trail system. Many regional endemic birds are found on the property, and many birds come to the feeders there.

S-10: San Vito airport lagoons and road from San Vito to Sabalito: Premontane wet forest. Elev.: 2,200'. From lat. 8°49.61' N, long. 82°57.80' W to lat. 8°49.80' N, long. 82°53.80' W. This is a good area for seeing the Gray-crowned (Chiriquí) Yellowthroat, Crested Oropendola, and Blue-headed Parrot.

S-11: Road from Paso Canoas to San Vito: Premontane wet forest. Elev.: 300'. From lat. 8°32.00' N, long. 82°50.30' W to lat. 8°49.61' N, long. 82°57.80' W.

S-12: From Sierpe on Río Térraba to Drake Bay: Premontane wet forest. Elev.: Sea level. From Sierpe at lat. 8°51.50' N, long. 83°28.20' W to the Río Sierpe estuary at lat. 8°46.50' N, long. 83°38.00' W. Local lodging includes Río Sierpe Lodge, where boat trips are available to Corcovado NP and Caño Island Biological Reserve. Telephone: 506-283-5573; fax: 506-283-7655; e-mail: vsftrip@racsa.co.cr.

S-13: Drake Bay Wilderness Resort (northwestern end of Corcovado NP): Tropical wet forest. Elev.: Sea level. Lat. 8°41.80' N, long. 83°41.00' W. Telephone/fax: 506-770-8012 or telephone 506-284-4107; e-mail: hdrake@racsa.co.cr; web site: www.drakebay.com.

S-14: Caño Island Biological Reserve: Tropical wet forest. Elev.: Sea level. Lat. 8°43.00' N, long. 83°53.00' W. Arrange for visits with local lodges like Río Sierpe Lodge, Drake Bay Wilderness Resort, Aguila de Osa Inn, La Paloma Lodge, or Marenco Lodge. This 741-acre island is six miles from the Osa Peninsula. It is possible to see Hump-backed Whales while en route between the mainland and the island.

S-15: Sirena Biological Station, Corcovado NP: Tropical wet forest. Elev.: Sea level. Lat. 8°78.74' N, long. 83°35.81' W. Accessible by air or by foot by hiking along the beach from La Leona or San Pedrillo. This biological station is one of the best examples of remote, wild rainforest in Costa Rica. It is home to significant populations of Scarlet Macaws, tapirs, White-lipped Peccaries, Great Curassows, Jaguars, Cougars, and other species characteristic of tropical wet forests. Telephone: 506-735-5282 or 506-735-5440 for reservations.

S-16: Corcovado Lodge Tent Camp; Carate; and southeastern end of Corcovado NP: Tropical wet forest. Elev.: Sea level. Lat. 8°26.91' N, long. 83°28.86' W. Address: Costa Rica Expeditions, P.O. Box 6941-1000, San José, Costa Rica. Telephone: 506-257-0766 or 506-222-0333; fax: 506-257-1665; e-mail: costaric@expeditions.co.cr; web site: www.costaricaexpeditions.co.cr. An excellent representative area for observing wildlife of the southern Pacific lowlands, including Scarlet Macaws, Mangrove Black-Hawks, parrots, King Vultures, many raptors, and four species of monkeys. Similar wildlife can be observed at nearby Marenco, Luna, Bosque del Cabo, and Lapa Ríos lodges.

S-17: Tiskita Jungle Lodge: Tropical wet forest. Elev.: Sea level to 200'. Lat. 8°21.48' N, long. 83°8.05' W. A 400-acre private forest reserve and tropical fruit experimental field station. Address: Costa Rica Sun Tours, P.O. Box 13411-1000, San José, Costa Rica. Telephone: 506-296-8125; fax: 506-296-8133; e-mail: info@tiskita-lodge.co.cr; web site: tiskita-lodge.co.cr. One of the best places in Costa Rica to see squirrel monkeys and White Hawks. Great concentrations of birds are present because of the variety of native trees and fruit trees on the grounds.

CENTRAL PLATEAU

P-1: Sarchí vicinity: Premontane wet forest. Elev.: 3,100'. Lat. 10°5.10' N, long. 84°20.80' W.

P-2: Xandari Plantation, Hotel Alta, Juan Santamaría International Airport/Pavas vicinity, and Tobías Bolaños Airport: Premontane moist forest. Elev.: 3,950'. Lat. 10°03.60' N, long. 84°13.01' W. Xandari Plantation Hotel's grounds are beautifully landscaped with many ornamental flowers and thus attract a wide variety of birds, including Red-crowned Ant-Tanagers, Long-tailed Manakins, and Rufous-naped Wrens. Blue-crowned Motmots are common, plus the shade coffee plantation on the grounds is one of the only places in Costa Rica to see the Buffy-crowned Wood-Partridge. Address: Xandari Plantation, Apartado 1485-4050, Alajuela, Costa Rica. Telephone: 506-443-2020; fax: 506-442-4847; e-mail: hotel@xandari.com; web site: www.xandari.com. Hotel Alta has beautifully landscaped grounds with a nice variety of birds typical of the Central Plateau. Telephone: 506-282-4160; fax: 506-282-4162; e-mail: hotlalta@racsa. co.cr.

P-3: San José vicinity and downtown: Premontane moist forest (urban). Elev.: 3,700'. Lat. 9°56.96' N, long. 84°04.05' W.

P-4: Curridabat; Tres Ríos: Premontane moist forest. Elev.: 3,900'. Lat. 9°54.14' N, long. 84°00.37' W.

P-5: Cartago vicinity; Parque de Expresión; Lankester Gardens; Las Concavas marsh: Premontane moist forest. Elev.: 4,700'. Lat. 9°50.20' N, long. 83°53.55' W. The Parque de Expresión in Cartago has ponds with waterbirds like Northern Jacanas; the private Las Concavas marsh can be viewed with permission and has wintering Blue-winged Teal, Killdeer, Eastern Meadowlarks, and Least Grebes. Hummingbirds and other birds can be seen along the trails at the Lankester Gardens.

CARIBBEAN LOWLANDS

C-1: Road from Los Inocentes Lodge east to lowlands by Santa Cecilia: Tropical moist forest. Elev.: 750' descending to 300'. From lat. 11°02.70' N, long. 85°30.00' W at Los Inocentes to lat. 11°03.70' N, long. 85°24.40' W at Santa Cecilia. This region has wildlife species of the Caribbean lowlands. Owls and Common and Great Potoos can be seen along the road at night with the aid of spotlights.

C-2: Caño Negro NWR and Río Frío: Tropical moist forest. Elev.: 175'. Lat. 10°54.50' N, long. 84°47.70' W. An exceptional refuge for wetland wildlife, including waterfowl and wading birds. There is a recent record of nesting by Jabiru storks. Lodging and boat trips can be arranged at the Tilajari Resort Hotel near Muelle. Address: P.O. Box 81-4400, Ciudad Quesada, Costa Rica. Telephone: 506-469-9091; fax: 506-469-9095; e-mail: info@tilajari.com; web site: www.tilajari.com.

C-3: La Laguna del Lagarto Lodge: Tropical wet forest. Elev.: 200'. Lat. 10°41.20' N, long. 84°11.20' W. Address: P.O. Box 995-1007 Centro Colón, San José, Costa Rica. Excellent wildlife characteristic of the Caribbean lowland rainforest, including the endangered Great Green Macaw and many aquatic species, can be seen here. Telephone: 506-289-8163; fax: 506-289-5295; e-mail: laguna-del-lagarto@adventure-costarica.com; web site: www.adventurecostarica.com/laguna-del-lagarto.

C-4: Tortuga Lodge and Tortuguero NP: Tropical wet forest. Elev.: Sea level. Lat. 10°34.36' N, long. 83°31.04' W. Address: Costa Rica Expeditions, Apartado 6941-1000, San José, Costa Rica, or Dept. 235, Box 025216, Miami, Florida 33102-5216. Telephone: 506-222-0333 or 506-527-0766; fax: 506-257-1665; e-mail: costaric@expeditions.co.cr; web site: www.costarica@expeditions.com. An exceptional area of lowland wet forest with great viewing opportunities to see wildlife like Great Green Macaws, parrots, monkeys, toucans, bats, crocodiles, tiger-herons, hummingbirds, and butterflies along the canals and along foot trails behind Tortuga Lodge. Night trips to see nesting Green Turtles can be arranged from July through October.

C-5: La Selva Biological Station, Puerto Viejo, Selva Verde, and El Gavilán Lodge: Tropical wet forest. Elevation 200'. La Selva Biological Station: Lat. 10°25.89' N, long. 84°00.27' W. Address: Organization for Tropical Studies, Apartado 676-2050, San Pedro de Montes de Oca, San José, Costa Rica. Telephone: 506-766-6565 at La Selva and 506-240-6696 for making reservations at La Selva at the main OTS office in San José; fax: 506-766-6535 at La Selva and 506-240-6783 in San José; e-mail: laselva@sloth.ots.ac.cr; web site: www.ots.ac.cr. Observations at Selva Verde Lodge and El Gavilán Lodge are

included with this site. Both are excellent places to observe wildlife of the
Caribbean tropical lowlands. Selva Verde Lodge address: Chilamate,
Sarapiquí, Costa Rica. Telephone: 1-800-451-7111 in the United States and
506-766-6800 in Costa Rica; fax: 506-766-6011; e-mail: selvaver@racsa.co.cr;
web site: www.selvaverde.com. El Gavilán Lodge address: P.O. Box 445-2010,
San José, Costa Rica. Telephone: 506-234-9507; fax: 506-253-6556; e-mail:
gavilan@racsa.co.cr; web site: www.gavilanlodge.com.

C-6: Road from La Selva to Guacimo lowland turnoff: Tropical wet forest. Elev.:
200'. From lat. 10°25.89' N, long. 84°00.27' W to lat. 10°13.00' N, long. 83°56.00'
W. Largely cleared pastureland and scrub, small ponds, and some rivers. Good
for herons, egrets, anis, and an occasional King Vulture.

C-7: Rara Avis: Premontane rainforest. Elev.: 2,000'. Lat. 10°17.30' N, long.
84°02.47' W. Address: Apartado 8105-1000, San José, Costa Rica. Telephone:
506-764-3131; fax: 506-764-4187; e-mail: raraavis@racsa.co.cr; web site: www.
cool.co.cr/usr/raraavis/ing/raraavis.html. This 1,500-acre reserve is an excellent place to observe wildlife of the Caribbean lowlands and foothills,
including the rare Snowcap Hummingbird. Lodge for sale. Call about status.

C-8: Rainforest Aerial Tram; lower levels of Braulio Carrillo NP; Tapir Trail:
Tropical wet forest. Elev.: 2,000'. Lat. 10°10.80' N, long. 83°56.60' W. Rainforest
Aerial Tram address: Apartado 1959-1002, San José, Costa Rica. Telephone:
506-257-5961; fax: 506-257-6053; e-mail address: info@rainforesttram.com;
web site: www.rainforesttram.com. WARNING: The Rainforest Aerial Tram is
an excellent and safe ecotourism destination. However, trails along the main
highway within Braulio Carrillo NP, like Sendero Botarama, have been the site
of armed robberies of tourists in the late 1990s. Visiting such trails in Braulio
Carrillo NP is not recommended.

C-9: Guacimo lowlands; Guapiles airport: Tropical wet forest. Elev.: 900'. Lat.
10°12.85' N, long. 83°47.35' W. The highway from Guapiles east to Limón is an
excellent stretch for spotting sloths in *Cecropia* trees. Rare Fasciated Tiger-
Herons can sometimes be seen in the water near the Río Roca bridge.

C-10: Road from Limón to Cahuita: Tropical moist forest. Elev.: 0'. From lat.
9°59.20' N, long. 83°02.00' W to lat. 9°45.00' N, long. 82°50.20' W. Along this
coastal highway it is possible to see Collared Aracaris, Blue-headed Parrots,
and many shorebirds and wading birds in the estuaries that flow into the
Caribbean. However, see safety warning in C-11 account.

C-11: Cahuita NP; Cahuita; Pizote Lodge: Tropical moist forest. Elev.: Sea level.
Lat. 9°45.00' N, long. 82°50.20' W. This NP encompasses 2,637 acres and was
designated for protection of the coral reefs there. It is the best example of coral

reef in the country, but it has suffered in recent times from pollution from banana plantations and siltation. This is one of the best places in the country to observe sloths, and a variety of raptors, shorebirds, tanagers, and other lowland wildlife can be observed. In mid- to late October the Cahuita and Puerto Viejo area is the major passage site for North American raptors migrating to Panama and South America. Over a million raptors were counted passing through this area during October of 2000 (Jennifer McNicoll, personal communication 2000). However, incidents of violent crime, armed robberies, and the murder of two tourists in 2000 make this drug-infested area relatively unsafe for tourism by lone tourists. Tourists should travel in groups of ten or more, and they should patronize only major hotels like El Pizote Lodge and avoid night outings, bars, and night clubs. El Pizote Lodge telephone: 506-750-0227; fax: 506-750-0226; e-mail: pizotelg@racsa.co.cr; web site: www.hotels.co. cr/pizote. Other good lodges in the area are Los Cocles, Suere, Shawandha, Villas de Caribe, and Casa Camarona.

HIGHLANDS

H-1: Monteverde Cloud Forest Reserve, Hummingbird Gallery, Ecological Farm, and vicinity: Lower montane rainforest. Elev.: 4,500'. Lat. 10°19.00' N, long. 84°49.19' W. Many excellent hotels in the vicinity. Examples include Monteverde Lodge (telephone: 506-645-5057; fax: 506-645-5126); Hotel Fonda Vela (telephone: 506-257-1413; fax: 506-257-1416); and Hotel Belmar (telephone: 506-645-5201; fax: 506-645-5135). For additional contact information on Monteverde Lodge, see details for Costa Rica Expeditions in account for site S-16. Excellent example of cloud forest, with Resplendent Quetzals, Three-wattled Bellbirds, Black Guans, and many hummingbirds, including the endemic Coppery-headed Emerald.

H-2: Poás NP: Montane rainforest. Elev.: 8,200'. Lat. 10°11.45' N, long. 84°13.95' W. Excellent example of montane forest, which includes 13,835 acres. It is a good place to see Sooty Robins, Yellow-thighed Finches, Large-footed Finches, Magnificent and Volcano Hummingbirds, Slaty Flowerpiercers, and Bare-shanked Screech-Owls. An easy day trip while staying in San José.

H-3: La Virgen del Socorro: Premontane wet forest. Elev.: 2,600', road descending to 2,200'. Lat. 10°15.68' N, long. 84°10.47' W. This road has been a popular birding trail in the Caribbean foothills. A wide variety of birds can be seen in the forest along this road, including White Hawks, Violet-headed Hummingbirds, and Black-crested Coquettes. At the bridge at the lower end of the road it is possible to see Torrent Tyrannulets and dippers.

H-4: Peace Waterfall (Catarata de La Paz), La Paz Waterfall Gardens, and Restaurante Catarata San Fernando: Lower montane rainforest. Elev.: 4,500'. Lat. 10°15.60' N, long. 84°10.70' W. The Peace Waterfall can be good for viewing local tanagers, hummingbirds, Torrent Tyrannulets, and dippers. La Paz Waterfall Gardens are well known for their nature trails and the diversity of hummingbirds that come to their feeders, including the uncommon Brown Violet-ear, Black-bellied Hummingbird, and endemic Coppery-headed Emerald. Telephone: 506-482-2720; web site: www.waterfallgardens.com. Not far from La Paz Waterfall Gardens is another exceptional birding site near the town of Chinchona. It is the Restaurante Catarata San Fernando. Feeders there attract a great variety of hummingbirds and the Prong-billed and Red-headed Barbets.

H-5: Hotel El Pórtico; San José de la Montaña in Heredia: Lower montane rainforest. Elev.: 5,800'. Lat. 10°05.00' N, long. 84°07.00' W. An excellent location for higher-elevation tanagers, hummingbirds, migrant warblers, and raptors on the slope of Barva Volcano. Hotel El Pórtico telephone: 506-237-6022; fax: 506-260-6002.

H-6: La Ponderosa farm near Turrialba: Premontane wet forest. Elev.: 3,760'. Lat. 9°57.31' N, long. 83°42.42' W. Private land; not accessible for tourism purposes.

H-7: Rancho Naturalista, near Tuís: Premontane wet forest. Elev.: 3,200'. Lat. 9°49.91' N, long. 83°33.83' W. Address: 3428 Hwy. 465, Sheridan, AR 72150. Toll-free telephone in United States: 1-800-593-3305. Telephone in Costa Rica: 506-267-7138 or 506-267-6104; fax: 506-267-7138; e-mail: mark@ ranchonaturalista.com; web site: www.ranchonaturalista.com. An exceptional site in the Caribbean foothills that has species of both the lowlands and higher elevations. It is one of the best places in the country to see hummingbirds, including the rare Snowcap. About fifty bird species come to the feeders in the courtyard each morning, and the viewing of hummingbirds at the hummingbird pools in the forest each afternoon is unique in the country. Sunbitterns and Black Guans have been seen from nearby roads. Excellent guides and trails.

H-8: Tapantí NP; Kiri Lodge: Premontane wet forest. Entrance/Kiri Lodge: Elev.: 4,300'. Lat. 9°45.62' N, long. 83°47.04' W. Bridge over the Río Grande de Orosí: Elev.: 5,000'. Lat. 9°42.21' N, long. 83°46.93' W. This NP covers 12,577 acres and is a great place to see wildlife of montane forests like Collared Trogons, Costa Rican Pygmy-Owls, Red-headed and Prong-billed Barbets, dippers, Emerald Toucanets, and Azure-hooded Jays. Kiri Lodge telephone: 506-533-3040.

H-9: Cerro de la Muerte/San Gerardo de Dota region (four sites):

Kilometer 66: Road descending to Finca El Jaular from 8,300' to 7,700'. Montane rainforest. Lat. 9°40.24' N, long. 83°51.92' W. The road to Finca El Jaular is a private road on the west side of the PAH that is closed by a large gate. The road can be birded on foot only with advance permission and by making arrangements to pay an entrance fee. Vehicles need to be left at the main highway. The land is owned by the Vindas family, who live down in the valley at the end of the road. Permission and payment should be arranged by calling Savegre Mountain Lodge at the telephone number listed for site H-10. This road descends through excellent primary montane rainforest and is a good place to see quetzals and other highland wildlife.

Kilometer 77, road to Providencia: At kilometer 77 on the PAH near Los Chespiritos Restaurant #1 is a turnoff to Providencia. Montane rainforest. Elevation: 9,400'. Lat. 9°35.68' N, long. 83°48.59' W. Along this road it is possible to see Silvery-throated Jays, Slaty Flowerpiercers, Yellow-thighed Finches, several hummingbirds, and Black-billed Nightingale-Thrushes. This road is 12 kilometers long, but some of the best birding is in the first two kilometers from the PAH.

Kilometer 86, Los Chespiritos #2: Montane rainforest. Elev.: 9,100'. Lat. 9°36.88' N, long. 83°49.07' W. This site is a trail on the west side of the PAH across the road and a couple hundred feet south of Los Chespiritos Restaurant #2. It is an excellent place for the Timberline Wren, the Peg-billed Finch, Sooty-capped Bush-Tanager, Volcano Hummingbird, and high-elevation wildflowers.

Kilometer 96, La Georgina, Villa Mills: Montane rainforest. Elev.: 9,300'. Lat. 9°33.46' N, long. 83°42.67' W. This site is west across the PAH from La Georgina Restaurant and is the site of an old highway construction camp where there is open and shrubby cover that is excellent for Volcano and Scintillant Hummingbirds and Timberline Wrens.

H-10: Savegre Mountain Lodge (Albergue de Montaña Savegre/Cabinas Chacón): The turnoff from the PAH is at kilometer 80 (at 9,400' elevation), and the road descends for 5.5 kilometers to Finca Chacón along the Río Savegre at 7,200' elevation. Lower montane rainforest. Lat. 9°33.02' N, long. 83°48.46' W. Telephone: 506-771-1732 or 506-390-5096; toll-free telephone in United States: 1-800-593-3305; fax: 506-771-2003; e-mail: ciprotur@racsa.co.cr; web site; www.ecotourism.co.cr/savegrelodge. Excellent road and lodge property to see Black Guans, Resplendent Quetzals, Long-tailed Silky-Flycatchers, Black-faced Solitaires, and resident Red-tailed Hawks.

H-11: Cerro de la Muerte transmission tower site (kilometer 90): Subalpine rain paramo. Elev.: 10,800'. Lat. 9°33.25' N, long. 83°45.16' W. The gravel road leading to the transmission towers from the PAH is approximately at kilometer 90 and is an excellent place to see Volcano Juncos, Peg-billed Finches, and resident Red-tailed Hawks.

H-12: Vista del Valle Restaurante: This restaurant is located at kilometer 119 on the PAH at 5,650' elevation. Lower montane rainforest. Lat. 9°27.78' N, long. 83°42.12' W. Telephone: 506-284-4685. This is a new site checked out in January of 2001. It is at the southeast end of Cerro de la Muerte overlooking the valley of San Isidro del General. This restaurant commands an excellent overlook above the San Isidro del General Valley where it is possible to see migrating Swallow-tailed Kites from January through April. They have a very successful bird-feeding station where it is possible to see Red-headed Barbets, Flame-colored Tanagers, Bay-headed Tanagers, and many other warblers and tanagers as well as the White-tailed Emerald and Violet Sabrewing.

ADDENDUM TO SOUTHERN PACIFIC LOWLANDS

New site: La Cusinga Lodge: Tropical moist forest. Elev.: sea level to 200'. Lat. 9°8.30' N, long. 83°44.30' W. An excellent ecotourism lodge with an abundance of lowland rainforest wildlife, good trails, marine birds, raptors, and the chance for boat trips to see humpback whales, mangrove lagoons, and Cano Island. On the Pacific coast near Dominical. Address: La Cusinga, Bahia Ballena de Osa, Apdo 41-8000, Costa Rica. Telephone/fax: 506-771-2465; e-mail: lacusinga@yahoo.com; web site: www.lacusingalodge.com.

APPENDIX C
Wildlife Vocalization Tapes and CDs

Following are cassette tapes and CDs referred to in the species accounts. Among the most comprehensive tapes and CDs for Costa Rican species are:

Voices of Costa Rican Birds: Caribbean Slope (BB)
Costa Rican Bird Song Sampler (CC)
Voices of the Cloud Forest (AA)
Songs of Mexican Birds (D)
Sounds of Neotropical Rainforest Mammals (H).

Most of the tapes and CDs are available from American Birding Association Sales, P.O. Box 6599, Colorado Springs, CO 80934. Telephone: 1-800-634-7736 or 719-578-0607; fax: 1-800-590-2473 or 719-578-9705; e-mail: abasales@abasales.com; web site: americanbirding.org/abasales/salescatal.htm. All listings are on audiocassette unless listed as a CD.

A. Anonymous. 1995. *A Selection of Birds from the Wilson Botanical Garden, Costa Rica.* C. Caparette, narrator. Borror Lab of Bioacoustics, Dept. of Zoology, 1735 Neil Ave., The Ohio State University, Columbus, OH 14210.

B. Anonymous. (1996?). *The Sounds of Belizean Birds.* The Belize Zoo & Tropical Education Center, P.O. Box 1787, Belize City, Belize.

C. Brigham, M. 1991. *Bird Sounds of Canada* (6 CDs).

D. Coffey, Ben B., and Lula C. Coffey. 1990. *Songs of Mexican Birds* (2 audio-cassettes). ARA Records, P.O. Box 12347, Gainesville, FL 32604-0347.

E. Coffey, Ben B., and Lula C. Coffey. 1993. *Bird Songs and Calls from Southeast Peru.* ARA Records and the Tambopata Nature Preserve, P.O. Box 12347, Gainesville, FL 32604-0347.

F. Cornell Lab. 1992. *A Field Guide to Western Bird Songs* (3 audiocassettes or 2 CDs). Library of Natural Sounds, Cornell Lab of Ornithology, 159 Sapsucker Woods Road, Ithaca, NY 14850.

G. Delaney, Dale. 1992. *Bird Songs of Belize, Guatemala, and Mexico.* Library of Natural Sounds, Cornell Lab of Ornithology, 159 Sapsucker Woods, Ithaca, NY 14850.

H. Emmons, Louise H., Bret M. Whitney, and David L. Ross, Jr. 1997. *Sounds of Neotropical Rainforest Mammals* (CD). Library of Natural Sounds, Cornell Lab of Ornithology, 159 Sapsucker Woods, Ithaca, NY 14850.

I. English, Peter H., and Theodore A. Parker, III. 1992. *Birds of Eastern Ecuador.* Library of Natural Sounds, Cornell Lab of Ornithology, 159 Sapsucker Woods, Ithaca, NY 14850.

J. Hardy, John W. 1983. *Voices of Neotropical Birds* (Audiocassette). ARA Records, P.O. Box 12347, Gainesville, FL 32604-0347.

K. Hardy, John W. 1990. *Voices of New World Jays, Crows, and Allies.* ARA Records, P.O. Box 12347, Gainesville, FL 32604-0347.

L. Hardy, John W. 1995. *Voices of the Wrens.* ARA Records, P.O. Box 12347, Gainesville, FL 32604-0347.

M. Hardy, John W., et al. 1989. *Voices of New World Pigeons and Doves.* ARA Records, P.O. Box 12347, Gainesville, FL 32604-0347.

N. Hardy, John W., et al. 1990. *Voices of New World Owls.* ARA Records, P. O. Box 12347, Gainesville, FL 32604-0347.

O. Hardy, John W., et al. 1995a. *Voices of New World Cuckoos and Trogons.* ARA Records, P.O. Box 12347, Gainesville, FL 32604-0347.

P. Hardy, John W., et al. 1995b. *Voices of New World Nightjars and Allies.* ARA Records, P.O. Box 12347, Gainesville, FL 32604-0347.

Q. Hardy, John W., et al. 1995c. *Voices of the Tinamous.* ARA Records, P.O. Box 12347, Gainesville, FL 32604-0347.

R. Hardy, John W., et al. 1995d. *Voices of the Woodcreepers.* ARA Records, P.O. Box 12347, Gainesville, FL 32604-0347.

S. Merrick, William. Undated. *Sounds of the Jungle.* The Book Stop II, Panajachel, Sololá, Guatemala.

T. Moore, John V. 1994a. *A Bird Walk at Chan Chich.* Bill Hare Productions, Milpitas, CA 95035.

U. Moore, John V. 1994b. *Ecuador, More Bird Vocalizations from Lowland Rain Forest.* Vol. 1. Bill Hare Productions, Milpitas, CA 95035.

V. Moore, John V. 1994c. *Sounds of La Selva, Ecuador.* Bill Hare Productions, Milpitas, CA 95035.

W. Moore, John V. 1996. *Ecuador, More Bird Vocalizations from Lowland Rain Forest.* Vol. 2. Bill Hare Productions, Milpitas, CA 95035.

X. Moore, John V., and Mitch Lysinger. 1997. *The Birds of Cabañas San Isidro, Ecuador* (2 audiocassettes). Bill Hare Productions, Milpitas, CA 95035.

Y. Murphy, William L. 1991. *Bird Sounds of Trinidad and Tobago.* Peregrine Enterprises, Inc., P.O. Box 1003, College Park, MD 20740.

Z. Parker, III, Theodore A. 1985. *Voices of the Peruvian Rainforest.* Library of Natural Sounds, Cornell Lab of Ornithology, 159 Sapsucker Woods, Ithaca, NY 14850.

AA. Ross, Jr., David L. 1992. *Voices of the Cloud Forest.* Library of Natural Sounds, Cornell Lab of Ornithology, 159 Sapsucker Woods, Ithaca, NY 14850.

BB. Ross, Jr., David L. 1999. *Costa Rican Bird Song Sampler.* Library of Natural Sounds, Cornell Lab of Ornithology, 159 Sapsucker Woods, Ithaca, NY 14850.

CC. Ross, Jr., David L., and Bret M. Whitney. 1995. *Voices of Costa Rican Birds: Caribbean Slope* (2 audiocassettes or CD). Library of Natural Sounds. Cornell Lab of Ornithology, 159 Sapsucker Woods, Ithaca, NY 14850.

APPENDIX D
Costa Rican Trip Preparation Checklist

This trip preparation checklist has been prepared by Carrol and Ethelle Henderson and is based on their experience leading fifteen birding tours to Costa Rica. The clothing and equipment listed are suggested for a two-week birding or natural history type of tour.

LUGGAGE

One or two pieces of soft, durable, canvas-type bags. Tagged and closed with small padlocks during air travel and storage at hotels. Think light!!! The less you bring, the easier your travel will be.

CLOTHING

Bring lightweight wash-and-wear clothes you can wash out yourself. Bring detergent double-bagged in Ziploc® or similar bags for places where laundry service isn't available.

- 3 to 4 sets of field clothes: shirts/blouses; pants/shorts/jeans, and one long-sleeved shirt
- Socks (4–5 pairs)
- Underwear (4–5 pairs)
- Handkerchiefs or Kleenex®
- Belt
- Sweatshirt/sweater/light jacket
- Towel
- Hat or cap
- Sleep wear
- One pair walking shoes/one pair tennis shoes
- Wash cloth
- Rain poncho or raincoat (lightweight)
- Swimsuit and beach thongs

TOILETRY ITEMS

- Pack of Wet Ones®
- Deodorant
- Toothbrush
- Toothpaste
- Dental floss

- Shampoo, without citronella base
- Comb/hairbrush
- Shaving cream
- Razor/shaver (Current is 110 ac, but some outlets don't take wide prong—bring adapter plug)

PHOTO AND OPTIC EQUIPMENT (OPTIONAL)

- Camera with flash unit or video camera
- Binoculars
- Camera bag
- Ziploc® or similar bags for camera (dust) and film (moisture)
- Extra batteries for camera and flash unit
- Lenses and filters
- Lens tissue
- Film: ASA 50, 64, or 100 for sunlight or flash; 200 or 400 for cloudy days or in rainforest; or telephoto lenses. Amount: 6-casual; 12-average; 20-eager; 30-enthusiastic.

OTHER EQUIPMENT

- Fingernail clippers
- Sunglasses
- Suntan lotion or sunscreen
- Chapstick®
- Insect repellent (up to 30% DEET)
- Aspirin
- Imodium® or Lomotil®
- Q-Tips®
- Notebook and pens
- Flashlight
- Field guides
- Knapsack/daypack/fanny pack
- Spending money, at least $350, in clean, undamaged bills
- Bag of detergent (double-bagged in Ziploc® or similar bags)
- Prescriptions for personal medication, including original containers
- Travel alarm
- Passport, plus photocopy packed separate from passport
- Tip for naturalist guide (about $7–$10 per day)
- Tip for driver (about $4–5 per day)
- Earplugs for sleeping near noisy highways or near loud surf
- Umbrella

OTHER OPTIONAL ITEMS

- Hunting or fishing vest for gear
- Spare camera!
- Mending kit
- Half gallon & gallon Ziploc®-type bags for film canisters, etc.
- Canteen or water bottle
- Lightweight rubber boots
- 20' cord for indoor clothesline
- Map: There is one exceptional map for Costa Rica that shows topographical features in great detail. It is published by the U.S. Department of Defense and is referred to as a "Tactical Pilotage Map." These are available for all regions of Latin America and are at a scale of 1:500,000. The map for Costa Rica is TPC K-25C. It can be ordered from the NOAA Distribution Branch (N/CG33), National Ocean Service, Riverdale, MD 20737.

INDEX

Phytolacca, 201, 235, 318
piapia, 360–361
Piaya cayana, 77, 255–256
picaflor, 376–377
picamadero barbirrayado, 329–330
piche, 179–180
pico chuchara, 157–158
picudo, 406–408
Pigeon: Band-tailed, 234–235; Red-billed, 235–236
pigüilo, 223–224
pijije común, 179–180
pinchaflor, 376–377; **plomizo,** 427–428
pinzón: cabecilistado, 430–431; **piquenaranja,** 429–430
Pionus: menstruus, 249–250; *senilis,* 248–249
Piper, 42, 399, 403, 410, 412
piririza, 225–226
pirrís, 432–433
Pitangus sulphuratus, 347–348
Pithecellobium, 63, 254, 282
pitorreal, 374–375
pizote, 477–479
Platymiscium, 59
Plover, Semipalmated, 220–221
Plusiotis resplendens, 80, 296
Poikilocanthos, 32
Poison Dart Frogs, 100–103
Polyborus plancus (see *Caracara plancus*)
pomponé, 207–208
pone-pone, 207–208
Porcupine, Prehensile-tailed, 445–446
Porphyrula martinica, 208–209
Pothomorphe sp., 42
Potoo: Common, 264–265; Gray, 264–265
Potos flavus, 476–477
Powell, George and Harriet, 7
Prehensile-tailed Porcupine, 445–446
premontane zone, 30–31
preservation, 5–8
Promar, 494
Protium, 252, 317–318, 320
Prunus, 60
Psammisia, 32, 395, 419
Psarocolius: montezuma, 389–391; *wagleri,* 387–388

Pselliophorus tibialis, 428–429
Pseudomyrmex spinicola, 74–75, 364
Psidium guajava, 65, 201, 236, 248, 250, 399, 416, 477
Psiguria, 53–54
Psittacanthos, 395
Psychotria, 53–54, 282, 339
Pterocarpus, 26, 59
Pteroglossus: frantzii, 318; *torquatus,* 316–317
Ptilogonys caudatus, 374–375
pucuyo, 266–267
puerco espín, 445–446
Puffbird, White-necked, 314
Puja dasylirioides, 15, 32
Pulsatrix perspicillata, 261–262
Puma concolor, 482–483
Purple-crowned Woodnymph, 278–279
Purple Gallinule, 208–209, 213
Purple-throated Mountaingem, 283–285

quebrantahuesos, 195–196
Quercus, 14, 30–31, 80
querque, 195–196
Quetzal, Resplendent, 294–296, 300
quioro, 321–322
Quiscalus mexicanus, 391–392

rabadillo tinta, 412–414
rabihorcado magno, 152–153
Rain Frog, 92
Ramphastos: sulphuratus, 319–320; *swainsonii,* 321–322
Ramphocelus: costaricensis, 412–414; *passerinii,* 414
rana, 93; **calzonuda,** 98–99; **de lluvia,** 92; **de vidrio,** 104–105; **ternero,** 94–95; **venenosa,** 100–103
ranita: piedrita, 92; **roja,** 101
Raphia, 23, 26
raposa, 443
rascón cuelligrís, 207–208
ratonerita, 364–365
Razisea, 271
Red-backed Squirrel Monkey, 20, 456–459
Red-billed Pigeon, 25, 235–236